M000216919

Uniter of Heaven
and Earth

SUNY Series in Judaica: Hermeneutics, Mysticism, and Religion
Michael Fishbane, Robert Goldenberg, and Elliot Wolfson, editors

Uniter of Heaven and Earth

Rabbi Meshullam Feibush Heller of Zbarazh
and the Rise of Hasidism in Eastern Galicia

Miles Krassen

State University of New York Press

Published by
State University of New York Press, Albany

©1998 State University of New York

All rights reserved

Printed in the United States of America

For information, address the State University of New York Press,
State Universty Plaza, Albany, NY 12246

Production by Marilyn Semerad
Marketing by Fran Keneston

Library of Congress Cataloging-in-Publication Data
Krassen, Miles
    Uniter of heaven and earth : Rabbi Meshullam Feibush Heller of
Zbarazh and the rise of Hasidism in Eastern Galicia / Miles
Krassen.
        p.   cm. — (SUNY series in Judaica)
    Includes biblographical references and index.
    ISBN 0-7914-3817-1. — ISBN 0-7914-3818-X (pbk. : alk. paper)
    1. Heller, Meshullam Feivush, d. ca. 1795.   2. Rabbis—Ukraine—
Galicia, Eastern—Biography.   3. Hasidim—Ukraine—Galicia,
Eastern—Biography.   4. Hasidism—Ukraine—Galicia, Eastern—
History.   I. Title.   II. Series.
BM755.H318K73   1998
296.8'322'092—dc21
    [B]   97-50607
                                                                            CIP

10 9 8 7 6 5 4 3 2 1

Contents

Introduction   1

1. Meshullam Feibush Heller and His Circle in Eastern Galicia   9

2. Sources of *Devequt* in Early Hasidism   43

3. Cosomological Bases for Meshullam Feibush's Concept of *Devequt*   81

4. The Barrier to Divine Aid   95

5. The Problem of Corporeality: Conditions for *Devequt*   107

6. The Remedy: Prayer, Torah, Sacred Calendar   123

7. Meshullam Feibush and the Maggid of Mezeritch   163

8. The Importance of *Zaddiqim*   187

9. Meshullam Feibush's Place in Early Hasidism   203

Notes   217

Bibliography   285

Index   301

Uniter of Heaven
and Earth

Introduction

Despite more than half a century of serious interest and contributions to the field by many of the most illustrious scholars in the history of Jewish thought and religion, the study of Hasidism remains in its earliest stages. As yet, no satisfactory history of the movement has been written and only recently has the groundwork been laid for a historically based understanding of Hasidism's founder, the Ba'al Shem Tov.[1] In general, phenomenologists of Hasidism, following Gershom Scholem, have spread a broad canvas in attempting to identify and clarify essential aspects of Hasidic teachings and piety.[2] Of particular note in this regard are the works of Scholem's students, Joseph Weiss and Rivka Schatz-Uffenheimer, and the work of Isaiah Tishby and Joseph Dan.[3] However, both the historians and phenomenologists mentioned above have approached Hasidism based on assumptions that are no longer tenable. Recent research has made it clear that the rise and success of Hasidism was neither a response to extreme social and economic deprivation among Jews in eastern Europe, nor a product of radical Sabbatian ideas and practices.[4] In fact, even Scholem's theory that Hasidism constitutes the last major trend in the history of Jewish mysticism has fallen from grace. More recently, a new approach, situating Hasidism within a broader panoramic context of historical influences and types of mysticism and magic, has been offered by Moshe Idel.[5]

On the other hand, detailed studies closely focused on specific figures, schools, and stages in the development of early Hasidism have been few. Although Abraham Joshua Heschel has written a number of essays on figures associated with early Hasidism, for the most part, the only schools that have received extensive attention are HaBaD and Bratslav Hasidism.[6] However, both of these schools only began to flourish around the turn of the nineteenth century. Consequently, our knowledge of the activities, teachings, and functioning of seminal figures in the early decades during which Hasidism was developing and spreading, remains quite limited. Yet it is in this early period that the formative teachings and interests of Hasidism are articulated. Thus, if we are ever to construct an informed view concerning the nature of this extraordinarily successful mystical religious movement and comprehend its deepest, most essential motives, and the earliest collections of its teachings, then the movement's first influential interpreters must receive our closest attention.

A particularly useful vantage point for examining Hasidism in its early stages of development can be found in the writings of Rabbi Meshullam Feibush Heller of Zbarazh. While Rabbi Meshullam Feibush never achieved the kind of celebrity associated with the charismatic and powerful personalities around whom the Hasidic communities took form, he is precisely the kind of figure from whom much can be learned. Scion of a prominent eastern European rabbinic family, descended from the famous Mishnah commentator, Rabbi Yom Tov Lipman Heller, Meshullam Feibush is both an interesting example of the type of person attracted to Hasidism in its early stages as well as a figure well equipped to represent and interpret its teachings. Heller seems to have been introduced to the teachings of the Ba'al Shem Tov by one of the founders of Hasidism's earliest disciples in eastern Galicia, the somewhat legendary Rabbi Menahem Mendel of Premishlan, who emigrated to the Land of Israel in 1764 with another close associate of the Ba'al Shem Tov, Rabbi Nahman of Horodenker. However, even more significant than R. Menahem Mendel's formative influence on R. Meshullam Feibush is the latter's relationship to Rabbi Yehiel Mikhel, the Maggid of Zlotchov, perhaps the prototype of the Hasidic Zaddiq in eastern Galicia. R. Yehiel Mikhel, himself a direct disciple of the Ba'al Shem Tov, seems to have begun to function as a charismatic and prophetic leader of a Hasidic conventicle centered in Brody in about 1772.[7] His activities as a Zaddiq, or perhaps more correctly, proto-Zaddiq, apparently begin around the time of the death of Rabbi Dov Ber, the Maggid of Mezeritch, who is generally viewed by the later Hasidic movement as the successor of the Ba'al Shem Tov.[8] R. Yehiel Mikhel's prophetic and redemptive, perhaps even messianic activities continued until his death in 1781, the year during which the first Hasidic book, by R. Jacob Joseph of Polnoy, Toledot Ya'aqov Yosef, appeared in print.[9]

Although the Maggid of Zlotchov seems to have attracted a certain measure of popular recognition as a Holy Man, for the most part his spiritual leadership involved an elite group of rabbinic figures who were mystics, pietists, and kabbalists. Many of his disciples were formerly to some degree students of the Maggid of Mezeritch who would themselves go on to become important communal leaders and authors of important Hasidic tracts. For this inner circle, R. Yehiel Mikhel was a spiritual master whose unique degree of adhesion to God (devequt) enabled him to accomplish extraordinary ends. His divinely inspired soul enabled him to reveal secret meanings of Torah, to enhance the efficacy of his disciples' prayers, to perfect their souls, to rectify flaws in the supernal worlds through retrieving and elevating fallen sparks of holiness, and in general to return the material world to its spiritual source.

When exactly R. Meshullam Feibush Heller became a member of the Zlotchover Maggid's close disciples is not certain. However, it is clear that

Meshullam Feibush was a central figure in this group during the last five years of the Zlotchover's life. Those of his writings that will be our principal concern, although not published until 1792, were all written between 1777 and 1781. To appreciate the great importance of these writings, two long pastoral letters written to a certain Rabbi Joel, possibly a member of the Hasidic community in Tiberias,[10] it is necessary to know something of the context within which they were written as well as the nature of their contents.

The year 1772 was a crucial one for the history of Hasidism for two reasons. First, this was the year in which R. Dov Ber of Mezeritch, the nominal successor of the Ba'al Shem Tov, died. While one must resist the tendency to project an anachronistic view of Dov Ber's activities based on later models of Hasidic leadership, it does seem that of the small number of most prominent rabbinic figures among the Ba'al Shem Tov's surviving disciples and associates, such as Rabbi Jacob Joseph of Polnoy and Rabbi Pinhas of Koretz, Rabbi Dov Ber was the most influential during the decade following the founder's death in 1760. The Maggid of Mezeritch's influence probably was the effect of his charismatic personality, homiletic skills, stature as a scholar, reputation as a mystic, and ability to inspire younger disciples. In addition, he seems to have organized a highly effective outreach program that succeeded in recruiting potential disciples. All of these qualities were attested to in the memoirs of the enlightenment philosopher, Solomon Maimon. Maimon was himself a potential recruit who experienced the charismatic qualities of the Maggid of Mezeritch firsthand. Nevertheless, he wrote as a critic of Hasidism, which he came to reject. Thus, his eyewitness account of a Shabbat with R. Dov Ber was an important piece of historical evidence.[11] R. Dov Ber's success in attracting disciples probably contributed directly to the problem that existed following his death. Despite Hasidic legendary accounts, there was as yet no tradition or custom for succession of Hasidic leadership or for communal organization.[12] Much scholarly attention has already been focused on the stages that resulted in Rabbi Shneur Zalman of Liadi's assumption of leadership in Lithuania and Belorus.[13] However, the assumption of leadership in eastern Galicia remains less well understood. Nevertheless, Galicia was initially at least equally important as an arena for the spread of early Hasidism. Not only did the Hasidic leadership achieve some of its first significant successes here, but also the sheer number of Hasidic masters, who emerged from this region, who were active within it, and who played important roles in spreading Hasidism westward into Poland, was substantially greater than those who were active further north.

One of the benefits that result from a careful reading of Meshullam Feibush Heller's letters is that they offer us a contemporary window into the views and activities of the emerging Hasidic leadership in eastern Galicia, for R. Yehiel Mikhel and his inner circle, which convened in Brody, were the center of Hasidic leadership in this area.

We should now recall that the second important event that affected the emergence of Hasidism in 1772 was the enactment of anti-Hasidic bans on the part of the Brody Kehillah.[14] It seems highly likely that the statements in that ban directed against Hasidic *minyanim* in the Brody region, were references specifically directed against the Zlotchover Maggid's group, which probably was only beginning to function at about that time. Further evidence for the prominence of R. Yehiel Mikhel as Hasidic leader was the fact that the first edition of *Toledot Ya'aqov Yosef* was burned outside his residence in Brody upon publication in 1781. This act was not merely a gesture directed against a symbolic representative of Hasidism, but was probably equally motivated by the fact that R. Yehiel Mikhel and his disciples were actively engaged in the controversial project of printing kabbalistic works.[15]

Among the interests of R. Yehiel Mikhel's group was the dissemination of Hasidic teachings that were attributed to the Ba'al Shem Tov and the Maggid of Mezeritch along with teachings emanating directly from R. Yehiel Mikhel himself. Although these teachings were not published until the 1790s, when they appeared in various forms in such anthologies as *Liqqutim Yeqarim*, *Zava'at ha-RYVaSH*, and others, Meshulam Feibush's letters made clear that these teachings were already circulating in manuscripts during the 1770s. These manuscripts, it appears, originated in R. Yehiel Mikhel's circle.[16] As such, they constituted a very particular account of Hasidism that represented the distinctive Hasidic outlook of the Maggid of Zlotchov and his followers. It would seem then that these formulations of the teachings and wont of early Hasidic practice, attributed ultimately to the Ba'al Shem Tov and his successor, R. Dov Ber, should be understood as an early interpretation of Hasidism, associated with the school of the Maggid of Zlotchov. This school was to a certain extent, independent of the one that flourished in Lithuania and Belorus, after the death of the Maggid of Mezeritch. The northern school was initially led by several of R. Dov Ber's disciples, most notably R. Menachem Mendel of Vitebsk.[17] It would soon come largely under the leadership of R. Shneur Zalman of Liadi, whose own interpretation of the teachings of the Ba'al Shem Tov and R. Dov Ber of Mezeritch, ultimately became the basis for HaBaD Hasidism.

What makes R. Meshullam Feibush Heller's letters so vitally important is that they not only offer an account of teachings and practices that emanated directly from R. Yehiel Mikhel and his associates, but they also contain a particularly interesting and influential critique and interpretation of many of the most problematic and controversial issues that appear in the early manuscripts. Central to this critique and interpretation is a viewpoint that distinguishes the spiritual practices appropriate for the Hasidic masters, the *Zaddiqim*, from what should be the aspiration and practice of their followers. Although similar in general terms to theoretical distinctions that were also made in the homilies of R. Jacob Joseph of Polnoy, R. Meshullam Feibush's directives reflect specific approaches that emerged from his involvement with the Maggid of Zlotchov and his group. Based largely on a personal response to the charisma of the proto-*Zaddiq*, R. Yehiel Mikhel, the letters emphasize the centrality of faith in the power and purity of the spiritual master's soul. As such, Meshullam Feibush's letters are among the earliest Hasidic texts to offer criteria for distinguishing genuine *Zaddiqim* from ordinary adherents of Hasidism. Moreover, they do so from the viewpoint of a follower who is motivated by his faith in a *Zaddiq* as opposed to texts glorifying the *Zaddiq* that were produced by the *Zaddiqim* themselves.[18] When viewed as an early attempt to distinguish in comprehensive and specific ways between the nature of the true *Zaddiqim* and others, R. Meshullam Feibush's epistle can be appreciated as a precursor of R. Shneur Zalman of Liadi's famous HaBaD Classic, the *Tanya*. However, where the HaBaD text has emphasized the efficacy of efforts made independently by the ordinary Hasid, the *beynoni*, R. Meshullam Feibush emphasizes the futility of spiritual aspiration without faith in the divine aid available only through the *Zaddiq*. This distinction, as we indicated, probably represents a crucial difference between two divergent tendencies in early Hasidism, the northern school that downplayed the charisma of the *Zaddiq* and the eastern Galician school of R. Yehiel Mikhel that, in a manner somewhat reminiscent of Guru worship in Tibetan Buddhism, has championed a path that was more devotionally dependent on the *Zaddiq*'s help.

Because of their comprehensiveness, a study focused on the letters of R. Meshullam Feibush of Zbarazh necessarily identifies and involves nearly all of the most important issues that concerned early Hasidic thinkers. These range from the most fundamental expression of a theology that embraces both transcendence and divine immanence to practical advice concerning how to pray, the meaning of Jewish holy days, and what sacred texts to study.

At the center of most discussions is an emphasis on the possibility of direct mystical apprehension of God, associated with the classical concept of *devequt*. The term is used in several senses by R. Meshullam Feibush. Its usage can range from a contemplative ascension which may culminate in a state of *unio-mystica* to the constant practice of keeping the mind aware of God's presence during even the most mundane aspects of ordinary experience. Because of the importance of this concept in early Hasidism, a substantial chapter is devoted to tracing some of the major lines of development of the concept of *devequt* in kabbalistic, philosophical, and ethical texts that seem to have informed the Hasidic concept. In order to facilitate an appreciation of the nuances in the eastern Galician approach to *devequt* represented by R. Meshullam Feibush, I also have offered a broader view of the term's usage in texts attributed to the Ba'al Shem Tov and two of his most important disciples, R. Jacob Joseph of Polnoy and R. Dov Ber of Mezeritch.

In addition to the mystical dimension, which has been recognized as fundamental at least since Scholem's studies, Meshullam Feibush Heller's approach to Hasidism places perhaps equally great weight on a concomitant ethical value, namely, humility.[19] The connection between the mystical and ethical values has to do with the fact that both mystical *devequt* and humility involve a degree of self-negation. To a certain extent, the ethical effacement of self may be a precondition for mystical states of adhesion to God and identity with the divine. However, even when the mystical dimension of experience is not present, humility as self-effacement is mandated by the central Hasidic theological position that only God really exists.

A third spiritual ideal, which is greatly emphasized as a quality of the *Zaddiqim*, is detachment from corporeality. This refers to the possibility of retaining an essential inner connection to God even when indulging in activities that involve physical pleasure.[20]

The existence of this ideal was fundamental for the development of the Hasidic *Zaddiq*, who, as a result, was enabled to have a closer relationship to disciples of less spiritual accomplishment. Through practicing detachment from corporeality, the *Zaddiq* extended the parameters of divine service and no longer required extensive periods of isolation and concealment in order to elevate fallen spiritual sparks. In a sense, detachment from corporeality was part of what might be termed a "tantric" tendency in Hasidic spirituality. Just as in tantric practice in Tibetan Buddhism, there was a possibility of using aspects of experience that at other levels might be considered outside of the parameters of the spiritual and holy, early Hasidism developed means of incorporating wider spheres of human experience into its highest spiritual practices. This tendency, which was highly controversial and often ridiculed by Hasidism's opponents, was clarifed and interpreted by R. Meshullam Feibush. His view, which would become highly influential, established very exalted criteria for adopting this practice that were so restrictive as to basically limit it to only the most accomplished *Zaddiqim*.

In addition to its championing of specific mystical and ethical ideals and practices for realizing them, eastern Galician Hasidim developed specific approaches to the mainstays of Jewish religious interest, Torah study, prayer, and celebration of the sacred calendar. In approaching these fundamental aspects of Judaism, Hasidism was informed by somewhat conflicting values which emanated from two major kabbalistic sources that developed in sixteenth-century Safed. On the one hand, early Hasidism embraced the redemptive, messianic attitude of Rabbi Isaac Luria's kabbalistic system. This was expressed in terms of an interest in retrieving holy sparks that fell into inappropriate locations as a result of a catastrophe that occurred during the initial stages of the theogonic and cosmogonic process. Characteristically, the restoration of these sparks to their proper locations in the upper worlds involved specific meditative intentions, or *kavvanot*, while performing religious acts. These *kavvanot* had a certain role to play in the Hasidism interpreted by R. Meshullam Feibush. On the other hand, they came into a certain measure of conflict with the emphasis on *devequt* that seems to have been adopted from a second kabbalistic stream, that was taught by Luria's teacher, Rabbi Moses Cordovero.[21] The eastern Galician Hasidic interpretation of *devequt* results in an emphasis on ecstatic prayer and particularly affected the ultimate conception of Torah study through subordinating intellectual aspects to contemplative ideals. The tension between competing Cordoverian and Lurianic values was also apparent in the spiritual meaning associated with the Holy Days.

In presenting all of the issues mentioned above, I have centered all of the discussions on the texts themselves. My method has been to collect all of the texts that seem most important for understanding a particular topic and to translate them in a manner that is both accurate and idiomatic, rather than literal. While I have tried to avoid anachronisms and expressions that might distort the historical contexts and meanings intended, I have also been concerned to render the texts in a form that is as readable as possible. For the most part this has involved making changes not only in word order and syntax, but also in seeking English idioms that express the meaning of the original more effectively than a more literal translation of the Hebrew would have. Wherever possible, I have tried to identify sources and significant parallels for the most important ideas, terms, and concepts utilized in the Hasidic texts. I have also directed the reader to many of the scholarly sources that deal with relevant issues. However, my main objective has been to make the spiritual world of an emerging eastern Hasidic school of the 1770s comprehensible to a contemporary reader. For me, the aspects of this school that deal with contemplation of the divine and spiritual transformation are most significant and interesting. Consequently, the work primarily seeks to clarify such issues and questions relating to them.

I began to study the material contained in this work more than ten years ago, as a graduate student at the University of Pennsylvania and at Hebrew University in Jerusalem. In 1990, I wrote a dissertation under the direction of Professor Arthur Green on R. Meshullam Feibush Heller of

Zbarazh's letters. Since that time, I continued to study this material and to work on the translations of Hasidic sources.

During the past six years, a number of very significant books and essays have been written on aspects of Hasidism that pertain to the subject matter of this book. Among these, four have particularly informed the present version of this work. Moshe Idel's *Hasidism: Between Ecstasy and Magic* broadens our understanding of the range of sources that may have been available to the formulators of Hasidic thought and practice. In addition, his discussion of the relationship between Cordoverian and Lurianic issues is essential for understanding the writings of R. Meshullam Feibush in particular and of the eastern Galician school in general. At the other end of the spectrum, Mendel Piekarz's Hebrew work, *Between Ideology and Reality*, offers a necessary corrective for the tendency to view Hasidism exclusively in terms of its mystical interests. While I cannot always agree with Piekarz's anti-mystical readings of Hasidic texts, his discussion of the extensive Hasidic literature that emphasizes the ethical dimension which complements Hasidic mysticism is very valuable. *Hasidism Reappraised*, edited by Ada Rapoport-Albert, contains many important contributions to the study of Hasidism. Essential essays by Ada Rapoport-Albert, Immanuel Etkes, and others clarify Hasidism's early history and spiritual character and also provide necessary critiques of the methodological foundations of earlier scholarship. Finally, Mor Altshuler's recent Hebrew dissertation, *Rabbi Meshullam Feibush Heller and His Place in Early Hasidism*, offers an esoteric reading of R. Meshullam Feibush's letters and of the activities of R. Yehiel Mikhel of Zlotchov and his school. Her work contains important new information regarding the Zlotchover and his associates and proposes a number of theories of potentially great importance for establishing the centrality of the R. Yehiel Mikhel and his eastern Galician school in the development of early Hasidism.

While the present work has benefited from the scholarly literature mentioned above as well as from numerous other sources, it remains an original contribution for which the author takes complete responsibility. In Arthur Green's essay in *Hasidism Reappraised*,[22] he observes that while Hasidism must certainly be understood within its historical context, it should always be remembered that the history of early Hasidism is a history of religious mystics. As such, it is especially important to understand the nature of the spiritual experience idealized and cultivated by the Hasidic masters. In *Uniter of Heaven and Earth*, I have intended to produce a work that contributes directly to that understanding.

1

Meshullam Feibush Heller and His Circle in Eastern Galicia

From the very first words of *Yosher Divrey Emet*, Meshullam Feibush Heller identifies himself as an adherent of Hasidism, the Jewish mystical school which traces its origin in the middle of the eighteenth century in the Ukraine to Rabbi Israel ben Eliezer, the Ba'al Shem Tov (c. 1700–1760).[1] However, while Meshullam Feibush clearly acknowledges the Ba'al Shem Tov as founder of the movement and occasionally cites his teachings, the major portion of the material that he presents is drawn from the teachings of three of the Ba'al Shem Tov's disciples, R. Dov Ber Maggid of Mezeritch, R. Menahem Mendel of Premishlan, and R. Yehiel Mikhel Maggid of Zlotchov. Of these three, there is no doubt that Dov Ber is generally considered the most important. Known by Hasidim as the Great Maggid, Dov Ber (1704–1772) is, according to Hasidic legend, the chosen successor of the Ba'al Shem Tov.[2] It is Dov Ber's disciples who are generally considered to have been most responsible for the spread and popular success of Hasidism in eastern Europe. Nevertheless, although Dov Ber's influence permeates Meshullam Feibush's writings, a close master-disciple relationship does not seem to have existed between them. Indeed, the nature and extent of Meshullam Feibush's relationship with each of the four Hasidic masters is suggested in the very opening of *Yosher Divrey Emet.*

> He asked me to write "upright words of truth"[3] and faith which were heard from the enlightened ones of the generation, wonder workers, full of the holy spirit, whom I had personally seen, their fear and awe [of God] was like that of an angel, and all of them drank from one stream, namely, the divine Rabbi Israel Ba'al Shem Tov . . . ,[4] However, I only merited to see the face of his disciple, the divine R. Dov Ber, and later I acquired sacred writings [containing] his holiness' words[5] [which] arouse the heart of [those] who tremble for the service of God in truth. Several times I was also in the presence of the oak, the divine R. Menahem Mendel of Premishlan. But most of all, to distinguish between the dead and the living, [I am expounding] what I heard from the mouth of the holy of holies, son of saints, *zaddiq* son of a *zaddiq,* the exceptional *rav,* our divine master and teacher, R. Yehiel Mikhel [of Zlotchov], may his light shine.[6]

This passage tells us much of Meshullam Feibush's background. We see that he associates himself with the school of Israel Ba'al Shem Tov. Although he has never met him personally, he has had the opportunity to learn from three of the Ba'al Shem Tov's direct disciples. Since one of these, Menahem Mendel of Premishlan, emigrated to the Land of Israel in 1764,[7] it may be that Meshullam Feibush only became interested in the teachings of the Ba'al Shem Tov during the period between the latter's death and Menahem Mendel's departure from Eastern Europe, that is, sometime between the years 1760–1764.

As for Dov Ber, although Meshullam Feibush did indeed meet him, his knowledge of the Maggid's teachings is very much influenced by posthumously circulated writings which he has but recently obtained. These writings must be the manuscripts that were indeed circulated by disciples of Dov Ber during the mid to late 1770s.[8] We may also note that, while Meshullam Feibush mentions encountering Menahem Mendel several times, he only states that he "managed to see the Maggid of Mezeritch." The wording suggests that the two may have met only once. This reading is supported by other evidence in the text. Although reference is often made to Dov Ber's teachings in our text, in many cases the teachings are quoted from the manuscripts. Otherwise, Dov Ber's teachings are usually presented as having been heard from one of his disciples. Only once does Meshullam Feibush actually quote a teaching of the Maggid as something that he himself heard directly.

> And I heard from the mouth of the holy of holies, the divine R. Dov Ber of blessed memory, on that *Shabbat* that I spent with him while he was alive, when they asked him about a certain midrash, and he spoke concerning an analogy there in midrash [Leviticus Rabbah] . . .[9]

The text implies that Meshullam Feibush visited the Maggid on only one occasion, a certain *Shabbat*, when Dov Ber was asked to interpret the midrashic comparison of a disciple of the wise to a golden bell with a clapper of pearls.[10]

As for Meshullam Feibush's visit, it is known that during the late 1760s and early 1770s, the Maggid of Mezeritch began to gain fame. During the last five years of his life, he received many visitors who were interested in his teachings. For the most part, such visits were the result of the propagandizing activity of Dov Ber's disciples who encouraged prospective adherents to visit the Maggid of Mezeritch. It is also known, that the Maggid had the custom of improvising homilies on themes spontaneously suggested by his audience.[11] Such might have been the case on the occasion recorded by Meshullam Feibush. At any rate, the evidence suggests that aside from the manuscripts that he had only recently received, Meshullam Feibush knew Dov Ber's teachings only indirectly. His great respect for the Maggid was due to the latter's reputation as a leading exponent of the teachings of the Ba'al Shem Tov. However, it is significant that Meshullam Feibush never explicitly referred to Dov Ber as the successor to the Ba'al Shem Tov. This may suggest the extent that Meshullam Feibush valued his own eastern Galician traditions concerning the Ba'al Shem Tov's teachings.

Indeed, the two other masters mentioned, Menahem Mendel and Yehiel Mikhel, are quoted frequently on the basis of teachings which Meshullam Feibush heard directly. Thus, it is clear that these Galician masters are his primary teachers. This is particularly the case in regard to Yehiel Mikhel who was the only one of the three still alive at the time Meshullam Feibush began to write our text.[12] He is treated with the elaborate terms of reverence which befit a living master. Moreover, some of his teachings had been heard during the holiday of *Shavuot*, 1777, only shortly before the time of writing.[13] Clearly, an important master-disciple relationship existed between Meshullam Feibush and Yehiel Mikhel who was certainly one of the most important figures associated with the teachings of the Ba'al Shem Tov in eastern Galicia during the late 1770s.[14]

In addition, both Menahem Mendel and Yehiel Mikhel were active in the same part of eastern Galicia where Meshullam Feibush lived and were themselves closely connected.[15] Thus, we must assume that Meshullam Feibush was primarily influenced directly by Hasidic leaders in his own area. This is born out by the fact that, aside from Dov Ber, virtually everyone that Meshullam Feibush quoted in *Yosher Divrey Emet* was active in eastern Galicia. Even where he cited figures, who were more directly connected to the Maggid of Mezeritch, they were leaders from his own locality. It is significant that not one of the leading disciples of the Maggid of Mezeritch, such as R. Levi Isaac of Berdichev, R. Menahem Mendel of Vitebsk, or even the peripatetic R. Menahem Nahum of Chernobyl, who flourished in other parts of eastern Europe, was quoted as a source of the Ba'al Shem Tov's teachings.[16]

Perhaps even more significant was the total absence of any reference to two other disciples of Dov Ber, R. Samuel Shmelke of Nikolsburg and R. Elimelekh of Lizhensk, both of whom had been active in Galicia by this time. While the Rabbi of Nikolsburg died in Moravia only shortly after Meshullam Feibush was writing,[17] his disciple, R. Elimelekh, continued to be fully established at that time as a *Zaddiq* in Galicia and functioned as such

only slightly to the west. Indeed R. Elimelekh's position would seem to parallel that of Yehiel Mikhel. Both were famous as *Zaddiqim* and important
for establishing early centers of Hasidic activity in Galicia.[18] Moreover, a
close disciple of Elimelekh, R. Zekhariah Menahem Mendel of Yaroslav,
wrote a defense of his master and of *zaddiqism* at about the same time that
Meshullam Feibush was writing his epistles.[19] Nevertheless, the only connection between these two major figures, which occurred in Meshullam
Feibush's writings, was indirect. One of the sons of Elimelekh's older
brother, the famous Hasidic master, Zusya of Anipol, was mentioned as having been present at the court of Yehiel Mikhel during one of Meshullam
Feibush's visits.

The evidence presented above suggests that the positions taken regarding Hasidic teachings in Meshullam Feibush's writings and especially the
specific attitudes expressed concerning Dov Ber's practices may not only
represent the views of a distinct eastern Galician school that operated somewhat independently, but also parallel to another influential Galician school
of disciples of the Maggid of Mezeritch, which may trace its origins to
Shmelke of Nikolsburg. Rabbi Shmelke's school had a profound influence
on the spread of Hasidism into Poland. Among Shmelke of Nikolsburg's disciples were Levi Isaac of Berdichev, Elimelekh of Lizhensk, and Israel of
Kozhenitz.[20] However, the eastern Galician school may have originated
with Menahem Mendel of Premishlan. Nevertheless, its central figure and
undisputed leader during the 1770s must certainly have been Yehiel Mikhel
of Zlotchov. While too rigid a distinction between the members of these two
schools should not be assumed, it seems highly likely that Meshullam
Feibush's epistles were addressed to a circle of eastern Galician Hasidim that
not only centered around the teachings of Yehiel Mikhel, but which was also
distinct from the Hasidic school in the north associated with R. Menahem
Mendel of Vitebsk and, later, R. Shneur Zalman of Liadi.[21]

However, this eastern Galician "school" was certainly not essentially
hostile to Dov Ber and his teachings. Important relationships between close
disciples of Dov Ber and members of this school were evident.[22] Meshullam
Feibush himself visited the Maggid of Mezeritch on at least one occasion
and it is clear that he was intensely interested in Dov Ber's teachings. Yet, it
is also apparent from Meshullam Feibush's writings that certain crucial differences existed between the teachings of the Maggid of Mezeritch and the
Hasidic path that Meshullam Feibush had learned directly from his eastern
Galician masters. It was precisely the tension that resulted from loyalty to
Dov Ber as authentic interpreter of the Ba'al Shem Tov's teachings and a
sense of urgency concerning the need to interpret his teachings in the light

of Menahem Mendel and Yehiel Mikhel's example, that motivated Meshullam Feibush to address certain key aspects of Hasidic practice in his tractates. Undoubtedly, Meshullam Feibush was also influenced by extra-Hasidic historical factors. He must have been at least partially motivated to tone down radical elements in Hasidic teachings as a result of organized and severe opposition to Hasidism in the Brody region.[23] Nevertheless, I have chosen to emphasize inter-Hasidic tensions which may have required resolution even without the added external pressures.

In the remainder of this chapter, the biographies of the two Galician masters who directly influenced Meshullam Feibush and formed the center of his circle will be discussed. After discussing the lives and selected teachings of Menahem Mendel of Premishlan and Yehiel Mikhel of Zlotchov, the discussion will turn to the life of Meshullam Feibush and his writings.

Rabbi Menahem Mendel of Premishlan

As in the case of many other early Hasidim, little is known concerning the life of R. Menahem Mendel of Premishlan. He has composed no works,[24] has founded no dynasty, and has figured only infrequently in Hasidic hagiographic sources. Nevertheless a collection of his teachings and several scholarly works, dealing with aspects of his life, provide a basis for drawing the basic lines of his character and teachings.[25]

Little is known concerning Menahem Mendel's early life. We have no sources concerning his place of birth, ancestry, or early teachers. It is only known that his father's name was Eliezer and his mother's name may have been Batsheva.[26] He had at least two brothers. One was known as Zvi the Hasid. He resided in Zlotchov as well as in Yampol and was closely associated with R. Yehiel Mikhel, the Maggid of Zlotchov. One of the most important editions of the teachings of Dov Ber of Mezritch, *Or ha-Emet*, was based on a manuscript that had belonged to Zvi the Hasid.[27] Another brother, Eleazar, helped support Menahem Mendel while the latter was in the Land of Israel.[28]

The earliest references to Menahem Mendel concern events that occurred during the period 1757–1764 when he was already an important disciple of the Ba'al Shem Tov. A story in *Shivhey ha-BeSHT*, a collection of legends dealing with the Ba'al Shem Tov and his disciples, indicates that Menahem Mendel was thirty-six years old in 1764.[29] Thus, he may have been born in 1728. One account indicates that Menahem Mendel met the Ba'al Shem Tov.

According to the *Sefer Vikuah* of R. Israel, the Maggid of Slutzk, Menahem Mendel joined the Ba'al Shem Tov and his brother-in-law, R. Gershon
of Kutov for a meal that occurred sometime between 1757–1760.[30] However, it is neither possible to determine how close a relationship existed between the Ba'al Shem Tov and his young disciple, nor whether Menahem
Mendel learned the Ba'al Shem Tov's esoteric teachings directly from the
master.

An anecdote in *Shivhey ha-BeSHT* indicates that Menahem Mendel
was astonished upon learning "the Ba'al Shem Tov's wisdom" from R. Nahman of Horodenka. The term "wisdom" possibly referred to the Ba'al Shem
Tov's new esoteric method for elevating wayward thoughts during prayer.[31]
Thus, it would seem that Menahem Mendel only learned this unique teaching of the Ba'al Shem Tov after the latter's death.[32] Indeed, although Menahem Mendel became a major Hasidic leader and follower of the Ba'al Shem
Tov, there is no indication in his extant teachings that he ever accepted or
taught the controversial method of elevating wayward thoughts.[33]

It appears that Menahem Mendel had gained considerable recognition
by the 1760s. In 1764, he visited R. Jacob Joseph of Polnoy, the Ba'al Shem
Tov's leading disciple. Although perhaps twenty-five years his senior, Jacob
Joseph treated Menahem Mendel with great respect, placing his own quarters at his guest's disposal. In addition, he made arrangements so that Menahem Mendel could lead the prayers in a private prayer quorum of his own.
Moreover, according to a legendary source, when Menahem Mendel reached
the town of Old Konstantynow, "the whole city went out to welcome
him."[34] A particularly important relationship existed between Menahem
Mendel and R. Nahman of Horodenka (c. 1680–1765). The latter became a
close associate and disciple of the Ba'al Shem Tov sometime during the
1740s.

R. Nahman's second son, Simhah, was later to marry the Ba'al Shem
Tov's granddaughter, Feiga. Among their children was the famous R. Nahman of Bratzlav.[35] In 1764, Menahem Mendel emigrated to the Land of Is-
rael with R. Nahman of Horodenka and several other Hasidim, including R.
Fridel of Brody.[36] From a contemporary account of the voyage, Menahem
Mendel was able to afford larger than average quarters on the ship. The
Hasidim reached Tiberias on the eve of *Sukkot*. They were favorably re-
ceived by the dominant Sefardic community and quickly became leaders of
the small Ashkenazic community. The flattering account of two Ashkenazic
Hasidim that appeared in a contemporary work by R. Hayyim Joseph David
Azulai is, in all probability, an eyewitness description of the two.[37] The same
author explicitly cited Menahem Mendel in his commentary to Psalms.[38]

While the aged R. Nahman only lived until the following summer, Menahem Mendel survived as leader of the Ashkenazic community in the Galilee for several more years. His prominence was indicated by two additional sources. In the summer of 1765, R. David Halperin of Ostrog, a wealthy disciple of the Ba'al Shem Tov, died. In his will, he bequeathed 200 thalers to Menahem Mendel and 150 thalers each to R. Nahman and R. Fridel.[39] In addition, Menahem Mendel's name appeared at the top of the list of signatories on an appeal for funds for the Jewish community in the Galilee.[40]

The exact date of Menahem Mendel's death is not known. According to one source, he died in 1771.[41] The tombstone in Tiberias indicates only that his death occurred on the 21 of Tishri.[42]

The reasons for Menahem Mendel's emigration to the Land of Israel are obscure. However, at least three factors may have influenced his decision. In the letter to his brother, R. Zvi the Hasid of Zlotchov, Menahem Mendel emphasizes the sanctity of the Holy Land and chastises his brother for remaining abroad. (Love for the Land of Israel was an important motive in early Hasidic thought. The Ba'al Shem Tov, himself, according to Hasidic legend, failed in two attempts to reach the Holy Land.[43] Other important figures like Jacob Joseph of Polnoy and Pinhas of Koretz also saw their dreams of living in the Land of Israel frustrated.) Thus, love for the Land of Israel, itself, might have been sufficient motivation for Menahem Mendel's emigration. While, the extant sources do not suggest that this motivation was tinged by messianism, *per se*, this motive cannot be entirely ruled out. It was a certainly is a factor in the thought of his disciple Meshullam Feibush, who explicitly mentions it in connection to the Hasidic emigration of 1777.[44]

A second factor may have been the desire to escape persecution by the opponents to Hasidism. However, such persecution is best documented and seems to have been most pronounced in eastern Galicia at a somewhat later period.

Beginning in the late 1760s and continuing into the 1780s, Hasidim were persecuted in the Brody region. In 1772, a ban against Hasidim was published in Brody. Less than a decade later, the first Hasidic publication, *Toledot Ya'aqov Yosef*, was publicly burned there, outside the residence of R. Yehiel Mikhel.[45] However, Meshullam Feibush indicated that opposition had already been directed against Menahem Mendel.[46] Although such early opposition probably did not equal the organized persecution later suffered by the Hasidim, it may yet have contributed to Menahem Mendel's decision to leave for the Land of Israel.

Abraham Rubenstein suggested a third reason. In the period following the Ba'al Shem Tov's death in 1760, various Hasidic leaders and factions vied for the role of successor to their master. Only sometime after Menahem Mendel's departure, R. Dov Ber of Mezeritch became the dominant Hasidic leader. Rubenstein speculated that Menahem Mendel may himself have been a candidate for Hasidic leadership and may have fled from the role due to his extreme modesty.[47] However, the plausibility of this theory is mitigated by the fact that Menahem Mendel was recognized as a leader almost immediately upon his arrival in Tiberias. The Ashkenazic community there was a small one and his role there could not have been commensurable to the position of authority he might have attained in eastern Europe. Thus, the desire to escape fame and its responsibilities could conceivably have motivated him to some degree.[48]

While Menahem Mendel's association with the Ba'al Shem Tov and his disciples, Jacob Joseph of Polnoy and Nahman of Horodenka is clear, his relationship to Dov Ber, the Ba'al Shem Tov's successor remains problematical. To my knowledge, only one Hasidic legend exists concerning their meeting.[49]

According to this account, when Dov Ber had become famous, Menahem Mendel wished to visit him. However, perhaps to test the Maggid, Menahem Mendel concealed his identity. His servant was instructed to introduce him as an ordinary Jew named Barukh. Dov Ber, nevertheless, welcomed him as R. Mendel of Premishlan. When Menahem Mendel protested that his name was Barukh, the Maggid replied with the verse, "*Barukh* (blessed) he shall be."[50]

While the historicity of this alleged encounter is difficult to verify, it is nevertheless worthwhile to take note of the relationship between the two Hasidic leaders that the story depicts. First, the legend indicates that Menahem Mendel only met Dov Ber after the latter had become famous. This would probably have occurred during the 1760s, since Dov Ber became associated with the Ba'al Shem Tov only shortly before the latter's death. Menahem Mendel, presumably, did not know much about Dov Ber or his teachings. Nevertheless, positive relations were established between the two. The story is curious for several reasons. Significant differences exist between the teachings of Dov Ber and the extant teachings of Menahem Mendel. The harmonization of these differences, indeed plays a central role in Meshullam Feibush's synthesis of conflicting early Hasidic approaches.[51] Nevertheless, the one work attributed to Menahem Mendel *Darkhey Yesharim*, is primarily a variant of material contained in a manuscript of Dov Ber's teachings.[52]

This text would seem to deny that important differences existed between the teachings of Menahem Mendel and Dov Ber. However, it is now apparent that *Darkhey Yesharim* may well have been edited by Meshullam Feibush. Thus, the tendency to harmonize the relationship and teachings of the two early masters may be the result of Meshullam Feibush's efforts. In this case our story would merely reflect this tendency.

The relationship between Menahem Mendel and Meshullam Feibush's other Galician master, R. Yehiel Mikhel of Zlotchov, is well attested. Menahem Mendel's letter to his brother, Zvi the Hasid, adds greetings to Yehiel Mikhel and his son, R. Joseph of Yampol. It also mentions Solomon Vilner, who is quoted by Meshullam Feibush.[53] The letter indicates that Menahem Mendel maintained close relations with Yehiel Mikhel and his school even after his move to Tiberias. Although no other letters are presently extant, the possibility must be considered that additional correspondence may have existed between Menahem Mendel and Meshullam Feibush's circle. While Mershullam Feibush is not mentioned in this letter, this may be explained by assuming that he was not in Zlotchov at the time. Other letters directed to him in Zbarazh may have existed which are simply lost to us at present. At any rate, one source claims that Menahem Mendel entrusted the spiritual guidance of the young Meshullam Feibush to Yehiel Mikhel before he embarked for the Land of Israel.[54] While the story may be apocryphal, there is reason to believe that Yehiel Mikhel was in some sense the successor of Menahem Mendel among the Hasidim in the Brody area.[55] Nevertheless, while Yehiel Mikhel may have shared certain attitudes with Menahem Mendel, he was also directly connected to the Ba'al Shem Tov and seems to have formed a relationship with Dov Ber of Mezeritch, perhaps after Menahem Mendel's departure.

Although the details of Menahem Mendel's life are scant, key aspects of his personality emerged rather clearly from the sources at hand. According to an anecdote in *Shivhey ha-BeSHT*, Menahem Mendel disliked the adulation his fame as a holy man brought him. When he visited R. Jacob Joseph in Nemerov in 1764, shortly before embarking for the Land of Israel, he was reported to have complained "about the great honor that was accorded to him."[56] When Jacob Joseph informed him that the Ba'al Shem Tov used to pray that people would disparage him, he replied that he had also considered such a course. Humility, of course, was a major theme in virtually all early Hasidic teaching. According to Meshullam Feibush's view, the Hasidic *Zaddiqim* never pursued fame and authority. Precisely because of their great humility, they were chosen and compelled by God to assume the mantle of leadership.[57] In all likelihood, Meshullam Feibush's concept of the Hasidic leader was modeled on the personal example of his teachers, Menahem Mendel and, especially, Yehiel Mikhel of Zlotchov.

Although a Hasidic account denied that Menahem Mendel ever practiced asceticism, his temperament must nevertheless be regarded as essentially ascetic in nature. The same account informed us that Menahem Mendel welcomed and prayed for afflictions which he considered signs of divine favor.[58] As for shunning ascetic practices, the meaning must be that Menahem Mendel deemphasized fasting and other practices that weakened the body. Excessive fasting as a basis for repentance characterized the kabbalists of Safed and was typical of pre-Beshtian hasidim in eastern Europe. Menahem Mendel, like several other early Hasidic teachers, was opposed to practices that afflicted the body. Nevertheless, it is clear that he followed a rigorous path of self-discipline and shunned physical pleasure. Detachment from corporeality was an essential element in his teaching and practice. According to Meshullam Feibush, Menahem Mendel was especially critical of those who believed that they could sanctify the act of eating by merely making use of Lurianic *kavvanot*.[59] As long as they continued to delight in the pleasure of their meal, he felt that their pious intentions were of no avail.[60]

Indeed, eating in sanctity seems to have been at least as important to Menahem Mendel as prayer. A Hasidic source tells us that he was accustomed to immersing himself in a ritual bath before meals, but not before prayer. Meals for Menahem Mendel were primarily an occasion for uplifting divine sparks.[61]

Menahem Mendel practiced an intense form of self-awareness. R. Abraham David of Buczacz reported that Menahem Mendel's spiritual perfection was the result of an unusual practice. He paused in the middle of each statement, presumably in order to detach himself and to rest his consciousness in *devequt*. He also practiced a similar form of detachment whenever he was looking at something.[62] Intense concentration on his inner state was accompanied by a concern for purity of speech that is reflected in a number of Menahem Mendel's extant teachings. Moreover, the importance of this concern may have impelled him to adopt another extreme and somewhat unusual practice. The author of *Shivhey ha-BeSHT* stated that when Menahem Mendel made his visit to R. Jacob Joseph, he had not spoken for twelve years. During that time, he communicated only by writing. Apparently, Menahem Mendel was so out of the habit of speaking that he was unable to respond coherently to Jacob Joseph's questions.[63]

Silence as a spiritual practice is well attested to in a number of spiritual traditions.[64] Nevertheless, the story concerning Menahem Mendel may exaggerate what was probably a definite tendency towards restraint in speech rather than a long-standing practice of silence. No reason is given for Menahem Mendel's breaking his silence in order to speak to Jacob Joseph. Nor is his practice of silence confirmed in other sources.

A document from the Asher Pearl library provided another interesting view of Menahem Mendel's behavior, shortly before he left eastern Europe.[65] As reported in *Shevhey ha-BeSHT*, before arriving at Nemerov to visit Jacob Joseph, Menahem Mendel spent some time in Cekinowka, a town on the left bank of the Dniester, in the region of Yampol. According to the document, while in Cekinowka, Menahem Mendel became very angry at people who were clapping their hands during prayer. He, himself, "stood still as a corpse," not moving at all while reciting the eighteen benedictions, except for the mandatory bows. He stayed up all night learning Torah. Shortly before dawn, he immersed himself in the ritual bath so as to be ready to begin his morning prayers precisely at dawn. The account bears out Menahem Mendel's rather severe demeanor. (Clapping and exhuberance during prayer is an Hasidic hallmark which frequently was criticized by the movement's opponents. However, it is clear that not all Hasidic masters favored excessive emotionalism.)

Menahem Mendel's approach to prayer emphasized concentration and sincerity through the unity of mind and utterance. This is the approach which Meshullam Feibush strongly advocated in *Yosher Divrey Emet*. Another practice for which some Hasidic leaders were criticized was delaying the beginning of prayer until the appropriate spiritual preparation had been achieved. Such clearly was not Menahem Mendel's habit. Like the Ba'al Shem Tov, he began his morning prayers at the preferred time, dawn. It is interesting that the account did not depict Menahem Mendel as having ceased his learning for the superogatory midnight devotions. This practice, *Tiqqun Hazot*,[66] appeared in most kabbalistic prayerbooks and was adopted by many Hasidim. Menahem Mendel, however, was depicted as having spent the entire night immersed in Torah study.

In general, Menahem Mendel was inclined to a rather austere life-style of self-discipline. His legendary silence and disdain for adulation indicated a dislike for social intercourse. According to the Asher Pearl document, Menahem Mendel left for the Land of Israel precisely because "[people] began to travel to him in order to receive a blessing."[67] Nevertheless, several of the teachings attributed to Menahem Mendel indicated concern for the less fortunate. An example of the extent of his compassion was also recorded in the Asher Pearl document. At the time that Menahem Mendel was visiting in Cekinowka, Bessarabia, which was located on the other bank of the Dniester, belonged to the Turkish Empire. Once, when Menahem Mendel went to immerse himself in the river, he heard a Jew calling to him from the other bank. The Jew was being held captive by the Turks in Soroki, Bessarabia. Menahem Mendel crossed the river and redeemed the Jew with the money he had received from his uncle for the trip to the Land of Israel. (The Ba'al Shem Tov and his disciples were famous for their efforts to redeem Jewish captives. However, such behavior was by no means typical.) Indeed, Menahem Mendel's uncle became angry at him when he learned of the good deed. Menahem Mendel regarded the religious obligation of zedaqah, aiding the unfortunate, in a special light.) An early Hasidic source preserves a teaching in his name which argues that divine commandments that are observed for ulterior motivations would be better left undone. The only exception was zedaqah.)[68]

Like many of the early Hasidim, Menahem Mendel was famous for the intensity of his prayer. Twice in Shivhey ha-BeSHT, it was mentioned that Jacob Joseph praised the prayer of Rabbi Mendel. Once he said: "I, too, became like one of the common folk and forgot the way to pray. They reminded me of the way of prayer."[69] Yehiel Mikhel of Zlotchov was also impressed by Menahem Mendel's manner of praying. Generally, Yehiel Mikhel always insisted on leading the prayers himself. He was reported to have told his disciples that only for the Messiah would he relinquish his position. Nevertheless, when Menahem Mendel visited, he was accorded the honor of standing before the ark. When Yehiel Mikhel was questioned concerning this, he replied, "for [Menahem Mendel,] Messiah would also relinquish the position of prayer leader."[70] On another occasion, Yehiel Mikhel is said to have fled from the room where Menahem Mendel was leading the prayers, lest his soul expire from the sweetness of Menahem Mendel's prayer.[71] According to an early Hasidic source, Menahem Mendel taught that prayer should be so intense that even the wicked who have never prayed in their lives, would feel compelled to pray.[72]

We have already mentioned Menahem Mendel's emphasis on eating as a sacred act. An interesting teaching reported in his name sheds light on his approach to eating and asceticism. According to Menahem Mendel, a person who ceases his meal while he still has desire for food attains a higher spiritual level than a person who fasts. For the former feels more intensely the desire to eat since he restrains himself precisely in the midst of his desire. On the other hand, while fasting, one's soul is not so afflicted, since he is not directly tempted by the taste of food.[73] The teaching seems to echo a radical tendency in the sixteenth-century popularization of Safedian Kabbalah, Sheney Luhot ha-Berit, where it is maintained that greater merit is attained when a mizvah is performed with both "urges." A higher level is attained when one acts after subduing the evil urge.[74] In general, Menahem Mendel seems to have disapproved of fasting as a spiritual practice for two reasons. First, it weakens the body and thus results in a reduced capacity to carry out other religious practices effectively. In addition, he seems to have seen in fasting a not very effective method of turning to God, which could easily be employed in an hypocritical manner. One might think that the merely physical deprivation of fasting atoned for spiritual deficiencies.

Menahem Mendel was more interested in a transformation of both one's inner state and outward behavior. Consequently, he recommended a spiritual regimen that began with the "fasting of the limbs." One began, for example, by a fast of the eyes. For one day a week, one refrained from looking at anything that is not essential. Gradually, the length of time is increased. Subsequently, the same principle was applied to hearing and the other senses. Only when the total process of transformation had been completed, was a single day of fasting, in the conventional sense, of great value.[75]

After leaving eastern Europe in 1764, Menahem Mendel spent the remainder of his life in the Land of Israel. It is clear that the Holy Land held great spiritual significance for him. In one teaching, he asserted that the second day of holidays (celebrated only outside the Land of Israel) was more important than the first day. The reason was that the sanctity of the holiday manifested in the Holy Land on the first day, but does not reach the Jewish communities abroad until the second day.[76] Despite the superior sanctity of the Holy Land, Menahem Mendel initially was not able to attain the spiritual level he had experienced in eastern Europe. However, he soon overcame his problems until even his simplest prayers in the Land of Israel were equivalent to his most intense spiritual experiences in eastern Europe.[77] In a famous dictim, Menahem Mendel was reported to have said that while he was still in eastern Europe, he used to beg God to allow him to pray one entire prayer properly. However, the atmosphere of the Holy Land made him wiser. Now he asked only that he be permitted to say a single word properly.[78]

Several of Menahem Mendel's teachings have been preserved regarding the problem of disturbing thoughts during prayer. The teachings indicate an approach to the problem that differs significantly from the teachings of Dov Ber of Mezeritch. According to Dov Ber, wayward thoughts or distractions that enter the mind while praying, are divinely granted opportunities for releasing holy sparks that have fallen captive to the external shells. When one becomes aware of the intruding thought, the divine source of the fallen spark can be identified. For example, a sexual thought ultimately derives from *hesed*, loving-kindness. Dov Ber advocates elevating the holy sparks

through concentrating on the appropriate divine source or root of the wayward thought.[79] However, according to Menahem Mendel, wayward
thoughts arise during prayer because one is not satisfied with his current
spiritual level. The desire for higher spiritual states interferes with the concentration that is required for true prayer. Only through self-effacement
and humble acceptance of one's present state can genuine communion with
God be achieved. Like Dov Ber, Menahem Mendel also sees the goal of
prayer as *devequt* through detachment from corporeality. But the practice of
elevating wayward thoughts plays no part in the process of attaining intimacy with God.[80]

Further evidence that Menahem Mendel did not advocate the practice
of elevating wayward thoughts, which was an innovation of the Ba'al Shem
Tov, can be deduced from a teaching found in *Degel Mahaneh Efraim*. Menahem Mendel recommended the practice of mentally visualizing the Tetragrammaton as a remedy for overcoming wayward thoughts.[81] In the passage cited, Menahem Mendel attributed the passage to the Safedian
kabbalist, Isaac Luria. This was a standard Hasidic practice which the Ba'al
Shem Tov wanted to replace by the new method of elevating rather than
merely dispersing wayward thoughts. The newer method was more appropriate for the non-dual tendency in the Ba'al Shem Tov's teachings, which
asserted that God was present in every thought. Interestingly enough, the
passage in *Degel Mahaneh Efraim* juxtaposed both approaches. After attributing the old approach to Menahem Mendel, the method of elevating wayward thoughts was recommended by the author as a teaching he learned
from his grandfather, the Ba'al Shem Tov. As suggested by the juxtaposi-
tion, the new method never entirely replaced the old.[82]

As a disciple of Menahem Mendel, who later came under the influence
of Dov Ber, Meshullam Feibush was accutely aware of the need to resolve
the inherent conflict between the two approaches. His solution in *Yosher
Divrey Emet* presented a position that would often be echoed in subsequent
Hasidic literature.

Although the available evidence strongly suggests that Menahem Mendel did not embrace the new method of elevating wayward thoughts during
prayer, he may, nevertheless, have accepted the principle of the Ba'al Shem
Tov's teaching, at least in part. A reliable early Hasidic source attributes a
teaching to Menahem Mendel that does explicitly mention elevating
thoughts that are tainted by impure motives. Possibly, he had in mind elevating impure thoughts that occur at times other than prayer. The implication
seems to be that vices need to be replaced by their corresponding virtues.[83]

Of the teachings that Meshullam Feibush brings in the name of Menahem Mendel, mention should be made of one passage which asserts that

mystical experience or *devequt*, is the essence of Jewish esoteric teachings. While *devequt* is, perhaps, the most fundamental teaching of early Hasidism, Menahem Mendel's position is extreme. He argues that the term *nistar* does not, as conventionally conceived, refer to the esoteric literature of the Kabbalah, per se, but rather to the ineffable inner experience of love and awe of God.[84] While Menahem Mendel continues to speak in Lurianic terms of elevating holy sparks as the primary religious task, *devequt* rather than the esoteric Lurianic meditative formulae is the essential element that accomplishes the goal.

Due to several factors, Menahem Mendel remained a somewhat obscure figure in the early annals of Hasidism. He left eastern Europe before Hasidism became a popular movement. Most of his mature period was spent in the tiny Ashkenazic community of Tiberias. He founded no dynasty to establish his teachings and immortalize his name. Nevertheless, Menahem Mendel must be regarded as one of the foremost early Hasidic figures in eastern Galicia. His teachings were preserved in several of the most important early Hasidic texts by such authors as Benjamin of Zalozitz, Abraham Hayyim of Zlotchov, Uziel Meisels, Moshe Hayyim Ephraim of Sudilkov, Raphael of Bershad, and others.[85] As for his disciple, Meshullam Feibush, in his view, Menahem Mendel was a divinely inspired spiritual giant of the same order as the Ba'al Shem Tov and his nominal successor, Dov Ber, the Maggid of Mezeritch.

Yehiel Mikhel, the Maggid of Zlotchov

Sometime after Menahem Mendel of Premishlan emigrated to the Land of Israel, Yehiel Mikhel of Zlotchov became Meshullam Feibush's spiritual master. A disciple of the Ba'al Shem Tov in his youth, Yehiel Mikhel became one of the most important and influential of the early leaders of Hasidism in Galicia.[86] Yehiel Mikhel was a spiritual aristocrat: the descendent of a long line of rabbis, ascetics, and charismatics, which dated back, according to family tradition, at least to the medieval French exegete, Rabbi Shlomo Yitzhaqi (Rashi). His paternal great-grandfather was Moses of Pistyn, Rabbi of Swierze (near Premishlan), whose martyrdom is described in Barukh of Kossover's *Amud ha-Avodah*.[87] The account of Rabbi Moses' death indicated the extraordinary level of religious dedication that Yehiel Mikhel was to inherit. It is said that although a wooden spike was driven through virtually the entire length of his body, he felt no pain. The murder took place just before the eve of the Sabbath. Since R. Moses fasted all week, his bowels were empty. He managed to avoid experiencing pain as a result of concentrating his mind exclusively on the fervent repetition of God's praises.[88] Yehiel Mikhel's grandfather, Joseph of Pistyn, was an ascetic like his father, Moses. In his later years, about 1742, he emigrated to the Land of Israel where he died. According to a story in *Mayim Rabbim*, Joseph encountered the Ba'al Shem Tov on the way to the Holy Land. He predicted that he himself would reach the destination, while the Ba'al Shem Tov would be compelled to return to eastern Europe.[89]

Yehiel Mikhel's father, R. Isaac of Drohobitch (before 1700–c.1758),[90] was famous in eastern Galicia as a religious judge and kabbalist. Primarily during the 1730s, he was a member of the rabbinic court in Brody that also included Isaac Horowitz of Hamburg and Ezekiel Landau, author of *Noda bi-Yehudah*. About 1754, he moved to Ostrog, where he was one of the ten subsidized scholars at R. Yospe's House of Study.[91] His final years were spent in Horochov.

As a member of the important rabbinical court in Brody,[92] Isaac of Drohobitch possessed great knowledge of religious law. Yet, a curious story indicates that his legal decisions were not always made merely on the basis of legal expertise. Once, in a case involving the demand for payment of a debt owed by a deceased merchant, Yehiel Mikhel's father disagreed with Isaac Horowitz's ruling. Although no legal evidence of the debt existed, Isaac of Drohobitch claimed that he had seen the deceased who admitted the debt.[93] As for his prowess as a kabbalist, an early Hasidic source reported that once Isaac lost his way in a forest. As a result of utilizing a special mystical combination of letters (*yihud*) to bless the spirit of the forest, the forest guided him safely to his destination.[94]

Isaac of Drohobitch did not become an actual follower of the Ba'al Shem Tov.[95] In all likelihood, R. Isaac, who was believed to possess prophetic powers,[96] was an ascetic kabbalist of the hasidic type that preceded the Ba'al Shem Tov's innovations. As such, he may initially have been opposed to the new Hasidic leader. Nevertheless, the two met on more than one occasion and Hasidic tradition indicated that they came to hold each other in high regard.[97] Isaac of Drohobitch's teachings were recorded by the authors of a number of early Hasidic works, including Benjamin of Zalozitz, Abraham David of Buczacz, Issachar Ber of Zlotchov, and R. Joseph Bloch.[98] In addition, several stories concerning Yehiel Mikhel's father were contained in *Shivhey ha-BeShT*.[99]

It is difficult to determine the exact year of Yehiel Mikhel's birth; several dates appeared in the sources, ranging from 1721–1734.[100] In all likelihood, he was born in Brody, probably in 1726. A fantastic story concerning the birth maintained that many sons had previously been born to Isaac of

Drohobitch and his wife, before Yehiel Mikhel. However, on each occasion, the father expressed disappointment when he viewed the baby. As a result, the infant died shortly thereafter. When Yehiel Mikhel was born, his mother refused to permit Isaac to view the child until he had promised to spare him. When the father finally saw the child, he lamented that many finer souls than this one had already been rejected.[101] Yehiel Mikhel was certainly born into a demanding environment. As a child, he was brought up severely and taught to disregard his needs. Although raised in great poverty, a tradition claimed that Isaac of Drohobitch slapped his son for complaining of his hunger.[102] Later, Yehiel Mikhel taught his own sons to pray for the welfare of their enemies, a practice highly recommended in *Reshit Hokhmah*.[103]

Yehiel Mikhel was raised in Brody, a town famous for its rabbis and kabbalists. While there he studied with leading rabbinic scholars like Ezekiel Landau and Isaac Horowitz of Hamburg. However, he was educated chiefly by his father. A Hasidic story claimed that once Yehiel Mikhel left his father in order to study in the *yeshivah* of Isaac of Hamburg. However, after three days he returned to his father. When asked why he abandoned the *yeshivah*, he replied, "Whenever I study Torah with my father, I see the letters flying forth from his mouth. This is not the case at the *yeshivah*."[104]

Sometime during the 1740s,[105] Yehiel Mikhel married Rekhele, or, perhaps, Yente Rekhel, the daughter of Rabbi Moses of Bialetserkov.[106] In order to fulfill the terms of the dowry, the father-in-law was forced to mortgage his wine press. However, when his wife complained bitterly over her father's poverty, Yehiel Mikhel renounced his claim to the funds.[107] His extraordinary character was further revealed by his behavior after the wedding. According to a Hasidic record, Yehiel Mikhel isolated himself for a period of a thousand days, during which he neither spoke to nor saw anyone, devoting every moment to "serving the Lord with marvelous *devekut* [sic]."[108] After spending the first years of the marriage with his father-in-law in Bialetserkov, Yehiel Mikhel lived for a short time in utter poverty and anonymity in Boreslav. From here, he returned with his family to Brody.

In Brody, Yehiel Mikhel worked as a teacher of young children. He also studied with Hayyim Tzanzer at the Brody *Klaus*, where many of the leading kabbalists not only gathered to pray according to the *kavvanot* of Isaac Luria, but also to learn Torah. However, while in Brody, Yehiel Mikhel became a focus of controversy. He drew criticism because of his custom of beginning his prayers after the legally established time for saying them had elapsed.[109] This was a custom adopted by a number of the early Hasidim who felt that spiritual preparation for prayer was more important than praying at the prescribed times. Although Yehiel Mikhel gained his reputation as a *maggid* or preacher, when he moved on to reside in Zlotchov and Yampol, he continued to visit Brody regularly. References to several important sermons that he preached in Brody can be found.[110] He maintained a residence and House of Study there, even after he ceased being a full-time resident. As late as 1777, Meshullam Feibush made reference to having heard a homily preached by Yehiel Mikhel at Brody.[111] Moreover, the first Hasidic publication, *Toledot Ya'aqov Yosef*, was burned outside his house in Brody in 1781. The choice of location, of course, indicated the prominence he had achieved by this time as the leading representative of Hasidism in eastern Galicia.

Most of Yehiel Mikhel's final years were spent in Yampol, a town near Ostrog, in Volhynia, where he served as preacher.[112] However, his reputation was established earlier in Zlotchov, a town in which a number of early proponents of Hasidism resided. Among the early Hasidim, there were Menahem Mendel of Premishlan's brother, Zvi the Hasid, Issachar Ber, author of *Mevasser Zedeq*, who was the town rabbi,[113] and his son-in-law Abraham Hayyim, author of *Orah le-Hayyim*.[114] It was in Zlotchov that Yehiel Mikhel became known as an itinerant preacher who had the power to discern a person's sins, merely by gazing at his forehead.[115] Despite the considerable support he must have had there, Yehiel Mikhel was forced to abandon Zlotchov. However, the precise nature of the problems he encountered there is not known.[116]

From Zlotchov, Yehiel Mikhel moved to Kalki. However, his stay there was a brief one. He soon relocated to Yampol, where he was to remain until his death. According to Hasidic accounts, Yehiel Mikhel served as preacher in Yampol while Ezekiel Landau was Head of the Rabbinic Court. Since Ezekiel Landau left Yampol for Prague in 1755, Yehiel Mikhel must have arrived sometime before that year.[117] Relations between the two were strained. Landau specifically objected to Yehiel Mikhel's habit of praying late. Pinhas ha-Levy Horowitz of Frankfurt intervened. His concern aroused the Head of the Rabbinic Court in Lissa, David Tevele, to write to Ezekiel Landau in defense of Yehiel Mikhel.[118]

Yehiel Mikhel spent the last twenty-six years of his life in Yampol. During that time he influenced many of the next generation's Hasidic leaders. He, himself, became, along with Elimelekh of Lizensk, one of the two most important Hasidic figures in the area. His death occurred in Yampol on the 25 of Elul, 1781.[119] According to family tradition, he was fifty-five years old at the time of his death.[120] A eulogy for Yehiel Mikhel appeared in the early Hasidic work, *Tiferet Uziel*, by Uziel Meisels.[121]

A rather detailed account of Yehiel Mikhel's death was written. According to this account, Yehiel Mikhel had become increasingly detached from interest in the material world during his later years. He was given to many fasts and he became famous for the degree of his mystical absorption (*devequt*) in the divine presence. The intensity of his adhesion to God reached its peak on the Sabbath. His family became increasingly concerned, lest he expire in his total disregard for what was occuring around him. They made a point of stationing someone with him every Sabbath afternoon for the third meal, in order to recall him from his absorbed state. However, on the final Sabbath of his life, no one was with him. His daughter heard him moving around his meditation chamber repeating over and over, "at this favorable moment, Moses died." She ran to summon her brother, Isaac of Radvil. Although the son arrived in time to arouse Yehiel Mikhel somewhat from his *devequt*, he was too late to prevent his death. According to sources, Yehiel Mikhel is said to have died precisely upon uttering the word "one" in the declaration of unity.[122]

It is not known exactly when Yehiel Mikhel became associated with the Ba'al Shem Tov. Since it is doubtful if his father, Isaac of Drohobitch, ever became a follower himself, it would seem that Yehiel Mikhel independently accepted the Ba'al Shem Tov as master. Nevertheless, he could have had contact with the founder of Hasidism already during his youth in Brody, during one of the Ba'al Shem Tov's occasional visits. According to the account in *Shivhey ha-BeSHT*, Yehiel Mikhel accepted the Ba'al Shem Tov as his master because he had been instructed to do so by Heaven. He was shown "'streams of wisdom' which led to the BeSHT."[123] According to other Hasidic accounts, this occurred only after Yehiel Mikhel was already a wandering preacher. Yehiel Mikhel only accepted his master after many efforts on the latter's part to demonstrate his spiritual eminence.[124]

It would seem that one of the most important lessons that the Ba'al Shem Tov taught to Yehiel Mikhel was compassion and understanding of the suffering of sinners. Yehiel Mikhel clearly adhered to exceptionally high spiritual standards. In his younger days, his own fervor for serving God as perfectly as possible was accompanied by a lack of tolerance for the short-comings of others. A Hasidic story recounted how once a person was compelled to violate the Sabbath laws as the result of an accident that occurred to his coach. When he told Yehiel Mikhel, who resided at that time in Boreslav, what had happened, the young rabbi prescribed a severe penance. The man was ordered to undertake many fasts, to roll in snow, and to perform other ascetic acts that were recommended in the early ethical works. However, such an approach was foreign to the way of the Ba'al Shem Tov. When the man complained to the Hasidic master about the severity of Yehiel Mikhel's penance, the Ba'al Shem Tov replied that he could atone for inadvertantly violating the Sabbath merely by lighting a certain number of candles in honor of the Sabbath at the synogogue. He also told the man to tell Yehiel Mikhel that he was expecting him to spend the following Sabbath with him in a neighboring town. As it turned out, the very same misadventure that had occurred to the other person befell Yehiel Mikhel. He was not able to arrive before the beginning of the Sabbath. When he appeared before the master, brokenhearted over being forced to violate the Sabbath, the Ba'al Shem Tov upbraided him for the severe penance he had prescribed. According to the Ba'al Shem Tov, Yehiel Mikhel should have realized that the suffering and regret that the man had experienced were sufficient to atone for the sin.[125]

Although Yehiel Mikhel seemed to have maintained his ascetic practices even after coming under the influence of the Ba'al Shem Tov, he may have somewhat softened his expectations of others. Meshullam Feibush portrayed him as a popular leader who attracted the masses. Nevertheless stories concerning his severity and ability to awaken the fear of heaven in others abound. Although his temperament seems to have been quite different from that of the Hasidic founder, Yehiel Mikhel became a strong supporter of the Ba'al Shem Tov. According to Hasidic tradition, it was Yehiel Mikhel's custom, every Sabbath, to relate a story concerning the Ba'al Shem Tov at the third meal, just before reciting the blessings after eating.[126]

According to Hasidic legend, Yehiel Mikhel was one of only a few of the founder's disciples who unequivocally accepted the leadership of Dov Ber of Mezeritch, after the Ba'al Shem Tov's death in 1760.[127] According to *Shivhey ha-BeSHT*, Yehiel Mikhel turned to Dov Ber because it was revealed to him that the very same "streams of wisdom" which had previously flowed to the Ba'al Shem Tov, now reached Dov Ber. Several accounts exist concerning visits Yehiel Mikhel paid to the Maggid of Mezeritch. According to one story, Yehiel Mikhel visited once with his young son, Isaac of Radvil. When they arrived, Yehiel Mikhel sent the boy several times to summon Dov Ber, but the latter did not respond. When Yehiel Mikhel went himself to investigate, he found that Dov Ber was closeted with Elijah the prophet.[128]

According to another account, Dov Ber held Yehiel Mikhel in the highest regard. Once Yehiel Mikhel came for a visit with his close disciple, Mordecai of Neshkiz. When the latter referred to Yehiel Mikhel as his "Rebbe," the Hasidic term for a spiritual master, he was mocked by Dov Ber's disciple, Solomon of Lutzk. When Dov Ber found out about this, he rebuked his disciple severely.[129] The high regard in which Yehiel Mikhel was held in the court of Dov Ber is also apparent from stories that are told in the HaBaD tradition. The founder of HaBaD Hasidism, Shneur Zalman of Liadi, was one of the youngest disciples of Dov Ber. According to a story told by his grandson, Menahem Mendel of Lubavitch, when Shneur Zalman first came to Mezeritch, he was not able to tell which of the two leaders was the greater, until Dov Ber explained that his soul emanated from a slightly higher source than the soul of Yehiel Mikhel.[130]

Shneur Zalman of Liadi was not the only one of Dov Ber's disciples to have adulated Yehiel Mikhel. Elimelekh of Lizensk, the other major Hasidic leader in Galicia both visited Yehiel Mikhel and sent his disciples to visit him. Other early disciples of Dov Ber, who are known to have acknowledged Yehiel Mikhel, included the brothers, Shmelka and Pinhas Horowitz.[131] By the 1770s, following the death of Dov Ber in 1772, a number of his disciples began to establish themselves in Galicia. Many of these younger disciples like Abraham Joshua Heschel of Apt, Abraham Hayyim of Zlotchov, and Zvi Hirsh of Nadberna, also regarded Yehiel Mikhel as their master. Thus, it is clear that, while Yehiel Mikhel's spiritual character was fully formed before he became associated with Dov Ber, he must have been well aware of Dov Ber's Hasidic approach. He not only visited Mezeritch, but was constantly exposed to Dov Ber's teachings through his disciples.

Nevertheless, the precise nature of Yehiel Mikhel's relationship to the Maggid of Mezritch is not certain. Legendary sources which emphasize Yehiel Mikhel's subordination to Dov Ber should be viewed with caution. This is especially the case in regard to the legend in *Shivhey ha-BeSHT*, which emanated from HaBaD sources that had a direct interest in establishing a Hasidic lineage that extended from the Ba'al Shem Tov through Dov Ber to Shneur Zalman, the founder of HaBaD.[132]

It is interesting that the only major Hasidic leader from whom Yehiel Mikhel was estranged was Pinhas of Koretz.[133] The latter was also an early associate of the Ba'al Shem Tov who seems to have supported Jacob Joseph of Polnoy, rather than Dov Ber, as successor to the Hasidic leader. However, the enmity between R. Pinhas and the Maggid of Zlotchov probably originated in a dispute concerning ritual slaughter in Koretz. The dispute involved a son of R. Pinhas and a follower of Yehiel Mikhel.[134] However, Yehiel Mikhel's growing influence as a spiritual master in Koretz seemed to further provoke Rabbi Pinhas who was finally forced to relocate to Ostrog.[135]

The picture that emerges of Yehiel Mikhel from the many Hasidic stories that are told about him is rather consistent. He is characteristically portrayed as a religious virtuoso, uncompromisingly dedicated to the service of God. The stories concerning his younger days emphasize the great poverty within which he lived. Yet, he considered it improper to pray for his and his family's material well-being.

According to one account, he once explained his practice by likening the world to a wedding feast from which the bride had been kidnapped. Although all the delicacies had already been prepared, would it not be insensitive and unworthy of the guests to demand their portions while the father was grieving over the lost bride? Similarly, as long as the *Shekhinah*, or divine presence, was in exile, Yehiel Mikhel could not bring himself to ask God for his worldly needs.[136] Nevertheless, he was very solicitous concerning the needs of others. Another account claimed that despite his poverty and constant involvement in prayer and Torah study, he was always ready to serve guests, even if it meant pawning whatever he owned.[137] On the other hand, his dedication to the Hasidic cause was so unswerving that it occasionally resulted in neglect of his own family's needs. A story in *Shivhey ha-BeSHT* recounts how Yehiel Mikhel left his son, Joseph of Yampol, in the throes of death, while he himself made an ascent to heaven in order to defend the Hasidic writings of Jacob Joseph of Polnoy. So intent was Yehiel Mikhel on his mission, that he forgot to intercede for his son. Only the pleas of the deceased Ba'al Shem Tov, who was present in heaven at the time, saved the life of Joseph of Yampol.[138]

Many of the stories concerning Yehiel Mikhel emphasized his asceticism and charismatic powers. Sources indicated that he continued his habit of prolonged and frequent fasting to the end of his life. In this, he chose to follow in the footsteps of his ancestors, rather than adopt the path of the Ba'al Shem Tov. The extent and nature of his asceticism distinguished his spiritual approach from that of Menahem Mendel of Premishlan. The latter, while very much opposed to indulgence, tended to transform his carnal activities into spiritual practices (*avodah be-gashmiyut*), while Yehiel Mikhel inclined to the older ascetic way of abstention. Another apparent difference in the personalities of the two teachers of Meshullam Feibush was that Menahem Mendel, while ready to exercise compassion for others, preferred obscurity. Yehiel Mikhel, despite all the evidence of his other-worldliness, was a public figure. He gained his reputation as a wandering preacher and managed to attract and influence a large number of talented disciples.

Virtually all of the Hasidic leaders who became prominent in Galicia towards the end of the eighteenth century, were, to some degree, disciples of Yehiel Mikhel. Among the more famous disciples and associates of Yehiel Mikhel were Abraham Joshua Heschel of Apt, Jacob Joseph, the Seer of Lublin, Naftoli of Ropshitz, Kalonymus Kalman Epstein of Cracow, author of *Maor ve-Shemesh*, Abraham Hayyim of Zlotchov, and Solomon of Karlin.[139] In addition, a number of figures must be considered as specially close disciples. The foremost of these were Mordecai of Neshkiz (born c. 1728)[140] and Yitzhak Isaac ha-Kohen of Koretz (1753–1788).[141] Others included, Abraham Mordecai of Pintshov and his brother Joseph of Zemigrad, Zvi Aryeh Landau of Alik, Zvi Hirsh of Nadberna, Meshullam Feibush of Zbarazh, and the young Hayyim Tirer of Tchernowitz, who died in 1818.

In a real sense, Yehiel Mikhel's closest disciples were his five sons, Joseph of Yampol (d. 1812), Isaac of Radvil,[142] Zev Wolf of Zbarazh, Moses of Zevil, and Mordecai of Kremenitz (1765–1820). [143] The eldest son, Joseph must have been born during the 1750s. The story of his birth appeared in *Shivhey ha-BeSHT*.[144] Another story indicated that he was old enough to have visited the Ba'al Shem Tov with his father. He became an important Hasidic leader after his father's death. In his later years, he shared the responsibility for administering funds for the Hasidic community in the Land of Israel with Barukh of Mezbuzh, to whom he was related by marriage.

Meshullam Feilbush Heller

Rabbi Meshullam Feibush Ha-Levi Heller was descended from a line of prominent east European rabbis. The most famous of his ancestors was the well-known commentator on the Mishnah and author of other legal works, Rabbi Yom Tov Lipman Ha-Levi Heller (d. 1654 in Cracow), author of *Tosefot Yom Tov*, which is printed in the standard editions of the Mishnah.[145] Yom Tov Lipman served as Head of the Rabbinical Court in Vienna and Prague. His great-grandson, Rabbi Meir ben Samson (d. 1745) was Meshullam Feibush's grandfather. Rabbi Meir served as Head of the Rabbinical Court in Brezhin, one of the principle Jewish communities in the Lemberg region of eastern Galicia.[146] His wife, Hadassah (d. 1732), had equally illustrious ancestors, most notably, R. Solomon Luria of Lublin, the MaHaRSHaL.

Meshullam Feibush's father, Rabbi Aaron Moses, served as Head of the Rabbinical Court in Senyatin.[147] His father's brother, Rabbi Yehudah ha-Levi Heller of Aleksenitz, was a member of the famous Brody *Kloyz*, where leading scholars and kabbalists studied and prayed. Indeed, several of Meshullam Feibush's close relatives were associated with the *Kloyz*, including his brother, Noah Abraham.[148] Meshullam Feibush's mother, Vechne, was the daughter of the Head of the Rabbinical Court in Tismenitz, Rabbi Israel Moses Yerushalmi.

While it is clear that Meshullam Feibush came from a highly learned family, little, if any, evidence exists that any of his relatives were associated with early Hasidism.[149] Of his siblings, little is known concerning his younger brother, Rabbi Judah, except that he died in Kalis and was known as Judah the Hasid.[150] The elder brother, Rabbi Noah Abraham (d. 1786 in Brezhin), served as Head of the Rabbinic Court in Dolina. He was a member of the Brody *Kloyz*, ordained by Rabbi Hayyim Rappoport, the Head of the Rabbinical Court in Lemberg.[151] Rabbi Noah Abraham was a prominent rabbinic authority in eastern Galicia. He authored a number of works, concerning both legal issues and midrashic legends. However, most of his writings were destroyed in a fire.[152] His descendents only recently succeeded in publishing *Zerizuta de-Avraham*, a collection of his homilies on the Torah and the first three chapters of *Avot*.[153] While later sources sometimes were inclined to view Noah Abraham as part of the Hasidic milieu, no references from his contemporaries were located that would support this view. All the approbations which were written by his contemporaries came from noted rabbinic authorities who were not supporters of Hasidism. The only exception was the approbation of Meshullam Feibush, himself. Significantly, Meshullam Feibush's praises made no mention of any connection between Noah Abraham and Hasdism.[154] Thus, it seems that Meshullam Feibush's association with Hasidism was not a result of his family's influence. He was the first member of his family to join the party of the Ba'al Shem Tov.

As for specifics concerning Meshullam Feibush's life, information was limited. In all likelihood, he was born in the region of Lemberg, perhaps in Senyatin, where his father was Head of the Rabbinical Court. However, it was not possible to determine the exact year of his birth. Since, as he tells us on the first page of *Yosher Divrey Emet*, he did not meet the Ba'al Shem Tov who died in 1760, one may speculate that he was perhaps fifteen years old or slightly older at that time. Thus, he was born sometime before 1745.[155] Details concerning his education also were available. Nevertheless, we should assume that he received a first-rate rabbinic education, since virtually his entire family functioned as rabbinic authorities. He learned, presumably, from his elder brother, Noah Abraham, whose expertise was highly attested. Meshullam Feibush, himself, remarked that he had "already learned a lot of Torah *she-lo-li-shemah*" (before adopting the Hasidic manner of study, which emphasized apprehension of the presence of God while learning, rather than intellectual mastery of the subject).[156] Moreover, in his later life, Meshullam Feibush was held in high regard precisely by those disciples of Yehiel Mikhel of Zlotchov who were experts in *halakhah*. Rabbi Hayyim Tirer of Tchernovitz quoted Meshullam Feibush in several of his works. In a section of Rabbi Hayyim's work, *Sidduro shel Shabbat*, Meshullam Feibush wass specifically cited for his *halakhic* expertise. Concerning the appearance of the letter *nun* in an inverted form in the biblical text before Num. 10:35 and after 10:36, Hayyim of Tchernovitz explained:

> I also heard something concerning this from the divine saint, the famous holy lamp of Israel, our late teacher and master, Rabbi Meshullam Feibush of Zbarazh, may his memory be a blessing for life in the world to come. For he was expert in the entire literature of the Codes and responsa literature concerning this matter.[157]

Similarly, Rabbi David Solomon Eybeshutz of Soroka, author of *Arvey Nahal*, referred to Meshullam Feibush in his commentary on the *Shulhan Arukh, Levushey Serad,* in the section on the laws concerning ritual baths.

Meshullam Feibush married twice. The name of his first wife does not appear in the family geneologies.[158] She was the mother of his first son, Rabbi Moses Aaron.[159] Meshullam Feibush's second wife, Yentl, was the daughter of Rabbi Abraham Hayyim Shor, the author of *Zon Qodashim*. The fruit of this second marriage were two sons: Rabbi Barukh Itzik Ha-Levi Heller of Zvanitch and Rabbi Samson of Uziran (1782–1848). Remnants of Samson's writings, entitled *Nezirut Shimshon,* were collected and published in the Munkacz edition of *Yosher Divrey Emet*. Descendents of these two sons continued to function as Hasidic leaders until the present day.[160]

Meshullam Feibush is characteristically identified with the town of Zbarazh. It is known that he died and was buried there on the 20 Kislev 1795. However, why or when he came to Zbarazh is not clear. He certainly never served as Head of the Rabbinical Court.[161] It is not known if Meshullam Feibush ever served any official religious function in Zbarazh. The town is also associated in Hasidic historiography with another Hasidic master, Rabbi Zev Wolf the son of Yehiel Mikhel of Zlotchov. While a connection between these two figures would seem likely, it is doubtful whether the son of the Zlotchover Maggid had anything to do with Meshullam Feibush's establishment in Zbarazh. He is neither mentioned even once in *Yosher Divrey Emet,* nor does his name appear in the extant later writings of Meshullam Feibush.

It seems clear that by 1777, when Yosher Divrey Emet was written, Meshullam Feibush was already functioning as some kind of Hasidic authority. However, it is difficult to determine how wide or extensive his sphere of influence was at that time. Nominally, the text was a letter written to a distant childhood friend. However, twice in the text, Meshullam Feibush used the expression "and to those who hearken to our voice," which indicates that he intended the recipient to circulate his writings among a larger following. Unfortunately, it was not possible to determine precisely either to whom the epistle was sent,[162] or where it was circulated.[163] What was clear, was that the intended readers held both the late Dov Ber of Mezeritch and Yehiel Mikhel in high regard. Nevertheless, they must have been located in an area somewhat removed from the burgeoning Hasidic centers. We may assume that their interest in Hasidism was in need

of both encouragement and clarification of certain basic principles and practices, particularly where contradictions between the teachings of Yehiel Mikhel and other Hasidic leaders like Dov Ber were apparent. Meshullam Feibush was uniquely qualified to address these needs. He was a direct disciple
of Yehiel Mikhel of Zlotchov and had earlier come under the influence of
Menahem Mendel of Premishlan in eastern Galicia. In addition, Meshullam
Feibush claimed to have personally seen the Ba'al Shem Tov's successor, Dov
Ber of Mezeritch. Morever, his ancestry and rabbinic background leant considerable weight to his arguments. Nevertheless, while Meshullam Feibush's
epistles were in large measure a defense and justification of faith in the Hasidic leader, the Zaddiq, he did not address his audience from a position of
superiority. Rather, he presented himself as a fellow disciple of the Hasidic
masters who comprehended the true spiritual basis of their authority.

It is difficult to determine whether the attitude that Meshullam Feibush
assumed, when he began *Yosher Divrey Emet* in 1777, reflected his actual
position in the Hasidic world of eastern Galicia at that time. Given the great
emphasis that was placed on humility in his teachings, it is possible that his
importance was already somewhat greater than he admitted. Nevertheless,
whatever degree of leadership he may already have attained, it is clear that
he was still functioning within the shadow of his master, Yehiel Mikhel of
Zlotchov.[164] Consequently, his early writings must be viewed, at least in
part, as propaganda for the Maggid of Zlotchov, who was at that time a central target of Hasidism's opponents.

Although it is clear that Meshullam Feibush never approached his master in importance as a Hasidic leader, it is reasonable to assume that in the
years following Yehiel Mikhel's death, Meshullam Feibush's influence grew.
We already noted the high regard that was posthumously paid to him by
such later leaders as Hayyim Tirer of Tchernovitz. While he did not assume
a public role as leader of a community, the evidence of several extant letters
attested to the role he played as a personal spiritual guide. The letters emphasized the importance of faith and joy in serving God as antidotes against
sadness, a primary weapon of the evil urge. They emphasized the need for
not only restricting one's thoughts to the meaning of the words when one
prays, but also the importance of Torah study. Both letters were written
after *Yosher Divrey Emet*. In both cases, Mushullam Feibush assumed the
role of an independent spiritual guide without attributing his advice to specific teachings cited in the names of his masters. In one case, he referred to
the writings of Jacob Joseph of Polnoy. This reference, however, supported
the late dating of the letter in question. Jacob Joseph was not mentioned even
once in *Yosher Divrey Emet*, despite the fact that his writings discoursed at

length with issues discussed in that text. The writings of Jacob Joseph were only published in 1780. Thus, it would seem that Meshullam Feibush was not aware of them before that time.[165]

Nevertheless, while Meshullam Feibush was highly regarded, he never established a major Hasidic court. From the fact that very few anecdotes concerning him appeared in the collections of Hasidic hagiography, we may infer that he never became a popular figure. His personal influence was limited to a rather modest number of disciples. Some of these, however, as indicated, became figures of prominence in the Hasidic world. Moreover, his literary influence on later Hasidism was great. His writings first appeared in print in 1792 and continued to be reprinted in various forms until the present day.[166] Moreover, modern scholarship tended to identify Meshullam Feibush as the editor of the important anthology, *Liqqutim Yeqarim*.[167]

Although references to Meshullam Feibush are few, key aspects of his personality emerged from the anecdotes told about him and from personal remarks that appeared in his letters. According to one account, Meshullam Feibush suffered from ill health. When he visited Rabbi Samuel, the Head of the Rabbinical Court in Zalishtik, his host made sure that his wife served Meshullam Feibush especially nourishing food, in order to restore his health.[168] If Meshullam Feibush, indeed, suffered chronically from a weak constitution, this might account, at least in part, for his relative lack of popularity. His health may have restricted his encounters with the public. However, it should be noted that whatever the nature and extent of Meshullam Feibush's health problems may have been, they were probably not the result of excessive asceticism. While his teachings strongly warn against the spiritual dangers of indulgence, they never counseled excessive fasting as a penance.[169]

While Meshullam Feibush does not seem to have practiced mortifications, it was clear that he was exacting in his pursuit of spiritual purity. This was apparent from the unusual emphasis in his writings on moral and ethical perfection as preconditions for the sublime mystical experience of *devequt*. Essentially, Meshullam Feibush strove to achieve sincere and pure-hearted worship of God. According to the same source quoted above, Meshullam Feibush once remarked that in his youth, he had been tempted by the devil to accept the experience of divine inspiration and other extraordinary mystical experiences. However, he rejected all of these temptations, preferring to pursue only the level of truth.[170]

Meshullam Feibush was very deliberate in his actions. Apparently, he paid close attention to all the impulses that entered his mind. Before embarking on a course of action, he examined his motivations to make sure that his reason for acting was not prompted by the wiles of the evil urge. This aspect of his personality was the theme of several other anecdotes. According to one story, Meshullam Feibush once felt an urge to fast, even though his condition was weak. So, he designated a certain day for the fast. However, from the moment that the time for the fast was fixed, his desire to undertake the fast constantly increased. Since it was clear to him that his desire for this voluntary fast was much greater than the desire he ordinarily felt to carry out an obligatory fast, he decided against it. He reasoned that the cause of such unnatural desire could only be the evil urge which wanted to further weaken his body.[171] Clearly, Meshullam Feibush's inner life was characterized by a kind of gnostic struggle between the forces of good and evil. The evil urge would attempt to trick him by concealing itself in the impulse to perform some superogatory practice. Only Meshullam Feibush's deliberateness of character and sober pursuit of authenticity in his religious life enabled him to distinguish the promptings of the evil urge. A somewhat similar story recounted that Meshullam Feibush was determined to reject his impulse to don *talit* and *tefillin* for the afternoon prayer. Here again, through closely observing the quality of his enthusiasm, he came to the conclusion that the impulse was caused by the evil urge. Such enthusiasm to carry out the commandment of donning prayer shawl and phylacteries was only appropriate for the morning service when this commandment was obligatory.[172]

In yet another area, Meshullam Feibush had to be on his guard, lest the evil urge diverted him from true service. He had to fend off the tendency to view imperfections in his religious life too negatively. According to one story, Meshullam Feibush once noticed during *Shabbat*, that one of the knots which bound the fringe of his prayer shawl came loose. The evil urge reminded him that such an occurrence was considered a sign that the wearer of the prayer shawl did not fear heaven. However, undismayed, Meshullam Feibush continued his prayers by assuring himself that his fear of heaven was undeniable. Otherwise, he could have easily retied the knot. It was only his fear of heaven that prevented him from doing so, since such an act was forbidden on the Sabbath.[173]

Like other early Hasidic masters, Meshullam Feibush was sensitive to the fact that depression and a sense of spiritual unworthiness seriously undermined a person's ability to fulfill his religious obligations. Consequently, in *Yosher Divrey Emet*, even though humility was Meshullam Feibush's cardinal virtue, he recommended that one arouse a sense of pride in one's worship so that an excessive sense of humility would not prevent one from praying altogether. In his own life, Meshullam Feibush seemed to have gone even further. He examined everything that entered his mind, until, as he related in one of his letters, he knew the root of every single thought. One may say, perhaps, that he took a cognitive approach to the psychological problems of the religious life. Trains of thought that seemed to lead in a direction opposed to his spiritual values and aspirations were countered by other more positive thoughts that diverted his mind back to the desired course.

The restricted range of Hasidic authorities cited in *Yosher Divrey Emet* suggests that Meshullam Feibush's Hasidism developed within a rather limited sphere of influence. Although the Ba'al Shem Tov receives pride of place in Meshullam Feibush's spiritual pantheon, teachings in his name are only occasionally quoted. These he knows, of course, primarily through the oral tradition, never having met Hasidism's founder. Once, for example, Meshullam Feibush cites a teaching which he heard from a disciple of the Ba'al Shem Tov, Rabbi David of Mikolajov.[174] However, as noted above, he does not yet seem to have been acquainted in 1777 with the homilies of the principal recorder of the Ba'al Shem Tov's teachings, Rabbi Jacob Joseph of Polnoy. (These only began to appear in print in 1780.) On the other hand, a great deal of Meshullam Feibush's thought seems to be rooted in the teachings of Dov Ber of Mezeritch.[175] However, most of the material Meshullam Feibush brings in the name of the Maggid of Mezeritch has come to him via manuscripts which were being circulated in the mid-1770s. Much of the content of this material, it now appears, originates in the teachings of Yehiel Mikhel of Zlotchov.[176]

In several cases, Meshullam Feibush has heard teachings from one of the disciples of Dov Ber. These are, for the most part, rather obscure figures about whom little is known. They include Rabbi Gershon of Lutzk and Rabbi Dov Ber of Hordikov. One notable exception is a teaching from Dov Ber that was explained to Meshullam Feibush by the Galician master, Rabbi Zvi Hirsh of Nadberna (d. 1802).[177] Only on one occasion, does he cite a teaching that he heard directly from Dov Ber of Mezeritch, himself.

Two other figures, mentioned by Meshullam Feibush, were associated in one way or another with Menahem Mendel of Premishlan. The first, Rabbi Solomon Vilner,[178] received greetings in Menahem Mendel's letter from the Land of Israel to his brother, Zvi Hasid of Zlotchov.[179] The second, "Rabbi Issachar Ber of our community," was explicitly identified as a disciple of "Rabbi Mendel." It is possible that he was the well-known author of *Mevasser Zedeq*, and one of the principal disciples of Yehiel Mikhel.[180]

Although he is not mentioned explicitly in Meshullam Feibush's writings, Hasidic sources indicated that Meshullam Feibush's closest friend was

Rabbi Ze'ev Wolf (Velvele) of Charny-Ostrog.[181] According to Hasidic accounts, Ze'ev Wolf turned to Meshullam Feibush after the death of Dov Ber of Mezeritch. Ze'ev Wolf was also reported to have been a follower of Rabbi Pinhas of Koretz, an associate of the Ba'al Shem Tov.[182] Meshullam Feibush may also have visited Rabbi Pinhas together with Ze'ev Wolf.[183] According to a Hasidic tradition, the ties between the two friends were so close that Ze'ev Wolf subdued his desire to emigrate to the Land of Israel as long as Meshullam Feibush was alive. In 1798, three years after the death of Meshullam Feibush, Ze'ev Wolf set out for the Holy Land. On the journey, he befriended the young Rabbi Nahman of Bratzlav.[184]

Ze'ev Wolf was one of the principle teachers of Rabbi Menahem Mendel of Kosov, the founder of the Kosov-Vizhnitz Hasidic dynasty. As a result of the close ties that existed between Meshullam Feibush and Ze'ev Wolf, Hasidic tradition also regarded Menahem Mendel of Kosov as a disciple of Meshullam Feibush.[185] If this tradition is true, Meshullam Feibush must be regarded as having had a direct influence on the founder of one of the major dynasties in later Hasidism.

The Writings of Meshullam Feibush

The principal writings of Meshullam Feibush of Zbarazh consisted of two independent texts that came to be known as *Yosher Divrey Emet* and *Derekh Emet*. However, the use of these titles in order to distinguish Meshullam Feibush's works can be misleading. First, the former text was not generally identified by this title until the edition of Meshullam Feibush's writings published in Munkacz in 1905. In all earlier editions in which this text was published as an independent work, it was also entitled *Derekh Emet*. Thus, references to *Derekh Emet* in Hasidic and academic writings referred to either of the two texts, depending on the edition being used.[186] Second, the text which has come to be known as *Yosher Divrey Emet*, originally appeared as part of an early anthology of Hasidic teachings, *Liqqutim Yeqarim*. In the first edition of *Liqqutim Yeqarim* (Lemberg, 1792), Meshullam Feibush's text appeared between pages 19d and 31a. However, his name did not appear on the title page and there was nothing within the text itself to indicate that he was the author of the material contained within these pages. Indeed, his authorship was apparantly not revealed until the first edition published after his death (Zholkva, 1800). Consequently, references to *Yosher Divrey Emet* were sometimes also indicated by the title *Liqqutim Yeqarim*. [187] Part of the confusion concerning the use of the title, *Derekh*

Emet, for both of the texts may be due to the fact that the shorter and later work was published earlier than the first independent edition of the material in *Liqqutim Yeqarim*. Since this title had already been associated with teachings of Meshullam Feibush, the publishers appropriated it when they decided to print the material in *Liqqutim Yeqarim* as an independent work.[188]

Meshullam Feibush's first principal work, *Yosher Divrey Emet*, consisted of two letters which were written to a certain Rabbi Joel. According to a manuscript in the possession of the Heller family, which formed the basis for the Munkacz edition, the first letter was written in the spring of 1777. Internal evidence would suggest that the second letter was essentially written during the fall of 1782.[189] Although the letters must have had a limited circulation in manuscript form, they were not published until their inclusion in the first edition of *Liqqutim Yeqarim* in Lemberg, 1792. However, in the Lemberg edition, the first letter was censored. On page 21a, a note appeared to indicate that the text was not complete.[190] In a third edition, published without imprimaturs in Zholkva, 1800, significant material was added. For the first time, Meshullam Feibush's name appeared on the title page with the following explanation:

> And now the Lord has brought into our possession holy teachings of the Holy Lamp . . . our divine master, Feibush of Zbarazh, [from a] manuscript written in his own hand, which were concealed among the possessions of one of our fellows . . .[191]

This edition does not seem to have received adequate attention on the part of modern scholars.[192] In this edition, Meshullam Feibush's epistles appear between the pages 20a–32a. Preceding them is the notation, "from the writings of the *Zaddiq*, our teacher and master, Feibush of Zbarazh." As for the text itself, where two earlier editions had indicated a hiatus, the Zholkva edition adds almost seven columns of additional text.[193] Since, aside from minor alterations and the correction of printer's errors, the text here is virtually identical to the version printed in the 1905 Munkacz edition, it should be considered the first complete edition of *Yosher Divrey Emet*.

Liqqutim Yeqarim continued to appear in a number of editions during the nineteenth century.[194] In the meantime, separate editions of this material began to appear under the title, *Derekh Emet*. The first such edition seems to have been printed in Tchernovitz in 1855.[195] The approbation written in 1851 by Rabbi Joseph Landau, the Head of the Rabbinical Court in Jassy, indicated that the text contained writings that had already been printed in *Liqqutim Yeqarim* and in "the pamphlet *Derekh Emet*" along with many additions. In other words, this edition contained the two principal works of Meshullam Feibush. Rabbi Landau was, perhaps, unaware of the 1800 Zholkva edition of *Liqqutim Yeqarim* and, consequently, assumed that the uncensored text of *Yosher Divrey Emet* contained additions not previously published. It was interesting to note that, although the work as a whole received the title of the pamphlet, *Derekh Emet*, in his imprimatur, Rabbi Landau referred to the first text as *Yosher Divrey Emet*. This may be the earliest designation of Meshullam Feibush's epistles by that title.

As for Meshullam Feibush's second and briefer ethical work, *Derekh Emet*, it appeared first in print in Lemberg, 1830. In that volume, it was preceded by Zekhariah Mendel of Jaroslav's *Darkhey Zedeq*.[196] The title page noted that *Derekh Emet* was being printed for the first time, having previously existed only in manuscript. It was subsequently reprinted many times in several forms: as an independent work, together with *Darkhey Zedek*, and, beginning with the 1855 Tchernovitz volume, together with *Yosher Divrey Emet*. It is not known exactly when Meshullam Feibush composed this short tract. However, it must have been written subsequent to *Yosher Divrey Emet* and, probably, no earlier than 1782.[197] In some of the volumes entitled *Derekh Emet*, *Yosher Divrey Emet* appeared as "*Derekh Emet*, part one" and the text originally called *Derekh Emet* appeared as "*Derekh Emet*, part two."

Nevertheless, there was no evidence that Meshullam Feibush, himself, ever considered these texts part of a single work. *Yosher Divrey Emet* was clearly conceived as a work involving two parts, the two letters.[198] Although *Derekh Emet* was written later, Meshullam Feibush made no reference in it to his earlier text. Nor does he continue or augment discussions that he was compelled to abbreviate in *Yosher Divrey Emet*. For these reasons, *Derekh Emet* should be considered an independent work. While the information presently available indicated that *Derekh Emet* was only published about thirty-five years after Meshullam Feibush's death, it must have received some circulation in manuscript.

The edition of *Yosher Divrey Emet* that was published in Munkacz, 1905, by Samson Heller of Kolymyja, is the most complete edition of the extant writings of Meshullam Feibush.[199] This edition is based on manuscripts that were collected by the Heller family. However, the texts of *Yosher Divrey Emet* and *Derekh Emet* that appear in this edition contain no new material. There are several other important additions, however. These include a text containing fragments of a commentary on the Pentateuch and other portions of the Hebrew Bible as well as comments on some Talmudic passages,[200] a kabbalistic prayer composed by Meshullam Feibush,[201] and a magical ceremony to be performed before dwelling in a new lodging.[202] Also included in this edition are the two letters written by Meshullam Feibush to unknown disciples,[203] and a document concerning the establishment of a group which has committed itself to study the entire Mishnah within the coming year.[204] The document is dated Monday, the 12 Kislev 1779. Meshullam Feibush's name is the first of the signatories.

In addition to material written by Meshullam Feibush, himself, the Munkacz edition also includes several texts written by his descendents. These include homilies on biblical passages and rabbinic comments by Meshullam Feibush's son, Rabbi Samson of Uziran. This material is entitled, *Nezirut Shimshon*.[205] A responsum written by Meshullam Feibush's great-grandson, Rabbi Abraham Samuel, the Head of the Rabbinical Court in Buzinov, also appears.[206] The responsum is written in defense of a kabbalistic *kavvanah* that Meshullam Feibush would say before preparing a parchment to be inscribed with the verses that are contained within the phylacteries.

Of the additional writings of Meshullam Feibush that are included in the 1905 Munkacz text, the fragments of his commentary are particularly important. In an introduction to these writings, the author informs us that he began recording these teachings on the 26 Tevet 1775.[207]

Meshullam Feibush decided to commit these teachings to writing because he was afraid that otherwise he would forget what he had previously learned from his teachers and books. Only a portion of the text survived. On several occasions comments alluded to are no longer extant. Due to the incomplete state of the printed text, generalizations concerning its content must be made with caution.

Nevertheless, a number of observations are in order. First, in the introduction, Meshullam Feibush expresses the hope that the writings may be of benefit "to my sons or to one of the fellowship that hearkens to my voice." A similar reference to a group that looked to Meshullam Feibush for guidance appears twice in *Yosher Divrey Emet*. From the introduction, it is clear that such a group was already in existence more than two years before Meshullam Feibush began *Yosher Divrey Emet*. Second, Meshullam Feibush's Hasidic masters are rarely mentioned in this apparently earlier text. Yehiel Mikhel of Zlotchov is not mentioned even once. On the other hand, Dov Ber of Mezeritch and Menahem Mendel of Premishlan are each mentioned only twice.[208] Moreover, both are cited in a form that indicates that they were still alive at the time of writing. This suggests that Meshullam Feibush may have begun recording his teachings some years before the date indicated in the introduction.[209] The absence of Yehiel Mikhel's name also suggests that much of this material might have been written before Meshullam Feibush's association with this master became decisive. However, since, unlike in *Liqqutim Yeqarim*, the general approach taken by the author in this text does not involve frequent references to his masters, this conclusion should not be too hastily drawn. Moreover, Yehiel Mikhel may well have been cited in sections that are no longer extant.[210]

While several teachings that are included in *Yosher Divrey Emet* already appear in these fragments, the text has a very different tone. Lacking are both the polemical justification of the Hasidic *Zaddiq* and the critique of the teachings of Dov Ber of Mezeritch. This also suggests a somewhat early date of composition. The two references to Dov Ber of Mezeritch present teachings that Meshullam Feibush has heard directly. There is no indication that Meshullam Feibush is aware of the teachings of Dov Ber that circulated in manuscript. The controversial material that would receive such importance in *Yosher Divrey Emet* is not at all in evidence. From the content of these early writings, we realize how provoked Meshullam Feibush may have been by the subsequent dissemination in eastern Galicia of Dov Ber's teachings. Their apparent failure to take into consideration the uniqueness of the *Zaddiq*'s soul is in direct conflict with teachings of Meshullam Feibush's master, Yehiel Mikhel. The attempt to resolve this conflict constitutes one of the principal themes of *Yosher Divrey Emet*.

In 1974, the late Grand Rabbi Abraham Isaac Kahn of *Yeshivat Toledot Aharon* published a new edition of *Liqqutim Yeqarim* with an introduction and notes. In this edition, Meshullam Feibush's epistles were removed from *Liqqutim Yeqarim* and printed as an independent text called *Yosher Divrey Emet*.[211] The shorter *Derekh Emet* also appeared as an independent text, following *Yosher Divrey Emet*. Kahn's *Yosher Divrey Emet* essentially followed the Munkacz edition. However, he presented the text in consecutively numbered sections and added notes and a summary of the contents. For the sake of convenience, we used Kahn's edition.

2

Sources of *Devequt*
in Early Hasidism

Nearly fifty years ago in a series of lectures delivered at Hebrew Union College in New York, Gershom Scholem identified *devequt*, or communion with God, as the focal point of early Hasidism and as the principal factor in determining its spiritual physiognomy.[1] Scholem's insight that Hasidism placed greatest emphasis on awareness of the "real omnipresence and immanence of God"[2] has gone until recently virtually unchallenged.[3] Yet, aspects of his treatment of the subject have been augmented, questioned, and, in some cases, refuted in the considerable scholarly research, which has dealt with the history and meaning of the term *devequt*.[4] In the face of so much new material on the subject, Scholem's article can no longer be considered a sufficient account of *devequt*. The quantity and importance of recent insights clearly call for a fresh presentation of our subject.[5] Our goal, then, will be to review those aspects of recent research that contribute to a new account of the antecedents of *devequt* in Hasidism and to present a preliminary phenomenology of *devequt* in selected early Hasidic texts.

Scholem begins his discussion of *devequt* with several very important medieval sources, Nahmanides' commentary on Deut. 11:22 and Maimonides' *Guide of the Perplexed*, part 3, chapter 51. However, the term had been interpreted even earlier in ways which would be of interest to Hasidic thinkers. Indeed already in rabbinic literature the meaning of those verses, which speak of cleaving to God, are the subject of discussion.[6] One trend of rabbinic interpretation is decidedly non-mystical.[7] Assuming the impossibility of direct contact between the human and the divine, the biblical injunction "to cleave to Him" is understood as calling for a clear commitment to the way of God or some type of *imitatio dei*.[8] On the other hand, a number of teachings in the name of Rabbi Akiva and his followers call for a literal reading of the verse. "And you who are cleaving to YHVH, your God— actually cleaving."[9] Here the meaning clearly goes beyond external action, no matter how God-like, and points to an inner state of connection to the deity. Thus, it is clear that in the early rabbinic period there was a tradition which understood biblical expressions of cleaving to God in a literal or mystical sense. Moreover, this inner mystical experience is already associated with the Holy Spirit. "Just as when someone is attached to impurity, an impure spirit rests upon him, it follows that when one is connected to the *Shekhinah*, the Holy Spirit rests upon him."[10]

However, one non-mystical rabbinic interpretation of *devequt* is also deserving of our attention since it is frequently cited in the early Hasidic writings of R. Ya'aqov Yosef of Polnoy and plays an important role in his theory of *devequt*. As an interpretation of Deut. 11:22, we find "and is it possible for a person to ascend to the supernal and cleave to fire?[11] . . . rather, cleave to the sages and their disciples."[12] This view recoils at the notion of intimacy between the divine and human. The best means of cleaving to God is not only an association with those who are experts in His Torah, but also to actively support them.[13] We shall soon see how R. Ya'aqov Yosef embraces both of these seemingly mutually exclusive understandings of *devequt*. For the present, however, we need only remark that while the interpretation which involves association with Torah sages has no apparent mystical connotation in the rabbinic sources themselves, there is nothing which would prevent it from being absorbed by mystical conceptions of the Torah that developed in the Middle Ages.

While rabbinic literature does contain evidence of belief in the possibility of mystical experience, such experience receives no sustained or systematic analysis. Fully developed theories which explain the ways in which contact between the human and the divine can occur appear only in the Middle Ages. These theories are extremely dependent on terminologies borrowed from non-Jewish philosophical sources.[14] The terminologies are, according to Moshe Idel, of three distinct types: Aristotelian, Neoplatonic, and Hermetic. However, in many cases aspects from more than one terminology are combined in a particular presentation of *devequt*. The terminologies differ as to the entities said to be involved in the divine/human contact and in conceiving the contact as a result of human ascent or divine descent. All three types are found in Hasidic sources.[15]

Approaches to *devequt* in early Kabbalah may also be distinguished in other ways: as theocentric or anthropocentric in emphasis and as nomic or anomic. In the first case, the distinction depends on whether the state of *devequt* is intended primarily to affect the divine or human realm. In the earlier stages of Spanish Kabbalah, the anthropocentric type predominates.[16] *Devequt* is a means of empowering the human soul. It may be a precondition for attaining prophecy, for bestowing blessing, or for producing holy progeny. At any rate, it functions as an aspect of personal perfection which renders an individual better able to serve the community. A particularly important example which later became a major characteristic of early Hasidism, is the notion that *devequt* transforms a person into a channel through which blessing can flow from the divine realm into the human.[17]

Where the focus of *devequt* is theocentric it tends to function as an element of theurgy. The Kabbalist's principal interest is to produce beneficent effects in the divine realm. Here the Kabbalist's thought has theosophic effect. Through concentrating on the Tetragrammaton, the letters can be activated as symbols of higher entities, or *sefirot*, which are brought into a state of union. When the Kabbalist cleaves to the unified totality, he is able to produce the same theurgic effect that was once dependent on the Temple service.

In all of the cases cited above, whether anthropocentric or theocentric, *devequt* serves primarily as a means to some other end and not as an end in itself. The mystical experiences involved are not sought for their own value, but because they are necessary in order to achieve some other extraordinary goal, whether theurgic, magical, or mediational.

However, there was another major trend which developed in Spain during the middle of the thirteenth century and which was anthropocentric in the extreme. This ecstatic school of Kabbalah cultivated certain types of mystical experience for its own sake. Here *devequt* was understood in its most extreme form as *unio mystica*. This approach, as expounded by its leading figure, Abraham Abulafia (1240–1291), had its theological basis in the Aristotelian epistemology of Maimonides rather than in the system of the *sefirot* which was central to Spanish theosophical Kabbalah.[18] The Aristotelian approach to *devequt* led to union between the human intellect and its divine object which was often identified as the Active Intellect. This mystical experience of union was cultivated by Abulafia and his followers as the ultimate goal of religion and a condition of prophecy. It was compared to the attainment of eternal life.[19] In order to attain the ecstatic union, Abulafia practiced and taught a system of spiritual exercises that involved letter combinations, visualization, controlled breathing, head motions, and singing.[20] Ecstatic Kabbalah was almost entirely anomic, its methods of practice occurring entirely outside the parameters of the divine commandments. This may be one of the reasons why Abulafia was condemned in Spain. At any rate, the school's influence spread to Jewish communities located further to the east and was incorporated in the sixteenth-century Safedian synthesis of earlier Kabbalistic trends. Abulafia's writings were included in Moshe Cordovero's (1522–1570) compendious *Pardes Rimmonim* and in Hayyim Vital's (1542–1620) important popular work of piety, *Sha'arey Qedushah*. Cordovero, moreover, considered Abulafia's letter and divine name mysticism to be a more advanced form of Kabbalah than the way of the *sefirot*. The Safedian attitude seemed to have been that the purpose and practice of

the Abulafian methods were respected, but restricted solely to the knowledge and usage of the spiritual elite.[21] Through such influential sources Abulafia influenced Hasidism.[22]

For some reason, Gershom Scholem's *devequt* article entirely ignores
Abulafia's school of Ecstatic Kabbalah and its basis in philosophical terminology. As a result, it was easier for him to argue that *devequt* excludes the
meaning of *unio mystica* or that such cases are at best marginal.[23] Idel has
shown that unitive descriptions recur in Kabbalistic literature quite frequently, just as in non-Jewish mystical writings. Moreover Kabbalists have
used images to represent *unio mystica* which are no less extreme than those
of their more notorious non-Jewish mystical counterparts.[24]

Bold expressions of *unio mystica* are by no means either rare or marginal in early Hasidic literature.[25] This fact is partially acknowledged by Scholem, especially in regards to teachings emanating from R. Dov Ber of
Mezeritch and his school. But even here we are cautioned "not to lose ourselves in his terminology, which is radical indeed, but to consider the context of his thought."[26] Indeed, it now appears that the context of R. Ber's
thought must indeed be reconsidered. Precedents for early Hasidic *unio
mystica* go back at least to the thirteenth century, and are not nearly as few
nor as eccentric as Scholem implies. Moreover, a direct source for the non-
dual tendency in R. Ber's Hasidic theology can be found in the Kabbalah of
Cordovero which was known to the Hasidim through a popular text which
Scholem himself mentions, *Sefer Hesed le-Avraham* of R. Avraham Azulai.

We already have made reference to the fact that recent research has
shown that Hasidic conceptions of *devequt* are extremely indebted to pietistic popularizations of Safedian Kabbalah. Scholem's article deals with at
least one of these sources, *Sefer Haredim* of R. Eleazar Azikri.[27] Other
sources, especially *Reshit Hokhmah* of R. Elijah de Vidas and R. Isaiah
Horowitz's *Sheney Luhot ha-Berit*, are equally important and an analysis of
their influence should be part of any discussion of *devequt* in Hasidism.[28]
Mordecai Pechter's research in the homiletical and ethical literature of
(sixteenth-century) Safed has disclosed that *devequt* was of major concern
to a number of the most important Kabbalists. It is prominent as part of a
metaphysical theory presented in the popular sermons of Rabbis Moses Alsheich, Elisha Gallico, and Solomon Alkabetz. In the diaries of R. Joseph
Karo and R. Eleazar Azikri it is described in terms of personal mystical experiences. In *Reshit Hokhmah* and in Vital's *Sha'arey Qedushah*, *devequt*
even merits a full systematic treatment which explains its metaphysical and
psychological bases as well as its ethical underpinnings. With the exception
of the diaries, all of these works are intended for popular audiences. The

Alsheich sermons, *Sha'arey Qedushah,* and *Reshit Hokhmah* are certainly known to the Hasidim.

In the Safedian texts a number of motifs are prominent which typify Hasidic approaches to *devequt.* First, in Alsheich's widely read sermons *devequt* is particularly associated with learning Torah. An essential identity between the inner nature of the Torah and of the human soul is posited. The assumption is that both are divine in their innermost essence, but are covered over by protective garments which conceal the essence. Thus, to the extent that a person, through concerning himself with the Torah can free his soul from its physical garments, he can approach a state of *devequt.* The metaphysical assumption is, of course, that in essence God and the Torah and the Jewish soul are one.[29] Several corollaries of this idea are worth noting. *Devequt* comes about through a process of moral perfection according to the guidelines of the Torah. This path is progressive and virtually endless. Thus, *devequt* is already understood here as a mystical path.[30] Second, due to the underlying assumption of the identity of God, Torah, and Jew, the path towards *devequt* with God through the Torah is essentially one of self-knowledge. However, at its higher stages, it is definitely associated with cleaving to the *sefirot* and with comprehension of esoteric matters.[31]

Also found in the homiletical literature is the notion that *devequt* is characterized by longing. Often erotic motifs are employed to describe the mutual desire of God and the soul to be reunited. At the ultimate stage of perfect *devequt,* a level that is associated with the first *sefirah Keter,* complete silence ensues. This is termed *asifat ha-mahashevah* (nullification of thought).

Azikri's diaries are also rich in material which is similar to typical Hasidic descriptions of *devequt* experiences.[32] Here one finds a range of ecstatic states. Emphasized are love, awe, and trembling in the presence of the Divine along with joy and humility. A record of how Azikri realized the ideal of constant *devequt* is detailed. The technique for remaining permanently in *devequt* consists in constantly performing *yihudim* (combining the letters of divine names).[33] It is worth noting that Azikri's concept of *devequt* extends to all times and circumstances. He expresses this ideal in conjunction with the verses, "I place YHVH before me at all times" (Ps. 16:8) and "the whole earth is full of His Glory" (Is. 6:3). *Devequt* has here the meaning of life in the presence of God. This is described as self-abnegation within a feeling of joy.[34] In order to maintain *devequt,* the habit of *hitbodedut* (mental concentration) must be mastered.[35]

The complete presentations of *devequt* in *Reshit Hokhmah* and *Sha'arey Qedushah* contain most of the ideas detailed above. However,

several additional aspects of importance are found there. In Elijah de Vidas'
work, *devequt* is associated with love. Its ultimate realization is tantamount
to total love of God in a state of *unio mystica*.[36] Progress towards this end is
attained in stages called *"deviqah," "hashiqah," "hafizah."* These refer to
increasingly closer stages of adhesion involving the three mystical dimensions of the human soul, *nefesh*, *ruah*, and *neshamah*. Adhesion occurs
when one has the sole intention of "uniting the *shekhinah* and removing all
the evil shells from her." However, this theosophical goal is accomplished
anthropologically through the suppression of alien thoughts[37] and through
hitpashtut ha-gashmiyut, complete withdrawal of the soul from material
interests and sensations. But this is more readily achieved through desire
and love for Torah than through the ascetic means of fasting and mortifications. De Vidas emphasizes the value of *devequt* for its own sake as a state of
union with the divine which is compared to sexual union. It does, however,
have the simultaneous theurgic effect of uniting all of the *sefirot*.[38]

Hayyim Vital also makes *devequt* contingent upon moral perfection according to the Torah. Here again it is associated with the theurgic process of
uniting all of the *sefirot* and raising them to *Eyn Sof*. But for Vital, *devequt*
is no longer ultimate. It is rather a precondition for prophecy. Nevertheless,
in *Sha'arey Qedushah* the influence of the values of Abulafia's ecstatic Kabbalah are evident.[39]

Another source that is highly regarded by the Hasidim is Isaiah
Horowitz's *Sheney Luhot ha-Berit*.[40] It, too, contains a number of distinctive motives which were to become hallmarks of early Hasidic thought.[41]
The ideal of constant *devequt* is related to the practice of holding the Tetragrammaton in the mind's eye at all times. This practice is identified as the
meaning of Ps. 16:8. It is emphasized that *devequt* constitutes a path of ever
increasing levels of holiness. *Devequt* can be maintained while learning
Torah. This is possible because the letters of the Torah have the power to en-
lighten one who gazes upon them even when the meaning of the words is
not understood.[42]

However, *Sheney Luhot ha-Berit* is, perhaps, most important for its notion of serving God with the "evil urge" itself. This idea contains a number
of aspects which are of relevance to us. First, it contributes to the ideal of
constant *devequt* through extending the range of opportunities for serving
God to such seemingly nonreligious activities as eating, drinking, and mari-
tal relations. More radical is Horowitz's advice concerning the need to perform the commandments in a state of arousal. In order to guarantee that the
mizvot will be fulfilled with great intention (*be-hit'orrerut ha-lev*), the *She-
LaH* advocates performing a positive commandment through its negative,

and a negative commandment through its positive. This means that when one is about to perform a certain commandment, he should first have in mind the reasons why he would prefer not to do it and even feel the body's reluctance to perform it. Through overcoming this inner conflict, the requisite intentionality is produced. This emphasis on including the evil urge is expressed in even more daring terms. We find that negative traits like jealousy, hate, and lust can themselves be means of serving God and need not be eradicated. Indeed the impure can be made pure. The more negative qualities are still available for transformation, the greater the degree of holiness of the divine service.[43] As in *Reshit Hokhmah*, alien thoughts or negative moral traits are recognized as a fundamental barrier to *devequt*. However, the only remedy proposed is their suppression. The possibility of transformation that is so praiseworthy in regards to negative traits does not seem to have been applied to negative thoughts per se before Hasidism.

The importance of the Safedian texts for the development of Hasidic ideas, in general, and *devequt*, in particular, cannot be overemphasized. Not only do they champion *devequt* as a religious ideal towards which one should constantly aspire, but their basic formulations of *devequt* bear most of the radical features which have been associated with Hasidism.[44] Their influence, however, goes beyond the originality of their views. They are also important as sources for earlier Kabbalistic thought.

In particular, one Kabbalist should be mentioned whose ideas were preserved in *Reshit Hokhmah* and in *Sha'arey Qedushah*. Rabbi Isaac of Acre, a proponent of both ecstatic and theosophic Kabbalah, was active in Spain from the late thirteenth until the mid-fourteenth-century.[45] He was perhaps the first to recommend a version of *devequt* that occurred at the initial stage of the spiritual path. Moreover, it was intended for everyone, not just the elite.[46] In a passage from his work, *Mei'rat Eynayim*, which is included in *Sha'arey Qedushah*, R. Isaac presented *devequt* as the first rung in a three stage process which eventually led to prophecy.[47] Prophecy was acquired through mental concentration (*hitbodedut*) which cannot be practiced until one first had become established in equanimity (*hishtavut*). But the method recommended here for attaining equanimity was adhesion (*devequt*) to the *sefirah Tif'eret*. This adhesion was accomplished through the practice of constantly directing one's thoughts to the letters of the Tetragrammaton which was identified with *Tif'eret*.

We noted earlier that Gershom Scholem begins his discussion of *devequt* and Hasidism by calling attention to Nahmanides' commentary on the Pentateuch and Maimonides' *Guide of the Perplexed*. There is no reason to question the centrality of these sources. In the first case emphasis is placed on the possibility that communion with God may take place even during ordinary public intercourse. As for Maimonides, he had already associated *devequt* with passionate love of God and divine providence. Moreover, in his theology which places so much emphasis on the knowledge of God, *devequt* has a particularly important role to play. Nevertheless while both Maimonides and Nahmanides directly have influenced Hasidic notions of *devequt*, it would be difficult to argue that their direct influence is greater than that of the Safedian texts. Moreover, in both of these cases *devequt* is discussed in the context of the most sublime spiritual levels, whereas the Safedian texts are clearly intended to popularize mystical-ethical concepts and values to a greater extent. Even if Scholem somewhat exaggerated the democratic character of early Hasidic ideas, there is no doubt that the more popular Safedian texts are much closer in spirit to the outlook of early Hasidism.[48] Furthermore, although Maimonides' passage on *devequt* is sometimes quoted directly in Hasidic texts,[49] the Maimonidean approach to *devequt* also entered Hasidism through the mediation of ecstatic Kabbalah. Indeed the ecstatic school, following Abulafia, has identified itself as the guardian of the technical methods necessary for attaining the prophetic goal of Maimonidean theology.

Devequt, then, does not refer to a single, general experience. It is applied to a number of intense, experiential encounters with the divine. These may be intellectual, emotional, psychological, contemplative, or social in nature. In virtually every case, the Hasidic approach is connected to some precedent in the history of Jewish thought, from the rabbinic period through the Middle Ages.[50] Moreover, Hasidic attitudes towards *devequt* are typical of their times and region. In many cases, these Hasidic attitudes are more moderate than those of their contemporaries.[51] If there is a uniqueness in Hasidic conceptions of *devequt*, it is more one of emphasis than innovation.

The Basis of Devequt

The concept of *devequt* in early Hasidism[52] emphasized the possibility and importance of human awareness of the Divine Presence. This idea, as already indicated, was in no sense new in the history of Jewish thought. Nor was it unique to the individuals who were instrumental in founding the movement which came to be known as Hasidism. The call for constant remembrance of God was passionately urged by many an east European preacher of the eighteenth century and found its way into the homiletical literature of the period, often in forms far more radical than those typical of Hasidic thinkers.[53] Thus, the intensity of Hasidic interest in *devequt* should be understood not as its distinguishing feature, but rather as an indication of the extent to which early Hasidism was rooted in the values of Safedian Kabbalah, both Lurianic and Cordoverian, which were popularized in several influential Kabbalistic-ethical texts.[54]

While Hasidic sources usually indicate that communion with the divine depends on certain methods for controlling thoughts, the spiritual techniques are themselves based in the fundamental aspects of Hasidic faith. The call for constant attachment to God is rooted in a radical application of the principle of divine immanence.

> One should think that the entire world is full of the Creator's Glory and that the Divine Presence (*Shekhinah*) is always with him [although] it is extremely subtle. . . . And he should think and believe with perfect faith that the Divine Presence is there guarding him, and that he and the blessed Creator are connected through all his limbs and powers, and that he and the blessed Creator are looking at each other. The Creator can do whatever He wishes. He can destroy the world in one moment and create it [anew] in another. In His Blessedness everything positive and negative in the world has its root. For everything contains His effluence (*Shefa*) and energy (*Hiyyut*) . . .[55]

The Divine is omnipresent, omnipotent, and providential. It is the cause of everything, both positive and negative, and the enlivening force in all that exists. While this faith tends towards pantheism, in fact Hasidic theology does not advocate worshipping the world as it appears to the senses. Indeed the senses tend to be deceiving for they do not perceive that the attractiveness of creation is only due to the divine which is present within it. They confuse the divine essence with the objects of this world in which it is partially contained.

> . . . One should keep from [taking pleasure in] looking at attractive things, especially at beautiful women, when one looks in order to satisfy one's lust. For in such looking one is like an idol worshipper . . . Rather this is the way to act in regard to what one sees. If one suddenly finds himself looking at a pretty woman, he should begin to reflect on the source of her beauty. When she is dead, surely she will no longer have such a face. So where does her beauty come from? It must come from a divine power which has emanated into her. It bestowed upon her this beauty and ruddiness. So the root of the beauty is a divine power. Why should I allow myself to be drawn after the part, when I can cleave to the root and essence of all the worlds where all beauty is located?[56]

Fascination with the world as it appears separates one from God, it is tantamount to idol worship. Paradoxically, this separation is, of course, only apparent. For the radical belief in immanence implies that existence can never be separated from its divine source. But, the Hasidic demand for *devequt* calls for more than mere assertion of faith in divine immanence, some degree of apprehension of the divine is required. This requires a mental process of constantly distinguishing the spiritual essence from its material container.

> Similarly, whenever one looks at other material things, such as a vessel, he should reflect on the source of the vessel's beauty and form. Thus [one sees that] matter is secondary. It is beauty and form that constitute the spiritual vitality of the vessel and are themselves a portion of the divine from above.[57]

Here the Hasidic analysis of creation resembles Platonism. However, unlike the more explicitly acosmic theology of the somewhat later HaBaD movement, it is not yet quite stated that the world of the senses is illusory.[58] The problem is that the senses tend to exaggerate the importance of matter as if its claim upon human attention were based upon its own inherent quality. In reality, material objects are attractive (or repulsive) only because they make manifest nonmaterial forces which are divine emanations from the supernal ontological source. The Hasidic emphasis on immanence widely extends the parameters of the arena within which the divine can be located.[59] However, since a definite ontological hierarchy separates matter and form, Hasidic faith in divine immanence must be classified as a type of idealism. This is expressed in Hasidic language, particularly in the writings of R. Jacob Joseph, by the notion that *devequt* pertains to the supra-natural, literally to that which is "above nature" (*lema'lah me-ha-tev'a*). Commenting on Abraham's response to the divine promise that his descendants would inherit the Land, R. Jacob Joseph states:

> Abraham himself immediately felt that he had managed to ascend the rungs which are above nature. These are the rungs of faith, thus it is written, "*and he believed in YHVH* . . . (Gen. 15:6). For faith in His Blessedness is the essence of *devequt*, to be joined to the blessed name *YHVH* which is supra-natural.[60]

The expression "above nature" indicates that the contact with the divine that constitutes *devequt* takes place in the mental realm within which a contemplative ascent is possible. The human being, situated in the physical realm or nature, has the opportunity at every moment to undergo a transformation through mental adhesion to the divine. Such a transformation brings one into a state of holiness which is supra-natural. For R. Jacob Joseph, holiness is ultimately identical with *devequt*.[61]

We have already indicated that *devequt* or communion with God, occurs within the human mind, although its arena is the natural world where the divine force which is the real source of the senses' interest in all material things and experience must be discerned. Still, at its highest stages, *devequt* is equated with love. This indicates that it is an experience mutually shared by God and man who manage to embrace and even unite despite the natural barriers that would seem to preclude such a union. In the writings of R. Jacob Joseph, a human being can approach intimate communion with God through a gradual process of sanctification which begins with separation from matter and continues through several stages of purifying the mind until nothing is left but an awareness of the divine presence.

> Now we shall explain what Maimonides wrote in the *Guide of the Perplexed,* that circumcision is for perfection of the moral attributes.[62] The meaning is that through removing the foreskin of circumcision, the foreskin of the heart and alien thoughts are [also] removed. Through directing the heart one can purify one's mind (*maheshaveto*) and fulfill "*and to Him you shall cleave.*"[63] For this is the root of everything: to cause one's mind to cleave to His Blessedness without any ulterior motive (*peniyah*) or separating screen for then the *Shekhinah* crowns his head. This is the esoteric meaning of "*and their king shall pass before them and YHVH at their head,*"[64] as is explained in *Reishit Hokhmah.*[65]

This state, moreover, can be maintained during all of the ordinary conditions of life, once the requisite stage of purification has been completed.

> The meaning of the verse, "He causes their king to pass before them" is that everywhere, whether while sitting at home or while traveling along the way, he causes their king to pass before them.[i.e.] nothing impure is permitted to enter their eyes or ears, only matters of holiness and commandment from the kingdom of holiness. And the reason is because "and YHVH is at their head,"[i.e.] their mind is always [focused on God]. Thus according to the [nature of the] thought in their mind, so is [the character] of what occurs before them . . .[66]

For R. Dov Ber, the human being's relation to the divine is, in a certain sense, *mutatis mutandis,* analogous to that of all other aspects of the natural world. Just as what is essential in everything else is the ray of divine energy which takes form in the object, so the very impulse to worship is itself a ray from the divine source.[67]

> And the verse continues, "great is *YHVH* and much praised [in the city of our God . .]."[68] In other words, we should magnify and praise Him for all the good that He bestows upon us. For all the pride and glory that He has from our

worship is entirely "*in the city*" (*ba-'iR*) , i.e. through the arousal (*hit'oReRut*) of our God. For it is He who arouses us to serve Him and to overcome [the obstacles] As our sages said, "were it not that the Holy One Blessed be He helps him [one could not succeed]."[69] Nevertheless His Blessedness [experiences] pleasure and pride and pays us a great reward. He rewards as if we had done it on our own. But in reality, true worship does have to be through our own arousal. For we are a ray of the divine from above (*heleq eloha mi-ma'al*). And this is the meaning of "*in the city*," through the arousal of our good impulse, the divine part that is within us— that is the meaning of "*our God . . .*"[70]

For R. Dov Ber, then, ultimately *devequt* can occur not only because "His Glory fills the entire world," but because anthropologically, there is an essential identity between the best human impulses and the divine itself.

Devequt, then, can occur in varying degrees, depending on the context,[71] the extent to which an individual has attained spiritual purity, and other variables. At times it means nothing more than keeping God in mind during circumstances that are not normally associated with religious acts. Typically this is accomplished through allotting a portion of one's consciousness to the visualization of the Tetragrammaton.[72] In other cases, *devequt* may entail a total obliteration of the sense of self, ecstatic immersion in the divine source of life. While a range of meanings and degrees of intimacy with the divine are indicated by the term *devequt*, its ultimate expression is *unio mystica*. The goal of union with God entered Hasidism through theories of *devequt* already formulated in popular Kabbalistic-ethical works, particularly those influenced by the sixteenth century Safedian Kabbalist, Moses Cordovero. Nevertheless early Hasidic writings should be recognized as a particularly rich source of unusually bold and original formulations of this phenomenon.[73]

Barriers to Devequt

The ideal of *devequt* calls for a fundamental transformation of human consciousness. According to the Hasidic view, mere gratification of the senses' cravings, and attainment of mundane pleasures are considered dubious goods. These, moreover, not only pale by comparison to *devequt*, but they also are seen as dangerous since they essentially undermine interest in its pursuit.

The only true good is *devequt* with His Blessed Name, as it is written, "*as for me, closeness to God is good.*"[74] But *devequt* with the *Shekhinah* cannot possibly be attained except through subduing matter and the evil urge. And this is only by means of suffering (*yissurin*), [i.e., through] the opposite of the verse, "and Yeshurun grew fat and balked"[75] which [alludes to conditions] that are a barrier to *devequt*.[76]

Devequt in early Hasidism is not merely a matter of faith or attitude, it is a value which is only realized within a generally ascetic approach to life. Hasidic asceticism should be viewed as moderate in comparison to the practices of certain contemporary eastern European Kabbalists who continued to be guided by the norms of Kabbalistic ethics that were typical of sixteenth-century Safed.[77] Nevertheless, there is a clear connection between *devequt* and asceticism in our sources.[78]

> Cause your thought to cleave above and do not eat or drink too much, only what health requires. Pay no attention to this-worldly matters, not thinking of them at all. But, always endeavor to separate yourself from corporeality, for through regarding this-worldly matters, one is coarsened. The sages said, "seeing leads to reflecting and [thus] to desiring."[79] And it is written concerning the tree of knowledge, *"pleasant to look upon and good to eat."*[80] Its attractiveness resulted from [Eve's] seeing it.[81]

Thus, attaining *devequt* initially demands control of the senses. The body's natural desires and impulses require disciplining lest they distract one from the interests of spiritual transformation.

However, early Hasidism's discussion of the obstacles to *devequt* does not concern itself with issues of corporeality in isolation, ultimately attention is given over to an analysis of inner qualities. Character defects are diagnosed which must be overcome and those which ought to be cultivated are identified. The basic assumption is that any tendency towards self-interest separates one from communion with the divine presence.

> In everything that one does he should think that he is giving pleasure to the *Shekhinah*. He should not think of his own pleasure at all, for this is mere vanity. Why should he act for his own pleasure? Even if he performs a number of practices and preparations so that he can worship in *devequt*, if he takes pleasure from this worship, this is also worshipping for one's own sake. But the basis of all his worship should be for the sake of the *Shekhinah*. Not even a little should be for his own sake.[82]

It is not merely a question of shifting the focus of one's attention and activities from worldly to spiritual matters. Even the latter will not lead to *devequt* as long as they are pursued out of selfish motivations. Self-interest is itself a fundamental barrier to *devequt*.

The problem with self-interest, even in the service of God, is that it ne-
cessitates a diversion of attention from its proper object, the divine presence.
In a value system that places *devequt* and experiential knowledge of God at
its summit, this is a serious flaw.

> From RYVaSH [Rabbi Yisrael Ba'al Shem]: "For my thoughts are not your
> thoughts and your ways are not My ways."[83] The meaning is that as soon as a
> person separates himself from God, he is immediately guilty of *avodah zarah*
> (idol worship). There is nothing In between. This is the meaning of *"and you
> turn away and serve [other Gods]."*[84]

Instead of self-interest, Hasidism recommends the development of an
inner state that is beyond all egotism.

> "I place YHVH before me at all times."[85] *"I place"* (*ShiViti*) is related to equa-
> nimity (*hiShtaVut*). No matter what happens, whether people praise or con-
> temn, one's inner state should remain in balance (*ha-kol shaveh ezlo*).[86] This
> applies also to food. Whether one eats delicacies or other things, it should make
> no difference because there is no longer any evil urge at all. And no matter what
> occurs, one trusts that it is from God, and if it seems fitting to Him . . . One's
> only intention is for the sake of Heaven. From the individual's point of view,
> there is no dissent. This is a very great level [87]

This condition of complete faith in God's will and total indifference to one's
own honor and the satisfaction of personal preferences is an ideal of Hasidic
ethics. Though not easily attained, it can be developed through practicing
the spiritual exercises that are associated with *devequt*.

> Equanimity is an important principle. The meaning is that it will be the same to
> him whether he is considered an ignoramus or as one who knows the entire
> Torah. What brings this about is the constant [practice] of *devequt* with the cre-
> ator. For due to the constant demands of *devequt*, he is not free to think of such
> things. For he is constantly occupied by his effort to attach himself to Him
> above.[88]

The contemplative exercises act as a kind of prophylactic against the mind's
ordinary tendency to think about personal interests. Here the term *devequt*
refers to the techniques of spiritual discipline rather than to the condition
that they are meant to produce, communion with God. The goal is here
identified as equanimity (*hishtavut*). These two distinct usages of *devequt*
reflect two different trends of thought which directly influenced Hasidism.
Where *devequt* refers to a technique that leads to *hishtavut*, the source is
that of the fourteenth century Kabbalist, R. Isaac of Acre.[89] Where *devequt*

means a mystical state, the sources can be any of several popular Kabbalistic-ethical works, especially *Reishit Hokhmah, Sheney Luhot ha-Berit,* and *Sefer Haredim.*[90]

In general all of the classical moral vices that can be construed as counter to the state of *hishtavut* are warned against. Anger and sadness are frequently singled out among the negative qualities which cause, or are in themselves, a separation from the divine presence. However, the vice which is most emphasized as a barrier to *devequt* is haughtiness (*gavhut*).[91]

> As for haughtiness, even a tiny thought of haughtiness is very serious. For every ulterior motivation (*peniyah*) is due to haughtiness. Since every thought is a complete structure,[92] haughtiness causes great harm above. It drives away the *Shekhinah,* as it is written, *"every proud person is an abomination of YHVH."*[93]

Every vestige of self-importance must be eradicated. Even accomplishment in *devequt* must not become a basis for feeling superior to others or a source of pride.

> One should not imagine that he is greater than his fellow because he worships in *devequt*. For he is like all other creatures who were created with the necessity of worshiping His Blessedness. The Holy Name gave his fellow an intellect just as he himself received one. And how is he more important than the worm that serves the Blessed Creator with all its mind and power? Man is also a worm, as it is written, "I am a worm and no man."[94] If the Blessed Name had not given him a [human] intellect, he would only be able to serve Him like a worm. So he is no more important than a worm, and certainly no more than another person.
>
> He should think that he is [like] a worm and that the other tiny creatures are considered as comrades in the world. For all were created and each has only that ability which the Blessed Creator gave to it. This matter must always be kept in mind.[95]

The Hasidic attack on haughtiness has two aspects. Especially in the writings of R. Jacob Joseph, haughtiness and arrogance are associated with the learned rabbinic authorities. In this analysis, which echoes homiletical complaints already resounding in non-Hasidic sources,[96] Torah learning is a cause of pride which weakens the moral caliber of the rabbinic leadership and alienates it from the people. In this context, *devequt* figures as a value which can bridge the gap between the learned elite and ordinary people. This is so despite the paradoxical nature of *devequt* which, while indeed demanding absolute self-effacement, transcends the limits of nature in its contact with the divine.

In the writings of R. Dov Ber of Mezeritch, the context within which the relationship between haughtiness and *devequt* is discussed is psychological rather than social. In this trend of thought, *devequt* tends towards *unio mystica*. It is typically associated with an ecstatic state called *"ayin"* (nothing), because consciousness is here entirely filled by the divine presence.[97] In the absence of all sense of self, only God is present. The mystic becomes as nothing.

> If during prayer one feels pride from his *devequt,* he should recollect that he is from the *shevirah,*[98] that he is feeling proud and thus aware of himself, so how can this be perfect *devequt?* This is the meaning of *"a sage should not praise himself for his wisdom . . . but in this one can take pride, in knowing Me."*[99] The meaning is as in [the verse], *"and Adam knew [Eve, his wife]."*[100] For since one is cleaving to *Eyn-Sof* and *Eyn-Sof* is not divided into parts, . . . And the enlightened will understand.[101]

Devequt is here likened to conjugal union which is called "knowing" in the Genesis account of Adam and Eve. But "knowing God" refers here to a union with *Eyn-Sof* the ultimate divine aspect which is beyond all differentiation. Since *Eyn-Sof* is indivisible, *devequt* as complete union with *Eyn-Sof* must allude to a state which likewise involves no division into parts. It is non-dual. For *devequt* to be perfectly realized in this sense, awareness of self must not be present. Since pride inherently involves a kind of reflection on self, it always indicates a separation from the divine presence. When pride is present, consciousness must be divided to some degree; both self and God are objects within it. Thus, perfect *devequt* cannot tolerate even the least degree of pride.[102]

Finally, it would seem that the most general barrier to *devequt* is lack of attention. It is by no means expected that perfect *devequt* will be realized at every moment. Yet, some degree of *devequt* is always expected.

> . . . [not only while learning Torah and during prayer but] even all day one should fulfill "I place YHVH [before me at all times]"[103] and [thus] he will have [at least] a bit of *devequt.* It may be compared to a lamp or coals: as long as a spark still remains in them, they can burn. But, when not even a single spark remains, a new fire must be brought. Thus the verse says, *"a constant fire."*[104] I.e., he should have some degree of *devequt* which is compared to a fire, the blazing fire, flame of YaH *"on the altar,"* for one who makes an inner sacrifice of his [evil] urge, *"that will not go out."*[105]

The ideal of constant *devequt* demands watchfulness under all circumstances.

Some attention always must be focused on one's inner state. Selfish motivations and negative character traits must be constantly identified. An inner connection with the divine must be continuously maintained. As long as this attentiveness continues, some degree of *devequt* is obtained.

Contexts of Devequt

Early Hasidism embraced the view, already advocated by the popularizers of Safedian Kabbalah, that contexts for communion with the divine should be widely extended beyond the normal parameters of sacred experience. Already in the sixteenth century the goal of constant *devequt* was pursued by mystics like Eleazar Azikri, author of *Sefer Haredim*.[106] However, unlike Azikri, early Hasidism was interested in promoting greater contact between learned mystics and the ordinary Jews. Thus, early Hasidic sources sought to persuade reclusive scholars that holiness or *devequt* can be maintained even when one was not engaged in learning Torah, performing *mizvot*, or prayer.

> A person should serve God with all his power. For everything is needed by God, since God desires to be served in every way. For example, sometimes a person goes and speaks with people and then he is not able to learn. So he needs to be connected to God in his mind and to perform *yihudim* (unifications).[107] Similarly, when a person travels and is not able to pray and study as usual, he needs to serve Him in other ways. One should not be troubled by this, for God desires to be served in all [kinds of] ways. Sometimes in this manner and sometimes in another. Accordingly, He arranges it that one has to travel or to talk to people in order that one may serve Him in another way.[108]

Thus, even when one was far from the *Bet Midrash* and involved in ordinary conversations, one can be serving God. The condition was that "unifications" be performed. The term referred to a contemplative technique, usually but not necessarily involving combinations of letters or Divine Names,[109] that maintained *devequt*.

The widening of the parameters within which divine service can occur particularly applies to those areas where necessary physical activities are involved. Although such acts as eating and drinking might seem to be too corporeal in nature to be a part of divine worship, the need to maintain *devequt* even when attending to physical needs is already explicitly demanded in *Sheney Luhot ha-Berit*.[110] This general demand for unceasing *devequt* is echoed in Hasidism.

> In all that a person sees he should remember the Holy One Blessed be He. If it is [a matter of] love, he should recall the love of God. If it is [a matter of] awe, he should recall the awe of God, as is well documented. And even when one goes to the toilet, he should think, am I not separating evil from good? And this is a unification and the good will remain for the Blessed One's service.[111]

However, Hasidic interest in eating[112] and drinking and the like is not only based on the general tendency to include everything in the demand to maintain constant *devequt*. Food and the other physical objects with which a person is confronted are important because they bear a particular relationship to his soul.

> The Torah shows concern for a Jew's property. Why is this so? For it is a great principle that with regard to everything that a person wears or eats or makes use of, he benefits from the divine energy (*hiyyut*) that is in that particular thing. Were it not for that spiritual element (*ruhaniyut*), the thing could not exist at all. There are holy sparks there that belong to the root of his soul. I heard that this is the reason why people have different preferences.[113]

Because of the hidden intimate spiritual connection between a person's soul and the material objects that he makes use of, activity involving those things itself constitutes a spiritual act.

> Whenever one makes use of that object, or eats food even because of physical need, he rectifies the sparks.[114] For afterwards he worships with the energy that comes to his body from that garment or food or other things. So through that energy with which he worships the Blessed Name, [the sparks] are restored. Thus it sometimes happens that something is lost. For when one has already completed the restitution of all the sparks in that object which pertained to his soul, then His Blessed Name takes the object from him and gives it to another. For the sparks that remain in the object belong to the other's soul.[115]

Although our passage uses the language of Lurianic Kabbalah, it is clear from the context that its author's interest was not primarily in the technical details of raising sparks. More important is the implication of divine immanence and the attitude of reverence for creation that presence in a world enlivened by holy sparks demands.

> The Ba'al Shem Tov, of blessed memory, said what one eats is a being(*beney adam*), what one sits on[116] is a being, and the object one makes use of is a being. In other words, [there are] sparks in those things. Accordingly, a person should have compassion for his possessions and for everything that is his, because of the sparks that are there—in order to have compassion for the holy sparks.[117]

But in order to experience such a relationship with one's personal objects, one must practice *devequt*.

> As a result of the energy of the Torah that he learned that day, if later something occurs to him and he does not know whether to act or not, he can understand what to do from the energy of the very matter that he learned. As long as he is constantly cleaving to His Blessed Name, then His Blessed Name will make sure that he can always know [what to do] as a result of the energy of [learning] Torah. But if a person is only occasionally with His Blessed Name, then He will also only occasionally be with him. Nor will He bring it about that his garments and food will contain the sparks that his soul is meant to restore.[118]

Another context for practicing *devequt* that is indicated in early Hasidic sources is solitary contemplation (*hitbodedut*).[119] The practice involves a form of meditation in which the journey through the four worlds of the Kabbalists that is ordinarily made during the morning prayers is replicated as an independent act of contemplation.

> In the beginning of prayer, one should feel in his mind that he is in the World of Making, later he should feel that he is in [the World of] Formation, the world of the angels and *ofanim*. Next [he should sense that he is] in [the World of] Creation, until he senses inwardly that he has flown very high in his thoughts to the World of Emanation. Just as a person moves from room to room, so he should move in his mind through the upper worlds. And he should take care not to fall from his very high state of consciousness (*mahashavto ha-gavoha*[!] *meod*) in the upper worlds. Rather he should make a great effort to maintain his high state [holding his concentration like] a rein and bridle as if establishing a boundary to keep from falling. And when he wishes to do this for the sake of *devequt* at times other than during prayer, it is necessary that no other person be [moving about] in that house, for even the chirping of birds could distract him, as could another's thoughts.[120]

Although this text suggests that ideal conditions of isolation are necessary for successfully practicing *hitbodedut*, another source indicates that solitary meditation of this type can be dangerous and should only be undertaken in pairs. Moreover, despite the fact that the desired state can easily be interrupted by external distractions, it seems there are occasions when it can be maintained even in company.

> When one desires to practice meditation (*lihyot be-hitbodedut*), another friend should be with him, but a solitary person is in danger. Rather there should be two in one room, and each should independently meditate on the Blessed Creator (*yitboded be-azmo im ha-Bore'*). Sometimes when one is [really] cleaving he can practice *hitbodedut* even in a house where there are other people.[121]

The extent to which a person requires isolation from others in order to practice *hitbodedut* depends on how strong his adhesion to God is. The danger of solitary *hitbodedut* seems to be that the soul in an intense state of *devequt* may expire in its longing to be reunited with its divine source. Hasidic legend attributes such a death to R. Yehiel Mikhel of Zlotchov.[122]

We have seen how *devequt* involves anomian practices and extends spiritual activity into areas of life that are not central to the fulfillment of religious law. However, the ideal of *devequt* also colors the Hasidic attitude toward the three foundations of religious life: learning Torah, prayer, and *mizvot*. These are considered particularly favorable opportunities for realizing *devequt*.

> Mishnah: "Whoever performs one commandment receives benefits."[123] ... [A] person should contemplate during study of Torah and prayer that the letters of the Torah and prayer are vessels like the body. One must draw into them *ruhaniyut* and within it the light of *Eyn-Sof* which is the true unity, like the soul in the body. And clearly when it comes to the performance of a divine commandment which is a physical act and a vessel, one needs to draw into it the *ruhaniyut* and unity of the *Eyn-Sof* ...[124]

When a *mizvah* is properly performed it is a means of connecting a person to God. However, the Hasidic attitude regarding proper performance of a *mizvah* is primarily concerned with the inner purity of the one fulfilling the commandment.

> Even if one fulfills a commandment for selfish reasons (*she-lo le-shem sha-mayim*), i.e. when one does it with some ulterior motivation, he causes a separation, God forbid. For the Torah and the Holy One, Blessed be He, are one. So when one does a *mizvah* properly, this *mizvah* and the Holy One, Blessed be He, become one. For everything is one [united] holiness from one spiritual force (*ruhaniyut*).[125] But, if one does it improperly (*she-lo ke-tiqqunah*), then he creates a *qelipah* (shell) around this *mizvah* so that it cannot be united with the holiness of the Holy One, Blessed be He. Thus a separation is formed between the holiness of this *mizvah* and the holiness of the Holy One, Blessed be He. This is called a *qelipah* for it forms a shell around this *mizvah* that prevents it from uniting with His Blessed Holiness. The enlightened will understand.[126]

The proper performance of a *mizvah* is, then, a mystical experience. Hence, the reference to the enlightened. This experience can occur because the external form of the *mizvah* is understood as a vessel that contains an inner spiritual force, *ruhaniyut*. This *ruhaniyut* can be activated and caused to return to its divine source through the intention (*kavvanah*) of the person fulfilling the *mizvah*. When the *mizvah* is performed in a state of *devequt*, there is a union of the person with the *ruhaniyut* of the *mizvah* which unites with the *ruhaniyut* of God. However, when an ulterior motive is present in the mind of the person performing the commandment, his consciousness is divided. The selfish motivation separates the person from the *ruhaniyut* of the *mizvah*. Thus, no union occurs.[127]

This mystical understanding of the commandments places great emphasis on the quality of the experience of performing each and every one. This means that the importance of fulfilling a *mizvah* lies primarily in the present, as an immediate opportunity for attaining *devequt*. This view is opposed to the one that emphasizes hoarding up the merit of as many commandments as possible for future reward in the world to come.[128]

The traditional emphasis on Torah study came into conflict with some Hasidic understandings of *devequt*. Already in the teachings of the Kabbalists of Safed the ultimate purpose of learning Torah was pneumatic and not primarily the acquisition of knowledge.[129] This attitude was discussed in detail in *Sheney Luhot ha-Berit*. One passage attributed to R. Isaac Luria the view that a specific period of time should be set aside for uniting one's mind with God, that is, *devequt*. Moreover, this practice was declared seven times more valuable than time spent on Torah study.[130] The passage seems to imply that Torah study and practices involving *devequt* are incompatible.[131]

Indeed when Torah study is understood as a fundamentally intellectual activity in which one's consciousness must be given over to the details of the subject studied, it would seem to directly conflict with the contemplative goals of *devequt*. The latter is presumed to involve dimensions of consciousness that are other than and beyond the discursive intellect.

However, *Sheney Luhot ha-Berit* also makes reference to a number of teachings of R. Moses Cordovero that involve a theory of *devequt* which can occur even during Torah study. Nevertheless, the Cordoverian approach assumes an understanding of Torah study that is not primarily discursive. At the basis of this view is a theory of sacred language which posits that the language in which the Torah is written is unique. Unlike other languages, the letters of the Hebrew Bible are not merely conventional signs that form words. They are vessels that contain a spiritual essence that originates in the divine source.[132] Thus, reading them with this spiritual essence (*ruhaniyut*) in mind leads to *devequt*. Contact with the divine is the true purpose of learning Torah. Hence, even when the sacred words are read without comprehension a degree of illumination is attained.[133] This view directly influenced the Ba'al Shem Tov's approach to learning, which involved a pneumatic interpretation of the rabbinic injunction to learn *li-shemah* (for its own sake).

Whoever learns *li-shemah* has love as his intention: to cause himself to cleave to the essence of the letters of the Torah through which he becomes a chariot for the Holy One, Blessed be He, who is the essence of life and the ultimate delight. For within the letters is the light of *Eyn-Sof.* And in the light of the King's countenance is life. So the Besht understood from the matter of *li-shemah*, for the sake of the letter itself, i.e. for the light of *Eyn-Sof* and the divine energy that is concealed within it.[134]

Nevertheless the question still remains whether such spiritualization of studying Torah can replace its intellectual aspects. With the increasing influence of Cordoverian Kabbalah during the eighteenth century in eastern Europe, the question has received considerable attention in the homiletical literature. The learned Kabbalists, who composed much of this material, have sought a formula that would include both the intellectual and pneumatic aspects of Torah. A typical solution has seen the discursive aspects as a kind of preparation for the ultimate spiritual satisfaction of *devequt* which is the result of learning *li-shemah*.[135] This approach is similar to that of R. Jacob Joseph who presents it via an erotic analogy. Learning is compared to lovemaking. The intellectual efforts can be likened to enticements, while *devequt* constitutes the act of intercourse itself.

As our sages said: "The Holy One, Blessed be He, has no other interest in the world than the four ells of the *haLaKhaH* (religious law) . . ."[136] The second explanation [alludes to] the word *KaLaH* (bride) . . . It concerns the sages permission to learn with ulterior motivation (*she-lo li-shemah*) . . . Not, God forbid, that one should remain at this level, but rather that one should ascend from level to level until he reaches learning for its own sake . . . The second interpretation notes that *halakhah* and *hakalah* have the same letters, for "*from my flesh I see God.*"[137] For the bride has all kinds of adornments in order to arouse the desire for intercourse. And at the time of intercourse, she removes her clothing. . . . Similar are the enticements of Torah, these are *pilpul* or when one learns in order to receive some benefit, even to acquire a place in the world to come. These are not the main thing. All of these constitute the adornments of the supernal bride[138] so that she may arouse the holy supernal coupling. . . . So when a person causes himself to cleave to the form[139] of the letters of the Torah, which is the *kalah*, and his essence is joined to the innermost essence of the letters of the Torah, this is the true intercourse, completely naked, without any garment or motivation or benefit or reward. Only for Her sake, for love of Her, that he might cleave to Her, that is the ultimate point of everything . . .[140]

Thus, R. Jacob Joseph does not reject virtuosic intellectual modes of study or the initial presence of personal motivations like the desire to enhance one's reputation or to gain a reward for one's learning. He sees them as necessary antecedents that enhance the real goal, *devequt*. Through these motivating factors one is stimulated to continue on in one's learning until it becomes an act of unconditional love, motiveless communion with the divine.

While the previous example probably expresses the view of the highly learned R. Jacob Joseph, teachings which seem to be authentic to the Ba'al Shem Tov also indicate that his method of learning in *devequt* did not exclude comprehension of the text.

> . . . and in order to clarify [how to cause something to ascend and to connect it . . . so all may be one], I will mention some of what I heard from my teacher [i.e. the Ba'al Shem Tov]. When one learns a deep matter and does not understand it, this is *Malkhut*.141 And when one has put his mind into it (*u-khe-she-natan da'at*) in order to understand and has descended to its depth, then he has bound and joined *Malkhut* with *Binah*.142

Thus, it would seem that the Ba'al Shem Tov's approach to Torah study combined learning and *devequt*. This was possible for two reasons. First, the type of learning usually specified in his authentic teachings did not involve intellectual exercises more complex than comprehension of the text's meaning.143 Second, the concept of *devequt* that pertained to Torah study, as Rivka Schatz-Uffenheimer noted,144 was more enthusiastic than strictly contemplative. What was essential was the awareness of divine immanence while learning.

> In this way one may explain [the passage in the Passover Haggadah] "and it is this (*hi'*) that has stood for our ancestors and for us, that not one alone stood over us to destroy us and the Holy One, Blessed be He, saved us from their hand." In other words, as we explained, one has to learn Torah *li-shemah*, i.e. for the sake of [the letter] *heh*. [But], *heh* can be spelled three ways, [with a *heh*, *yod*, or *alef* and these letters collectively spell] *hi'* (this). Thus it says "and it is this," i.e. Torah study *li-shemah*, for the sake of the *heh* and its three spellings, that stood for our ancestors and for us. "That not one alone" [means] because the One who is the principle of the world is not present in the Torah that one learns, [therefore] they stand against us to destroy us. [But] "and the Holy One, Blessed be He," i.e. when the Holy One, Blessed be He, is there [in our consciousness while we are learning] "saves us from their hands." [This is] in accord with what I heard from my grandfather . . . [the Ba'al Shem Tov] on "one who repeats his learning a hundred times is not like one who repeats his learning a hundred times and one."145 In other words, the One who is the principle of the world is present in his learning.146

However, in the teachings of R. Dov Ber the concept of *devequt* becomes more deeply contemplative. This leads to a potential undermining of the value of Torah study. On the one hand, the Maggid of Mezeritch affirms the theory of *devequt* with God by means of the Torah that was articulated in the homiletical writings of sixteenth-century Safed.

> One has to make a greater effort towards *devequt* while speaking than during Torah study.[147] For when one speaks, it is necessary to have in mind only *devequt* with the Blessed Creator. But when one is learning one should fill his mind with the subject being learned (*zarikh lahshov maheshevet ha-limud*) through this one achieves proper *devequt*. One should always be occupied with Torah for it is "*a tree of life for those who hold fast to it.*"[148] But when one is only involved in conversation and relies on [a meditative practice to maintain] *devequt*, he has to be very careful never to fall from *devequt*.[149]

The Torah itself brings about *devequt* with the divine source of life when the mind of a person studying it is totally absorbed in the lesson. On the other hand, there is a clear preference in R. Dov Ber's thought for contemplative states over the discursive exercising of the intellect even when it focuses on Torah.

> "Whoever multiplies words brings sin."[150] The meaning is lack. For even when one's speaking with others involves the wisdom of Torah, nevertheless silence is much better. For in silence one can contemplate His Blessed greatness and connect himself to His Blessedness more than when he joins himself through speech.[151]

Thus, while R. Dov Ber's mystical conception of the Torah seems to allow for Torah study with *devequt*, his emphasizing of contemplation over intellectual learning recalls the teaching of R. Isaac Luria concerning *devequt*.[152]

> At any rate one should not be constantly learning without any pause. This was fine for the first generations. For their minds were very strong and they corrected their moral qualities and awe of the Lord. They were constantly cleaving to Him[153] without any pause and did not have to exert themselves at all over this. For awe was constantly on their faces and they learned [in a state] of supernal holiness and love. They were concerned with esoteric matters (*hayu mit'askim be-shiur qomat ha-Bore'*) even in their study of the exoteric. For the Torah and the Holy One, Blessed be He, are one. Thus they became a chariot for the *Shekhinah*. So they were able to engage in a lot of Torah study. But as for us whose minds are weak and whose moral qualities are abhorrent, if we will constantly study Torah without pause, we will forget awe of the Lord and correction of the moral qualities and the uniting of our deeds to his Blessed name ... And the ARI of blessed memory (R. Isaac Luria) wrote that one who is sharp and expert should learn [only] one or two hours ... Therefore, one should rest a

bit from learning in order to contemplate the greatness of the Blessed Creator in order to love Him and be in awe of Him and to be ashamed in His presence and to long for His commandments. One should not think many thoughts, but only one.[154]

Here R. Dov Ber does not argue that Torah study and *devequt* are mutually exclusive. The pious men of old were able to learn in a state of *devequt*. But the present generation is intellectually, morally, and spiritually on a lower level and will not be able to overcome the various selfish motivations that pertain to Torah study. Thus, if they are to cultivate the higher goals of religion, they must set aside specific times from their learning for contemplative practices.

Nevertheless the Maggid of Mezeritch had no intention of encouraging neglect of Torah study. On the contrary, he was concerned that the contemplatives among his disciples might be inclined to overemphasize meditation. Thus, he presented a justification of Torah study which must occur along with separate periods for contemplative practice.[155]

When one learns he should rest a bit during each hour in order to attach himself to the Blessed Creator. As for learning, despite the fact that it is not possible to cleave to His Blessedness, for not every mind can manage to study in love and awe, [but] only the [spiritual] elite like R. Shimon ben Yohai and his comrades, nevertheless one must always study. For the Torah purifies the soul and is a tree of life for those that hold fast to it. If one will not study, he will not have the intelligence to cleave to his Blessedness. As the sages said, "an uncouth person does not fear sin and an ignoramus is no *hasid*." [156]

Two things are clear from these texts. First, R. Dov Ber is very interested in promoting Torah study. Indeed he struggles to find arguments to justify it.[157] However, it is also clear that his conception of *devequt* is more contemplative than the enthusiastic version we saw above in the teachings of the Ba'al Shem Tov. For the Maggid of Mezeritch, *devequt* can only be practiced during Torah study by a very restricted spiritual elite. It is R. Dov Ber who advises separate periods for *devequt* and for study, while the Ba'al Shem Tov emphasizes *devequt* during Torah study.

In regard to prayer, virtually all early Hasidic sources agree that *devequt* is essential.[158] However, the techniques that are advocated for attaining *devequt*, the spiritual goals attained thereby, and the nature of the experiences described are varied.

In general, Hasidism inherited a Kabbalistic outlook regarding prayer that was greatly influenced by prayer books that followed a Lurianic approach. In effect, this meant that, despite the literal meaning of the liturgy, prayer was not primarily conceived as an act in which God was petitioned to fulfill an individual's needs. Fundamentally, prayer functioned theurgically. Through prayer, one elevated divine sparks that had been trapped in materiality and, through uniting various components of the divine realm, caused shefa' (spiritual beneficence) to descend into the world from the divine source.[159]

However, although Hasidism adopted the basic framework of Lurianic prayer, some early Hasidic texts are ambivalent towards Lurianic kavvanot.[160] In such cases, little interest is evinced in the myriad specific details that characterize the transformations that occur in the supernal worlds during Lurianic prayer. Instead, apparently under the influence of ecstatic values transmitted by Cordoverian Kabbalah, emphasis is placed on the subjective experience of the person praying.

The Hasidic conception of devequt during prayer is directly connected to the belief in divine immanence. Fundamentally, the person praying is asked to relinquish all self-interest in order to cleave to the omnipresent reality or the divine presence. Since the liturgy itself contains petitions for fulfilling individual needs, some Hasidic texts take the position that such needs really apply to the divine presence which is suffering in exile with Israel. A person who prays for his own needs separates himself from the divine presence.

> I heard from my teacher[161] that the Shekhinah is called prayer, as the Kabbalistic texts interpret the verse, "and I am prayer."[162] It is also explained there that when one prays, the focus should be on the Shekhinah, to unite her with her spouse, and not to have one's own benefit in mind. For, God forbid, concerning the latter it is written, "God placed me in the hands of [my enemies], I cannot rise."[163] My teacher, may his memory be a blessing for life in the world to come, further explained this. If a person has his own material interests in mind, intending that his prayer be answered for his material benefit, then a separation [between himself and the Shekhinah] is created there, through his introducing the material into the spiritual. Then he will not be answered at all.[164]

However, it should be noted that early Hasidism was not entirely indifferent to the needs of the individual and the community. However, here it is emphasized that the mind of one praying in devequt must be focused on the deity's needs. The implication in our text is that only then can prayer be effective. Nevertheless, other Hasidic texts are less extreme in denying the efficacy of petitionary prayer.[165]

The injunction to pray for the needs of the Shekhinah is not merely a strategy for realizing *devequt* during prayer. It is also directly related to the central Kabbalistic concern for freeing the *Shekhinah* from the external evil forces that afflict her. However, the Hasidic approach to this problem emphasizes the importance of the quality of a person's consciousness while praying, rather than esoteric knowledge of the meditative formulae advocated by Lurianic Kabbalah. The subjective experience of the one praying is a determining factor in the process of liberating the *Shekhinah* and restoring her to her divine spouse.

> It is known that in *Sefer Ez Hayyim*, an association is made between circumcision and the *hashmal*. It seems to me that the matter can be applied more generally to all aspects of Torah, prayer, and fulfilling the commandments. This is the esoteric meaning of *hashmal* that I received from my teacher, the Ba'al Shem Tov. It refers to the mystery of subduing and separating [the evil forces] and sweetening [judgments] that is necessary in all aspects of learning Torah and prayer. He said [*hashmal* should be understood as two words:] *hash mal*. For one needs to be silent (*laHSHot*) until he has cut off (*mal*) the external shell. Then he should speak [words of prayer] in order to sweeten judgments in their root, which is the secret of prayer that my master explained in the name of his teacher.[166] Consequently, [those who pray in this manner] are called "pruners of the field."[167] So one should remove intrusive thoughts from his mind [during prayer] and thus separate the external shells from the *Shekhinah*. Consequently, the word *mal* bears two meanings, speech[168] and cutting off.[169] One follows from the other. Thus *hash mal* implies that one should first cut off the external shells and then speak the words of Torah and prayer. This is separation and sweetening.[170]

From the above examples, it is clear that early Hasidism remained interested in several goals that had long characterized the Jewish approach to prayer. Despite the emphasis on *devequt*, some of the basic interests of Hasidic prayer remained petitionary. In addition to the mystical and ecstatic motives, theurgic and magical interests were also of great importance.[171] Needs were to be fulfilled, although they were conceived as needs of the deity. The *Shekhinah* required liberation from the clutches of the external forces, but this was accomplished through purifying the mind during prayer. Prayer had as one of its principal goals, "sweetening of [divine] judgment" and the stimulation of sources of beneficence. Nevertheless, the Hasidic emphasis on *devequt* also brought into the foreground another goal—prayer for its own sake.

Prayer is, from this viewpoint, understood as the opportunity par excellence for encountering God. This encounter constitutes perhaps, the highest expression of *devequt* and thus the apex of religious life.

From the Ba'al Shem Tov concerning the verse, *"Prayer of a poor person when he is weary and pours forth his conversation before God."*[172] [It may be explained through] an analogy. On the day of his rejoicing, a king proclaimed that whoever wanted something from the king would have his request fulfilled. There were those who requested power and honor and others that sought riches. Each one received according to his request. But there was one wise person there who said that his request was that the king would personally speak with him three times a day. It pleased the king very much that someone preferred speaking with him more than riches and honor. Thus his request was granted that he be permitted to enter the king's chamber and to speak with him. Moreover, there the treasuries were opened for him so that he might also acquire wealth and honor. So this is the meaning of the verse: the *"prayer of a poor person . . . [is that] before God he will pour forth his conversation."* For that is his desire.[173]

The text indicates that God clearly prefers the prayer of one whose only interest lies in sharing intimacy with the deity. Nevertheless, the analogy implies that less spiritual interests are also served. All those who turn to the king have their requests fulfilled. Moreover, while the highest type of prayer involves no ulterior motivations, God makes sure that his favorite also receives wealth and honor. This is but one of a number of early sources attributed to the Ba'al Shem Tov that view petitionary prayer with a certain measure of approval. The need for material benefits from God is not particularly disparaged. However, in the writings of Dov Ber of Mezeritch and his disciples, the tendency to deny the validity of petitionary prayer becomes far more explicit. In some extreme cases it is even denied that a Hasid has material needs.[174]

As indicated in the previous text, the highest form of prayer is conceived as a private audience with God that takes place in the deity's chamber. However, entrance to this chamber is not immediate. It is only reached via a contemplative journey through the four worlds that constitute the spiritual cosmos.

The Kabbalists had already conceived of prayer as such a journey and had assigned sections of the morning liturgy to each of these worlds. However, according to the Lurianic approach, access to the supernal worlds depended on focusing the mind on appropriate combinations of divine names and recalling the specific Kabbalistic processes that were occurring at every stage. These extra liturgical aspects of prayer were called *"kavvanot"* (or intentions). However, in early Hasidism interest in Lurianic *kavvanot* began to be replaced by another notion of intention.[175]

Hasidic texts emphasize *kavvanah* in the earlier rabbinic sense of concentration on the object of prayer. Hasidic *kavvanah* thus indicates the intensity with which one turns his consciousness from materiality to the divine presence. It refers then, to the active component of *devequt* during prayer, the increasing effort to achieve intimacy with the divine. At the highest stage of prayer, a state of pure receptivity is reached in which the effort becomes superfluous. However, this goal of prayer can only be attained through an increasingly active effort of intentionality, which is called "female waters."[176] This effort is conceived as a simultaneous contemplative ascent through the stages of the liturgy and the four spiritual worlds.

> From the Ba'al Shem Tov, concerning daily prayer. It should be in accord with the rabbinic saying, "I arouse the morning and the morning does not arouse me."[177] The meaning is that one should gradually increase his efforts [to concentrate on the divine presence] until [the prayer,] "blessed is the one who spoke ..." [This stage of the liturgy] corresponds to the world of *assiyah* (making), which is located below near the external shells. Afterwards, he should continue with greater *kavvanah* from "blessed is the one that spoke" until "may Your Name be praised," which is in the world of *yezirah* (formation). There the external shells are not as much in evidence as in the world of *assiyah*. From "may Your Name be praised" until the standing prayer, he should increase his *kavvanah*, until during the standing prayer the true embrace and coupling [of the divine male and female] occurs. Here] he should divest himself of corporeality, as indicated in the *Shulhan Arukh, Orakh Hayyim*, sect. 98. Thus, female waters are generated first and then male waters follow, [as in the verse], *"and she gives birth to a male."*[178]

"Female waters," which in Lurianic contexts generally refers to the soul's ascent to the divine, here indicates the initial efforts at *devequt* that are made as the stages of prayer proceed. The term "male waters" indicates the divine response, the ultimate stage in which the efforts of the pray-er can be relaxed.[179]

The contemplative ascent requires great concentration in order to prevent the mind from wandering. Unless the mind can be firmly fixed on the act of prayer, it is difficult to enter the meditative state that is called for. Hasidic sources fully acknowledge the difficulty of the task. Thus, a variety of strategies are offered for dealing with the problem of concentration. A typical approach, attributed to the Ba'al Shem Tov, involves focusing the mind on the letters of the prayer being said.[180]

In addition, early Hasidism has employed two Lurianic terms, *qatnut* and *gadlut*, in order to distinguish between degrees of contemplative concentration. They can be compared to states of lesser and expanded consciousness. In the expanded state, *gadlut*, one is conscious of being present in the upper worlds. However, it is not always possible to enter this state.

Thus, one needs to know how to practice *devequt* even in the lesser state, *qatnut*. In Lurianic Kabbalah the terms refer to stages in the formation of a *parzuf*. Each *parzuf*, when complete, contains all ten *sefirot*. However, in order to become complete, a *parzuf* must undergo a process analogous to the development of a fetus. In the initial stage of *qatnut*, the *parzuf* lacks the higher *sefirot* that are called "*mohin*" (brains), and must depend on a higher *parzuf* for these "intellectual" qualities. In *gadlut*, the *parzuf* receives its own independent *mohin*. Thus, Hasidism has appropriated the term *gadlut* to indicate the state in which a person praying receives *mohin* in the sense of expanded consciousness or apprehension of the divine realm.

> A wise person is capable of discerning whether the time is propitious for focus-ing his mind on the inner mystery and delighting in it as explained.[181] But, if he sees that he is in the lower state (*sod ha-qatnut*) and is not able to focus his mind because he is overwhelmed by extraneous thoughts, he should pray from the prayer book like a little child. My master testified that he himself had been for some time in "another land" in this sense.[182] The [higher state] eluded him. So he employed the technique of cleaving to the letters. Moreover, he said that when he prayed from the prayer book and employed the technique of cleaving to the letters, he elevated the aspect of *assiyah*.[183] Thus he advised individuals to use this technique until they returned to their higher level.[184]

Intense concentration on the letters diverted the mind from the literal meaning of the text. The technique seemed to open the mind of the person praying to a dimension of consciousness that was more pneumatic in nature and not dominated by the concerns of discursive thought. A person's con-sciousness in this state was, as a result, less accessible to intrusive thoughts since it was turned away from all discursive interests. Once the person's consciousness had been firmly fixed in this state, it was easier to introduce the contemplative objects of awareness, probably Lurianic *kavvanot*, that formed the content of the higher state. The technique of atomization of the letters thus constituted a kind of bridge between ordinary consciousness and the expanded state of *gadlut*.

The choice of letters as an appropriate object of meditation was also rooted in earlier Kabbalistic conceptions that viewed the Hebrew letters as vessels that contained divine potency. As least as early as the thirteenth cen-tury, meditative Kabbalistic systems regarded the letters as a primary means for attaining contact with divine immanence.[185] Since the divine potency was often represented as light, meditation on the letters led to a particularly vivid, visual meditative experience.

He should concentrate his entire mind in the potency of the words that he utters until he sees the lights of the words, sparkling one from another. From them a number of [additional] lights are produced. This is the meaning of the verse, *"light is extended to the righteous and joy to the upright of heart."*[186] The letters of the Torah are chambers of God, for he extends the emanation of his light into them, as written in the *Zohar,* "the Holy One, blessed be He, and the Torah are one."[187] Thus a person should direct all his spiritual energy and soul(*kol ha-kavvanah she-hi' ha-neshamah*) into [the words of his prayer], for it is the soul that is concentrated (*ki ha-kavvanah hu' ha-neshamah*). This is *devequt:* the Holy One, blessed be He, the Torah, and Israel form a unity.[188] This is detachment from corporeality: his soul divests itself from his body and clothes itself in the thoughts that he utters, and he will see many supernal worlds.[189]

Thus, the early Hasidic understanding of *devequt* during prayer involved intense concentration of one's consciousness on the words of the liturgy to such an extent that all extraneous thoughts were effectively prevented. This entailed a certain lack of involvement in the meaning of the liturgy. Attention was concentrated on the divine emanation that was believed to be present within the letters and words.

The texts that we have been considering emphasized the visual aspects of the prayer experience. However, other texts indicated that the aural dimension of the prayer experience also played an essential part in producing the desired contemplative state.[190] Thus, it would seem that atomization of the words of prayer involved both visual and aural components which together created a kind of pneumatic field. Concentration on this pneumatic field enabled the person praying to apprehend the divine emanations contained in the words of prayer.

Thus far, we discussed some of the strategies recommended in early Hasidic texts for transforming prayer into a contemplative experience of *devequt.*[191] However, it was also recognized that even in deep contemplative states, undesired thoughts could occasionally enter into the consciousness of the pray-er. This problem became one of the major focuses of early Hasidic texts dealing with prayer. In response to this problem, strategies and theological positions were developed that are among the most original aspects of early Hasidic thought.

In general, Hasidism inherited the view that extraneous thoughts are a hindrance to prayer. (The object of prayer is to turn away from the material concerns of ordinary consciousness and to ascend into the spiritual realm. To the extent that the mind is preoccupied by materialistic concerns it is prevented from returning to its spiritual source). Thus, the conventional position regarding extraneous thoughts was that they should be rejected. One should forcefully turn the mind to the spiritual objects of contemplation. This strategy made perfect sense as long as the underlying theological position was dualistic. As long as a rigid distinction was made between sacred and profane, between God and the world, extraneous thoughts played no role in worship. They were essentially a distraction caused by the "evil urge" that a spiritual person was enjoined to reject. Although, the problem of "extraneous thoughts" was not as important an issue for Lurianic kabbalists, before Hasidism, both the Sabbatian kabbalist, Nathan of Gaza, and Elijah ha-Kohen of Smyrna already called for abrogation of Lurianic kavvanot because extraneous thoughts made it impossible to employ them.[192]

Early Hasidism did not entirely reject the established position regarding extraneous thoughts. Texts do exist that counsel rejecting such thoughts under certain circumstances and particularly during its initial stages, when contemplation or devequt is still weak. However, two factors seem to have conspired to cause early Hasidic masters to change their attitude concerning the problem and to develop an alternative approach that was unique to Hasidism. First, while Hasidism nominally associated itself with the dualistic Kabbalah of Isaac Luria, its theology was, also significantly influenced by the more pantheistic Kabbalah of Moses Cordovero.[193] Faith in divine immanence was essential to the early Hasidic concept of devequt. This faith directly influenced the Ba'al Shem Tov's teachings concerning extraneous thoughts.

> Thus he explained the meaning of assuming the yoke of the Kingdom of Heaven. A person is obligated to believe that "the entire creation is full of the divine Glory,"[194] "there is no place where He is not found."[195] Thus all of a person's thoughts contain [an emanation] of the divine reality. For each thought is a complete structure.[196] Consequently, whenever during prayer a negative or extraneous thought arises, it comes to the person in order to be transformed and elevated. If a person does not believe this, he does not completely accept the yoke of the Kingdom of Heaven. For he limits, God forbid, the divine reality.[197]

Faith in divine immanence was applied directly by the Ba'al Shem Tov to the phenomenon of disturbing thoughts. Complete acceptance of the yoke of divine sovereignty involved the belief that God was to be found everywhere, even in seemingly undesirable thoughts. Thus, such thoughts should not be rejected, but rather elevated to the realm of the divine. By viewing them as vessels which also contain a divine emanation, extraneous thoughts could be included in the contemplative experience of prayer. On the other hand, their rejection implied a diminution of the divine power which in theory must be unlimited.

In addition to the theological framework that contributed to the early Hasidic position regarding extraneous thoughts, a more practical consideration may also have been a factor in developing the technique of elevating such thoughts. As we indicated, the Lurianic approach provided the kabbalist with *kavvanot*, detailed instructions concerning the appropriate meditative focus of each stage of the prayer service. In contrast, Hasidism increasingly emphasized *kavvanah*, or *devequt* with the divine emanation concealed within the words of prayer. Here the meditative focus was much more subjective. The specific content of the contemplative mind was not precisely prescribed, but rather defined in spiritual-emotional terms like love and awe of God and apprehension of the divine presence or by somewhat vaguely described visual experiences. In general, emphasis seems to have been placed more on the pneumatic aspects of the prayer experience than on its specific content. As a result, the content of the contemplative experience could vary considerably from one prayer to another, unlike the Lurianic experience which was rather precisely orchestrated. Since the content of the Hasidic prayer experience was, in this sense, more open, the status of extraneous thoughts was more problematical. As a result of the change in emphasis from Lurianic *kavvanot* to the Hasidic notions of *kavvanah* and *devequt*, Hasidic thinkers were compelled to deal with the issue of extraneous thoughts. As indicated, the Hasidic solution to the problem was to apply the principle of divine immanence and thereby encompass seemingly extraneous thoughts within the parameters of the contemplative prayer experience.

Nevertheless, the practice of elevating extraneous thoughts involved certain restrictions. Despite his all-encompassing affirmation of faith in divine immanence, the Ba'al Shem Tov did not infer that all thoughts were, in practice, to be treated as vessels containing divine emanation. In the continuation of the preceding text, a criterion was offered whereby a person can determine whether an extraneous thought should be elevated or rejected.

> However, sometimes extraneous thoughts arise that should be rejected. If you wish to know which thoughts to reject and which to draw in and elevate, [here is the criterion]. At the time that an extraneous thought arises, a person should observe whether a way to transform and elevate it immediately occurs to him. If so, he should draw in and elevate the thought. But if a way to rectify the thought does not occur to him, then, presumably the thought came to annul a person's prayer and to confuse his mind. If so, it is permitted to reject that thought. For, 'if one comes to slay you, rise up and slay him first."[198]

The Ba'al Shem Tov conceded that two types of extraneous thoughts existed. One type indeed contained a holy spark that was in need of release and elevation. The other was the type known to earlier periods of Jewish thought, a weapon of the "evil urge" whose only intent was to nullify a person's prayer. The criterion offered for distinguishing between the two involved noticing whether a basis for elevating the thought immediately presented itself. In other words, if the extraneous thought can be immediately related to one of the *sefirot*, it can be elevated to that divine source and thus play a role in the process of prayer. However, if no connection to the *sefirot* or divine attributes spontaneously appeared, the thought must be rejected before it can destroy a person's *devequt*.

Thus, it would appear that the criterion ultimately is based on contemplative considerations. The determining factor is whether the solution immediately arises. Theoretically, any thought can be considered a derivative of one of the *sefirot*. For example, thoughts of lust may be viewed as remote extensions of the divine quality of love that is rooted in the *sefirah, Hesed*. Thus, the content of the thought is not the issue, but rather whether the relationship of the thought to its root in the *sefirot* is immediately apparent. If so, the thought constitutes no threat to maintaining the contemplative state. The pray-er is, in effect, not disturbed by this thought, despite its content. Since the thought's divine root is recognized, the appropriate *sefirah* can immediately become the object of contemplation and the person's *devequt* may continue. In some cases, contemplative concentration may even be enhanced by the opportunity to elevate the extraneous thought. However, if the solution does not immediately arise, elevation would require diverting the mind from its contemplative state in order to discursively determine an appropriate divine root. Since maintaining the contemplative state of *devequt* is most important, the second type of thought must be rejected. It does not function as a vessel containing the divine, but rather as a potential disturbance.

The practice of elevating extraneous thoughts was a major innovation of the Ba'al Shem Tov. It served well two of his principal interests, the pantheistic tendency in his thought, which was expressed by an extreme form of faith in divine immanence, and the concomitant emphasis on *devequt*, or contemplative adhesion to emanations of the deity.[199] Nevertheless, the practice was considered dangerous and, consequently, restricted to a spiritual elite.[200] Hasidism's opponents viewed the practice as pretentious and hypocritical. Thus, it became one of the central focuses of anti-Hasidic propaganda. As Hasidism became a popular movement, the practice or elevating extraneous thoughts was deemphasized. Among the first Hasidic leaders to argue strongly against the practice was Meshullam Feibush of Zbarazh.[201]

Dov Ber of Mezeritch continued to promote the basic interests that characterized the Ba'al Shem Tov's approach to prayer. However, the Maggid emphasized implications that were only latent in his master's teachings. As we have seen, the Ba'al Shem Tov emphasized *devequt* in the sense of intense concentration on the divine emanations that were contained in the words of prayer. This involved a gradual advance through the liturgy which was conceived as a contemplative journey through the four worlds. The contemplative dimension of prayer was entered through a process of increasing detachment from corporeality. Nevertheless, little attention was given to the metaphysical condition reached in the ultimate stage. Despite his pantheistic tendencies, the Ba'al Shem Tov did not tend to draw the ultimate conclusion that man's individuality was completely effaced at the height of the prayer experience.[202] This step was, however, taken by his disciple, Dov Ber. The ultimate stage of prayer was considered an ascent to the *sefirah*, *Hokhmah* (divine wisdom), which in Dov Ber's kabbalistic system was called "*Ayin*" (Nothing).

> During prayer, one should place all his energy into saying the words (*ba-dibburim*). Thus one proceeds from letter to letter until corporeality is forgotten. One should think that the letters are combining and joining together. This is a great delight. For if there is delight in corporeality, how much more so in spiritual experience. This stage is the world of *Yezirah* (formation). Next, one reaches the letters of thought and will not hear what he is saying. Thus one reaches the world of *Beri'ah* (creation). After this, one arrives at the quality of *Ayin* (nothing), for all of his physical senses (*kohotav ha-gashmiyim*) are annulled. This is the world of *Azilut* (emanation), the quality of *Hokhmah* (divine wisdom).[203]

In Dov Ber's text, attention is given to the various stages that constitute the process of detachment from corporeality. Gradually, all physical senses are effaced until one reaches a state of pure spirituality. This state of physical annihilation, or nothingness, is identified with ascension to the divine Nothing, the metaphysical stage where no differentiation exists. Ascension to the mystical state of *ayin* has become a hallmark of Dov Ber's thought.[204]

Identification of the ultimate level of mystical experience as *Ayin* or complete annihilation of one's corporeal powers, allowed Dov Ber to draw out another implication that was only implicit in the Ba'al Shem Tov's teachings. If the mystic was called upon to attain a state of complete annihilation, or passivity, then the power that actively functioned during prayer must be recognized as the *Shekhinah*, the divine presence itself.

> This is the meaning of the verse, "*he gathered stones . . .*"[205] For it is known that the stones are the letters.[206] Thus when the *Zaddiq* prays through the

letters and binds himself to the supernal *Hokhmah*, i.e., when he has already entered the gate of *Ayin*, he realizes that were it not for the divine power within him, he would be absolutely nothing. Therefore, everything [active at this level] is the divine power. The prayer being spoken (*ve-ha-dibbur*) is the divine world of speech with which the world was created.[207] The world of speech is drawn from *Hokhmah* which is [the stage of] delight and the pleasure that God derives from creation. So here as well [when he has reached *Hokhmah*] he utters the prayer only for God's pleasure.[208] Thus he returns the letters to their root, i.e., to *Hokhmah*, from which they were drawn.[209]

According to Dov Ber's approach, the *Zaddiq* attaches himself to the creative power which has descended into the letters of prayer. As the *Zaddiq* ascends in *devequt* to the level of *Hokhmah*, the divine emanations are returned to their source. Experientially at this stage, the *Zaddiq* enters an ecstatic state in which all aspects of his own powers are eradicated. It is as if the divinity itself is uttering his prayer. The *Shekhinah*, or the "world of speech," pronounces the words. This ultimate character of Hasidic ecstatic prayer is summed up in another example of Dov Ber's teachings.

> He should think that the world of speech is speaking through him and that otherwise it would be impossible to utter the prayers. As it is written, "*O Lord, open my lips*."[210] Similarly, it is only possible to think because of the world of thought. He is like a *shofar* which only brings out what is blown into it. If the one blowing into it were not present, it could not make a sound. Thus if, God forbid, God were not with him, he could not speak or think.[211]

Thus, in Dov Ber's thought, the ultimate implications of faith in divine immanence are realized contemplatively through *devequt* during prayer. The ecstatic ascent culminates in a virtual union with the divine presence. Every vestige of human independence is conceded. One becomes merely a passive vessel empowered by God.

In conclusion, one further point needs to be made. The Hasidic concept of *devequt* as unmediated contact with the deity was essentially an esoteric teaching. It was not assumed that all Jews could or should endeavor to attain such a state.[212] The various techniques that were recommended for realizing *devequt* were meant to be practiced by a spiritual elite that could lead ordinary people back to God.

Early Hasidic sources often compare the Jewish community to a single body composed of many limbs. The spiritual leadership, or *Zaddiqim*, are likened to the head of that body. It is they who are expected to maintain a mental state of adhesion to the divine presence. Already in the writings of Jacob Joseph of Polnoy, a distinction is made between two types of people, those whose concerns are essentially spiritual and those who are primarily involved with corporeal matters. Only the former practice the unmediated form or *devequt*. The latter are not expected to cleave directly to the divine presence, but rather to those who maintain the state of unmediated *devequt*.[213] However, in the writings of Dov Ber of Mezeritch, the social implications of the theory of *devequt* are not delineated.

With the popularization of Hasidism and the dissemination of Dov Ber's writings during the 1770s, much confusion arose concerning who should practice these teachings. Hasidism's opponents maintained a theory of *devequt* that, in certain essential ways, conflicted with the Hasidic approach.[214] They were particularly offended by abuses that arose from a vulgarization of Dov Ber's teachings. Moreover, not all early Hasidic leaders advocated the practice of elevating foreign thoughts that was presented in detail in Dov Ber's writings. As a result, issues concerning the esoteric aspects of the Hasidic theory of *devequt* became a central concern among disciples of Dov Ber of Mezeritch. Among the first to address these issues critically was Meshullam Feibush Heller of Zbarazh.

3

Cosmological Bases for Meshullam Feibush's Concept of *Devequt*

Tensions associated with Meshullam Feibush's conception of *devequt* reflect a trend that developed during the eighteenth century. Over the course of the two preceding centuries, Lurianic Kabbalah was established as the dominant kabbalistic school in eastern Europe.[1] So pervasive was the influence of this school, that its basic concepts, terminology, and religious outlook became normative elements in most contemporary approaches to Jewish theology.[2] However, in the second half of the eighteenth century, religious figures of various types began to express reservations concerning Lurianic Kabbalah.[3] Issues that troubled critics of the Lurianic approach included concern over its excessively anthropomorphic language, its lack of rationality, and the unreliability of the manuscripts in which its teachings were presented.

As the influence of Lurianic Kabbalah waned, the earlier Kabbalah of Moses Cordovero, was in a position to capitalize.[4] The Cordoverian writings were less anthropomorphic in character and composed along generally rationalistic, scholastic lines. In addition, many kabbalists felt that knowledge of the Cordoverian sources was, at least, a prerequisite for understanding the Lurianic approach. Cordoverian Kabbalah was particularly accessible. Some of Cordovero's own principal works were readily available in printed editions. Moreover, several influential works, written by his disciples, served to popularize the Cordoverian approach. Elijah De Vidas's *Reishit Hokhmah*, Isaiah Horowitz's *Sheney Luhot ha-Berit*, and Abraham Azulai's *Hesed le-Avraham*, all written in a predominantly Cordoverian vein, were among the most important disseminators of Safedian Kabbalah in eastern Europe.[5] All three works served as important kabbalistic sources for early Hasidism. All were prominently quoted by Meshullam Feibush in *Yosher Divrey Emet*. The influence of Cordoverian Kabbalah had especially important implications for Meshullam Feibush's theory of *devequt*.[6]

While it is clear that Cordoverian Kabbalah had a decisive influence on Meshullam Feibush's thought, Lurianic Kabbalah remained a major element in Meshullam Feibush's thought. Although he frequently argued that its methods were too sublime for use by men of his generation, he continued to acknowledge the value of studying Lurianic writings as a source of inspiration.[7] Moreover, Meshullam Feibush's thought relied on key concepts in Lurianic Kabbalah. However, as we shall see, while he never explicitly called into question the basis of Lurianic Kabbalah, Meshullam Feibush's use of Lurianic concepts sometimes suggested the influence of the Cordoverian outlook.

Among the major points of divergence of the two Safedian systems was the cosmological model used to account for the process of creation. According to the Lurianic account, creation required a prior withdrawal of the *Eyn Sof*, or unmanifest God, from the space which creation would subsequently occupy. This initial act of divine withdrawal was called "*zimzum*." Lurianic writings concede that a certain divine residue, or *reshimu*, remained in the vacated space. Nevertheless, the theory of *zimzum* tended to emphasize the remoteness of the transcendental God and mitigated pantheistic tendencies that were already present in the classical kabbalistic writings of thirteenth-century Spain.[8] Divine elements were only present in the lower worlds to the extent that they had fallen below as a result of a cosmic catastrophe, the *shevirah*, which had occurred during the process of creation. In contrast, the Cordoverian Kabbalah presented a predominantly emanationist model of creation.[9] The divine essence was not withdrawn in order to make room for creation.[10] Rather, it was progressively concealed in a series of vessels that became increasingly dense as the process continued through the four worlds that composed the kabbalistic cosmos. This approach gave greater emphasis to divine immanence, which was present at all levels of creation, despite its increasing concealment.

The major differences in the cosmological outlooks of the two systems had important implications for the concept of *devequt* and the nature of mystical experience. While *devequt* as contemplation of the divine does play a role in Lurianic Kabbalah, it does not constitute its principal method. Far greater emphasis is placed on theosophical and theurgic interests. The Lurianic kabbalist is primarily concerned with bringing about unions between various *parzufim* in the supernal worlds and in refining out and elevating the divine sparks that had become entrapped within the lower levels of creation. These goals are achieved through the contemplative combination of divine names (*yihudim*) and, more generally, through having in mind the intention of producing the specific theurgic effect that is accomplished by performing *mizvot*. The Lurianic Kabbalist participates in a gradual messianic process that depends essentially on *berur*, the retrieval of those particular divine sparks that can be elevated on any given day.

The Cordoverian approach had somewhat different priorities. Cordovero's system also involved theosophic and theurgic interest in affecting relationships between *sefirot*. However, for Cordovero, the highest level of kabbalistic activity involved drawing divine emanations(*ruhaniyut*) into the letters of the Hebrew alphabet and then restoring them to their divine root.[11] This could be accomplished both during prayer and Torah study. The *ruhaniyut* contained within the letters could be returned to its divine source via the breath of the person speaking the words. Consequently, a supreme kabbalistic goal could be accomplished through a contemplative practice that did not depend on possession of the type of abstruse esoteric knowledge that was required in the Lurianic practices. Cordovero explicitly wrote that the method of drawing *ruhaniyut* into the letters is effective even when a person does not know the meaning of the words he is uttering.[12] Since contact with divinity could be accomplished through fixing attention on the sounds one was uttering, Cordovero's approach greatly increased the opportunities for practicing *devequt*. Indeed, Cordovero's theory became one of the bases for early Hasidism's approach to *devequt* during prayer and Torah study. The Hasidim only added the notion of a person's entering the letters. As a result, the Cordoverian contemplative practice was transformed into a truly mystical experience in early Hasidism, since the consciousness or soul of the person himself and not merely *ruhaniyut* enters the letters.[13] In addition, the pantheistic tendency of Cordovero's cosmology also tended to increase the possibility and importance of *devequt*, or apprehension of the indwelling divine presence. Cordovero's emphasis on the unity of the *sefirot*, the Torah, and the souls of Israel further contributed to the prominance of *devequt* in his thought.[14] Cordovero's disciples particularly emphasized the moral dimensions of religious life. *Devequt* is a supreme value in the ethical sections of De Vidas's *Reishit Hokhmah* as well as in Horowitz's *Sheney Luhot ha-Berit*.[15] Thus, the tendency to emphasize *devequt* as a religious value in Hasidism was more the result of Cordoverian than Lurianic influence.

Despite the important role that Cordoverian Kabbalah plays in Meshullam Feibush's cosmology and conception of *devequt*, Lurianic Kabbalah remained a major component of his overall religious outlook. Meshullam Feibush continued to define the fundamental historical role of the Jew in terms of the Lurianic goal of refining out divine sparks and restoring them to their divine source. However, he emphasized that this process of *berur* depended primarily on detachment from corporeality (*hitpashtut ha-gashmiyut*) and *devequt*.

Refining out [the sparks that fell during] the *shevirah* cannot possibly be accomplished as long as one cleaves to and desires corporeal delights. For how can one refine out [the holy sparks] when he lusts for the residue in his heart. But *berur* is accomplished when one cleaves to God in awe and love and elevates this quality of awe to the level of *Ayin* which is *Hokhmah* (wisdom). This entails understanding with a powerful apprehension that the corporeal delight is to be despised. One would never willingly partake of such physical pleasures as eating, drinking, and sex, if he were not compelled by God [to do so]. For a spark of the divine love and delight has become corporealized [in the pleasurable act] and [the spark] has become residue and material. By means [of this apprehension of the true nature] of the delight, one separates himself from the residue. Thus desire for the residue is rejected because of wisdom.[16]

Although Meshullam Feibush utilizes the Lurianic concept of uplifting divine sparks in order to explain the religious significance of certain corporeal acts, he avoids mention of the Lurianic *praxis*. The process of elevating sparks is understood primarily in mystical-ethical terms. What is of utmost importance when performing acts that involve physical pleasure is the motivation with which the act is carried out. One should see the physical pleasure contained in the act as something to be despised and carry out the act solely for the sake of the concealed divine spark. The Lurianic metaphysical goal of refining out divine sparks is accomplished through a refinement of consciousness that involves rejection of the external physical pleasure and cleaving to the divine element which can be apprehended as the essence of the experience. We might also note that Meshullam Feibush uses the concept of reaching a state of *Ayin* in order to designate the transformation of consciousness that is required in order to perform *berur*. This concept and its association with the *sefirah*, *Hokhmah* (divine wisdom), is not at all typical of Lurianic Kabbalah, but follows the usage that is characteristic of Dov Ber of Mezeritch's teachings regarding the ultimate level of *devequt*.[17]

Meshullam Feibush's treatment of the concept of *berur*, then, retains the general framework of the Lurianic myth. However, by emphasizing how much *berur* is dependent on *devequt*, he underscores the element in this process that is most consistent with his Cordoverian interests. This approach involves an explicit rejection of the magical efficacy of Lurianic *kavvanot* which, in his view, are not sufficient to accomplish *berur*. The latter, as we have seen, can only be achieved through detachment from corporeality and, more particularly, through *devequt*, cleaving to the immanent divine element.

The matter is not as the ignorant in our generation suppose, who learn Kabbalah and think that while eating they can elevate the sparks by means of the *kavvanot* that apply to eating. How is this possible, if they have not reached the spiritual level that we mentioned, which requires raising the quality of awe to the level of wisdom? They have the *kavvanot* in their thoughts, but nevertheless [continue] to enjoy [physical pleasure].[18]

In Meshullam Feibush's thought, the Lurianic myth is most useful as an explanation for man's fallen state. In general, Lurianic techniques are not recommended because they have no immediate magical effect. Their efficacy is entirely dependent on the spiritual state of the person employing them. Since Meshullam Feibush believed few people of his own generation had achieved the requisite ethical development, the Lurianic *kavvanot* are not appropriate for general use. Moreover, it is clear from the above discussion that interests of a more mystical-ethical nature take precedence in Meshullam Feibush's scale of values. Nevertheless, the Lurianic myth of cosmic catastrophe, *shevirah*, continued to interest him as an explanation for the presence of evil in the world.

> Indeed, were it not for the *shevirah*, there would be no evil or materiality. All elements of creation would be cleaving to the blessed Creator, just like the *ofanim*, *serafim*, and holy *hayot*. [19] Even animals [would be cleaving], just as it will be, God willing, during the messianic age, may it speedily occur in our days. For the good will be retrieved, while evil and impurity will cease to exist. . . . For God's holiness will be revealed from the external shells. Even inorganic matter, plants, and animals, according to their capacity, will apprehend and cleave to the blessed Creator, how much more so we Israelites, His favored people. The *shevirah* caused distancing, coarsening, forgetting, and separation from God. But it was all in order to test us, for our ultimate benefit, when we are purified through our actions and good is retrieved from evil through cleaving to the blessed Creator.[20]

Evil is explained as the direct result of the Lurianic myth of *shevirah*. However, we should note that in the passage, evil is primarily understood as separation from God, the absence of *devequt*. Were it not for the *shevirah*, everything would be cleaving to God. Thus, evil could not exist.[21] Nevertheless, the *shevirah* and the separation from God which it caused were meant for humanity's (and creation's) ultimate benefit. In the messianic age, as a result of good deeds and *devequt*, everything will return to an apparently permanent state of cleaving to God. Again we see the great emphasis that is placed on *devequt*, not only as characterizing the ideal and ultimate states of existence, but also as the means through which the goal of the Lurianic myth is realized.[22]

It is important to note that Meshullam Feibush's presentation of the Lurianic myth describes a historical process that culminates in the messianic age, a time when every aspect of creation will experience *devequt*. The concept of *shevirah* is useful for accounting for the fact that most of the beings that inhabit the world do not yet experience *devequt*. Indeed, the difficulty of overcoming the evil urge is maximized in Meshullam Feibush's writings.[23] Since the Lurianic concept of *shevirah* tends to enhance the prominence of the evil external shells in which divine sparks are held captive, it is compatible with Meshullam Feibush's basically pessimistic moral outlook. Nevertheless, it seems significant that the Lurianic concept of *zimzum* is not discussed in this context.[24] We may recall that *zimzum*, in its Lurianic usage, emphasizes withdrawal of the divinity from the space occupied by creation. Thus it does not serve the interests of a mysticism that emphasizes *devequt*, or apprehension of divine immanence.

Although Hasidic reinterpretations of *zimzum* already existed, in this context, Meshullam Feibush chose to ignore this aspect of Lurianic Kabbalah.[25] It may be that his avoidance of the Lurianic concept here, was also due to his general preference for a more Cordoverian cosmology.

While the aspects of Lurianic Kabbalah that Meshullam Feibush retained bring the problem of evil into sharp focus, the Cordoverian trend of his thought tends to view that problem as essentially epistemological. Meshullam Feibush adopted from Cordoverian sources, a cosmological model that viewed creation as acosmic in nature.[26] Although the world appears to be made up of a multiplicity of independent elements, in reality only the divinity and its emanated power exists.

> For surely you know what is written in *Sheney Luhot ha-Berit*,[27] concerning the verse, "*you shall know this day and take it to your heart that the Lord is God . . . there is no other.*"[28] There, it is written, that the intention of the verse was not to state that there is no other God beside Him. For that is obvious. Rather, the meaning is that nothing exists in the world except God. For before creation, everything already existed within the divine potency. God emanated His powers and created spiritual and material garments for them. But the divine emanated powers sustain all of them. Otherwise, if the divine powers would return to their source as before creation, the spiritual and material garments would be entirely unable to exist. [It would be] just as before creation, [when] God alone was exalted. . . . Consequently, there is really nothing in the world other than God and His emanated powers which are a unity. Other than [the divine unity] nothing exists. Although it seems that there are other things, everything is really God and the divine emanations. See there in *Sheney Luhot ha-Berit*, tractate *Shavuot*.[29]

Meshullam Feibush's authority for his acosmic view of creation is a text written by the turn-of-the-seventeenth-century kabbalist, Isaiah Horowitz.

Although Horowitz tended to view Lurianic *kavvanot* as deeper than other systems, he generally chose to conceal the mythical aspects of Lurianic Kabbalah, and preferred to emphasize the system of Cordovero.[30] The Horowitz text interpreted a biblical verse to mean that humankind was charged to realize that, despite the appearance of multiplicity in the world, everything depended on the divine unity for its existence. Although things appeared as independent entities, they were vitalized by emanated divine forces. These forces, moreover, although projected into creation, remained connected to their divine source. Thus, the divine unity that preceded creation was maintained even after the world was created. The seemingly independent and multitudinous objects of creation were in reality, only garments that contained and concealed an underlying divine unity.

The acosmic nature of creation defines the ultimate meaning of life. Humankind's purpose is to uncover the hidden divine reality, to discover God from within the corporeal world that conceals Him. The apprehension of God from within the midst of corporeality is *devequt*, cleaving to the hidden divine reality rather than its ephemeral garments. Religious life may be compared to a game of hide and seek. However, although God is well concealed within the world, He really wishes to be discovered. God experiences great pleasure when humankind succeeds in finding Him. Indeed, as Meshullam Feibush states in the name of his teacher, Yehiel Mikhel of Zlotchov, the world was only created for the sake of the delight God experiences when a person finds him through *devequt*.

I heard this directly from the holy Rabbi, the Maggid,[31] on *Shavuot*, when he preached a great sermon concerning the verse, *"the soul of Shadday will grant them understanding,"*[32] and [the rabbinic comment], "He is called *Shadday* because He said to His world, *"Day"* (that is enough!)."[33] The world, [he explained], was going through the various stages of creation [which involved a gradual transformation] from [pure] spirituality to corporeality. This occurred so that God would be able to receive pleasure when a righteous person returned the world [to Him], by means of his pure thought. For, *"news from a distant land is good"*[34] and a person is very pleased when he discovers a treasure in the midst of refuse. Similarly, it is a pleasure for God when a person purifies himself from the midst of great corporeality and returns [to a state of divine unity], such as existed before creation. Therefore, the world wanted to extend [the process of creation] even further and to become more corporeal, so that God could experience even greater delight). But God told the world, *"Day* (that is far enough!)," because He understood that it would no longer be possible for a person to return to *devequt* if the world were more corporeal. In that case, what purpose would creation serve? "For the world was only created in order to be connected,"[35] i.e., for the sake of *devequt* with the Creator.[36]

In its most basic sense, *devequt* is attained through adhering to the way of Torah, prayer and good deeds. One cleaves to the Creator through rejecting worldly interests and desiring to serve God through the divinely mandated methods. However, in order to cause God the pleasure mentioned above, one must not only follow the established practices, but also cultivate faith in the divine omnipresence.

> The essence of *devequt* through which God will receive pleasure from us involves all that we have said concerning distancing ourselves from evil and cleaving to the good. In other words, we must fulfill *"I constantly place YHVH before me."*[37] We must train ourselves in faith to believe, whenever we can concerning God, that *"the entire world is full of His Glory"*[38] and *"there is no place where He is not found."*[39] For the physical is no barrier to the spiritual, as is readily apparent. Thus each of us, depending on his spiritual level and the time and place, will experience awe of God. As a result of this awe, we can realize a state of true humility, to be as nothing compared to God's power.[40]

Faith in divine omnipresence leads to a state of awe before the divine presence. This state has different degrees of intensity that depend on a person's spiritual development and also on exigencies of time and place. When this state of awe is sufficiently developed, one becomes truly humble. All sense of self-importance is effaced by the recognition that God's power is limitless and unconditional. When this is fully recognized, one reaches the quality of *Ayin*.

The term *Ayin* is used here in an ethical sense. Along with rejecting the evil of worldly interests and pursuing the good that is found in the religious life, one cultivates faith in God's presence. This ultimately results in the understanding that one is *"as nothing (ke-ayin)"* compared to the omnipresent divine power.[41] However, the problem of attaining true humility goes beyond the ethical sphere and becomes essentially epistemological. In order to reach the level of *Ayin*, rejecting evil and doing good is not sufficient. Merely ascribing to the belief that God's presence fills creation does not lead to *devequt*. One must come to actually experience creation as a medium which, in all its manifold aspects, reveals God. This is accomplished by constantly thinking of God in all circumstances, until one comes to recognize the divine presence in all aspects of life.

> It is not possible to understand [the divine basis of creation] so that it will be established in our heart, unless we constantly think of the blessed Creator . . .[42] Thus it depends on *devequt*, clearly perceiving [God's power] with a pure heart. [This is] not like our present condition in which everyone imagines that he understands this, but such understanding is no understanding at all. True understanding means that a person comprehends that this is certain, even if he had

not seen or heard of it from another. He will understand [the divine basis of creation] independently, through *devequt* and his soul's constantly thinking of God. For whoever does not constantly think of God, even if he believes [that only God's power exists], will not experience creation this way. For the world is constantly on his mind, unaccompanied by thoughts of God. However, one who never thinks of the world [alone], but realizes that everything he sees depends on God, [truly comprehends the divine basis of creation].[43]

In order to constantly practice *devequt*, one must have God in mind at all times. As a result, one never experiences the world without at the same time maintaining a sense of the divine presence. Thus, the world is never perceived to exist independently. It is continuously related to God through the thought of a person practicing *devequt*.

The possibility of this experience, of course, essentially depends on faith in the Cordoverian pantheistic cosmology. If one does not believe that creation entirely depends on the emanated divine power for its existence, there would be no basis for connecting each aspect of experience with the thought of God. Nevertheless, what is important here is not primarily faith, but its epistemological implications. Comprehension of the matter involves training the mind to view the world in a new way, to see it as a garment that contains the emanated divine power. God's pleasure derives from the process of transforming human consciousness to recognize only the divine presence in creation. This process very much depends on making the discovery of God the true object of one's desire. In order to illustrate this, Meshullam Feibush makes use of a bold analogy that compares worldly lust and passionate desire for the divine presence.

> There is an analogy concerning this from the case of a person who looks at a woman's beautiful garments. Whoever is attached to his desire for women, God forbid, pays no attention to the golden, embroidered garments. Immediately, his heart falls to lusting for the woman who wears them. But another person whose heart is pure of this lust, simply looks at the clothing. So while both are looking at the same thing, each sees something different. It is similar, *mutatis mutandis*, in this holy matter. Whoever constantly desires God, perceives God in all that he sees in the world. For the divine power enlivens [whatever he sees], as the verse says, "*You enliven everything.*"[44] But it is otherwise for one that does not have a desire for God in his thought. He only perceives the material [aspects of creation]. Although, if prompted and questioned, he would say that God enlivens everything, he does not truly comprehend this through *devequt*.[45]

The passionate desire to discover God within the concealing garments of material creation ultimately affects one's self-perception as well. When the world is viewed as dependent on divine power, material objects are denied independent existence. Only God and the divine emanations truly exist. When this realization is applied to the self, it also must be understood as entirely dependent on God. The self is, as we have already seen, perceived as nothing (*Ayin*). However, now it is clear that the concept of *Ayin* goes beyond the ethical implications of humility and signifies a fundamentally mystical eradication of self.

> Consequently, if we attain *devequt*, we will conceive of ourselves in the same way [that we conceive of creation in general]. We are nothing (*Ayin*), but [it is] God [who] enlivens us. He is what exists and, besides Him, there is no other.[46]

Thus, it is ultimately this mystical nullification of the independent existence of the self that causes God supreme pleasure. God is discovered not only in the external world, but ultimately within the self. This inner apprehension of the divine presence is likened to the meeting of a parent and child. When the offspring returns to the presence of its parent, it receives kisses and other signs of affection. Similarly, God is delighted when a person returns to the divine source through realizing that God is the force that enlivens the self. Since the ultimate discovery of God takes place within the self, it is likened to an intimate embrace.

> Consequently, when we recognize that we are really as nothing and apprehend that there is nothing in the world besides God, just as before creation, then God, as it were, experiences the true delight that He hopes for from us. Just as a father and mother hope to give birth to a child and to bear it in their arms, so God, as it were, experiences delight from His children who come to His arms for kisses and embraces . . . [47]

While the analogy of a parent's joy in being recognized by its offspring is consistent with the anthropopathic notion of divine delight, it does not fully reveal the nature of the relationship between God and man that occurs when a person becomes *Ayin*. The analogy is helpful for underscoring the divine origin of the human soul which is represented as God's offspring. We may also infer, although this is not explicitly highlighted in our texts, that God's delight is shared by an individual who discovers his other divine origin, just as a child takes delight in the refuge he or she finds in his or her parent's arms. Nevertheless, in the analogy, a distinction between the parent and child remains. However, Meshullam Feibush's conception of *devequt* goes beyond this model of intimate communion. As a disciple of Yehiel Mikhel of Zlotchov, he views the ideal relationship to God as nothing less than *unio mystica*.[48]

> [Yehiel Mikhel of Zlotchov] said, according to [the implications of the divine basis of creation], things are exactly the opposite of the way people imagine. For when they cleave to the world rather than to the blessed Creator, it seems to them that they exist [independently] and are great. But in what sense are they great? One day they are here and the next they are gone. Their days pass like a shadow. Even during their lives they are vanity. Hence, if they think they are something, in reality they are nothing. But, if one considers himself as nothing because of *devequt* with the Creator, as we mentioned, one mentally causes all his powers to cleave to the blessed Creator, as before creation (*ke-mi-qedem*). Hence such a one is very great. For the branch comes to its root and is in a state of complete unity with its root. Since the root is *Eyn Sof*,[49] the branch is also *Eyn Sof*. For its existence [as a separate entity] has been voided like a single drop that fell into a great sea. It returned to its root and thus is one with the water of the sea and cannot be distinguished at all.[50]

Reality is exactly the opposite of the way it is ordinarily perceived. According to ordinary consciousness, creation consists of a multiplicity of independent objects. Because of this apparent independence, a person considers himself important. However, when measured against the great scale of history, an individual life fades into insignificance. On the other hand, although a person in *devequt* considers himself to be as nothing, he is really very great. For he has become identified with the underlying divine reality. By negating his separate existence, he becomes indistinguishable from the divine unity.

This expression of *unio mystica* is particularly bold in its use of Jewish mystical terminology. One might have expected the assertion that unity with the divine presence or *Shekhinah* had been attained. Such claims are more typical of Hasidism. In most kabbalistic systems, the *Shekhinah* is associated with the lowest of the *sefirot*, *Malkhut*, the bridge between the divine and lower worlds.[51] Adhesion to somewhat higher *sefirot* is also sometimes described in kabbalistic literature. However, union with the *Eyn Sof* is less common. The term usually indicates the supreme degree of divinity that ontologically precedes all manifestation. It is prior even to the distinction between transcendent and immanent aspects of the divinity that are respectively represented by *Tiferet* and *Malkhut*.[52] Indeed, *Eyn Sof* is generally considered to stand ontologically far above the entire world of the *sefirot*. As such it does not ordinarily function as an object of human experience. However, its usage here should not be interpreted with too much metaphysical rigor. Here the term seems to underscore the acosmic character of Meshullam Feibush's cosmology. Everything that exists is potentially contained within the divinity before creation. The externalization of this potentiality constitutes the multiplicity apparent in creation. However, such multiplicity is misleading. As Meshullam Feibush tells us elsewhere, "creation is a multiplicity from its external perspective, but from its inner perspective, it is a unity."[53] Thus, through an act of contemplating the indwelling divine reality, the illusion of external multiplicity, including the separate self, is penetrated, leaving only the divine unity which ontologically precedes creation.[54]

To better illustrate the possibility and character of this extraordinary experience, Meshullam Feibush employs two metaphors, the root and the branch"[55] and the drop motif.[56] The root and branch elucidates the pantheistic trend in Meshullam Feibush's cosmology. Behind this metaphor is the well known archetype of the cosmic tree as *imago mundi* or *Ez Hayyim*, as it is termed in Kabbalah.[57] All of reality is likened to a single organic unity. Although creation appears to be composed of a multiplicity of discrete individual units, every entity is only an offshoot, projected from a single source that continues to sustain it. Every branch can be traced back to its source, the root from which everything emerges.

However, the "root and branch" motif is not so helpful for understanding the nature of the transformation of consciousness that occurs in *unio mystica*. This transformation involves a fundamental loss of identity as separate individual. In order to illustrate this, Meshullam Feibush is aided by the "drop" motif. An individual consciousness that overcomes its sense of self-identity is like an isolated drop that falls into the sea. Just as the drop has become indistinguishable from the sea itself, so the transformed consciousness becomes, in some sense, identical with divinity.[58] Meshullam Feibush's ideal of religious experience as *unio mystica* is more or less consistent with the non-dual tendencies in the teachings of Dov Ber of Mezeritch.[59]

Nevertheless, the bold expression of *unio mystica* here attributed to Yehiel Mikhel was still controversial at the end of the eighteenth century. Although written in 1777, the passage was excluded from the first edition of *Liqqutim Yeqarim* (Lemberg 1792). It first appeared in print in a subsequent edition (Zholkva 1800) that was published five years after Meshullam Feibush's death in 1795. The Zholkva edition was the first to acknowledge Meshullam Feibush's authorship of at least a portion of the material contained in *Liqqutim Yeqarim*. Nevertheless, this edition was ignored by all previous scholars beginning with Simon Dubnov and including Joseph Weiss, Rivka Schatz-Uffenheimer, Zev Gries, and Moshe Idel.[60] Simon Dubnov "discovered" Meshullam Feibush's role in preparing the anthology, partly as a result of remarks made by Aaron Walden in *Shem ha-Gadolim he-Hadash*.[61] Joseph Weiss relied primarily on the 1905 Munkacz edition of *Yosher Divrey Emet*.[62] Moshe Idel quoted the text from *Mayim Rabbim*, a late collection of teachings attributed to Yehiel Mikhel of Zlotchov.[63] None of these scholars commented on the exclusion of the text from the earliest (and several later) editions of *Liqqutim Yeqarim* or on the fact that Meshullam Feibush's name was connected with the anthology as early as 1800.

We have seen how the pantheistic and acosmic tendencies that Meshullam Feibush drew from Cordoverian sources has provided a cosmological basis for mystical experience. Since, despite the appearances of multiplicity in creation, only God truly exists, *devequt*, or discovery of and adhesion to the divine, constitutes the principal religious goal and experience. Ultimately, this experience is construed as nothing less than *unio mystica*. Through the attainment of *devequt*, God's ultimate purpose in creating the world is fulfilled. Thus, the Cordoverian cosmological trend tends to promote *devequt* as valuable for its own sake.

Nevertheless, Meshullam Feibush did not advocate an anomian form of mysticism. He continued to view normative traditional aspects of religious life as the primary means for realizing *devequt*. Moreover, Meshullam Feibush continued to uphold certain Lurianic interests that depended on adhering to the framework of traditional Jewish life. The process of uplifting divine sparks in order to realize the messianic age was also very important to him. In this context, *devequt* was not an end in itself, but an essential means for accomplishing the Lurianic goal.

As we shall subsequently see, the attainment of *devequt* was subject to stringent conditions which promoted classical ethical values and guarded against immoderate mystical claims that were not accompanied by extraordinary spiritual development. While Meshullam Feibush was quite extreme in regarding the highest level of *devequt* as *unio mystica*, the criteria he presented for attaining *devequt*, ultimately restricted the experience to an exceptional spiritual elite. Since Meshullam Feibush identified this elite as the Hasidic *Zaddiqim*, his theory of *devequt* as *unio mystica*, based in pantheistic-acosmic cosmology, became, essentially, a basis for distinguishing the spiritual superiority of the Hasidic leadership.

4
The Barrier to Divine Aid

In a world in which only God and the emanated divine forces are real, spiritual perfection must ultimately be understood as the result of divine aid. Since spiritual perfection, for Meshullam Feibush, is defined as attaining a state of *Ayin* in which all sense of self has been voided through total immersion in the divine reality, the root cause of the human inability to reach this state is pride. This condition renders the human situation paradoxical, if not hopeless. On the one hand, an effort must be made to overcome those natural tendencies which characterize spiritual imperfection. Yet, success in such efforts themselves may lead to pride. On the other hand, as long as any sense of pride or self-interest remains part of the effort, spiritual perfection cannot be attained. Meshullam Feibush is acutely aware of this problem. A discussion of the inherent connection between moral development, spiritual perfection, and divine aid is not only central to his analysis of the religious life, but also contributes directly to his argument for faith in spiritual *virtuosi*, the true *Zaddiqim*.

The contemporary situation that Meshullam Feibush describes is one that is wracked by contention and jealousy. Although true religious giants are present in the generation who could provide spiritual guidance, pride is so prevalent that their leadership is spurned.[1] Indeed hypocrisy is so ingrained that false humility is pursued as a virtue.

> In fact, I just heard during this *Shavuot*, directly from the Rabbi and preacher [of Zlotchov], our Master and Teacher, Rabbi Yehiel Mikhel, may his light shine, the following. The world thinks it is a *mizvah* to be a humble person. But, actually, this "*mizvah*" is not mentioned in the Torah. The Torah only speaks in praise of Moses. In reality, the "devil"[2] put this matter into their hearts, that it is a *mizvah* to be a humble person. For first, he causes everyone's heart to swell with pride and makes him think that he is a great scholar, well-descended, rich, a *Hasid* and *Zaddiq*, full of moral virtues and upright, God fearing, pleasant and charming, and according to his degree, truly worthy to be greater than everyone else, [too superior] to turn to them or associate with them. But this [would be] an unseemly way to act (*raq she-zo midah geruah*) which would cause him to be despised by others. For they would take him for a conceited person. [And he thinks] it is really a *mizvah* also to be humble and self-effacing, and to speak with everybody, and to [allow oneself to] be insulted by all. So he pretends to be

humble. All this is the seduction of the devil.[3] For first he puffs up his heart within him and it blazes to Hell below, and afterwards he adds this "*mizvah*" as a virtue (*le-ma'alah*),[4] to add pride to his pride.[5]

However, this problem of pride is not merely a contemporary issue. It is a perennial problem that every would-be spiritual person must confront. In short, egotism is a natural condition of human birth.[6] It is so deeply rooted in human consciousness that one is not ordinarily aware of its presence. Meshullam Feibush helps bring the nature of this problem into focus by way of an analogy.

> God inspired me with an apt analogy concerning this.[7] A person travels along a road in a coach and falls asleep. [While he is asleep], the coachman transports him over a high mountain. Once the top of the mountain has been reached, the road is straight, for the ascending slope has already been passed. So, later, when the sleeping person awakens and is told that he is on a mountain, he cannot believe it. For he sees nothing that would indicate [that he is on a mountain]. If he had seen the slope on which he had previously traveled and ascended, he would know. But now everything appears level to him. So how can he acknowledge that he is on a mountain? But he will realize it later when he has descended from the mountain via the second slope that leads from the mountain to the valley. [Only] then will he understand that he has been on the mountain.[8]

Pride is not distinguishable as long as a person has known no other state. One is simply born into it with no recollection of how it arose. The state of sleep, of course, alludes to the fact that we are unaware of the divine basis of life. If one could remember the stages of creation from its root in divinity, then pride would be discernible. However, due to this sleep, it is only possible to become aware of pride through a transformation of consciousness which is characterized by its opposite, self-effacement.

> Pride is really comparable to a high mountain. If a person would sense when his heart is swelling within him, surely he would distinguish this, that there is pride and arrogance and that he has ascended on the mountain. But a person is born on this mountain which is pride. . . . So it seems to him that there is no pride or mountain at all. How can he distinguish this unless he descends from the mountain completely, to the very foot of the mountain in the valley. In other words, he must train himself in submission and effacement (*be-kheni'ah ve-shiflut*) in heart and in deed, and above all in the heart, and [then] the truth will be known to him.[9]

Pride, then, may be understood as the condition of spiritual blindness. It is the state of one who has no real sense of the nature of reality. Pride is an indication of the fundamental lack of awareness of the divine presence.

For, in reality, whoever has had the eyes of his awareness (*hakarato*) opened by God, always sees his insignificance and constantly is ashamed of himself. All the more so when he considers the greatness of the Blessed Creator, may his name be blessed. As a result of his shame in His presence, he is as absolutely nothing compared to Him.[10]

But this spiritual blindness is the condition into which all have been born. It is the direct result of Original Sin.

Because of the pollution of the serpent which blinds the eyes of man from seeing the truth, man is born with this pollution. [It is] because of the sin of Adam. Thus all the [causes of] pride appear in his heart. His eyes are blinded from constantly seeing God in his heart with awe and fear. He neither knows nor senses the pride in his heart at all. He is born [with this] and grows, little by little every day, greater than his fellow.[11]

Since pride is understood as the fundamental condition which separates humankind and God in the human consciousness, the eradication of pride plays a central role in spiritual development. As the principal barrier to *devequt*, it must be entirely uprooted. The more one overcomes pride and realizes his fundamental insignificance, the more the divine will be present in his consciousness.

But whoever wishes to cleave to God, truly to Him alone, realizes that it is impossible to cleave to Him unless he drives out pride from his heart and constantly recognizes his shortcoming and insignificance to such an extent that it will not seem to him that he has any virtue (*ma'alah*). For in reality, so it is to one who knows (*le-maskil*). For in addition to this it says, "*YHVH loathes all pride of heart*,"[12] that is, even in the heart, and even the tiniest bit ... The more he understands his insignificance and dwells on this constantly in thought and deed, the more he will experience (*margish*) the *devequt* of his soul with God.[13]

Since pride is so deeply rooted in the human condition, it is no small task to uproot it from the heart. Meshullam Feibush's analysis of pride and his emphasis on the importance of totally eliminating it as a condition for realizing the primary religious goal, *devequt*, sets a virtually impossible standard. Of this he is well aware.

In reality, not everyone can merit [to constantly uproot pride from his heart]. But "you are not responsible for completing the work ..."[14] So we should detach ourselves as much as possible, in every possible way, whenever we can, from all worldly matters, and truly cleave to God through Torah and good deeds. [It is] all [accomplished] through self-effacement (*shiflut*).[15]

Although the ideal of true humility[16] can rarely, if ever, be achieved, one must aspire towards it as best one can. Indeed, while one may speak of humility as an ideal, which has already been established in the heart, the term also applies to earlier stages of spiritual development during which the moral virtues are still being perfected.

> By means of the Torah one can reach humility, just as our sages said, "and it clothes him with humility."[17] Although they said that one of the ways of Torah is humility,[18] [which implies that] humility comes first, in reality, there is humility at the beginning and humility at the end. For the first [type of] humility refers to ridding oneself (harhaqat) of pride and the offshoots that it produces, e.g., anger and the like. Humility at the end refers to the establishment of effacement in the heart because of genuine awe for God . . . [19]

The distinction between the two types of humility illustrates the important relationship between moral development and spiritual perfection. The latter refers to the intimate relationship between the human soul and God, the various stages of devequt. But one cannot really speak of the attainment of devequt as long as the moral virtues have not been perfected. Negative character traits are too much a part of human nature. Their very presence stands in the way of communion with God. This is a theme which is repeatedly emphasized in Meshullam Feibush's writings.

> Whoever learns and ponders well the moral literature[20] knows that it is impossible to cleave to the good before he has rejected the evil. Concerning this, it is said, "and you will sow your seeds in vain and your enemies will eat them."[21] For the portion of good that one does, evil takes for itself, God forbid. For it is its own. According to the measure of his distancing [himself] from evil, so is the measure of his approaching the good.[22]

Moral development proceeds slowly and requires great vigilance. It is essentially a process that is based on self-awareness. In order to eliminate pride and its offshoots, one must first become aware of them through training oneself to be constantly attentive to all that is occurring within his consciousness.

> For this, great deliberation (metinut) is required, so that one will not become confused through the dispersion of the soul after other objects of attention (be-fizur ha-nefesh be-yedi'ot aherim). Rather, one should inquire within, examining with the measure of his soul[23] the intention and essence (tokho) of every matter and deed, [in order to determine] if it is for desire or for truth. He should carry this out at every single moment and in all that he does. For this is the beginning and basis of everything. "For one sees every defect except his own."[24] [He] chastises and is not chastised.[25]

Nevertheless while vigilance can raise the existence of pride and other negative character traits to consciousness, it still is not sufficient for uprooting them entirely from the heart. At this point, the human situation would be desperate indeed were it not for the possibility of divine aid. But divine aid is not possible as long as pride remains in the heart. We are now in a position to understand the solution to this paradox. While the most diligent attempt to uproot pride from the heart may be doomed to failure, the very recognition of one's inability to succeed in this effort produces a deep sense of effacement. In such a state, one may legitimately cry out to God for aid in utter sincerity.

> It is impossible to receive aid from God before one has put off pride from the heart. For "YHVH abhors all pride of heart,"[26] and "it and I cannot dwell together."[27] So how is it possible that He will aid him? Yet without help it is impossible to stand against the evil urge. So you see how our sages said that pride of heart is the root of all. Concerning this, they said, "whoever comes to purify himself receives aid."[28] Therefore, the beginning depends on the person's putting off pride of heart, recognizing his insignificance, how his eyes are sealed from seeing and his heart from understanding, and he lacks the power to stand against the petty and foul desire. [As a result], he will increase submission and effacement in heart and deed. Then he will be able to ask for aid from God, when he understands that it is not within his ability to stand against the evil urge. But as long as he considers himself great, then God is far from him . . . [29]

Thus, effacement is the key to salvation. The religious effort leads inevitably to the realization that one's own powers cannot prevail. Through the deep sense of one's limitations and insignificance, the absolute dependence on God is realized.

However, this deep realization can come only after a long period of great effort. Few are they who would even undertake to fulfill the demanding spiritual regimen that is required. Meshullam Feibush is too aware of the limitations of his contemporaries to expect those who turn to him for spiritual guidance to live up to the ideal standards that are detailed in the classical ethical texts. Instead, one must believe, he will argue, that there are great *Zaddiqim* who can indeed measure up to these standards.[30] However, the conditions of contemporary life, themselves, make it impossible for most people to follow so austere a spiritual path.

> In reality, the issue of human conduct in the ways of serving God is beyond measure. Although the many ethical works which were revealed in this period have gone into great detail, not every person can comprehend them (*la'amod aleihem*) and fulfill their words which were said in truth. For according to their

words, a person would have to be free from everything, without work, without care or troubles, and then perhaps he would be able to fulfill and do [what is required]: to "turn away from evil and do good."[31] By turning away from evil, I mean from every aspect of evil, whether in thought or in deed, and the same for doing good in all of its details. But "many tried to follow Rabbi Shimon ben Yohai's example and did not succeed."[32] In this generation, everyone has to be occupied with his trade and with his subsistence. As a result, the soul is greatly deprived of the opportunity to truly serve God, as we know. But, God forbid that because of this we should become negligent in keeping and fulfilling as much as we can.[33]

The demands of a genuine spiritual life are indeed daunting. Even under the best of circumstances few would be able to measure up to them. When one adds to this the difficulties caused by poverty and the time required to attend to the exigencies of life, the prospects for spiritual development become very slim. Since Meshullam Feibush's writings are directed primarily to individuals who are not capable of meeting the ideal standards of divine service, much attention is given to encouraging his reader to do what he can, despite the great disparity between what is possible and ideal conduct. Indeed, the need for encouragement becomes especially acute within the context of this non-dual theology in which man is basically nothing.

We have seen already how the inevitability of failure and human imitation forms a central part of Meshullam Feibush's thought.[34] This condition ultimately allows for the development of a sense of effacement in which God can be found. However, his uncompromising demand for total humility and the emphasis that Meshullam Feibush constantly places on recognition of human insignificance runs the risk of provoking a sense of futility and despair. Effacement is a positive virtue when it is a concomitant of the realization that only God and the divine powers exist. But, in those earlier stages of the spiritual path, during which the divine is still a stranger to human consciousness, a sense of powerlessness is very much liable to be counterproductive. Meshullam Feibush employs a number of strategies to offset this danger.[35] As we shall see, his recommendation of faith in Zaddiqim is one of the most important. However, our discussion of the problem of pride would be incomplete if we did not take note here of one particular argument which directly confronts the danger of negligence as a result of the sense of futility.

The strategy which Meshullam Feibush employs to ensure that too overwhelming a sense of humility will not prevent a person from performing his religious duties is one which is familiar in early Hasidic literature.[36] Divine service does require pride as well as humility. An excessive sense of humility, which causes a person to feel that he is not worthy or capable of performing a religious act, is only a device of the *yezer ha-ra* which will resort to any measure in order to keep a person from his religious obligations.

The argument has several key aspects. First is the general observation that we are indeed full of imperfections and far from the ideal of purity, nevertheless, the little that one does is precious to God.

> As for you, my beloved, don't allow your [evil] urge to seduce you [through saying], "for according to [the standards of the *Zaddiqim*], we cannot succeed (*lo maza'nu yadeinu ve-ragleinu*) and are comparable to beasts. What is our worship worth if we lack even the least speck of this path?" My beloved brother, the matter is indeed so. But a person needs to be very wise in every way to combat his [evil] urge and to weigh everything in measure. For the fact is that a person has to serve God with both qualities. Just as it is impossible to serve with pride, God forbid, for "YHVH abhors all pride of heart,"[37] so it is impossible to serve with [complete] effacement, as is known. For this would be negligence and abandonment of His worship. The evil urge will say "what difference does it make if you pray or if you concentrate, it is all vanity . . ." and other arguments like these. But it is not so. For the least bit from a person is very important to God, as long as it is sincerely offered for God's glory. It has a great effect above.[38]

Not only is the little that can be done effective, but there really is no other choice. If one is truly concerned about his faults and distance from God, he should perform his religious obligations. For that is the only way spiritual progress can be made. If one were to become negligent because of his sense of unworthiness, he could never hope to improve. Such negligence is based in the extreme of nihilism and essentially self-defeating.

> Even if a person's heart will become so disheartened as to think, "who are you to enter God's chamber when you are full of bad qualities and serious transgressions." In truth, so it is. One ought to rectify every quality and turn from transgression. But this can only be done through approaching God. For without this nothing is possible. . . . So a person must constantly force himself to approach God in his thought. If he is full of bad qualities and wishes to break them, it is only possible through drawing close to God. Even though he is not able, God sees his very great longing and helps him [to overcome his negative qualities] little by little, and also to repent of the transgressions that he has committed.[39]

God is so pleased by sincere human effort that He comes to the aid of the one who makes it. This is reflected in the gradual progress that is made along the spiritual path.

There is another extremely important aspect of the argument which we have yet to note. Whereas unconscious pride is the great obstacle to truly serving God, there is a type of pride which may be deliberately resorted to in order to ensure that the quality of effacement will not become excessively morbid. This pride in serving God is not only permissible, but even necessary. It is ordained by the ancient rabbinical sages.

> But if he would be totally egoless (shafal-mi-kol-ve-khol) perhaps his [evil] urge is liable to seduce him, saying, "who are you to speak before God and to serve Him . . ." and similar taunts. To [offset] this one has to take hold of pride, as the verse says, "and he will raise up his heart in the ways of YHVH."[40] As our rabbis said, "accordingly, Adam was created unique . . . so each and every one is obligated to say, for me the world was created."[41] Our rabbis also said, "A person should always regard himself as if he and the world are half innocent and half guilty. If he does a single mizvah, fortunate is he. For he rendered himself and the world into the scale of merit . . ."[42] At first glance this is great arrogance, that a person would imagine in his mind that the world was created for him, and that all the world depends on him. But our sages compelled us to use this pride. For otherwise there would be great disheartenment in our souls over the pursuit of divine service.[43]

Pride and humility are not absolute virtues. In reality there are positive and negative versions of each. This is the result of a duality that is inherent in the structure of reality. The evil urge is seductive because it represents the positive virtues in their negative forms. That is, it strives to persuade a person that what is in reality a negative course of action or attitude is in fact a virtue. For every positive virtue there is a parallel form that distorts it. This psychological polarity reflects a fundamental structural antinomy between holiness and pollution which is represented in Kabbalistic cosmology by the external shells (qelipot).

> But, "God created one alongside of the other,"[44] good alongside of evil, etc. All the qualities that are found in good are also in evil, only in good they are for the good and in evil they are for evil. One is the opposite of the other. Evil is always called, according to the verse in Proverbs, "the perverse way of a person foreign [to righteousness]."[45] . . . Thus the quality of the shell is the opposite of every true matter, to make what is good [appear to be] evil and what is evil [appear to be] good, just as the verse said, "woe to those who call evil good and good evil . . ."[46]

While in general, humility is a positive virtue and pride negative, this is only the case insofar as they bring a person closer to God. However, the arguments of the evil urge lead to the opposite, further estrangement, by concealing the fact that excessive humility is a vice and that there is a virtuous use of pride. In reality, the evil urge supports stagnation in religious life, advocating a kind of false humility that is, in actuality, only a concealed form of pride.[47]

> The "shell" seduces a person also with the two qualities, pride and humility. But it is exactly the opposite [of what one claims]. For example, when one wants to rebuke someone for not taking up the true way of serving God through Torah and prayer with genuine awe and love, without ulterior motive, etc . . . , the foolish person, seduced by his [evil] urge, will respond, "who am I to approach those ways." I recognize my iniquity. Who am I to pursue the greatness and wonders of the path of the *Hasidim*? I do what my fathers did and that is enough for me. The rest of the humility he expresses is all [an excuse] to be lax in worship. This is a seduction from the side of humility. Would that it were really so, and that he was humble in his mind toward himself and towards all. But, in fact, when someone argues with him and scorns him, he puffs up his heart and believes that he serves God through his learning and *mizvot* more than all the *Hasidim* in the world. He will become audacious and insult and humiliate [his opponent]. Even his heart is constantly filled with pride. For it seems to him that he succeeds in his worship. But actually, all this is the seduction of the evil urge and serpent, to uproot him from the land of the living and cast him down to the well of destruction with two contradictions.[48]

There is, then, a place for pride in the service of God. It may function well as an antidote to excessive self-abasement and thus serve to motivate a person to perform his religious duties. As such, it promotes genuine spiritual aspiration and can offset the inertia of complacency. On the other hand, what passes for conventional humility may really only mask a depth of pride which, though unacknowledged, is the dominant factor in one's consciousness.

As we have seen throughout our discussion, pride or egotism, is the primary obstacle in the way of spiritual realization, according to Meshullam Feibush's vision. If a certain use for this fundamental flaw has been mandated by the sages as a concession to human limitation, it is not without reservation. It is only acceptable as a motivator, before the fact. However, once one actually begins to perform a religious act, no trace of pride may be tolerated.

> But, God forbid, after the fact, and even while doing something for God, one should not imagine that there is really [any place for] pride [in the act], only submission and effacement, through recognizing that he is as nothing before God. He [himself] does not perform any deed. For all that he does is through the

power and aid of God, who helps him and gives him power. Without God, he would be nothing.[49]

Again we see that pride has no real place because salvation ultimately depends on divine aid. This is not merely the necessary corollary of a fundamentally negative appraisal of human potential. Some human beings, the true *Zaddiqim*, have great potential[50] and even the little that the average person does, accomplishes wonders. However, since all that really exists according to Meshullam Feibush's acosmic-pantheistic cosmology is God and the divine powers, God is always the true agent. In this sense, the spiritually developed individual realizes that he in fact does nothing and thus has no basis for taking pride in his spiritual accomplishments.[51]

This radical assertion of the exclusivity of divine agency gives rise to a further paradox. If human beings are powerless without divine aid, then they really accomplish nothing through their worship. If salvation comes through the recognition that divine aid is required, then religious worship, per se, would seem superfluous.

> This is what King David said, "*the salvation of the righteous is from YHVH, their refuge in time of sorrow, and YHVH will help them and rescue them, he will rescue them and bring them salvation, because they had faith in Him.*"[52] In other words, their salvation in righteousness and rescue from wickedness is certainly from God. For they have no power to withstand their [evil] urge. Indeed, our weak minds are far from [understanding that] God would help us without any worship on our part. For [our understanding] is too limited to comprehend God's bounty at every moment, as a gift and act of mercy. If we really knew [the extent of] our insignificance, we would know that we are not [really] doing any service.[53]

Although a person can really do nothing towards his salvation without divine aid, human beings tend to believe that their acts of worship are effective. It is difficult for the human mind to comprehend that salvation comes as a free gift of God and not as a result of human effort. However, in reality salvation is paradoxical. It is not the act of the worshipper that gives rise to salvation, but rather the quality of self-effacement that accompanies the act. One is saved by God precisely because, in turning to God, the notion that one can bring about his own salvation has been entirely surrendered.

> But [salvation does not come as the result of our actions, but] because we realize that we are as nothing, as is known to all who really inquire [into this] by themselves. That is what [King David] said [in this verse]. Although one realizes the

very truth, that without divine aid, it is not within his power to withstand his [evil] urge even for a single moment, nevertheless "*He will save them, because they had faith in Him*"[54] that He would save them.[55]

Ultimately, self-effacement and faith are closely related. The more one realizes human powerlessness, the closer he comes to recognizing that it is only divine power that is operative in creation. Thus, only faith or reliance on divine grace remains as a basis for salvation. Overcoming pride is a prerequisite for apprehending God.

5

The Problem of Corporeality: Conditions for *Devequt*

We have seen in the preceding chapters that, according to Meshullam Feibush's teachings, the world was created for the purpose of *devequt*. This means that God created the world in order to delight in human souls that would succeed in overcoming the limits of corporeality through discovering the divine presence and cleaving to it in their minds. The fundamental obstacle in the way of *devequt* is pride, an innate condition of life in which a person fails to recognize his dependence on divine power. Although overcoming pride is of fundamental concern for one pursuing *devequt*, it cannot be achieved until one has first disciplined his natural impulses. Self-mastery is a prerequisite for spiritual development. The idea that one can perform genuine spiritual acts without first confronting his passions is an illusion.

> There are fools who think they are giving over their souls to God in certain places during prayer. This is completely false. As our sages of blessed memory explained, "the impulses of the righteous are under their power and the wicked are under the power of their impulses . . ."[1] For a righteous person masters his desire while desire gets the best of a wicked person. [The latter] is subject to his impulses[2] and inclines toward whatever he desires. . . . So how can he give over something that is not under his power? For the soul is not under his power. Concerning this, it is said, "*we will raise up our hearts in our hands to God in heaven.*"[3] In other words, when the heart is under our power (*masur le-yad-dayim*), then [the verse says,] "*to God in heaven.*" Then we will be able to sanctify it and give it over to heaven.[4]

In the present chapter, we will examine more closely the psychological connection between detachment from physical desires and *devequt*. As we shall see, the emphasis on detachment not only contributes to the understanding of the state of consciousness which occurs during *devequt*, but also helps define the nature of true *Zaddiqim*. Meshullam Feibush's extreme demand for detachment as a precondition for *devequt*, increases the disparity between the spiritual potential of an ordinary person and the awesome attainments of the religious virtuoso.

According to the Hasidic viewpoint, all religious practices and obser-

vances are means for cleaving to God. However, these means are only potentially effective. In order to attain *devequt*, it is not sufficient merely to learn
Torah and observe the *mizvot*. Such practices only lead to *devequt* when
certain preconditions have been met.

> In reality, cleaving to God by means of the Torah and *mizvot* requires many
> preconditions. Our generation, including great masters of Torah, has over-
> looked these conditions which are enumerated in the Mishnah. . . .[5] Now the
> conditions are many, but the least of them is to be detached from temporal de-
> sires [such as] eating, drinking, sleeping, and intercourse, and to break the bod-
> ily powers, even when such things are necessary, because of one's heart's enthu-
> siasm for Torah and serving God for His name's sake in love. The worldly
> pleasure which comes from that matter will not be important to him (*lo yeha-
> shev elav*), just as a businessman who is happy because of his profit does not
> find the least pleasure in eating.[6]

In order to experience *devequt* through the Torah one must first attain a certain level of spiritual development. This development involves a great many
attributes, the very least of which is to be so filled by the desire to serve God
that one has no interest in the ordinary pleasures of this world. It is not
merely a matter of ascetic discipline. The desire to serve God must become
so strong that, by comparison, corporeal desires pale into extinction.

> This is "through excluding desire."[7] The Mishnah does not say "through a little
> desire," but "through excluding (*be-mi'ut*)." For the importance of reducing de-
> sire does not need to be mentioned. But he will limit even what is necessary.
> That is, he will increase the delight and desire of divine *devequt* in his heart
> through the Torah, until [other pleasure] is extinguished like a lamp in the af-
> ternoon [sun.] If he does experience a bit of pleasure, then it will be as our sages
> said, "pleasure that a person experiences against his will. . . ."[8] This all pertains
> to what is permissible to eat and drink and necessary for him. The same applies
> to necessary intercourse[9] at the necessary time.[10]

The path to *devequt*, then, involves a certain conscious effort towards
suppression of ordinary corporeal gratification. Indeed, one must choose to
overcome the power of such ephemeral desires through the recognition that
they are temptations that prevent one from fulfilling his sacred task. While
initially this process requires denial of pleasure, ultimately one's efforts are
rewarded by a spiritual delight which is far greater.

> But whoever is wise and longs to serve God, "*and the spirit of YHVH begins
> to inspire him*,"[11] then, although his soul desires the evil things we have

mentioned, if his soul clearly recognizes that something is evil, he realizes that he should break [this desire]. Although he receives no pleasure in this [suppression], in place of it he will attain the hidden good. Even in this world he will merit to taste a great delight in prayer, Torah, and the pleasantness of desiring to perform the *mizvot*. Thus he will experience a worthy desire in exchange for an evil one.[12]

The antinomy between good and evil desires parallels a fundamental division in the structure of the cosmos between the sacred and profane. This duality is also present in the human psyche. Part of the soul has its root in impurity, while the higher part is a product of the holy source. The profane is ephemeral and bound for destruction. The holy, on the other hand, is eternal. Thus the impure soul in man longs for ephemeral gratifications which only serve to separate him from eternity.[13]

For, in reality, a person's evil soul craves evil desires and qualities because it is from the side of death, destruction, and impurity which, God willing, will swiftly perish. It longs for its root, for dust and destruction and separation, all of which are the antithesis of His Holiness which is eternal and united, blessed be He and His name, and the epitome of spirituality (*ve-ruhani takhlit ha-ruhaniyut*).[14] Thus [the evil soul] seduces the holy spark in a person so that it will also be drawn after him, in order that they will dwell together in the dust.[15]

If the seduction of the evil soul leads to destruction and separation from holiness, detachment from corporeality leads directly to the various degrees of *devequt*, including, ultimately, *unio mystica*.[16]

This matter [of *unio mystica*] requires further explanation by way of an analogy. This is according to a metaphor that appears in the *Ra'aya Meheymna*[17] which likens God's ten attributes to a source, a spring, a sea, and seven tributaries. It is written there, "and if the artisan will break these vessels that he made, the water will return to the source." . . . The matter is the same with regard to man. Although he is a limited, created entity, this is entirely from his point of view, from the perspective of the creation into which he was created. However, when he detaches himself from corporeality [then his soul returns to its divine source].[18]

Here we have an excellent example of the Hasidic tendency to interpret mystical cosmological issues anthropologically. A passage in the Zohar, which explains the existence of the ten *sefirot* as depending on the divine essence that is emanated from the *Eyn Sof*, here becomes a metaphor for explaining *unio mystica*. Just as breaking these vessels would cause the divine essence contained in them to return to its source, detachment from corporeality causes the soul to return to its origin in God.

However, the path of return encompasses a number of degrees of intimacy. Initially, this intimacy is itself already present in the very longing for God which replaces corporeal desires. For when such longing is genuine, it contains within it some measure of awe and love for God. These are the experiential symptoms of *devequt*.

> For all the desires and cravings after this world's conceits and jealousies are vanity for one who has managed to truly taste even the tiniest bit of this desire in his soul. That is, [for one who has experienced] the state of awe and love. For when awe and fear are not present in the heart, it is nothing but external love ...[19] But, concerning awe, it is said, *"this is the gate to YHVH."*[20] For whoever enters the gate in which the king is found, naturally experiences awe. Similarly, when a person experiences fear of God in his heart, it is a sign that in his thought he has entered the King's gate. This is the attribute called *Malkhut*.[21]

This experience of awe in the presence of God further reinforces the effort to detach oneself from physical pleasures. A person in a state of *devequt* is ashamed of anything that separates him from God. He is embarrassed by his corporeality.

> When one constantly trains himself in this awe, then he will automatically despise all desires and evil lusts out of shame of God and fear before Him. This is [the meaning of] detachment from corporeality and strengthening the intellectual power which is explained in the *Shulhan Arukh, Orah Hayyim*.[22]

Genuine awareness of God produces an intense feeling of awe. One is so overwhelmed by the thought of God's presence that a state of acute self-consciousness is aroused. In such a state, one is, as it were, ashamed to indulge his carnal appetites in a compulsive way. Deliberation is required in order to examine the motivation of every tendency.[23] Due to this constant pursuit of purity in deed and in thought, a person who is truly practicing *devequt* is not capable of sinning.

> For it is impossible for a person who is cleaving to God in love and awe to commit a minor transgression, even less a serious one, and certainly not to be attached to some desire, God forbid. For is not God holy and separate from all materiality?[24]

However, *devequt* is never merely a matter of external behavior. It is always judged by the inner feelings of awe and love and not merely by outward appearances of piety.

But certainly He has no need for appearances (*le-fanim*), for love and awe of God are a different matter which [occurs] in a person's heart. His heart will constantly fear and be in awe of God. Love will constantly burn in his heart as Maimonides wrote.[25]

However, the emphasis on detachment from corporeality does not ultimately lead to a severe asceticism. Since it is primarily a condition of inner experience, once this level of spiritual development has been attained, corporeal acts can take place. This is the case even when the performing of such acts appears to violate the principle of detachment. Meshullam Feibush illustrates this possibility through an interpretation of an unusual passage from the Talmud.

> According to this, I understood a passage in the *Gemara*, tractate Shabbat.[26] "Ulla used to kiss his sisters' breasts . . . and he contradicts himself . . ."[27] See the comment of the *Tosafot* that ends "and the writer did not care to explain here at length why he would do this." On the face of it, it is perplexing that the *Gemara* would mention a contradiction and not answer in detail where an explanation is warranted. But, it seems to me, that with their holy spirit, their words did allude to an explanation, for one that understands. Their words were formed like a sapphire. In other words, according to what we have written above, if a person is detached from corporeality, then [his consciousness] is divided within (*hu muhlaq be-azmo me-azmo el azmo*). Within he cleaves to the blessed Creator with great longing. But, externally, he performs corporeal acts, such as eating and intercourse and the like. So within he is like an angel separated from the physical, while externally he appears like a beast. But this is not the case, God forbid, if he is not [detached from corporeality]. Then he is one with the animal desires and is not divided or detached from them at all.[28]

Detachment from corporeality involves a kind of split consciousness.[29] One does not totally avoid corporeal acts, but when one participates in them, they are done with a consciousness which is not motivated by a desire for carnal pleasure. Within, a person is wholly maintaining the awe-inspiring sense of God's presence.

> That is why they said in the *Gemara*, "when Ulla was coming from Rav's house." For then he was in an extreme state of detachment due to *devequt* of the Torah. [Then] "he would kiss his sisters . . ." The *Gemara* explains "and he contradicted himself."[30] In other words, why did he do this? Because [his consciousness] was split and his [inner state] was divided from his [external action] in other words, his spiritual consciousness (*ruhaniyut*) was detached from his corporeality. For were this not the case, how could he have done this? For it says [elsewhere] in the *Gemara*, "Ulla said all physical contact whatsoever is

forbidden." In other words, this is the strongest possible proof that he was divided from himself, i.e. spiritually detached from his corporeality. For "Ulla said [explicitly that all physical contact is forbidden] . . ." If so, it is forbidden to do this, but surely [he could only do this] because he was detached . . .[31]

As we shall see below, Meshullam Feibush makes clear that such extreme cases can only arise among the greatest spiritual adepts, the *Zaddiqim*. However, the need to practice detachment from corporeality, in the sense of a bifurcated consciousness, applies to everyone during necessary carnal acts. This is particularly the case in regard to the biblical injunction to reproduce.

> For the Maggid [R. Yehiel Mikhel of Zlotchov] explained the concept of *"be fruitful and become great."* . . .[32] God commanded us to be fruitful and to produce offspring. But He cautioned us concerning this matter for it is very corporeal and material. God forbid, we should be like animals. Indeed God's intention was [that this act] would lead to His blessed spirituality. So how could He command us to become corporeal?[33] For this reason, He added, *"and become great."* In other words, the act of procreation should not become a [merely] carnal act, through attachment to ephemeral desire. For then, what are you considered? You would be worthless. For your insignificance and lowliness would be just like the other animals and beasts whom you consider of little worth, through their inclining completely to matter.[34]

If the sexual act were merely a response to a physical desire, then human beings would be no higher on the scale of spiritual values than all other living creatures. However, reproduction is a divine command. As we have seen, the purpose of all commandments is *devequt*. Ultimately, fulfilling the commandments in *devequt* implies *unio mystica*, for human consciousness is filled by the divine presence. Thus, the individual human soul or branch, turning away from corporeality, returns to its divine root in which its separate identity is canceled. It is this potential for union with the divine which distinguishes human sexuality from that of the animals.

> Because of [the animals complete inclination toward matter], they walk with a bent posture. For even their souls are only of a quality that is worthy of dust and no more. So what are they considered? If you will [act] like them, you will be insignificant and lowly like them. Even though your bodies are upright, you will be considered as if you walked bent over.[35] But this is not the case, if you detach yourselves from corporeality and greatly cleave to God. Then your sexual union will be for His blessed name, and will be as detached from materiality as possible. Then you will be very great. For you will be cleaving to God. So the

branch will be connected to its root, forming one complete unity with it, just as I wrote for you above, in the analogy from the *Ra'aya Meheymna*.[36] "And if the artisan would break these vessels that he made, the water would return to its source."[37]

However, no matter how spiritually developed a person becomes, he cannot completely separate himself from corporeality. As long as he is alive his soul remains in the body. Nevertheless through breaking his mind's fixation on the craving for carnal satisfaction, he can become united with God. This is possible because of the divine element within his own soul which has only to be released from the tyranny of sensual craving in order to establish a continuum with God.

> If a person will break himself of all the desires that his will craves so that they are despised, he will constantly only long to be joined to the blessed Creator. However, it is not possible to accomplish this completely, since God created him to be a separate creature. Nevertheless his desire will always be for its root. Thus it is as if he were there.[38] For he directed his body after its root, since there is no break between them. This, then, is called an upright posture which is associated with man. For he was created to be adhering to God, like the ministering angels . . .[39]

Spiritual union can be attained because the body's limitations do not ultimately obstruct the continuum between the divine source and the soul. In order to protect humankind from the danger of corporeality, which is intrinsic to human life and especially to the sexual act,[40] God placed the divine spirit in humankind. It is this divine element which prompts a person to return to his/her spiritual origin.

> This is the meaning of "*I will cause you to be fruitful.*"[41] But it is a shortcoming to be concerned with corporeality. God forbid that we should be reduced to insignificance. Thus God promised us, "*and I will make you great.*"[42] Rashi explained, "with an upright body." In other words, I will emanate holy effluence into you, and I will put my holy spirit in your midst. Through this, my spirit will draw you to Me, so that you do not cleave to corporeality, God forbid . . .[43]

We have already noted[44] that Meshullam Feibush refers to two purposes for the creation. According to one approach, humankind is meant to detach him/herself from corporeality in order to give God the pleasure of receiving his/her soul as it returns to its divine source in *devequt*. This approach emphasizes the eternal possibility of *unio mystica*. The second approach concerns the historical process of retrieving the holy sparks which became trapped in impure shells as a result of the shattering of the vessels. This second approach, with its basis in Lurianic Kabbalah, also depends on detachment from corporeality. When such detachment is genuine, indulgence in acts that ordinarily involve carnal pleasure can be transformed into a spiritual act. Thus, in this Lurianic context as well, the efficacy of the spiritual intention to refine out the sparks depends on *devequt*. The sparks are released as a result of the inner detachment from the external corporeal pleasure. As consciousness is focused on the divine, the religious emotions of awe and love arise. These emotions ultimately lead to the state of *Ayin* (nothing) where, in choosing the divine, one utterly rejects all desire for corporeal gratification.

> In other words, he understands with a very powerful awareness (*hakarah*) that this pleasure is abhorrent (*nim'as*) and worthless. Of his own will he would not indulge in such corporeal pleasures as eating, drinking, and intercourse. But God compels him [to indulge in such pleasures] because they contain a spark of the Creator's love and delight that have taken on a physical form (*she-nitgashem*) as refuse and matter. [When partaking of] this pleasure, he separates himself from the refuse. Desire for the refuse is abhorrent because of *Hokhmah* (wisdom).[45]

The experience of *devequt* that occurs as a result of detachment from corporeality produces a kind of discriminating wisdom. The inferiority of corporeal pleasure is recognized by one who has tasted the far greater delight of *devequt*.

> It is like bringing a wise person something inferior, such as a coin or garment. Since the item is coated with a very good veneer, a fool would imagine that it is entirely good. But the wise person understands that, [while] the veneer is good, the main part is bad. So through his wisdom he separates the good from the bad.[46]

However, this process is not merely a matter of intention. The sparks can only be retrieved when one is truly indifferent to the desire for sensual pleasure.

> So it is for one who cleaves to the Creator through awe which leads to wisdom, i.e., to the awareness of wisdom that is expanded consciousness (*da'at*),[47] as I will explain below,[48] God willing. This means that [through wisdom], he will truly cleave [to God] in his thought and not merely say that [something] is vanity and worldly pleasure and nevertheless receive pleasure from it. [He should not be like all of those] who say [that they are indifferent], while their hearts delight in evil desires. They long for them, at least while indulging in

them, if not beforehand. That is foolishness. But the basis of wisdom is that it shall really be so. Then through this wisdom he will be able to succeed in refining out [the sparks]. This is alluded to by the Zohar: "everything is refined through wisdom."[49] Sometimes it says "refined in thought."[50]

Meshullam Feibush's demand for a genuine experience of detachment from corporeality is an aspect of his general preference for the mystical experience of *devequt* over the magico-theurgic *praxis* of Lurianic *kavvanot*. The implementation of esoteric knowledge does not in itself accomplish the Lurianic goal of releasing the sparks. What is decisive is the inner state of the person acting. Proximity to God through a heightened sense of awe in the presence of the divine effects the release of the sparks.

This position is an explicit criticism of contemporary, would-be, Lurianic kabbalists and a defense of the Hasidic scale of spiritual values which, possibly under the influence by Cordoverian Kabbalah, particularly emphasizes *devequt* through detachment.[51]

It is not like the foolish ones of our times who learn Kabbalah and think that they can refine out sparks while eating, by means of the *kavvanot* of eating.[52] How is this possible if they are not on the [spiritual] level mentioned above, experiencing the awe that leads to the wisdom that we have mentioned? In their thoughts they think the *kavvanot* and nevertheless take pleasure in [the food]. As the saint, our master and teacher R. Menahem Mendel [of Premishlan] of blessed memory said, from eating *li-shemah* (for the sake of a spiritual purpose) they come to *she-lo li-shemah* (for the sake of their own pleasure), as you know.[53] But the essence is as we have explained.[54]

As we have seen, detachment from corporeality is an indispensable condition for *devequt*. Nevertheless, detachment alone is not sufficient for transforming ordinary creation-centered consciousness into one which is pervaded by awareness of the divine. The attainment of *devequt* also requires a certain contemplative process through which one verifies and gains conviction in his belief in God's presence. One begins with knowledge of God that is received through tradition. However, such knowledge involves no verifying experience. One must come to understand the meaning of God's existence by testing its implications against the evidence of experience. When an unshakable conclusion is drawn that indeed God's presence pervades all existence, then one is said to have attained experiential knowledge of God, *Da'at*. This conclusion is the result of the mind's having become habituated to actually regarding all that it encounters as a manifestation of the Divine. *Da'at* is the transformed consciousness that is the basis of *devequt*.

Whoever wishes to attain *devequt* with God has to have *Hokhmah* (wisdom), *Binah* (understanding), and *Da'at* (experiential knowledge). *Hokhmah* means tradition from one's ancestors and teachers that there is a God in the world. This is merely an undeveloped thought (*maheshevet golem*). After this one has to understand one thing from another. [This involves using his] understanding to constantly consider how God watches over everyone and fills all the worlds. This is considering and understanding: from everything that he sees in the world, he realizes with his understanding and considers that God's power has to be present here. This is [what is meant by understanding [one] matter [from another], specifically, the matter of God from the matter of the world. Later, when this [stage] is completed, the idea (*ziyyur*) [remains] constantly in his consciousness. Now his consciousness is never free of this idea. For during the stage of understanding, the matter is only occasionally in his thought so that he understands and thinks about it a lot. But at other times he only thinks about other matters, God forbid. But when he determines [how] his thought and understanding concerning this [should be] and his mind has great conviction (*ve - nigmar me'od*) concerning it indeed, this [stage] is called *Da'at* (experiential knowledge). For he is constantly connected to this [consciousness] and does everything with it (*ve-holekh tamid ba-zeh*). So, no matter where he looks, he always sees God, as I wrote above[55] in the analogy of the woman's garments.[56]

This experiential knowledge of God cannot be obtained without detachment. For if one lacks detachment, the attractions of creation are liable to distract one from focusing on God in his consciousness. But when one has attained detachment from corporeality, it is possible to keep the mind constantly on God until one's consciousness is entirely accustomed to an awareness of the divine presence.

This is [attained] through detachment from corporeality. Everything depends on this. For, without it, desires will attract him to material things of the world and its vanities, and he will not have *Da'at*. Concerning this, it is written in the *Gemara*, "it is forbidden to have compassion for anyone who lacks *Da'at*."[57] This is [the meaning of the verse], "*know the God of your ancestors.*"[58] Know [God experientially]. Be connected to Him through your knowing Him. Constantly think that God's glory fills the earth. If you think of Him constantly, His existence will be confirmed in your heart, as if you were really seeing Him with your own eyes. Then this is called awareness[59] (*hakarah*).[60]

The experiential knowledge of God that is required for *devequt* is the result of deep contemplation. It is not merely a specific kind of faith or intellectual comprehension of any particular set of theological principles. *Da'at*, implies knowledge in the sense of arriving at a realization and direct experience of God's presence. Thus, it has an immediate and ineffable quality that is lost upon reflection. For this reason it cannot be described to someone who lacks this experience in a way that would adequately convey its nature. A person who possesses *Da'at* understands the great secret of how God can be present in a world which seems to be primarily material because he has located the divine as a living presence within his own consciousness. It is *Da'at*, the experience of God's accessible presence, which is the true basis of all the important mystical texts. Consequently, only those who share the experience of the texts' authors can hope to understand their content. This theme recurs several times in our text. Since it is precisely such existential knowledge of God which is attributed to the Hasidic *Zaddiqim*, the argument supports Meshullam Feibush's central position that the Hasidic leaders are the sole authentic interpreters of the Kabbalah.

> This is what is meant by concealed wisdom. For I heard directly from the Saint, our Master and Teacher, Menahem Mendel [of Premishlan] of blessed memory, that concealed (*nistar*) refers to something that one cannot [quite] explain to someone else. For example, it is impossible to convey the flavor of food to someone who has never tasted [anything like it]. It cannot be made clear to him, [merely] through talking about it. Such a matter is called hidden. Similar, is the matter of love and awe of the blessed Creator. It is not possible to explain such love in the heart to a friend [who has never felt it himself]. Thus it is called concealed. But as to calling the study (*hokhmat*) of Kabbalah concealed,[61] how is it concealed? Whoever wishes has only to pick up a book and learn it. If he cannot understand it, he is an ignoramus. For such a person the *Gemara* and *Tosafot* are also "concealed." But, actually, all the concealed matters in the Zohar and the Lurianic writings are entirely based on *devequt* with the Creator. [They are] for those who are worthy to cleave and gaze at the supernal chariot, like the divine R. Isaac Luria, for whom the pathways of the firmament were illuminated. He constantly traveled through them with his mind's eye, like the four sages who entered *PaRDeS*, as explained by the *Tosafot* in tractate *Hagigah*,[62] and see the Maimonidean glosses.[63]

The basic difference between the consciousness of those who have attained *devequt* and the consciousness of ordinary human beings is that those who possess *Da'at* have become accustomed to the presence of God in their minds through constantly focusing on it. For a person who is limited to ordinary consciousness, God remains a stranger, precisely because so little attention is given over to becoming familiar with the divine presence. Ordinary people may occasionally turn toward God, but these brief and superficial encounters leave no clear and lasting impression. On the other hand, one whose mind is constantly occupied with God, becomes accustomed to the feelings of awe and love which are products of his spiritual interest.

Since these feelings already contain within them a certain sense of divine presence, the more one cultivates them, the more familiar the presence of God becomes.

> However, the difference between someone who constantly thinks of the Blessed Creator and someone who does not [can be explained] through an analogy. It is a bit like someone who for a brief moment (pit'om) saw a stranger from another city and subsequently encounters him again. When he passes by him the second time, he will not recognize him. Even though he saw him earlier, he still will not be able to recognize him. For the [person's] form was only before him for a moment and did not make any [lasting] impression (ve-lo nehkakah berayonav). It did not become embedded in his memory. He cannot cleave to him on the second occasion, since he has formed no familiarity or friendship with him at all. So it is for one who never thinks of the Blessed Creator, or only occasionally when he pleases. He will be entirely unfamiliar with God,[64] love, and devequt. But one who thinks constantly of the Blessed Creator, or, at least, thinks of Him as often as he can, is like someone who has seen a person frequently. [As a result, the person's] form is deeply impressed in his heart. So even when the person is no longer present, his image, which is called reshimu in the Lurianic writings, remains in his heart. The next time he sees him, he is able to recognize him. His longing and love for him is very great and his connection with him (hithabruto) is very firm. [The experience of recognition] depends on the person's quality, whether he is forthright and worthwhile to be connected with, and the amount of time the two have previously been connected. Accordingly, the image, by which he subsequently recognizes him, will be fixed in his heart. This is what is meant by recognition (hakarah).[65] So it is for one who always thinks of God. It seems to him as if he stands before Him constantly, as in the analogy. This is the meaning of awareness [of God] (hakarah).[66]

A consciousness that is both always detached from corporeality and constantly thinking of God is an expanded consciousness. The experiential knowledge (Da'at) of its possessor is complete. It is expanded in the sense that wherever one looks, signs of the divine presence are found. This condition may be contrasted with ordinary limited consciousness which only perceives a creation that is bereft of divinity. In contrast, the possessor of Da'at has immediate awareness of God's presence within creation.

> Consequently, a person whose Da'at is complete has experiential knowledge or awareness of the Creator. As our teachers said, "the patriarch Abraham was aware of (hikir) his creator."[67] Now they meant this literally . . . But all this is only possible when one longs for and thinks constantly of God and is detached from corporeality. Such a person is said to have an expanded consciousness (Da'ato rehavah). He possesses a level of Da'at that "fills all the rooms." As the

verse says, *"and with Da'at the rooms will be filled."*[68] In other words, all the chambers of his heart and all the movements of his limbs turn and are filled with this [consciousness]. All his movements are for the sake of heaven. This is the meaning of [the verse],[69] *"Know Him in all your ways."*[70]

For a person with expanded consciousness, creation is experienced as truly pantheistic. God is not merely an idea that is held constantly in mind, but an in-dwelling reality. Once this presence has been recognized for what is real within an individual's consciousness, it is realized that such a presence is essentially unlimited. It is to be found everywhere.

> Also, no matter what he sees in the world, he sees that everything is God, as we wrote above in the analogy of the woman's garments.[71] Then he really sees that God's Glory fills all the world. This is the meaning of *"the rooms will be filled with Da'at."* In other words, whoever has *Da'at*, sees that all the rooms of the world are filled with God's Glory. So he is able to learn divine wisdom from everything he sees. As the verse says, *"He teaches him from the beasts of the earth."*[72] Then he connects the world to God and God to the world. Upon him the world rests. For the world can only sustain itself through divine effluence (*shif'o yitbarakh*). But who is it who draws forth [the divine effluence] and sustains [the world]? humankind, by means of his *devequt* and enlightenment (*hasagato*).[73]

A person who attains *devequt* in its ultimate sense becomes the link between God and the world. His consciousness overcomes duality, uniting Creator and creation in one continuous whole. Only a person who experiences creation in this way comprehends the meaning of the esoteric teachings. For, as we have seen, Meshullam Feibush, following the teaching of his master Menahem Mendel of Premishlan, considers all of kabbalistic literature to be based on the mystical experience of *devequt*.[74] For those lacking this consciousness, however, creation is experienced in the dualistic way in which it is described in the Bible.

> This [person] is called *Zaddiq* because he has the attribute of connection (*hitqashrut*).[75] For he is connected to God [while] he is in this world. Thus he connects God to this world. [He] is called "covenant" which connects the bestower with the receiver.[76] [He] is referred to in the verse, *"for all is in heaven and earth."*[77] This, the Targum Yonaton translates, "for he connects heaven and earth."[78] It [refers] to the *Zaddiq* who is connected to God, who is called heaven, while he is on the earth.[79]

The consciousness that is described here is indeed extraordinary. It is moreover, the kind of consciousness that the greatest *Zaddiqim* of the past possessed. Meshullam Feibush's mystical analysis of this consciousness is the key which explains the spiritual greatness of both the patriarchs and the talmudic sages.

> Then, before such a person, the whole world is full of God and full of Torah. For [the name] Torah means "teaches (*morah*) what was concealed," as we explained. Every creature teaches such a person wisdom how it was created and with what it was created. Abraham the Patriarch, of blessed memory, grasped this and composed *Sefer Yezirah*. The sages of the Mishnah and Talmud also [attained this level]. But to those who lack this [consciousness], God forbid, the world appears empty and devoid of God. They think that "*God established His throne in heaven*,"[80] as the apparent meaning of scripture suggests.[81]

Detachment from corporeality initially involves resistance to the attractions of corporeal delights which must be rejected as a condition for experiencing delight in serving God. To this extent, it is a value that all should seek to acquire. However, as Meshullam Feibush's presentation of this virtue proceeds, it is ultimately revealed to be an aspect of mystical consciousness rather than a merely ascetic-moral discipline. Detachment from corporeality does not imply total avoidance of carnal matters, but rather indifference to them as sources of pleasure. Such detachment requires a split consciousness. While one part of the self is involved in a physical activity, a deeper part of the soul takes spiritual delight in the concealed divine spark that is being released by the consciousness' attachment to God. However, such attachment also assumes that one has first attained *Da'at*, the ability to enter states of consciousness in which one is aware of God's presence. Detachment and *Da'at*, then, are two aspects of the same phenomenon, *devequt*. The former refers to the fact that fascination for and craving after the sensual delights that creation offers have been transcended. The latter term refers to the redirection of interest and awareness from the corporeal to the divine. Meshullam Feibush does not present this type of transformed consciousness as something to which all can aspire. He represents it as the very special quality which distinguished the legendary heroes of Jewish sacred history, patriarchs, tannaim, amoraim, and so forth.

The association of this extraordinary mystical consciousness with the outstanding figures of Judaism was not meant to encourage the average person to aspire to detachment and *devequt*.[82] On the contrary, by drawing out the full implications of this mystical consciousness—total indifference to the pleasures of creation, on the one hand, and union with God, on the other—Meshullam Feibush effectively established a spiritual basis for religious leadership that was meant to emphasize the superhuman attainment of the religious virtuoso and the spiritual poverty of the average person.

As we have seen in the previous chapter, much of Meshullam Feibush's teaching is based on the position that a human being is absolutely dependent on divine aid for salvation. To grasp the full social significance of Meshullam Feibush's theory of *devequt*, one needs to add one further detail which plays an extremely important role in his argument. Meshullam Feibush's teachers and heroes, the Hasidic leaders of his time, are spiritual *virtuosi* of the very same degree as the outstanding figures of the past. When he asserts that a consciousness characterized by detachment and *Da'at* is the mark of a *Zaddiq*, the person who connects heaven and earth and sustains the world, Meshullam Feibush has in mind, as we shall see, his own teachers.

6

The Remedy:
Prayer, Torah, Sacred Calendar

In each of the three preceding chapters, we have looked closely at one of
the most significant issues which together define the problem of life. According to Meshullam Feibush's theory of creation, there is a divine basis
for all existence. Creation exists because of God's desire to be discovered and
loved by humankind within the material world itself. We saw, however, that
because pride is so deeply rooted in human nature, the ordinary state of
human consciousness, itself, constitutes a virtually overwhelming barrier to
fulfilling this purpose. Indeed, the goal may only be realized as the result of
great spiritual effort towards breaking the power of carnal desires and attaining a mystical consciousness in which the divine presence is experientially known. In reality, human effort is inadequate to the task without divine aid. Only the greatest spiritual adepts have ever reached the goal, *unio
mystica*.

In the following chapter, we shall examine the remedies that are offered
in order to overcome the basic problem of existence, separation from God. In
the broadest sense, the general remedy is the way of Torah, itself, in all that
this concept implies. However, three specific areas are particularly emphasized and discussed in detail by Meshullam Feibush: prayer, Torah study, and
holidays.[1] In each of the following three sections, Meshullam Feibush's
treatment of one of these areas will be analyzed.

The Centrality or Prayer

Meshullam Feibush's religious ideal involves directly experiencing the
presence of God under any and all circumstances, as a result of learning
Torah. He, nevertheless, views prayer as the best of all possible means for attaining the spiritual goal. Genuine *devequt* cannot be attained by someone
whose prayers are performed in a perfunctory manner.

A person cannot obtain [passionate love for God][2] and be attached to it except
by Torah *li-shemah*,[3] and above all [through] prayer in *devequt* and ecstasy

(*u-ve-hitlahavut ha-lev*). . . . But the way they are conducting themselves, underestimating the importance of prayer,[4] how can they have *devequt* with God through the Torah?[5]

Prayer is especially important for several reasons. For one thing, the complete path of spiritual development which is outlined in the classical ethical works requires more time to fulfill than is available to the average person of Meshullam Feibush's day.[6] On the other hand, prayer is performed thrice daily by everyone. However, Meshullam Feibush has deeper reasons for emphasizing prayer which is based in his theory of *devequt*. As already noted, a transformed consciousness that is focused on God at all times is the desired goal. However, the deepest mystical experience of this consciousness occurs during prayer.

> In [the writings of Dov Ber of Mezeritch] the matter of [mystical] awe is treated at length in a number of places. From this awe one can reach genuine love [of God] until his soul cleaves to the daughter of Jacob. . . .[7] When he is constantly in this *devequt* through prayer, Torah, and good deeds, he will reach genuine detachment from corporeality, so that his existence will be canceled in his mind during prayer. He will not sense at all that he is in a body.[8]

Detachment from corporeality can be practiced at all times by great spiritual adepts. However, its ultimate degree, a state in which no awareness of physical existence whatsoever is experienced, can best be realized during prayer. This is the case, because Meshullam Feibush's conception of prayer, following the teachings of Dov Ber of Mezeritch, essentially involves a contemplative ascent to worlds that are beyond the physical.[9] While persistence in learning Torah and doing good deeds in a state of *devequt* may condition the depth of detachment that is achieved during prayer, the less contemplative nature of these activities calls for a state of consciousness in which there is a greater degree of awareness of corporeality and the intellectual and physical faculties that accompany it. However, when prayer has the strictly contemplative goal of intimacy or even union with God, consciousness must be so exclusively focused on the divine that intellectual and physical activities are virtually excluded. The difference in degrees of detachment from corporeality is illustrated by a teaching in the name of Menahem Mendel of Premishlan.[10]

> As the divine Saint, R. Menahem Mendel, of blessed memory, said concerning the statement in the Mishnah, "if he was riding on a donkey, he should dismount and pray."[11] The meaning is, if a person always rides on the donkey[12] and is

always detached from corporeality, nevertheless he is still aware of his corporeality. But during prayer, when holiness increases in the soul through the *mizvot* and words of prayer that are said in awe and love, he can "dismount and pray." He dismounts from the donkey, and is detached from the body completely.[13]

Nevertheless, the ideal state of consciousness which may be reached during prayer is far beyond what can be expected from the average person. For most people the attempt to reach *devequt* through detachment from corporeality requires a constant battle against the evil urge.

But we are totally obligated to encourage each other like wounded soldiers who are losing the war, God forbid, and need to be stout hearted (*le-hithazeq be-lev shalem*). They must hold their positions and avoid fleeing. For flight is the beginning of defeat. Similarly, the war against the [evil] urge is a very great war that constantly gains in intensity.[14]

Prayer is exceptionally important because it constitutes an especially favorable battlefield upon which one can wage the spiritual war. Inherent in the *mizvot* that accompany prayer and the arrangement of the liturgy itself is a source of divine aid that can help one to overcome the evil urge. As such, prayer presents a unique opportunity for realizing one's spiritual objectives.

For does not the essence of the war against the evil urge take place in the service of the heart which is prayer? All day long it is impossible to fight against it because we have no weapons. But during [morning] prayer a person wears a prayer shawl and is crowned by phylacteries. They are the battle garments for [encountering] Satan. So one girds himself in might to conquer his [evil] urge, preparing his soul with pure thought and directing it toward its Creator by means of the double-edged sword, the holy words of the sacrifices and verses of praise.[15] He takes a spear (*RoMaH*) in his hand, the 248 (*ReMaH*)[16] letters of the declaration of unity (*de-qeri'at shema'*) until he knocks down much of [the evil urge's] army. Then it becomes easy for him to direct his soul with a stable thought (*maheshavah nekhona*) during the silent prayer . . .[17]

The accouterments which are worn during prayer act as a kind of armor which offers some protection against the evil urge. The order of the prayers themselves is arranged in a way that progressively distances one from the range of the evil urge's attacks.[18] Having fought the preliminary battles against distraction, one has attained the degree of concentration that is appropriate for the main part of the service.[19]

While divine aid, as we shall see, is especially available during prayer, nevertheless, victory over the evil urge is rarely achieved. The reward for taking up the struggle is not in the ultimate result, but in the measure of the effort itself.

> For most of the people are already caught in the trap of the evil urge so that their urge rules over them. Few are they who wage war against it. Fewer still are those who succeed in their war, vanquishing and destroying [their evil urge]. Most of the Zaddiqim who battle against it do not complete their war. However, this does not deny them their reward, God forbid. God even enjoys this war greatly.[20]

Although even spiritual masters are ultimately unsuccessful in their attempts to overcome their evil urge, God enjoys their efforts. In effect, God delights in human spiritual failures, for each failure indicates an increased effort against the evil urge. Spiritual progress, under these conditions, is measured not so much by one's successes as by the formidability of one's opposition. This dynamic is reflected in the problem of disturbing thoughts that distract one during prayer. The problem is illustrated by an analogy which Meshullam Feibush borrows from Dov Ber of Mezeritch.[21]

> But we can make use of this analogy.[22] [Dov Ber] explained that sometimes the more one makes an effort to pray, the more one is bothered by evil and strange thoughts. It can be compared to the case of a person who has a fine son whose sharp mind comprehends Torah. He enjoys him very much and wishes to have even more pleasure from him. When a great scholar comes as a guest, [the father] asks him to try out this child. So the guest tests him by posing questions. He complicates the plain meaning in order to make it hard for [the son], (le-ha'aqimo) in order to test him. But the youth responds to everything and does not permit himself to be defeated. Thus the father's delight is increased.[23]

Like the father in the analogy, God's delight increases in proportion to the difficulties that have to be overcome. According to Meshullam Feibush's nondual creation myth, everything exists for the sake of God's pleasure. Thus, the evil urge also cooperates in the collective effort of serving God, by complicating one's difficulties so that God's delight may increase.[24] Thus, the proliferation of distracting thoughts during prayer may indicate that one has already succeeded in causing God pleasure through one's prior efforts to concentrate and that an opportunity to increase the divine pleasure has now been produced.

> He gave us one tester, the evil urge, to put us to the test, just as one tests a child in religious practice. He questions and objects and complicates the plain meaning in order to throw us off (le-hasibanu le-derekh aqum). If we are wise and do not permit ourselves to be diverted, then God has great pleasure. So, when the evil urge, who was also created for God's sake, sees that God has pleasure, he

determines (*mekhavven et azmo*) to test and mislead us even more. This is the reason for the proliferation of distracting thoughts during prayer . . .25

In effect, Meshullam Feibush concedes that it is impossible to completely eliminate distracting thoughts. But one should not think that God expects this of him. As long as one does not give up and continues to make an effort, God is pleased.

> Although we are not able to defeat the evil urge with his countless devices for increasing disturbing thoughts that encompass us like hills around a field, nevertheless we should do whatever we can. God will still be pleased, just as in the analogy. If the youth is not able to defeat [the guest] through arriving at the truth, but at least advances some kind of argument, even though he did not arrive at the truth, his father can still derive some pleasure from him. For he reasons, "I see that he at least is doing his best (*mitgabber et azmo*)." But, if when the youth was examined, he had remained dumbfounded and silent as a stone, then the father would be embarrassed by the son, God forbid. For he would see that he has no understanding at all.26

Meshullam Feibush's approach to disturbing thoughts during prayer is a model for dealing with the evil urge in other contexts. Every effort should be made to overcome the negative thought or quality, even though it is impossible to entirely succeed.27

> From this analogy evidence can be derived for subduing the evil urge in several other matters. For this is required in every act and quality. It is true that subduing the evil urge applies above all to prayer, but whenever an evil quality arises, one must subdue it as much as possible. God will derive great pleasure from this, as we have written. For this we were created, even though we cannot complete the battle . . .28

Because of Meshullam Feibush's various religious interests, his position regarding the employment of Lurianic *kavvanot* is somewhat equivocal. Already in the teachings of Dov Ber of Mezeritch a strong critique of the use of Lurianic *kavvanot* is evident.29 This critique is rooted in the commitment to the mystical experience of *devequt* as the primary objective of religious practice. According to the Lurianic method, the goal of prayer is reached through a gradual ascent through all of the supernal worlds which form the kabbalistic cosmos. At each stage of the ascent, a specific *kavvanah* or meditative object must be employed. The *kavvanot* usually consist of some divine name or the combination of letters which unite two divine names. Meshullam Feibush, following a tradition of the Ba'al Shem Tov, presents a version of this practice as it applies to the *mizvah* of ritual immersion.30 However, the practice requires absolute command of all the detailed combinations of letters which must be projected in the mind at the proper time. If the practitioner cannot immediately produce the proper *kavvanah*, his concentration will be interrupted. It is not the inherent magical power of the *kavvanot* alone which accomplishes the spiritual goal. Most important is the *devequt* of the person who applies them.

> But you must learn this [series of *kavvanot*] and rehearse them with a good friend many times until they are fluent in your mind (*be-libeha*) for immediate use (*le-khavven be-rega' 'ahat*). For our minds are too limited to hold all that one must meditate upon (*lekhavven*). Above all [one should concentrate on] *devequt* with God. If we [will primarily] concentrate on the *kavvanot* of [divine] names, we will not be able to concentrate on what should be most important. For this reason, the *kavvanah* has to be produced instantly. Now the most important *kavvanah*, in actuality, should be directed to God who examines what is within (*ha-bohen kelayot ve-lev*), [and knows] if one really attached himself to God without ulterior motives, God forbid. For this one must rehearse the *kavvanot* of [divine] names many times.[31]

Although Meshullam Feibush wholeheartedly endorses the use of *kavvanot* of a Lurianic type when it comes to the *mizvah* of ritual immersion, his advice concerning the need to fully master them before attempting to put them into use already suggests the basis for his reservations concerning their application in prayer itself. More important than any divine name is the need to direct the mind towards the divine presence itself. The mystical experience of *devequt*, involving the inner qualities of awe, love, humility, and the like, takes precedence in religious acts, particularly when speech is involved.[32] When employment of Lurianic or other similar *kavvanot* requires a lot of mental energy and attention, the concentration that is required for *devequt* is liable to be sacrificed. In a case like ritual immersion, it may be possible to combine both. For the *kavvanot* can be memorized without too much difficulty before hand and the amount of time *devequt* must be maintained, in order to complete the *mizvah*, is not prohibitive. However, when it comes to prayer with its extensive liturgy and extremely complex array of *kavvanot*, the task of mastering both the Lurianic practice while at the same time maintaining *devequt* can only be attempted by an unusually gifted pneumatic virtuoso.[33]

Dov Ber of Mezeritch's critique of Lurianic *praxis* reflects a clear preference for the mystical experience of *devequt* and the contemplative annihilation of self-consciousness. This is expressed in a famous analogy that compares the new mystical Hasidic approach to the activity of a thief.[34]

In fact, the essence of *kavvanah* is breaking the heart through submission and *devequt* with God. This is illustrated by an analogy in the writings of the Master R. [Dov] Ber, of blessed memory. For every lock has a key which opens it through turning.[35] According to the lock, so turns the key. But there are thieves who open without a key—they break the lock. Similarly, every concealed matter has a key and that is the *kavvanah* that is directed toward that matter. But the essence of the key is to be like a thief who breaks everything—to thoroughly break the heart through great submission. [Then] the supernal barrier will be broken which blocks a person [from God].[36]

However, Meshullam Feibush cites Dov Ber's analogy not in order to assert that the single *kavvanah* of *devequt* is ultimately as effective as all the Lurianic *kavvanot*. His primary interest lies in demonstrating that what is really operative is not the *kavvanot* themselves, but rather the inner state of the person praying. According to this view, the practice of Lurianic *kavvanot* demands great purity of heart and spiritual development. Lacking these qualities, one cannot even begin to practice the *kavvanot* properly.

In truth, you know that in my youth I learned some *kavvanot*. But [when I pray], I don't concentrate on them at all. For the essence of *kavvanah* is breaking the heart, as we said, and love and awe and honesty (*temimut*) and overcoming [the evil urge]. . . . If we would merit this [level of spiritual development], we could easily practice R. Isaac Luria's *kavvanot*. But, in reality, they were only meant for people like him, or [at least only] a bit less [developed] than he, whose hearts are already pure of all harmful dross that craves all the corporeal pleasures and [also] non-material (*ruhani*) pleasure, like honor. For this includes everything, jealousy, hate, anger, lust, vengeance, etc. For this is readily apparent (*zil qerei bei rav*) in those who approach God in truth and faith and not in a distorted way, God forbid.[37]

Here is no implied critique of the method or basis of Lurianic *praxis*. Indeed, Meshullam Feibush's thought is strongly influenced by Lurianic concepts. It is true that certain aspects of Lurianic Kabbalah, for example, the process of retrieving holy sparks (*berur*), are modified by the emphasis on *devequt*. However, this occurs without any indication that the author is aware that the Hasidic emphasis is in any way greater than Luria's.

Indeed, despite accepting the basic values of Dov Ber's contemplative method of prayer, Meshullam Feibush continued to occasionally employ Lurianic *kavvanot*. His emphasis on *devequt* did not, then, lead him to reject Lurianic *kavvanot* on principle. Rather, his conception of *devequt*, as conditioned by a degree of moral development, which only the great *Zaddiqim* can evince, led him to conclude that he and his readers were simply spiritually unprepared and unworthy of attempting the Lurianic method.

Here a definite tendency towards viewing the potential efficacy of a religious practice as dependent on the appropriateness of the person undertaking it is expressed. Practices, which are by definition inferior, may yet be effective if undertaken sincerely by those who are not capable of acting on a higher level.[38]

> But we are afflicted, from head to toe we lack even one sound limb. "*Every head is ill and every heart is sick.*"[39] Our hearts are not pure of corporeal desires at all, and certainly not from the subtler desires. For we enjoy and delight in being praised and celebrated and hate reproach. Thus we are far from God and cannot turn our minds to Him at all, not even in the simple sense (*ki-feshuto*). So how can we intend *kavvanot* that stand in the upper reaches of the world? For this reason, I choose, for myself, to have in mind one *kavvanah*, to turn the heart to God as much as possible, in accordance with the words and phrases [of the liturgy]. Nevertheless, occasionally, when I am able to instantly intend some easy *kavvanah*, i.e., some [divine] name, without effort (*she-lo le-troah al zeh*) and without diverging from the true *kavvanah*, then it is fine.[40]

Meshullam Feibush's acceptance of the Lurianic system is apparent from two other considerations. First, he recommends employing the *kavvanot* when *mizvot* are observed which involve action rather than speech. In these cases, as in that of the ritual immersion, the possibility of the mind being distracted from its concentration on the divine presence is greatly reduced. Second, although Lurianic *kavvanot* are so difficult to employ during prayer, it is worthwhile to learn them. Familiarity with the theoretical basis of this *praxis* will inspire one to pray. Nevertheless, an approach to prayer is recommended that is, at least to some degree, more pietistic than kabbalistic. God is not simply compelled to respond to prayer because of human mastery of specifically theurgic practices. God does what is necessary at a level beyond human understanding in response to sincere supplication.

> But when it comes to *mizvot* involving action, like phylacteries and *sukkah*, waving the four species, and blowing the ram's horn, it is good to intend the *kavvanot* of [divine] names. For in such cases, there is only action and no speech. But when it comes to [*mizvot* that involve] speech, such as prayer, there are so many *kavvanot* that must be [mentally] intended along with what is said, that it is practically impossible to speak [the words at the same time] without great effort. How can one neglect the plain meaning [of the liturgy] in favor of the [esoteric] *kavvanot*? Nevertheless, it is worthwhile to learn the *kavvanot* of all the prayers. For thus the soul will be aroused when it knows how far the words [of prayer] reach. For they have a very great and awesome effect above (*metaqqenim tiqqun gadol me'od*). Thus through [knowing] this we will be

greatly inspired to direct our minds and to focus all our powers on intending the direct *kavvanah*. Our mouths and hearts will be united (*shavim*) in love and awe. Thus God will accept our prayers. He will cause them to have the necessary effect (*ve-yif'al ba-hem ha-pe'ulah ha-zerikhah*), even though we do not know what we are doing. [This is indicated in the verse,] "*establish for us the work of our hands.*"[41] As written in the Zohar,[42] "establish it [means] cause it to accomplish your rectification (*ve-ateqqen tiqqunekha*) . . ."[43]

What we have, then, in Meshullam Feibush's position regarding the Lurianic *kavvanot*, is an approach to prayer that continues to be based on the theory of the *kavvanot*. The theurgic effects of prayer which are described in kabbalistic literature indeed occur. However, they occur through God's hidden powers as a result of faith. This is not an approach that is directed to sacred technicians who know how to produce the desired effects. Rather, it is addressed to those who are acutely aware of their spiritual shortcomings and their need for divine aid. It is an approach which might well appeal to someone who is in awe of the spiritual *virtuosi* and yet incapable of aspiring to be one of them. For, according to Meshullam Feibush's approach, even if one cannot practice the esoteric theurgic techniques, his prayers may still be effective, if they are offered with great concentration and sincerity. This unusually optimistic position became typical of Hasidism. The earlier propagandistic literature of Kabbalah tended to deny value to the religious efforts of those who do not possess esoteric knowledge. Here a way was found which did hold out hope for the average believer.[44]

Ideally, the experiential qualities, which should be present during prayer, are the inner states which indicate *devequt*. However, according to Meshullam Feibush's approach, even those who do not succeed in experiencing these emotional signs of intimacy with God, can offer prayers which are accepted. The important thing is that the mind be concentrated on the words of the liturgy that are being spoken and not thinking about other matters. As long as this is the case, the prayer may reach its destination. However, if *devequt*, as indicated by the qualities of love and awe, does not accompany the prayer, it cannot ascend on its own power. The hopes for such a prayer depend on its being offered by someone who is spiritually connected to the great *Zaddiqim*.

[Because of the earlier stages of the service,] it will be easy for him to direct his soul with a stable mind during the whispered prayer, so that thought and utterance will be united. Even though he is not able to experience awe and love [of God], the words of his prayer ascend as a result of the spiritual bonding he affects through saying, "I hereby accept upon myself the *mizvah* of '*and you shall love your fellow as yourself.'*"[45] Thus he connects himself in complete love with the holy souls of the generation's *Zaddiqim* whose images he knows.[46]

A person who cannot independently offer a prayer in a deep state of *devequt*, needs to rely on his great faith in the spiritual power of the *Zaddiqim*. Since their prayers are offered in *devequt*, they are sure to reach their destination. If one can manage to connect his prayer to those offered by the *Zaddiqim*, his prayer can then ascend along with theirs. This spiritual bonding is accomplished through a visualization technique that, while unusual in the history of Judaism, is comparable to meditative practices that are well known to the historian of religions.[47]

> He should imagine [the images of the *Zaddiqim*] before him at the time [that he affirms the *mizvah* of loving your fellow] in his mind. For this is a powerful spiritual practice (*segulah*) and has great benefit, as explained in *Hesed le-Avraham*.[48]

The practice of *hitqashrut* (spiritual bonding), seems to have been adopted from the literature which popularized Safedian Kabbalah. It was indeed practiced by Meshullam Feibush's principle teacher, Yehiel Mikhel of Zlotchov.

> In fact, I heard from the Saint, the divine Master, our Teacher and Rabbi, R. Yehiel Mikhel [of Zlotchov], . . . that he said before every prayer, "I connect myself with all of Israel, whether greater than myself or on a lower level than myself. The benefit of spiritual bonding with those who are greater, [is] that through them, my thought will be elevated and the benefit of bonding with those who are less great, [is] that they will be elevated through me . . ."[49]

Although it does not specifically mention the unusual visualization technique, *hitqashrut* is recommended in another source that derives from R. Abraham Hayyim of Zlotchov, who was also an important desciple of Yehiel Mikhel. In a manner similar to Meshullam Feibush, this text, does not recommend general use of the Lurianic *kavvanot*, but does express great respect for those who can employ them.

> . . . before prayer, a person should connect himself with the whole of Israel and especially with those who know the *kavvanot* of prayer. . . . As I have been taught to say before every prayer. . . . I hereby send my prayer from here to the land of Israel . . . with all the prayers of the prayer houses and study houses and the unifications of all Israel and especially with Your sons who know the

kavvanot of prayer and its secrets. With this intention, I pray in awe and love and love and awe in the name of all Israel. Thus the great ones have instructed me to say before every prayer . . .[50]

Hitqashrut seems to have been practiced particularly among the school of the Maggid of Zlotchov in Galicia.[51] Meshullam Feibush offers an explanation of how this spiritual bonding can occur. It is essentially no different from other forms of love which spiritually connect people even when they are apart.

> When, for example, a person is aroused to love his son, even though the son is not present, the father's love burns in his heart. That aroused love connects the soul of both of them in that moment, even though they are separated from each other. [There are] two reasons [for this]. First, when it comes to non-physical matters (*be-ruhaniyut*) distance is not relevant . . . Second, and this is connected to the first, love can only occur between two people who know each other, who have seen each other face to face . . . Then when they see each other and are joined together in love, each one's image is inscribed in the other's thought, and every thought is a complete structure.[52]

The problem is that people tend to think that only what occurs in the physical universe is real. However, according to Meshullam Feibush's idealist acosmic cosmology, the truth is exactly the opposite.[53] The less corporeal a phenomenon is, the more it is real and the greater its potential impact. In reality, the corporeal world depends on concealed spiritual forces for its existence.

> Although it seems that whatever is corporeal is real (*hu yesh*) while noncorporeal things (*ve-ha-ruhaniyut*) seem to lack reality (*she-eyn bo mamash*), all this falsehood is [only] from our point of view. For we are material creatures and constantly concerned with corporeality. But, in truth, it is the opposite. For the spiritual sustains the physical, and without it, the [physical] would be nothing. Now that spiritual force (*ruhaniyut*) which is not in a body is greater in quantity and power than [a spiritual force] which is in a body. For the one in the body is exhausted by the presence of its opposite which is corporeality. Consequently, a person's power of speech is more effective than the power of action. For it extends beyond human corporeality and becomes a spiritual force without a body. . . . Therefore, how much more so in the case of thought, which is more spiritual. It possesses more and greater power. As we know, in thought a person can reflect on his wisdom. All the work that he has in the world can be contained in a person's thought. For it is a power which is higher than the body. It begins in the body and continues beyond it in every place where a person wishes to extend it.[54]

Hitqashrut is possible because of the vast power of the mind. Separation in space does not prevent it from being joined to any object of which it has formed a distinct impression. Moreover, the nonphysical mental image is more real than the physical form. As long as one has seen a true *Zaddiq* and thus managed to implant in his mind a distinct impression of the *Zaddiq*'s countenance, he can unite his soul with the *Zaddiq*'s by recalling the *Zaddiq*'s image in his mind. The love one bears for the *Zaddiq* is the power which unites the two souls in this mental act.[55]

> Consequently, this mental image is the spiritual form (*hu' qomah ve-ruhaniyut*) of that person which he saw, only it was concealed within him. When love is aroused for him, that love connects and unites him with the image that is in his heart. And the *gematria*[56] for love is one . . .[57]

Knowledge of the *Zaddiqim* and the intention to bind one's prayer to theirs is sufficient for establishing *hitqashrut*. However, more spiritual effort is still required if that prayer is to be effective. One must indeed imbue the prayer with vitality. This is accomplished, as we have seen, through the effort that is made in order to unite thought and utterance. When the mind is fully involved in the words which are being spoken, prayer is offered in a state of sincerity (*temimut*). It is this quality which determines the viability of the prayer.

> Consequently, a person [should first] connect himself with the *Zaddiqim* and with all Israel whose hearts are sincere. Then, when he prays, he may only have in mind the simple meaning of the words,[58] concentrating exclusively on [the words of prayer] that he expresses in the form of its letters.[59] Nevertheless, if he has attained a state of sincerity (*be-temimut*) through gaining control of himself, although his [evil] urge [may continue] to trouble him with other motivations, he breaks it as much as he can. He compels himself to think sincere thoughts directed to God. Even in so slight a [degree of intentional] thought as this,[60] his words contain a bit of vitality. For the vitality of an utterance depends on the thought [behind them] and the vitality of thought is [measured by] love and awe. So if the utterance contains a bit of vitality, it can be elevated. On its own [such a prayer] would not be able to ascend, since it lacks the wings of love and awe with which [prayer] flies. Nevertheless, it may ascend through being included with the [prayers of] *Zaddiqim*. However, if, God forbid, the utterance is not accompanied by [intentional] thought, [then] it is dead, "*and the dead will not praise YaH.*"[61]

The emotional components of *devequt*, love and awe, are like wings which cause a prayer to ascend. When one cannot manifest these qualities, he must depend on the spiritual power of *Zaddiqim* who pray in *devequt*, if he wants his prayer to ascend. Nevertheless, as long as one has at least offered a sincere prayer, through mentally intending the words that he utters, and has bound himself to the *Zaddiqim*, they will see that the prayer is elevated.

> I heard a fine analogy concerning this . . .[62] A large party of people are traveling by foot to some destination and one of them becomes ill, God forbid. Although they have to travel on, they certainly will not leave him to perish there. If he is unable to walk, they will take hold of him in their arms and bring him along. But it is otherwise if, God forbid, one of them should die. What [good] is a corpse to them? They simply bury him there. So the moral is, when the utterance and the mind are united [in prayer], even without fear and love, it is like a sick person who has a bit of vitality. The *Zaddiqim* will aid him, as we said. But, if his thought is not focused on the utterance at all, [then the prayer] is treated like a corpse, God forbid. They throw it into the garbage.[63]

According to Meshullam Feibush, all prayers nevertheless have some value, since a divine command is fulfilled through offering them. All prayers are ultimately a source of sustenance for some aspect of the cosmos. However, one should aspire to offer as lofty a prayer as possible. Prayers that entirely lack vitality cannot ascend and sustain any aspect of the higher worlds. They become sustenance for the evil forces which are likened to dogs.[64]

> [Issachar Ber] also said that if, God forbid, [the prayer is like a corpse], nevertheless, one still does the King's will, [even if] it is not acceptable (*efshar*) at all.[65] For the King needs dogs also and is responsible for their sustenance. But this [comes from] the prayers which are completely rejected. However, it is not for us to provide the portion of dogs, better for us to give sustenance to the King himself or at least to His close servants, the holy worlds.[66]

As we have seen, Meshullam Feibush's theory of *devequt* has as its ultimate purpose the goal of providing God with pleasure through returning the emanated divine forces from their state of concealment in corporeality to their spiritual root.[67] Meshullam Feibush's theory of prayer operates according to the same principle. Divine vitality has been emanated into the letters of prayer and can be returned to its source in the Godhead when prayer is offered in *devequt*. The process by which God infuses vitality into the letters is analogous to human speech. Just as human speech, issuing from deep within the soul, produces words composed of invisible letters, so the creative power of God's will expresses itself through divine utterances that cannot be perceived.[68] Because this divine vitality is present in the letters of the liturgy and Torah, prayer and study are the primary means of realizing *devequt*.

But how is it possible to come close [to God]? It is by means of the letters of Torah and prayer. For God created the world with the twenty-two letters of the Torah as is explained in the *Sefer Yezirah*.[69] As for the matter of the letters of God, it is, *mutatis mutandis,* analogous to speech which issues forth from the human mouth which is divided into five sources [of speech]. From [these five sources], twenty-two letters [are produced]. When a person speaks, the entire utterance is produced from his soul as a spiritual emanation. The entire soul goes out in the utterance, just as the verse says, *my soul went out in his speaking*.[70] As written in *Reishit Hokhmah*, Gate of Holiness,[71] it is like kindling one candle from another. Even myriad candles can be kindled from one candle and yet the candle remains in its place. So it is with the breath that emerges from a person through speech. Therefore, speech is an emanation from the soul. But it is the last stage. For first came the thought, [the letter] *Yod*, [then] reflection (*hirhur*), [the letter] *Hey*, next the pure voice, [the letter] *Vav*, and after this the five sources of speech, the second *Hey*.[72] It is all a spiritual vitality of the human soul (*ha-nefesh ha-medabberet*).[73]

When a person speaks, he/she externalizes what was contained in his/her soul. In the same way, a divine element or force that was concealed within God is emanated during the process of creation which is analogous to speech. Although these forces are completely spiritual and cannot be perceived, they are contained within the letters of sacred writ. The letters, then, operate as vessels in which the divine forces can be apprehended in much the same way that the spiritual soul is only discernible when contained by the body.

Now I cannot write to you concerning the forms of the letters of thought, reflection, and speech. For I know nothing of them at all and such matters cannot be written. But in general terms, the matter is as follows. Just like a human mouth, [divine] speech which is called the mouth of God, emanated vitality in the form of ten utterances through which the world was created. These utterances contained all creatures and the entire Torah. For the Torah is contained in ten commandments that parallel the ten utterances, as is known.[74] The form of this vitality is not known to us at all, just as we do not know the form of the letters that are produced through a person's breath. One cannot see any image of them and they certainly [cannot be represented] in thought. Only, God gave us a form [for representing them] by means of writing the twenty-two letters. Nevertheless, this [written] form does not exist above at all, except by way of analogy, just as there is absolutely no resemblance between the form of the body and the soul. Rather, the body has a form and the soul enlivens that body. So it seems that the soul also has a form. But without the body, the soul has no form at all. It is [entirely] spiritual in essence.[75]

Just as God has chosen the form of the human body as the appropriate vessel for containing the soul, the written forms of the letters are divinely selected because of their suitability for containing the spiritual forces.

God, in His wisdom, desired precisely this form of the body, so that the spiritual entity that He created to enliven it could rest upon it. So it is in the case of the letters. God gave us precisely the form that His concealed and primordial wisdom desired. In each letter, one particular and necessary spiritual force (ruhaniyut ve-hiyyut) is contained. Through the combining of letters to form a word, one complete entity [is formed].[76]

Although the written forms of the letters are the perfect vessels for the twenty-two spiritual forces, they do not automatically contain them. The letters have to be filled with these forces through the holy intention of the person who writes them.

Thus there is a reason for writing a Torah scroll and [the parchments inserted in] phylacteries and mezuzot with the proper kavvanah. [They must be written] in a state of holiness, according to the law of our holy Torah, so that the spiritual force (ruhaniyut) will rest on the bodies of the written letters.[77]

The object of prayer is to draw down the supernal divine forces, or ruhaniyut,[78] into the letters of the liturgy and then to cause it to return to its source. This process is activated when one prays with devequt.

So when a person gives utterance to the letters, [he] activates (mena'ne'a) the supernal vitality. When he cleaves to God with an undivided mind (be-maheshaveto bi-temimut),[79] he returns the vitality that emanated down from the supernal thought until it reached [the level of] speech and was placed in the person's mouth. Through his longing for God with the words of the prayer, he causes the letters to fly to their root, if he manages [to pray] with a pure thought in love and awe. This is called female waters. It [occurs] if he is able to draw ruhaniyut from above into his speech, to cause the letters to fly above, as written in Pardes and quoted in the introduction to the prayer book, Sha'arey Shamayim [sic]. But, if not, as long as his thought, at least, is pure, this is also called uniting, for he unites the utterance with the thought.[80]

The determining factor in prayer, then, is the extent to which the mind has been compelled to focus itself on the words being offered in prayer. This emphasis, which diverges somewhat from the teachings of Dov Ber,[81] follows the position that is presented in Isaiah Horowitz's earlier commentary on the prayer book, Sha'ar ha-Shamayim.

As it is written in the prayer book, Sha'arey Shamayim [sic], this is why prayer is called work (avodah). It is a great work to gain control of a mind that is troubled with worldly concerns and to bring it under the domination of the intention to concentrate on the words of the prayer. Indeed, this requires great power . . .[82]

If one is successful in this effort to compel the mind to focus on prayer, a measure of the concentration acquired remains even after prayer is completed. It is this residue of the prayer state that indicates that the prayer has been accepted.

> For a sign that prayer was a bit acceptable before God is submission, if after prayer, submission remains in the heart. This is called the residue (reshimu) of prayer which is mentioned in the Lurianic teachings. After prayer an impression of the brains remains.[83] In other words, after prayer the intellect cannot remain as dominant in the mind as it is during prayer, in each person according to his measure. Nevertheless, the impression remains as submission and humility. But, if, God forbid, this is not the case, then certainly [the prayer] is not desirable at all . . .[84]

Although Meshullam Feibush's approach to prayer is very much informed by kabbalistic sources, it is clear that his real interest is not in the theosophic-theurgic aspects which are emphasized there, but rather a more pietistic inderstanding of berur. The crux of his attention is focused on what happens within the human soul. Indeed the supernal kabbalistic processes are but a reflection of the process of self-purification that is undertaken through the struggle against the evil urge.

> The process of retrieving (berur) holiness from evil appears entirely in man. Just as one purifies himself from the evil urge and negative qualities, so his portion in the supernal worlds, the holy, is drawn out from the shell. The essence of the purification (berur) occurs during prayer. For then, if he merits, he can purify his thought which is the essence of the soul. Then, immediately, the utterance will be clear and pure and clean of all dross of evil thought. If he does not merit this during the entire prayer, he will merit it in some of it. It depends entirely on the hour, time, and person.[85]

Torah Study as an Extension of Prayer

Early Hasidism's attitude toward Torah study and the manner in which it was performed was one of the movement's most important defining features.[86] The Hasidic attitude did not emphasize the intellectual aspects of study. Rather, it saw merely intellectual efforts as potentially harmful to Hasidism's central goal, devequt. The danger lay in the tendency towards pride that typically resulted from intellectual accomplishments. Since pride was conceived as antithetical to attaining an awareness of God's presence, learning for the sake of intellectual rewards or honor was condemned. Instead, an attitude towards learning was developed which was very much influenced by the Hasidic theory of prayer. Essentially, Torah study and prayer shared the very same goal, *devequt*, and were explained by means of the same theory of *ruhaniyut* of the letters. This was particularly evident in Meshullam Feibush's writings.

> The most important intention during study is just like the [fundamental] intention during prayer. For the soul cleaves to and approaches God by means of the letters of the Torah and the letters ascend to God, through the breath [of the person uttering them]. He receives great pleasure from this.[87]

The inner experiential qualities which characterize *devequt* during prayer are also required during Torah study. Although theories of *devequt*, which were developed in Safed during the sixteenth century, suggest that Torah Study in itself implies attachment to God,[88] Meshullam Feibush denies this. *Devequt* during Torah study occurs only when love and awe of God are experienced. This requirement marks an important distinction between the early Hasidic approach to Torah study and that of certain contemporary kabbalists.[89]

> In truth, [there are] many of our people who are considered by themselves and others to be great sages in the revealed and concealed Torah. They imagine that they are in awe [of God] and [that they possess] all the other qualities, imagining that they have attained a bit of Torah and awe. But, in reality, they still have not merited the least knowledge of the Torah of God. [For it] is called Torah because it teaches (*Morah*) what is hidden, namely, God. Just as the divine saint, R. Menahem Mendel [of Premishlan] of blessed memory, said perceptively, concerning the verse, "*the Torah of YHVH is perfect*,"[90] [it means] that the Torah which is of YHVH is perfection itself. For as yet, not a single person has even touched the tip of it. For they learn only the external part of the Torah. It is not in their minds to cleave to God and to be a chariot for Him, to be in awe of Him, and to love Him by means of the Torah. . . . They do not know at all what *devequt* with God is, nor what love and awe are. For they think that the learning which they are doing itself constitutes *devequt* and love and awe . . .[91]

Devequt, then, does not automatically occur during Torah study. Rather, it is both the ideal and goal of learning. Torah study should be undertaken primarily in order to become a vehicle upon which God may rest and not in order to seek wisdom for oneself.

> In truth, they only learn in a perfunctory manner in order to become wise. Concerning this, the verse says, *woe [unto those who are] wise in their [own]*

eyes . . ."[92] This, the Zohar calls, kindness that they do for themselves,"[93] as is known. But the essence of [learning] Torah for its own sake is to reach *devequt* with Him who is hidden within it. As we said, to be a chariot for Him.[94]

Torah study, then, like prayer, depends on directing one's mind to God. There are, therefore, two aspects to the process of learning, one exterior and the other interior. The words of the lesson are not merely material to be learned and applied. Although this function is not totally denied, the words serve a more important function. They are external garments or vessels within which the inner experience of the divinity can take place.

It says in the Midrash, to what may a disciple of the sages be compared? To a bell of gold and a clapper of pearls . . [95] Now [Dov Ber] said [it refers to] one who learns Torah *li-shemah*.[96] Cleaving to God, all the stirrings of the mind (*kol hegeyon libo*) are constantly directed to God. As the verse says, "*this Torah scroll shall not depart from your mouth, and you shall meditate upon Him day and night*,"[97] precisely upon Him![98] In other words, your thoughts will be upon God. For He is concentrated in *ruhaniyut* of the breath of Torah that comes out of a person's pure mouth, if he merited to purify his mouth and heart so that it will be a chariot for God. Consequently, the *devequt* with which one cleaves to God is the inner part [of Torah study] and the words of Torah which one learns constitute the outer part and garment for this *devequt*, and this is correct.[99]

In Torah study, motivation is all important. Any purpose which is present within the mind of the person learning other than the desire to cleave to God is unworthy. As in the case of prayer, *devequt* during Torah study requires the overcoming of all temporal desires and especially pride.

[However, it is not proper] if his love and desire are not for God, but he still cleaves to ephemeral desires, and craves even the least bit of honor. Then the honor is the internal part of his thought, and the [words of] Torah are external to the thought. How shameful when one renders words of Torah a garment for the inner folly of his thought. Thus the Midrash said, "to what may a sage's disciple be compared? To a bell of gold."[100] For, as is known, the bell is the external part and the clapper is the inner part[101] that reverberates within like a clapper within a bell. The Torah is called gold, according to [the verse], "*her garment is golden filigrees*."[102] In other words, the verse says, "*the princess's glory*"[103] which is awe of God and the presence of His *Shekhinah*, '*is within*,'[104] in the heart of all Israel. "*Filigrees of gold*," which are the letters of the Torah, are her garment and "*a clapper of pearls*," refers to *devequt* with God [which] is called "*a clapper of pearls*." For *devequt* with God is only possible through true humility. For "*YHVH abhors all proud of heart*."[105] So the verse says, "*and to the*

humble, He bestows grace."[106] Pearls are an expression (*mesugal*) of grace.
Thus [the Midrash] said *"a clapper of pearls"* which means this *devequt* which
is pleasant with grace.[107]

The problem of pride and humility is a central issue in Meshullam
Feibush's thought.[108] It particularly concerns him in regard to Torah study.
For he feels that his generation suffers from an excessive emphasis on acquiring intellectual knowledge of Torah at the expense of piety and experiential knowledge of God. Learning Torah is an essential remedy for overcoming pride, for it results in greater *devequt* and awareness of God.
However, it is only effective to the extent that one has first purified himself
from negative qualities.[109]

> By means of the Torah one can acquire effacement and humility. As our sages of
> blessed memory said, "and it clothes him with humility."[110] But they said that
> one of the ways of acquiring Torah is through humility.[111] Consequently, hu-
> mility comes first. Now, in reality, there is humility as a precondition and hu-
> mility as a result. . . . But, above all, Torah study for its own sake requires *deve-*
> *qut* with God and to surrender and efface oneself before Him and before all. So
> the more a person learns Torah, the more he will cleave to God and come close
> to Him, and the more meek of spirit he will become. "Spirit" here refers to
> [one's personal] will. His [personal] will will be meek.

Since Torah study increases *devequt*, it reduces one's sense of self-importance,
which is replaced by knowledge of God. Nevertheless, scholars who lack
character development tend to become even more haughty as a result of
their proficiency in Torah study.

> Thus one may understand a saying of our rabbis of blessed memory, "whoever
> teaches Torah to an unworthy student is like [a person] who hurls a stone at
> Mercury.[112] As it is written, *'giving honor to a fool is like wrapping a stone in*
> *sling.'*[113] At first glance, this comparison seems strange. Why precisely this
> analogy and not another? But, in reality, it seems the Gemara had this in mind.
> For it is known[114] that whoever exposes himself before [Ba'al] Pe'or and hurls a
> stone at Mercury is guilty [of idol worship] even though he meant to scorn [the
> idol]. For this is the manner in which it is worshipped. Although he intended to
> scorn it, it receives honor from [his action] and is enhanced, since thus it is wor-
> shipped. It is very similar if a person teaches Torah to an unworthy student. The
> intention is to cause him to cleave to God and to remove pride from his heart,
> . . . just as our rabbis of blessed memory said, "and it clothes him with humil-
> ity."[115] Consequently, one intends to make the student more humble through
> this. But, if he is an unworthy student, then, God forbid, he will acquire more
> pride from his studies. For he wants to be [known as] a scholar. His intention is

not at all for the sake of heaven, but merely for his own sake, so that he will become advanced in Torah, sharp and erudite. Consequently, although his teacher intends to humble his heart through the words of Torah that he teaches him, he puffs himself up through this, [so, it is] precisely like one who hurls a stone at Mercury . . .[116]

As we have seen, Meshullam Feibush repeatedly stresses the rabbinic ideal of Torah study for its own sake. His mystical interpretation of this concept is presented by means of several puns on the Hebrew form of the expression, li-shemah. Although the conventional meaning is "for its own sake," the Hebrew can also be taken to mean "for its name," and "for the sake of Hey," that is, God. By utilizing both of these meanings, Meshullam Feibush is able to make the rabbinic ideal of Torah study imply devequt, or discovery of the hidden divine immanence.

He gave us His Torah to contemplate for the sake of God (li-shemah), in order to cleave to God who is concealed in His Torah. As it says in the Zohar, "it is called Torah because it teaches and reveals that which was concealed."[117] For God is concealed and revealed. [He is] concealed from every eye and revealed in the hearts of those that desire [Him], who constantly long and search their minds and hearts in order to cleave to Him by means of His Torah and commandments. Through this, God, who is concealed in His Torah, which is His name,[118] reveals Himself in the hearts of His people. So [when] the heart most feels His love and awe, this is called Torah for its name (li-shemah). Like its name, Torah, it will teach (Moreh) and reveal to them the concealed, which is God.[119]

Another meaning of li-shemah indicates a level of Torah study which is even beyond delighting in its pleasures. This ideal is connected to the basic kinship that exists between the holy human soul and the Torah. Both are essentially emanations from the same divine source. Thus, the soul and the Torah can be considered as brother and sister. One should love the Torah, then, for its own sake, that is, as a natural result of this relationship which is permanent and not dependent on any particular charms that the Torah might possess.

In truth, [there are] many, even the most advanced (sheleymim) who desire the Torah and meditate on it day and night. They are sure that they are cleaving to God and to His Torah and delighting in its study more than in all matters of this world. Thus they suppose that they are fulfilling the verse, "say to wisdom, you are my sister."[120] But the light has yet to shine upon them. For why did the verse make this comparison to wisdom, saying, "you are my sister," implying that he should cleave to her in love? Why didn't it compare wisdom to a wife, as it is written, "*a valorous wife . . . ?*"[121] But the meaning is that there is [one kind of] delight between a man and wife and [another kind of] delight [in the love] a brother [bears for his] sister. The difference is that one depends on something which is ephemeral (*batel*). Later, if they hate each other, they can separate with a bill of divorce. But the other does not depend on something [external]. It is the necessary result of their being born from the power of one father and mother.[122]

The two levels of Torah study can be compared to the two types of love. A person who loves Torah study because of its pleasantness is like a person who loves because of the attractiveness of his spouse. However, when one's love for Torah study is based on the appreciation of its true nature, this is like the love between two siblings.

> This applies to wisdom. For it is possible to love the Torah because of the pleasure that comes from learning wisdom constantly and reveling in its beauty. This is similar to the pleasure a man derives from an attractive wife. It depends on an ephemeral matter. But true love of wisdom has to be due to its being breath from the mouth of God. It is a part of His very essence. As it is written, "*For YHVH will grant wisdom from His mouth, knowledge and understanding.*"[123] We, [His] sons, are emanated from His will. Consequently, we are brothers to His will and to wisdom, and it is impossible to separate from it.[124]

God's wisdom, the Torah, and the holy soul are both emanations from the same divine source which were originally united in a state of *devequt* within God. Their separation is the result of creation. Nevertheless, the intrinsic kinship between the Torah and holy soul guarantees that a permanent affinity will continue to exist between them even when they are separated. This natural love can be realized through Torah study which becomes a means of returning to the primordial condition of *devequt*.

> For this love, Torah study is required. Although we have been distanced from this [primordial] *devequt* through being clothed in a body and are guilty of sins and transgressions, nevertheless, we must break our whorish heart and return and cleave to God through the kinship that exists between us and [God's] wisdom. Through it we can reach our Father in heaven.[125]

Devequt during Torah study only occurs when it is intended and consciously pursued. Even if ulterior motives for learning are not present in the mind of a scholar, as long as *devequt* is not intentional, it must be presumed that he is not learning *li-shemah*.

In truth, whenever one learns in order to acquire pleasure, honor, and pride from the Torah, even though unaware of [these motivations], nevertheless, they are presumed to be present. As the Rav, Our Master and Teacher, Rav Menahem Mendel of Premishlan of blessed memory said, "presumably it was not *li-shemah*." As the Gemara ruled concerning a bill of divorce, it has to be explicitly intended for the woman named (*she-zarikh lomar li-shemah*).[126] One has to make this matter explicit and to be constantly thinking of it [while preparing the bill of divorce]. How much more so in the case of our holy Torah. If the person does not crave God as much as is fitting, and, God forbid, forgetting God in his heart, does not fulfill the saying in the *Shulhan Arukh* concerning the verse],[127] "*I place YHVH before me constantly*,"[128] but [merely] learns in a perfunctory way, then this is presumably not *li-shemah*.[129]

Meshullam Feibush strongly admonishes his readers against the dangers and even impropriety of studying Torah for the sake of the pleasures of learning. He goes so far as to compare someone who learns for the sake of pleasure to an adulterer who takes illicit pleasure from a woman's body.[130] Nevertheless, he concedes that Torah study is an inherently enjoyable activity. Ultimately, his admonition is only intended to emphasize that the highest motivation for learning is for the sake of *devequt* and not for pleasure.

> In truth, it is impossible not to receive pleasure from Torah [study], for it is sweeter than honey. However, although this is permitted for us, we should not learn because of this, but, rather, because *it is a pure divine utterance*,[131] and we are siblings, our Father's children.[132]

Meshullam Feibush's understanding of Torah study as primarily a basis for attaining *devequt*, rather than a means of acquiring information, applies to all aspects of the traditional curriculum. The proper study of all texts and subjects that are included under the general heading of Torah enhances one's ability to serve God.

> For [in] our entire Torah, both written and oral,[133] there is not a single word or even letter which has any other purpose than [to indicate] how to serve God. For that is the reason [the Torah] was given. It is called Torah because it indicates the way in which to go. Even in the laws concerning financial transactions and the other laws that do not seem to have any implication [in this regard], if it is lacking, the problem is yours.[134] But whoever serves God perfectly has secrets of the Torah revealed to him. These are secrets concerning how all six hundred thirteen *mizvot* can become means of serving God, even when it is not possible to fulfill them, as in the case of *mizvot* which depend on [being in] the Land of Israel. . . Thus the Zohar calls the six hundred thirteen *mizvot*, six hundred thirteen pieces of advice."[135] For they advise a person how to cleave to his Creator . . .[136]

Furthermore, the study of both exoteric and esoteric texts has the same purpose. There is no distinction in this regard between the study of legal texts and the mystical literature of the Kabbalah.

> I heard the saint, the Rav, the Maggid [Yehiel Mikhel of Zlotchov], say that all his life, it never made any difference to him whether he was studying Gemara or Kabbalah. [In every case], he never saw anything other than how to serve God. Indeed it is so.[137]

Nevertheless, there is a distinction between exoteric and esoteric subjects. While both require and lead to *devequt*, esoteric study involves a qualitatively superior degree of *devequt*.

> Thus our rabbis of blessed memory said, "a great matter and a small matter: a great matter [refers to] the Work of the Chariot[138] and a small matter [refers to] the debates of Abbaye and Rava."[139] But, God forbid that the sages meant that the debates of Abbaye and Rava are a small matter. For this is the essence of our Torah which was spoken at Sinai by the Blessed Creator's mouth. As for calling the Work of the Chariot a great matter, is it not the case that in our day practically everybody is well versed in the writings of the divine R. Isaac Luria of blessed memory, who revealed all aspects of the Work of the Chariot? But, in reality, both the revealed and concealed Torah are one category. For everything depends on a person's intention in learning. If one's intention is to become familiar with the contents, he will not attain anything. As it says in *Reishit Hokhmah*, "for concerning [such a person] it is said, 'for all his goodness is like a sprout in the field.'"[140] But if his intention [in learning a text] is that he desires to cleave to God [in order] to be a chariot for him and can only accomplish this through Torah and *mizvot*, then, whether by means of the revealed Torah or the concealed Torah, he will cause himself to cleave [to God]. The only difference is that through [studying] the concealed Torah, he will attain a more wondrous *devequt*.[141]

The saying of the rabbis concerning the relative merits of debates compared to the Work of the Chariot is not ultimately a comment on subject matter. Rather, it is a comment on approaches to Torah study, intellectual versus mystical. Learning as a basis for cleaving to divine immanence is a great matter. In comparison, delighting in intellectual exercises is insignificant.

> This, in my opinion, is what they meant [by saying] "a small matter [refers to] the debates of Abbaye and Rava." In other words, [if] the intellect [is] merely [involved] in the argumentation of the Gemara, such as the debates and problems of Abbaye and Rava, it is a small matter. Whoever learns for the pleasure of this intellectuality is small and insignificant. He does not contact God (*ve-eyno*

noge'a la-Shem yitbarakh).[142] It is only like desiring some other matter of wisdom. But when one desires to be a chariot for God by means of the Torah, this is a great matter. Thus [they said], "a great matter [refers to] the Work of the Chariot," i.e., to make oneself a chariot for God by means of [studying] Torah.[143]

Meshullam Feibush's teachings are very much influenced by sixteenth-century Kabbalah. As we noted in regard to his attitude concerning *kavvanot* of prayer, while the practice can be undertaken only by a spiritually advanced, it is nevertheless worthwhile to study the texts in which the *kavvanot* are presented. However, Meshullam Feibush recognizes that the Lurianic texts may be too difficult for his readers to master. Consequently, he recommends studying several basic texts from the thirteenth-century Spanish Kabbalah.

> As for studying the Kabbalah of the Lurianic writings, I know that you, yourself, do not wish to study [these] without someone more advanced than yourself. But this you will not find. [So] study only *Sefer Sha'arey Orah* (Gates of Light) and *Ginat Egoz* (The Garden of Nuts),[144] and above all, *Sefer ha-Zohar* and the *Tiqqunim*.[145]

It is most important that Torah study occur as a kind of extension of prayer. Indeed, the optimum time for study is immediately after finishing the service.

> Now immediately after the prayer, without any pause or conversation, learn a portion of Torah, Prophets, and Writings, Mishnah, Gemara, and Codes, as time permits. If possible, it is very good to learn publicly, a lesson from the ethical texts. However, I do not know if this is possible, since people tend to run out immediately after *Aleynu*.[146] Determine this for yourself.[147]

Whatever the content and length of the lesson may be, study must be undertaken with the same concentrated attitude of mind that is required for prayer. Indeed the quality of Torah study depends on the success one had in achieving *devequt* during the preceding prayer. In addition the worshipful character of the study experience is evoked by preceding the lesson with a *kavvanah* and appropriate prayer.

> But prior to all Torah study, focus your mind (*teyashev et azmekha*) so that it will not be a matter of routine (*mizvat anashim melumadah*) but only for God's sake. Yet not every occasion will be equal. Sometimes you will be able to learn with great desire, for God's sake, if you merit to pray with a pure thought. At other times [you will only learn] with less intensity (*be-maheshavah qetanah*). But always intend to learn for God's sake, because *mizvot* require *kavvanah*.

> And say orally, "for the sake of uniting the Holy One, blessed be He and His *Shekhinah*."[148] Also, before [studying] Kabbalah, you should say the prayer of the divine R. Isaac Luria, of blessed memory, which is printed in the *Tiqquney Zohar*.[149]

Meshullam Feibush's pietistic approach to prayer was directly influenced by popularizations of sixteenth-century Kabbalah. (The prayers that he recommends uttering before Torah study are found in Nathan Hannover's *Sha'arey Zion*). This small collection of prayers was an important vehicle for disseminating the fundamental motives of Lurianic Kabbalah in popular form. Even though Lurianic Kabbalah itself was not part of the recommended curriculum, its basic themes were accepted and affirmed. Although Hasidic piety elevated the importance of *devequt* beyond all other values, the quest for *devequt* continued to be pursued within the context of a universe that was understood in generally Lurianic terms.

> You should say the prayer that is written in *Sha'arey Zion* before all Torah study, even though you do not concern yourself with the Lurianic writings to understand the Names that are contained there. For they are the basic Names (*shemot peshutot*) of God which sustain the worlds . . .[150]

Ultimately, then, Torah study, like prayer, is an especially favorable opportunity for mystical experience. Through Torah study with the proper intention, one can fulfill the ultimate religious goal of returning to God. Thus, Torah study and prayer have essentially the same purpose. Indeed, since this ideal of Torah study cannot be fulfilled without divine aid,[151] Torah study, itself, becomes a form of supplication.

> For you, whom God has not permitted to be entirely free to study all day, surely a little [learning] after prayer with *kavvanah* and with a focused mind is better than a lot [of study] without *kavvanah*, God forbid. Most important is the *kavvanah* that we mentioned.[152] For we have already learned a lot for selfish reasons (*she-lo li-shemah*). Now let us put the thought in our hearts to learn for God's sake. Even though it is impossible to direct our minds to this, God will help us. We need to beseech Him concerning this. Indeed we should ask Him for everything that we lack. For who is greater than He?[153]

The Sacred Calendar and Devequt

Discussion of the sacred calendar receives considerable attention in Meshullam Feibush's writings. One reason for its prominence is the fact that Sabbath and holy days are occasions when homilies are preached. Much of Meshullam Feibush's discussion of the sacred calendar consists of homilies that were probably presented orally. However, there is a deeper reason for the emphasis Meshullam Feibush places on holy days. They are viewed as providential opportunities when higher consciousness is more readily accessible to those who seek it.[154] The sacred calendar is conceived as a kind of spiritual corrective to the otherwise excessively material character of creation. The holy days make *devequt* possible by restoring to the world some of the hidden divine essence which was concealed in order that a material creation could emerge.

The process of creation involved two fundamental stages.[155] First the idea of creation arose in the divine mind. At this stage everything that would subsequently exist in the material world was already present as ideas in God's thought. However, the purpose of creation was so that God could receive pleasure through His creatures' recognition of their divine origin. In order to maximize this pleasure, the creatures had to be further removed from their source. This entailed a second stage of creation in which the spiritual ideas were transformed into physical forms. The transformation occurred through a gradual process of materialization which entailed the progressive obscuration and limitation of the original spiritual essence. The material world only emerged at a stage when its spiritual basis was greatly concealed. Under such conditions, God indeed took pleasure in His creatures' efforts to find Him.

> Consequently, the *ruhaniyut* of everything is what was emanated in the primordial divine thought. This is the vitality (*hiyyut*) of everything. Afterwards, when everything was created in actuality, through a gradual process of materialization (*hit'abut ve-hishtalshelut*), this *ruhaniyut* nevertheless remained above, concealed in its root and was not at all revealed. But the vitality that is within creation (*she-ba-beru'im*) is a very limited vitality which has been gradually contracted until it could be contained in material bodies.[156] That concealed light could not be revealed nor shine upon creation, because God was still busy with the process of creation and contraction until things would become material entities.[157]

However, since this process of concealment resulted in the severe reduction of the quantity of spiritual energy that sustains the world, creation's very existence was in jeopardy. Thus, when the six days of creation were completed, God had to inject an additional quantity of spiritual energy into the world so that it could continue. Since this supplemental energy came from within the divine mind itself, it constituted a revelation of the divine essence.

After everything was completed on the sixth day, if the world had remained in [this state of] creation, it could not have continued [to exist] because of the small [quantity of] vitality that it contained. For the vitality that is in materiality is constricted. Therefore, after completing all the work of creation, God projected an illumination from the concealed [level of] creation.158 It emanated from [the stage] where creation existed in His thought as a very spiritual being and is really the divine essence itself.159 He projected His glorious splendor from one end of the world to the other throughout the entire work of creation. Above all, God sent an illumination (behirut) from its concealed root in divine thought to man, His chosen creature.160

The pure spiritual essence of creation remained concealed above when the physical world was produced. It is a ray from this concealed spiritual essence which is slightly revealed on the Sabbath.

The Sabbath, or seventh day, is most important because it is the time when the concealed divine essence, which sustains the universe, is made manifest throughout all creation. This process is repeated every week.

You already know and have heard that what initially occurred (pa'am ehad), constantly recurs at the same time (in the cycle of time). Especially in regard to Shabbat, it has to be so. For "in His goodness, he perpetually renews each day the work of creation."161 With the creation of each day, the creatures of that day were brought into existence: minerals, plants, animals, and humans, until Shabbat arrived. Then the source is aroused to send them [sustaining] energy, just as it was at the time of creation.162

The Sabbath is primarily a manifestation of divine will which allows the world to exist.163 All existence, then, depends on God's will. But this divine will desires devequt, since the only purpose for existence is so that the creatures will cleave to their creator. Consequently, through the additional revelation of the divine essence which occurs on Shabbat, devequt is fostered, as creation is enabled to return to its divine root. Shabbat is thus sacred time in a truly cosmological sense.164 The human celebration of Shabbat is merely the recognition of the changed cosmic state.

Consequently, the name Shabbat means returning (hashavah),165 for the creatures returned to their root. The meaning is that no creature can exist except through God's will. There is no creature in the world that exists [independently]. For they were created after non-existence (ahar ha-he'eder), i.e., non-existence preceded them. But whatever was preceded by non-existence can only exist through God's will which exists forever [and] which precedes everything. For He is eternal: He never has not existed nor will not exist (lo sar ve-lo yasur). Now the idea of the creatures was in His will for He wanted them to be.

Since without His will, they [would] perish and have no existence at all, just as they did not exist before they arose in His will.[166] But His will [concerning] the creatures was for the pleasure He [would have] from them when they would cleave to their root through their longing. Through this they would exist because they are cleaving to Him and He exists eternally, and also [because] they would fulfill His will which He desires from them. So His will would be in its place and creation would exist. For they have no existence except through fulfilling His will for them.[167]

Through the revelation of *Shabbat*, the desire for *devequt* is aroused. Were it not for *Shabbat*, creation would not be able to discover its divine root because of its great concealment. However, when the divine root discloses itself, creation is filled with longing to cleave to its source. Through this longing, the original unity which existed within the mind of God is restored.

Now this [divine] will [for the creatures] to cleave to their root is impossible [to fulfill]. For, as a result of creation, they have become distant from their root, as we have explained, through the physicality (*gufaniyut*) of human beings and separated through this from the root which is one spiritual unity (*ruhaniyut ve-ahdut ehad*). Therefore, after creation, God wanted them to [continue to] exist. But they could not because of their distance from Him. So He projected an illumination of their concealed being which is from His blessed essence, through a slight emanation (*hishtalshelut*).[168] Then they were filled with desire and will for them. It is like a small child who pursues foolish games and forgets his father. But later, when he sees his father, because of his desire for him, he throws everything aside and cleaves to him. He runs to him because he is a part of [his father's] essence (*she-hu' netah mi-netahav*). Similarly, so to speak, when God shines His glorious splendor at creation, then their faces are turned toward Him in great longing. This is what His will hopes for from them. It is the cause of their existing for the two reasons we mentioned.[169] This is the meaning of *Shabbat* which is returning to the root. The root shines upon the branches and the branches desire and delight in Him and long for Him and [this situation] is a unity with God.[170]

Through the revelation of *Shabbat*, the multiplicity which externally characterizes creation is overcome. Since everything participates in the inner cleaving to the revealed divine root, a condition of mystical unity is produced.

Through this you can understand a saying in the Zohar, "the mystery of *Shabbat* is *Shabbat* which is united through the mystery of one . . . for the holy throne of glory is united with the mystery of one . . ."[171] For the creatures, in their totality, are called a throne for God, as the verse says, *The heavens are my throne* . . ."[172] The creatures are outwardly a multiplicity, but within they are one. But when are they one? When they are cleaving to and desiring one thought, *devequt* with God. Consequently, all of their desiring has one direction, one will, one longing, to cleave to one. It is this *devequt* which unites and connects God with the creatures so that they may be sustained by God who is one.[173]

The unity that characterizes *Shabbat* is essentially a union that occurs between the transcendent and immanent aspects of God. This union is represented by a myth of *hieros gamos* which is described in the Zohar.[174] Although the Zoharic text deals with a theosophical union involving two of the *sefirot*, Meshullam Feibush interprets it as a reference to *devequt* between the human soul and God.

> Now this connecting [of creation with God] is called covenant. Therefore, *Shabbat* is called covenant of the world,[175] for at that time intercourse between the Holy One, blessed be He, and His *Shekhinah* takes place. You already know what is meant by the Holy One, blessed be He, and His *Shekhinah*. The Holy One, blessed be He, refers to divinity which is concealed from the creatures and His *Shekhinah* is divinity which dwells below [among them]. But the union (*hitqashrut*) of the two of them occurs on *Shabbat*, as I wrote above. Understand this well, for it is the true meaning of *Shabbat*, as written in the Zohar, *Terumah*,[176] and *Tiqquney Zohar*,[177] and in the writings [of Dov Ber].[178]

The revelation of *Shabbat*, then, is a means of attaining *devequt*. This revelation, however, varies in its intensity, depending on the spiritual level of each person. Although the illumination of *Shabbat* affects all of creation, it primarily is apprehended by the Jews.

> The principle that arises is that *Shabbat* is a holy day for it shines and reveals an illumination from the Holy, which is God, the Holy of Holies. It shines on all the creatures, and especially on His people, Israel. This is the secret of spreading the canopy of peace.[179] For *sukkah* (canopy) means *yiskeh* (he will see) which is a verb that denotes seeing. [This] refers to the illumination which is revealed so that the souls will long for Him; all eyes will gaze at Him. "Peace" (SHaLoM) refers to the connecting of the creatures with God. For this is wholeness (SHeLeMut) and peace, everything is one. The reason it is called SuKKah is [because] it is like thatch (SekKhaKh) which has openings in it. The sun's light shines into [the *sukkah*] through the openings. Similarly, God's illumination is revealed to everyone according to his level, to one as a tiny spark, to another as a greater one, to a third as an even greater one. Thus it is called *sukkah*.[180]

The various levels of apprehending the divine illumination are reflected by the varying degrees of corporeality that characterize a person's Sabbath joy. For a highly evolved *Zaddiq*, the delights of *Shabbat* have no physical aspect whatsoever, since his *devequt* is purely spiritual in nature. For others, the pleasure of *Shabbat* is experienced primarily through eating and drinking. However, since these activities are carried out in a spirit of holiness, they still maintain a spiritual quality.

> But, note, the apprehension of *Shabbat* and holidays is not equal for every-one.[181] For a *Zaddiq* it is a pleasure of [apprehending] an intellectual light, *deve-qut* with the Creator in the pleasantness of His blessed splendor. This is a great joy, beyond measure. But whoever is not a *Zaddiq* feels a physical joy, expansion of the heart through enjoying food and drink. Thus Rashi wrote in [his com-mentary on] tractate *Beyzah*, concerning the remark of our rabbis of blessed memory, "an additional soul is given to man ..."[182] This is the material form of the joy and love at its lowest level. Yet, it is also holy, since [the person] is not able to attain the highest level of *devequt*. God forbid profaning it with anger or sadness for that is the opposite of holiness, which is the shell, as is known.[183]

Three levels of Sabbath delight are indicated in the Sabbath liturgy. While the higher levels can only be comprehended by those who have experienced them, the lowest level guarantees that all may participate in the holiness of the Sabbath experience.

> This matter is alluded to in the prayer book ... "those who delight [in *Shabbat*] will always inherit glory, those who taste [*Shabbat*] merit life," and also "those who love the words [of *Shabbat*] chose greatness." For there are three levels. Now the first two are hidden and concealed and known only to those who ob-tain them. But they are concealed from those who have no knowledge of the souls' *devequt* with God, but only of the third level. For they love the words [of *Shabbat*], i.e., the revealed words that we can speak about and explain, such as the pleasure of food and drink etc. Also, [in this case], if they do this for the sake of Heaven, according to their understanding, they choose greatness.[184]

The divine illumination of *Shabbat* is revealed throughout the entire day and, thus, all *Shabbat* activities including the three meals are opportu-nities for attaining *devequt*. Nevertheless, as in other days, the primary oc-casion for realizing *devequt* is during prayer. The divine illumination is ex-perienced as an additional more spiritual soul which is not present during the week. The presence of this additional soul is especially apprehended dur-ing Shabbat prayers. This emphasis on prayer underscores the heightened spiritual character of the day and offsets the vulgar notion that *Shabbat* is a time for physical pleasures and rest.

> Accordingly, if you are intelligent, you will understand that the basis of *Shab-bat* is to cleave to God in prayer and Torah.[185] Thus the Zohar proclaims, "this

day is a day of souls and not a day of bodies."[186] The souls' root shines upon the embodied souls and they surrender to it. This is called the addition of a *Shabbat*-soul. All of this is felt during prayer.[187] Accordingly, one must be exceedingly careful with Shabbat prayer. For this is the essence of *Shabbat*, not as the masses, including even the learned, think, who do not tremble over the word of God and undervalue prayer. *Shabbat* in their eyes is something else, I know not what. But the truth is as I have written . . .[188]

The *devequt* that can be attained on *Shabbat* and the festivals depends on two factors. First, through the dispensation of the additional soul a divine illumination is revealed which may be apprehended. Were it not for this light, there would be no arousal and *devequt* could not occur.

Devequt with God is only possible by means of God Himself. Just as the verse says, "For with You is the source of life, in Your light we see light."[189] It is impossible for the eyes to see in darkness and at night. Why is this? Although the eyes have the power of sight, it is not possible for them to see in darkness. They are only vessels which are capable of drawing the light. With this light they [are able to] see. Consequently, it is only possible to see during the day, or at night by means of a candle. For the eyes draw from the light of the candle or a lamp that shines. Then the eyes will see.[190]

However, even though the divine illumination is available on these holy occasions, it is not apprehended equally by everyone. Indeed, it can only be apprehended at all when the organs of apprehension have been duly prepared. This preparation involves fulfilling the conditions of spiritual development that are necessary for *devequt*.[191] Without a purified heart and mind, the revelation of the Sabbath and festivals cannot be apprehended.

Similarly, in the case of *devequt* with God, a person has to have vessels in his heart and mind, i.e., eyes of the intellect. In other words, the mind and heart must be clear and bright and free of all dross of desire and negative qualities, as I wrote above. Then, when God shines His light upon us on the holy occasions, in His light we will see light. But this would not be the case, if, God forbid, we had no eyes. Like the blind, we would grope about in darkness, like a blind person who cannot see even at midday, because he does not have vessels [for drawing light]. Similarly, we who lack a pure mind and heart, do not see even at the time of the illumination of *Shabbat* and festivals.[192]

Although the divine essence is revealed in greater measure during *Shabbat*, this revelation is not perceived by ordinary people whose spiritual state has not been sufficiently refined. That the light is indeed present on sacred occasions is attested by *Zaddiqim*, but ordinary people simply cannot detect it, since they lack the requisite spiritual organs of apprehension.

The Sabbath and festivals, then, are, like the Torah, means of attaining *devequt,* because they contain within them the hidden divinity itself. While each of the festivals is characterized by its own unique kind of revelation of divine light, the joy of these sacred occasions is in every case fundamentally a rejoicing in the divine immanence.

> The essence of the Torah and the commandments is the *devequt* of the soul and will with God, and especially [in the case of] the *mizvot* that depend on [specific] times such as *Shabbat* and festivals. [For they] are days when God reveals and projects an illumination of the additional souls to His people, which is the essence of *devequt* for those who know, as I wrote above. But the character of *devequt* during *Shabbat* and Passover and *Shavuot* and *Sukkot* is not the same. [Yet], in each case their joy and pleasure is in God's presence in the day itself. This is what the Zohar wrote on the verse, *"this is the day God made, let us rejoice and be happy in it,"*[193] *"'bo'* (in it), i.e., in the day, *'bo'* (in him), i.e., in the Holy One, blessed be He, and it is all the same thing.'"[194]

The divine illuminations that are revealed on Sabbath and festivals are manifestations of *Hesed,* God's benevolence. This means that as a result of the illuminations, additional vitality is released into creation in order to sustain it. When the outpouring of God's *Hesed* is apprehended, the creatures are filled with the joy that characterizes the celebration of Sabbath and festivals. The High Holy Days, New Year's Days and the Day of Atonement, are also occasions when a divine illumination is projected throughout creation. However, in these cases, the illuminations are not manifestations of *Hesed,* but rather of *Gevurah,* God's might. Instead of increasing the sustaining vitality, the light is now contracted and the existence of creation is called into question. When the illumination of *Gevurah* is apprehended, the creatures are not filled with joy, but with fear. For it is a time of judgment.[195] The protection of divine judgment that is released during the Days of Awe causes everyone to experience some degree of fear and awe.[196] For most people, this involves at least some degree of fear of punishment. However, the most spiritually developed experience a species of awe that is not primarily concerned with judgment and one's personal fate.[197] This level depends on a more selfless appreciation of divine power which leads to genuine repentance, involving complete effacement in the presence of God's overwhelming might.

Just as in the case of *Shabbat* and festivals, the Days of Awe mark a cyclical recurrence of an original cosmic event. The sacred calendar operates according to a myth of eternal return.[198] According to this, every New Year replicates the cosmic conditions which pertained during the act of creation. The beginning of a new year in time marks the recreation and renewal of the cosmos itself.

You already know what the divine R. Isaac Luria of blessed memory wrote. On every occasion, the divine manifestation (*hit'orerut*) that occurred [on this occasion] in the past, is aroused [anew]. For example, during the holy *Shabbat*, the manifestation of the light of returning is aroused which God sent at the time of the first *Shabbat*. It shines in the same way now, as one says, "who in His holiness bestows rest upon His people Israel during the holy *Shabbat*." At Passover, He releases an illumination which shined when Israel went out from Egypt, and at the Feast of Weeks, the illumination [that accompanied] the giving of the Torah. Similarly, now during the Days of Awe, He releases the illumination of the beginning of creation, which is judgment with which the world was created. As the verse says, "*in the beginning Elohim*[199] (*God*) *created*,"[200] which is a beginning, and all beginnings are difficult.[201]

New Year is primarily an occasion for awe and fear of God because it occurs at a time of *zimzum*, or divine contraction. This term is particularly associated with the Kabbalah of Isaac Luria. However, Meshullam Feibush presents it according to one of its usages in the system of Moses Cordovero.[202] According to this usage, *zimzum* is associated with a process in which the forces of judgment are recalled to their root in order to be neutralized, or "sweetened." This act of causing the forces of judgment to ascend beyond their designated location in the hierarchy of creation fills them with fear.

For the creation of the world took place through [an act of] *zimzum*, and *zimzum* involves withdrawing the vitality [from below to a place] above. We know what is written in *Reishit Hokhmah*,[203] in the name of R. Moses Cordovero, on the verses, "*for behold, the kings assembled [and] passed together, they gazed, and even wondered, were confused, trembled, fear gripped them.*"[204] This referred to the removal of the celestial palaces above.[205] What one learns from its context applies in general. For the displacing of something from below to above, and that is the meaning of *zimzum*, is very frightening for something that was below [which] has to occupy a place that is higher than its own. Who can bear such fear?[206]

The reference in *Reishit Hokhmah* is to a passage in Cordovero's commentary on the prayer book, *Tefillah le-Moshe*. There, Cordovero interprets the kabbalistic meaning of Ps. 48 which is recited on the second day of the week (Monday). According to tradition, on the second day of the week, Gehinnom was created. Through this psalm, the forces of severe judgment which are the basis of Gehinnom are neutralized. During this process of "sweetening judgment," the previously emanated chambers of the World of Creation are elevated back to their root in the World of Emanation. The elevation fills them with fear since anthropopathy is ascribed to even the highest elements in the divine realm.

The retraction of aspects of the divine realm which occurred during creation is repeated during New Year. The quality of light that is emanated at this time recalls the emanated sources of the souls to their point of origin in God. The fear that these sources experience above is mirrored below in the fear that individuals sense during this period.

> Now the existence of this light is what the Zohar calls the "black spark" (*bozina' de-qardinuta'*)[207] which is a light of the power of contraction. It is called "returning light" (*Or Hozer*).[208] Now this light is aroused and shines at the time of New Year just as during the creation of the world. As one says, "this is the day of the beginning of Your work, a memorial to the first day." Because of this, fear falls on the souls. For the sources of the souls are gathered together above, and are very frightened. As the verse says, "*they were confused, they trembled, fear gripped them . . .*"[209] And their branches below which are in the body sense this somewhat, each according to its [degree of] consciousness (*da'at*).[210]

The fear which fills the souls at this time reestablishes God's sovereignty in the world. For as the souls are returned to their divine source, they recognize God's lordship.

> This is the meaning of our saying, "and in it Your sovereignty will be raised up." For God is called King as a result of the manifestation of awe and fear of lordship over the branches which are emanated, created, formed, and made by Him.[211]

However, the restoration of the souls to their source is not only meant to instill in them fear of divine lordship. As a result of this contraction, they are prepared for a re-emergence in a state which is appropriate to them.

> Just as at the time of creation there was a contraction above in order to later bestow vitality (*le-hashpi'a*) below in measure and proportion, as it says in the Zohar, "with the black spark He measured out the allotment,"[212] i.e., measure, weight, balance and allotment for every [aspect] of creation, spiritual, and physical, so during this day [something] very much like it is aroused over all creation as at first.[213]

The gathering up of the soul roots is compared to human pregnancy. The souls in the divine source are like an embryo in the womb which undergoes the necessary stages of formation before birth can take place.[214]

> This is the meaning of "this is the day the world was born,"[215] i.e., (creation may be understood as) the pregnancy of the world.[216] Just as a pregnant woman gathers up the embryo within her and there, during the period of pregnancy, all

of a person's limbs and powers are measured and proportioned until he is born, so it is at New Year's, the birth of the world . . .217

Because of this ascension of the souls and their preparation for rebirth, New Year is an especially important time for *devequt*. The exceptional proximity between the souls and their divine source calls for a special effort of purification. Those souls which have become tainted by their misdeeds during the preceding year cannot expect to be welcomed above, nor will their New Year's prayers be answered with favor.

So whoever has a brain in his head and wishes to serve God in truth, understands this matter correctly. He asks himself how he can enter and cause the root of his soul to cleave above, if he is tainted in his deeds. Thus he performs true acts of complete repentance. On New Year's day, his only desire and longing is to beseech God. Since this is a time of favor and remembering, and visitation of every spirit and soul which ascends from its place to the lofty heights above, perhaps God will have pity upon us and remove from us all of the clouds and darknesses that separate us from Him. Then we will cleave to Him with a pure heart on this day. . . . As a result of this *devequt* on New Year's day, we will derive merit for the entire year in all aspects of our conduct in the way of God.218

The purity of one's worship during this period determines one's fate during the coming year. However, concern for one's material well-being is not nearly as important as praying for *devequt*, the opportunity for the soul to return to its divine source. The judgment that occurs has definite implications for one's fate in the world, but of greater consequence is the judgment which determines how closely the soul may approach God. This judgment rests upon a review of one's deeds.

This is the meaning of the inscribing,219 i.e., the impression that is recorded when the divine soul approaches and cleaves [to God] in this *devequt*, everything is reviewed at once: matters [pertaining to] one's soul and body, his wife and children, his garments and food, his business and all that pertains to him. For everything is included in the desire of the branch as it approaches its root. There its [fate] is determined and the entire judgment is pronounced at that very time and moment. According to a person's path, so he will find [his judgment]. For matters pertaining to a person's body, his wife and children, food, and all that occurs to him, are all secondary to what concerns the soul's *devequt* with God. According to one's deeds, they will either bring him near or cast him off. It is all [according to] a true judgment and providence.220

The prayer for *devequt* is what God really desires. For God's pleasure is the result of creation's recognition of and returning to its divine source. Judgment and the fear it arouses serve to reveal God's sovereignty. The wise seize upon this opportunity for fulfilling the divine will through their *devequt*.

> Whoever is wise emphasizes what is essential and begs with all his heart for God to help him attain *devequt* of the soul and to reveal the glory of His sovereignty and lordship upon us, which is awe of God. For this is the reason the world was created. Accordingly, one says in [the] New Year [liturgy], "so arouse Your fear . . . and all creatures will be in awe of You." For we ask for what is essential, that He remove all the obstacles and reveal the glory of His kingdom . . . , just as [it was] at the time of creation on, before the sin [of Adam]. God has great pleasure from this when we are wise [enough] to place what is essential first and to de-emphasize what is secondary. But if, God forbid, the opposite [occurs] and we do not desire *devequt* with Him at all, but are only [concerned] for our bodies like the masses, and we beg for physical sustenance, this is the opposite of the desired intention. For physical sustenance spoils creation, as the verse says, "*and Yeshurun grew fat and kicked.*"[221]

The manifestation of divine judgment, which occurs during the Days of Awe, is ultimately an act of divine mercy. Through the revelation of judgment, the world is paradoxically saved. This is the case because the root of judgment in its divine source is no other than benevolence. When this root is revealed the destructive powers of judgment are tempered and transformed into agencies of divine love.

> God saw that His people Israel required a great salvation and release at this very time, through sweetening Judgment and [curtailing] its dominance so that the world would not be destroyed, God forbid. We already know what the divine R. Isaac Luria of blessed memory wrote. Sweetening of judgment does not occur through a manifestation of mercy, but through a manifestation of judgment. This is because the root of judgment in its ultimate [source] above is a great [manifestation of] mercy. This is the case of God's first *zimzum* for the sake of revealing His love for His people Israel. . . . The *zimzum* is really love and great mercy. Even though it is contraction and judgment, nevertheless it is really mercy. For it is sweetened judgment. It sweetens all judgments which are beneath it.[222] For it is their root and they are its branches. But [the judgments] themselves are not mercy as it really is. Thus we say [in the High Holy Day's liturgy], "to pardon sins through judgment, to overcome His anger through judgment." In other words, it all takes place through supernal judgment which is very sweetened.[223]

However, according to kabbalistic theology, supernal forces are only activated by sacred objects and acts in the created world which mystically correspond to them. Thus, the soteric root of judgment is aroused through the sounding of the *shofar*, or ram's horn. When this commandment is fulfilled with the proper intention, it becomes a vehicle for divine aid and the merciful roots of supernal judgment are revealed.

> But with what is this root of judgment which is great mercy aroused? It is by means of the *shofar*. Everything supernal has something which corresponds to it below, [which is] a subtle spark from it. Through the arousal below, when we take up the object below at God's command [in order] to fulfill His commandments, the supernal power is really aroused. God who gave His people this [commandment], Himself arouses the power of the person who does these things for their Maker's sake (*le-shem po'alan*), and not for any other purpose, only for God's sake. For this is the essence of the intention and desire of the [divine] will (*ve-hefez ha-razon*).224

The sounding of the *shofar* expresses the remorse of the human heart which recognizes its sinfulness. Through this breaking of the heart, the power of judgment is broken.225 Through contrition, the soul returns to God and the forces of judgment return to their root where they are sweetened.

> This is the meaning of repentance to which the *shofar* alludes. Repentance is the returning of a person in his heart and soul to God through very great breaking of his heart. It is the returning of the judgments to their root. For the judgments are [manifestations] of the strengthening of the power of the *sitra ahara*226 through the sins. Through breaking the heart in submission and true repentance to God, [the judgments] are broken and come to their root. The root is a supernal light over everything. It is the *SHoFaR* which perfects (*ha-me-SHaPeR*) everything. It is the power of repentance. For from there all the powers and thoughts of repentance are emanated to all people.227

Human repentance is itself essentially the result of divine aid. For it is aroused in people by God from a source within the divine world. This source is the *sefirah* called "*Binah*" (understanding) which is associated with repentance in the Zohar.228

> Now the divine aid of repentance is entirely from [that source] which is called *Binah*. In other words, the essence of repentance is an arousal of understanding in the human heart which understands the greatness of the Creator, blessed be His name. One feels great submission in recalling that he enters soiled into the chamber of the King of the Universe. Through this, he returns to Him in truth . . .229

Just as in the case of prayer and Torah study, the breath, which is expressed during the act is essential for returning the soul to its divine source, so it is in the case of repentance. The breath which is expelled into the *shofar* contains the imprint of all the misdeeds which were committed during the year. By releasing the breath into the *shofar* in a state of contrition, it is enabled to reach the supernal source of repentance, *Binah*, and from there is returned as purified vitality.

> The secret of the commandment [of blowing the *shofar*] is to bring out from one's heart the sound of submission and breaking the heart through the *shofar*, i.e. to return the judgments to their root. For in the breath of the heart and mouth of each person, all the flaws that are in his soul (*nefesh, ruah, u-neshamah*) are recorded. All the strengthening of the *sitra ahara* and the judgments are recorded in the breath. So he puts it into the *shofar* which alludes to God's supernal light, the light of repentance, to which all return who return to Him. It is the light of understanding which sends forth an illumination of understanding and recognition of His greatness to all the worlds. . . . When they return to Him, he sends below the rectified vitality of the souls of all creatures from the supernal *shofar*.[230]

Essentially, then, the Days of Awe enable a person to obtain an especially heightened experience of *devequt* through the arousal of divine judgment. The special divine dispensation of the season helps human beings to overcome the barriers to fulfilling God's will. The blemishes in human nature, which separate a person from God, are wiped away through the contrition that is stimulated by the divine revelation. Thus, through the institution of these sacred occasions and the divine commandments through which they are observed, God provided means for fulfilling the purpose of creation. The holidays afford an opportunity to provide God with the pleasure that He receives when creation returns to Him.

> The meaning of all this is that the essence of our efforts (*megamatenu*) during these days is repentance and returning to our root, to God, and cleaving to Him in order to cause Him pleasure. As I wrote above, God has great pleasure from this repentance and returning, just like the pleasure a father has from a son who returns to him after being distant. Most important is to beg God for strength. Just as one was wholeheartedly attached to Him during these days in truth, so may He be inscribed in our souls. We will receive the imprint of divinity in our souls as an aid and to help guide us during the entire year so that we will not turn away entirely (*le-bal nateh ashurenu mi-kol ve-khol*), God forbid.[231]

The special opportunity for *devequt* that is offered during the High Holy Days can spiritually strengthen a person during the following year. The proximity to God that can be attained during this season leaves an imprint which continues to aid a person to overcome the barriers to *devequt* that will arise throughout the following year.

Meshullam Feibush goes on to discuss aspects of the Day of Atonement and the Festival of Booths which are part of the general experience of this sacred season. However, the basis of his approach to the holidays can already be understood from the discussion concerning New Year. Because creation entails a separation from God, a corrective is necessary if man is to have any hope of returning to his divine source. Human beings are by nature essentially drawn after worldly interests. The transformation of consciousness that is necessary if *devequt* is to be realized requires extraordinary efforts that are beyond most people's abilities. Moreover, the attainment of *devequt* is paradoxical. Returning to the divine root involves transcending the sense of self-existence. Thus, human effort towards *devequt* may itself be counterproductive and only serve to reinforce pride. For all of these reasons, human salvation is ultimately dependent on divine aid. This aid is, to a large extent, available through the sacred calendar which provides periodic remedies that relieve the inherent limitations of human nature.

> Everyone's [evil] urge constantly overcomes him. So God provided a wondrous solution (*hifli' ezah*) and increased aid, holy days and times for the souls to come close to Him by means of the illumination that shines and illuminates these times. [This is] especially [the case] during these days, New Year and the Day of Atonement, which are the mind and heart of the whole year . . .232

7

Meshullam Feibush and the Maggid of Mezeritch

As we have seen in the preceding chapters, one of the major sources for Meshullam Feibush's teachings is R. Dov Ber, the Maggid of Mezeritch. The Maggid is identified as a disciple of the Ba'al Shem Tov, the founder of the lineage whose teachings Meshullam Feibush upholds. Moreover, Dov Ber is clearly identified as one of the greatest *Zaddiqim*, who has perfected the quality of detachment from corporeality, attained experiential knowledge of God, and attained true *devequt*. Nevertheless, Meshullam Feibush differs with Dov Ber in his presentation of several key issues. Since the establishment of Hasidism in Galicia during the last two decades of the eighteenth century is generally attributed to the efforts of Dov Ber's disciples, the question of Meshullam Feibush's relationship to Dov Ber is an important one. In this chapter, we shall examine Meshullam Feibush's attitude towards the Maggid's teachings.

The teachings which Meshullam Feibush attributes to Dov Ber may be divided into two general categories, those which are familiar from other sources and those which cannot at present be located in other collections. Three cases of the latter appear in our text. In one case, Meshullam Feibush refers to a teaching he has found in the manuscripts.

> And in truth it is written in the new writings of the Rav, Rabbi Dov Ber . . . which are in my possession, that the indication that a prayer has found some favor before God is submission (*hakhna'ah*), i.e., if submission remains in the heart after prayer, this is called the *reshimu* (imprint) of the prayer which is mentioned in the Lurianic writings . . .[1]

In view of the fact that Meshullam Feibush explicitly cites the manuscripts as the source of this teaching, it is surprising that it does not appear in any of the extant collections of Dov Ber's teachings. While an interpretation of the Lurianic concept of the *reshimu* does appear in several of Dov Ber's extant teachings, it is not to be found with this particular meaning.[2] While it is difficult to rule out this teaching as authentic, it is important to note that Dov Ber's teachings do contain other criteria for determining the quality of one's prayer. These criteria tend to emphasize what occurs during the experience of prayer itself rather than its aftermath. For example, the uninterrupted character of *devequt* during prayer is emphasized.[3] Meshullam Feibush's selection of the criterion of submission (*hakhna'ah*) after prayer rather than the quality of *devequt* during prayer is consistent with the general orientation of his teachings. His writings are directed to individuals whom he feels are incapable of fulfilling the extreme demands of Dov Ber's teachings. Thus, he emphasizes the effort to subdue one's desires and external interests and to direct one's thoughts toward God, rather than the various aspects of higher contemplative experience. The success of this effort during prayer is evident in the state of humility that remains even when the prayer has been completed.

Also attributed to Dov Ber is a teaching concerning *devequt* which involves an interpretation of a verse that does not appear elsewhere. This teaching emphasizes the efficacy of *devequt* as an essential means for both subduing desires and repenting transgressions.

> And as the holy Rabbi, our Teacher and Master, Dov Ber   . said, this is the meaning of the verse, "*YHVH is good for all.*"[4] It means that it is beneficial for a person to flee from every problem (*le-khol davar*) and to bring himself near to God. If he wishes to subdue his desires and [negative] qualities, it is only possible through accustoming himself and compelling his thought to cleave to God. Even if he is not able [to do so], nevertheless it is good [to make the effort]. Or, [in the case of] one who wishes to turn from transgressions that he has committed, it is all [accomplished] through drawing near (*hitqarevut*) to God . . .[5]

Although a comment on this particular verse does not seem to exist among the extant writings of Dov Ber, nevertheless the teaching that appears here does contain certain basic ideas that are readily found in his teachings. The association of repentance and *devequt* appears, for example in *Maggid Devarav le-Ya'aqov*: "one who repents requires awe and intimacy (*hitqasherut*) with the Creator, and above all, repentance is in the heart."[6]

As for *devequt* and desires, while *devequt* is not generally presented in Dov Ber's teachings as a remedy for desires per se, it does have at least a prophylactic effect because of the shame it induces.[7]

The third case of a teaching that is not found elsewhere is the one example in which Meshullam Feibush explicitly states that he heard something directly from Dov Ber. The teaching involves an interpretation of a rabbinic analogy between a sage and a golden bell with a clapper of pearls.[8] The interpretation emphasizes the need for *devequt* during Torah study. For a person who studies properly, the letters of the Torah constitute a golden exterior within which the mind can cleave to God. While no other record of the Maggid's interpreting this midrash can presently be located, it is important to observe that the point which the interpretation wishes to make is typical of Dov Ber's thought. Torah study in itself is not meritorious if it is not undertaken for the purpose of *devequt*. Studying Torah for the honor that knowledge brings is shameful.

> If he managed to purify his mouth and heart so that he will be a chariot for God, then the *devequt* with which he cleaves to God is the inner [aspect of studying Torah] and the words of Torah that he learns are the external [aspect] and a garment for this *devequt*, and this is correct. But this is not the case if his desire and love is not for God, but he still cleaves to temporal desires and craves even the least bit of honor. Then the inner [aspect] of his thought is the honor and the Torah [that he is learning] is external to his thought. How shameful it is when one makes of the words of Torah a garment for his thought's inner foolishness.[9]

A very similar teaching appears in a fragment that is found in the collected sayings of Dov Ber. Although the verse interpreted is different, the same essential point is made.

> *"A clever person acts with knowledge and a fool spreads folly."*[10] The meaning is, whoever is wise, even when he attends to his own needs, acts with knowledge (*Da'at*), in other words with *devequt* with God. Now *Da'at* is a term which implies connecting and *devequt*, as in [the verse], *"and Adam knew (yada') [his wife, Eve.]"*[11] Similarly, it is said, *"know the God of your fathers."*[12] In other words, connect yourself and cleave to the God of your fathers constantly in all your deeds. *"And a fool spreads (yiFRoSH) folly."* In other words, even though he is separated (*PaRuSH*) from the world and constantly studies Torah, he only learns and prays without *devequt* with the Creator, only to aggrandize himself and to be called Rabbi, [then] it is folly for him.[13]

The material that is attributed to Dov Ber, but not found elsewhere, does indeed make points that are typical of Dov Ber's thought. Nevertheless, we cannot assume that the formulations of these teachings are direct quotes from Dov Ber. Meshullam Feibush tells us explicitly that while his teachings are entirely based on what he has learned from his teachers, he does, nevertheless, occasionally provide his own explanations in order to better explicate their teachings.

> All that I write is entirely from their words and the meaning of every aspect of wisdom that I write is entirely from them. Only, occasionally I explain their words to you with a ready example (*be-mashal ha-qarov*) and sometimes I

interpret here (*ba-zeh*) some verse or matter in the Gemara. But the essence of
the wisdom is from their words, from what God granted me to understand of
them . . .[14]

The claim is, then, that the basis of all that Meshullam Feibush writes is
from his teachers. He does not consider himself an innovator as far as the
meaning of the fundamental ideas are concerned. However, he is clearly
much more than a passive vessel for the transmission of his masters' teachings. He is more than willing to introduce his own examples, analogies, and
interpretations into the text. Although he denies diverging from the meaning found in his sources, Meshullam Feibush's viewpoint is indelibly
stamped on all that he writes. In the cases cited above, it is difficult to determine to what extent Meshullam Feibush may be coloring authentic teachings of Dov Ber to suit his own purposes. Since no variants are available, one
can only speculate on the extent that Meshullam Feibush's interests may
have influenced the transmission. However, when we turn to those examples of Dov Ber's teachings which do exist in other sources, we can more
readily detect the hand of Meshullam Feibush.

In certain cases, Meshullam Feibush presents teachings in a manner
that is very faithful to what we find in other sources of Dov Ber's thought. A
good example, is his emphasis on *yir'ah* or awe of God as a prerequisite for
genuine religious experience.

> For all the desires and lust of this world [with its] conceits and jealousy are van-
> ity for one who has managed to taste even the least bit of this longing [for God]
> in his soul in a genuine manner. I.e., [for one who has] experienced awe and
> love. For if awe and fear [of God] are not in his heart, it is only external love, as
> explained in the writings of the Rav, our Teacher and Master, Dov Ber. . . . As
> long as a person serves God and learns Torah without awe, i.e., as long as fear of
> God does not enter his heart, it is all [only] external [learning]. But concerning
> awe, it is said, "*this is the gate to YHVH*,"[15] For whenever one enters the king's
> gate, fear naturally overcomes him. Similarly, when a person is overcome with
> fear of God in his heart, it is a sign that he has entered the King's gate in his
> thought. This is the attribute of *Malkhut* (sovereignty). . . . When one accus-
> toms himself to constantly feel this awe, he immediately despises all of the de-
> sires and evil qualities because of shame before God and fear of Him. This is de-
> tachment from corporeality . . . I did not want to elaborate on this matter which
> deserves to be treated at length, but [the details] are found in the writings which
> I mentioned. . . . There he treats this matter of awe at length in several places.[16]

During prayer and Torah study, a person should be overcome by awe in
the presence of God. Genuine love of God is not possible without awe. It is

not sufficient to make a pretense of these pious emotions. They must be
the direct result of faith in or apprehension of God's presence.[17] The existence of this genuine awe in the heart is associated with the lowest of the ten
sefirot, Malkhut. The awe that is an indication of genuine *devequt* renders
one ashamed to be drawn after corporeal interests. Thus, one attains detachment from corporeality as a result of awe. As Meshullam Feibush makes
clear, his presentation of this subject is a digest of material which is found in
several sections of the circulating manuscripts. Meshullam Feibush's first
reference to a teaching of Dov Ber that concerns the difference between
genuine and external awe is found in *Liqqutim Yeqarim*. This text seems to
be the primary source for Meshullam Feibush's teaching.

> There are those who pray in sadness because melancholy overcomes them and
> they think they are praying with great awe. There are also those who think they
> are praying out of great love for the Creator, although it is really [only a case of]
> excitability (*marah adumah*).[18] However, when one prays with [genuine] love
> of God and consequently shame overcomes him and he wishes to glorify God
> and to conquer his evil urge for Him, then it is good. For a person is only said to
> serve God when he feels fear and awe. And "[with] awe" means that awe over-
> comes him and not that he causes himself to feel awe, for this is only raising up
> *Mayyin Nuqbin*.[19] But, genuine awe means that fear and trembling overcome
> one and because of [this] fear, one does not know where he is. The brains are pu-
> rified, and tears automatically descend. But when this is not the case, although
> one thinks that he [is feeling] love for the Creator, it surely is not anything. For
> this is the gate to *YHVH*, awe is the gate to love. If one has not entered the gate
> of awe, how can he be experiencing [genuine] love? Whoever is not on such a
> level that awe overcomes him, only serves God by rote. He thinks he is loving
> God and serving Him with joy, but this is not joy, but merely revelry. Therefore
> he should return to God with all his heart and soul.[20]

This text, attributed to the Maggid of Mezeritch in *Liqqutim Yeqarim*, presents the basic position that Meshullam Feibush asserts, awe of God must
precede love and must be a genuine response to the encounter with God's
presence. Awe is the existential gate through which one enters into the divine presence. As Meshullam Feibush tells us, Dov Ber does go into greater
detail. However, the essential point is the same. Only two key aspects of
Meshullam Feibush's text are lacking here, the association of awe with
Malkhut and the connection of awe to a sense of shame which detaches one
from corporeal desires. However, Meshullam Feibush has also indicated that
the subject of awe is discussed in a number of places within the corpus of
Dov Ber's writings. Indeed this is the case. We need cite only one example
from *Maggid Devarav le-Ya'aqov*.

The essence of wisdom is awe. Although one has to serve God with [both] love and awe, it is only necessary to acquire awe, and immediately love of the Creator will rest on him. For it is the way of a male to follow after a female.[21] Through this one can examine himself [to see] whether his awe is complete. We can understand this by way of an analogy. If one of the ministers standing before the king were offered something exceedingly desirable, which, under other circumstances, he would crave, nevertheless, since he is in the king's presence, he will not have desire for that thing. This is because his shame and fear of the king have become so great that he is not aware of himself and his qualities. They are all canceled out by his awe of the king. . . . Now awe is the king's lowest level, for the king [himself] has no awe, but awe flashes out from the king and rests on his servants. Thus awe is certainly the king's lowest level and it joins the king and his people. . . . So the essence of *Malkhut* (sovereignty) is awe. For the essence of the king's delight in his kingdom (*Malkhut*) [comes from his subjects'] fearing him and thus they obey him . . .[22]

In this passage, awe is again presented as a prerequisite for love, which in this case follows automatically when awe is complete. However, we also see here Dov Ber's association of awe with shame that renders one immune to even the greatest of ordinary desires. We also find the other motif that occurred in Meshullam Feibush's text, awe is identified with *Malkhut*. One essential element in Dov Ber's text, which appears to be lacking in Meshullam Feibush's presentation, is the aspect of self-annihilation that is part of the experience of awe. However, we would be wrong to assume that Meshullam Feibush has censored out this aspect. Indeed, it does appear in the continuation of his argument.[23]

From this awe, one will reach genuine love, until his soul will cleave to the daughter of Jacob, as explained in *Reishit Hokhmah*.[24] When one has become constant in this *devequt* through prayer and Torah [study] and good deeds, he will reach genuine detachment from corporeality, for his existence will be annihilated in his mind during the time of prayer and he will not at all feel that he is in the body.[25]

This passage is a good illustration of Meshullam Feibush's method of presenting Dov Ber's teachings. As we have seen, he has culled through several distinct sources in order to present the material in one coherent whole. The elements that he includes are indeed faithful to Dov Ber's teachings, but are selective rather than complete. The result is a general presentation of basic hasidic issues rather than an exhaustive analysis of all their kabbalistic implications.

Another area in which Meshullam Feibush's method of presenting the teachings of Dov Ber is apparent is found in his essentially faithful though incomplete interpretation of the concept of *Ayin* (nothing). The concept is discussed in two passages. In the first case, Meshullam Feibush makes reference to an analogy which appears frequently in Dov Ber's teaching. The analogy compares the state of *Ayin* to the intermediate stage of transformation which occurs when an egg becomes a chick.

> And concerning [the return to *ayin*], the *Rav*, R. Ber, interpreted the passage in the Gemara which [explains why] a chick which hatches from a non-kosher egg may be eaten. The reason is that it does not grow until the egg rots. The moment it begins to grow it is merely dust.[26] In other words, it is impossible for anything in the world to change from one state of being (*mezi'ut*) to another unless it reaches [the state of] *Ayin*, i.e., the state of being which is intermediate. Then it is nothing (*ayin*) and cannot be apprehended at all (*ve-eyn adam yakhol la-amod alav*). For it has reached the level of *Ayin* as before creation. Then it is created as a new creation, just as [in the case of the transformation] from egg to chick. That moment in which the destruction of the egg is completed, [but] before the beginning of the constitution of the chick is *Ayin*. In philosophy, it is called *Hyle*, which cannot be apprehended at all, for it is the power that precedes creation and is called *Tohu*. Similarly a growing seed such as the five types of grain and other seeds, will not begin to grow until that seed has perished in the earth and lost its being, as is known, so that it can reach [the state of] *Ayin*, which is the level that precedes creation. It is [also] called *Hokhmah* (wisdom) or thought which is not revealed. After this it is created. For "*you made everything in Hokhmah.*"[27] As for the Gemara's expression "merely dust," this means *Hyle* is called dust, according to the verse, "*all was from the dust,*"[28] which is the *Hyle*, as is known. It is called dust because it is the primal matter (*Hyle*) for material things. This is the meaning of "*everything came from the dust,*" i.e., the *Hyle* , "*and all returns to the dust,*"[29] i.e., the *Hyle*. Consequently, if a person wishes to be a new creation, not a [merely] physical and material [one that] desires material things, but [one that desires] only God, he must try as often as possible to attain this level of awe in his thought which leads to humility so that he may arrive at the quality of *Ayin*. Then God will create him as a new creation and he will be like a source that increases and a stream that never ceases."[30]

Although the analogy of the chick and the egg and the idea that transformation requires passing through an intermediate state of *Ayin* are taken from the teachings of Dov Ber, this is clearly an original exposition by Meshullam Feibush. The analogy and the association of *Ayin* with *Hokhmah* and the primordial matter (*Hyle*) are found in several contexts within Dov Ber's writings.[31] However, in none of the texts does the Maggid concern himself with explicating the Gemara. Nor does he make use of the verse from Kohelet as a proof text for explaining the meaning of Hyle.

Moreover, in all cases, details appear which Meshullam Feibush omits. For example, Dov Ber characteristically refers to the capacity of *Ayin* or *Hyle* to unite opposites. It is the power which allows the four elements to be combined into the composite entities that characterize creation.[32] Another theme which Meshullam Feibush fails to mention concerns the *Zaddiq's* capacity to effect a change in the divine thought as result of the association of *Hyle* and *Hokhmah*.[33] As for the transformation that occurs when a person reaches *Ayin*, Dov Ber's exposition differs somewhat from Meshullam Feibush's text.

> It is known that when one brings anything in the world to its root, one can cause it to change from what it was at first. For example, when one wants to transform a grain of wheat into a quantity of wheat, one brings it to its root, which is the growing power that is in the earth. Consequently, it will only grow in the earth and not in any other place. Even there it will not grow until rain falls and moistens it and causes it to lose its form and to reach the quality of *Ayin*, which is the primordial matter (*homer ha-Hyle*) or *Hokhmah*, as is known. Moreover, it is the root of all, as it is written, "*you made everything with Hokhmah.*"[34] Then the growing power can effect it, and much wheat will grow from it. Similarly, when a person brings himself to his root, i.e. to *Ayin*, he reduces himself, like *Hokhmah* which reduces itself. Then the qualities of love and awe, etc., will be transformed in him, [so that] all will be directed to God alone. For when the qualities are cleaving to material things, they are separate branches, for when one loves something one does not fear it and one does not love what one fears. But, when [the qualities] are cleaving to God they are entirely a unity, as is known. For the aspect of *Ayin* unites everything. And it is impossible to reach the level of *Hokhmah* until he is in a state of awe, for without awe there is no *Hokhmah*. When he has attained complete awe of the creator, love will automatically rest upon him . . .[35]

Although the passage does contain many of the ideas and motifs which Meshullam Feibush includes, its emphasis is different. In both texts, the transformation involves a change of focus from involvement with material objects to an exclusive interest in God. In both cases, awe is required in order to reach the level of *Ayin* where the transformation occurs. Dov Ber's text, however, occurs within a context that views the transformation from materiality to *devequt* as moving from a state of multiplicity and conflicting emotional qualities to one of unity in which all the qualities are harmoniously balanced. Meshullam Feibush does not concern himself with this issue. Nevertheless, an echo of the idea that *devequt* transforms the world from multiplicity to unity does appear in his discussion of *Shabbat*.[36]

Meshullam Feibush's text concludes with the idea that the transformation that occurs when one reaches *Ayin* renders one "like a spring which increases and a stream that never ceases."[37] This quotation from *Avot* does not appear in any of the texts in *Maggid Devarav le-Ya'aqov* that deal with the *Hyle*.[38] It is difficult to determine Meshullam Feibush's meaning. However, he probably does not have in mind merely the idea that an individual's power increases as a result of the transformation that occurs when it comes to *Ayin*, as is illustrated in the Maggid's analogy of a single seed of wheat which becomes abundant as a result of the power of growth. The motif is more fully developed in another passage in *Maggid Devarav le-Ya'aqov*.[39] There, the point is made that an individual has greater capacity to act as a channel for divine effluence (*shefa'*) when it ascends to its root. However, it is quite possible that Meshullam Feibush has in mind a somewhat different idea. Later in a text, that may have been influenced by the thought of Moses Hayyim Luzzatto, he indicates that a person who has realized *Ayin* becomes capable of sanctifying even nominally secular objects and activities. This idea is supported by an interpretation of the same mishnah from *Avot*, which is attributed to the Ba'al Shem Tov, but which was heard from Menahem Mendel of Premishlan.[40]

It seems, then, that Meshullam Feibush has, in general, explicated genuine elements of Dov Ber's teachings, although he has combined and selected them from various sources, choosing only those emphases which pertain to his interest in *devequt*. He has also felt free to explain them with scriptural and talmudic references of his own.[41] His presentation is, in general, very faithful to Dov Ber's teachings. Nevertheless, his language does add a characteristic emphasis that is not found in the Dov Ber texts. While in the latter, there is a tendency to emphasize the transformation that occurs as a result of *Ayin*, the theistic aspect of the process is not stressed. Meshullam Feibush, on the other hand, says explicitly that when one reaches the level of *Ayin*, "then God will create him [as] a new creation."[42]

Although Meshullam Feibush does not concern himself with all of the ramifications of Dov Ber's theory of *devequt*, the basis of his conception of *devequt* is, nevertheless, essentially faithful to Dov Ber's teachings. Consider, for example, the following well-known text.

> The Holy One, blessed be He, underwent (*asah*) many contractions through many worlds so that He could be a unity with man, for [otherwise man] could not bear His brilliance (*behirut*). And a person has to separate himself from all corporeality to such an extent, until he ascends through all the worlds and becomes a unity with the Holy One, blessed be He, until his existence is entirely negated . . .[43]

Union with God is possible because the path to God retraces the same stages of divine emanation through which creation was produced. Just as God had to progressively contract the divine essence in order for a material world to exist, so man must divest himself of the various levels of corporeality in order to return to God. *Devequt* leads to self-annihilation through which one becomes a unity with God. These aspects are all retained in Meshullam Feibush's teachings.[44]

Nevertheless, Meshullam Feibush has given Dov Ber's interpretation of the Gemara a different emphasis. The superiority of the deeds of *Zaddiqim* over the act of creation lies not merely in their capacity to return sparks of holiness to their divine source, but in their own efforts to return in their minds to the conditions which preceded creation. While it would be incorrect to infer that Dov Ber places any less emphasis on *devequt* and unity, it is clear that Meshullam Feibush's position is colored by other influences as well.[45] Moreover, we see clearly that Meshullam Feibush, while very much informed by Dov Ber's teachings, nevertheless, feels free to change their context.

Another case in which Meshullam Feibush removes a teaching of Dov Ber from its original context involves an early hasidic interpretation of the Midrash, "what was the world lacking [at the end of the six days of creation]? *Menuhah* (rest). When *Shabbat* came, *menuhah* came."[46] The point of the Midrash is to resolve an apparent contradiction. On the one hand, the work of creation was completed in six days. Yet Gen. 2:2 states that God completed his work on the seventh day. The midrashic solution is that the work was completed on the seventh day with the addition of *menuhah* (rest) which is not additional work. Dov Ber's version appears within a context that emphasizes the power of repentance.

> Our Rabbis of blessed memory said, "whoever observes *Shabbat* properly is pardoned, even if he is guilty of idol worship like the generation of Enosh."[47] For there is [a midrash], "what did the world lack? *Menuhah*. When *Shabbat* came, *menuhah* came." The world was created during the six days of action, and by means of God's speech, i.e., the letters of the Torah, and all came to be from *Ayin*. But creation still did not contain the power of the creator, which maintains it. For the Holy One, blessed be He, is called *menuhah* because movement does not apply to Him, since movement only applies to something in time and space. But the Holy One, blessed be He, is infinite and is not transferred from place to place and is also not bound by time . . .[48]

Although Meshullam Feibush quotes and explicates several parts of this passage accurately, he makes use of it for a different purpose. His context is the stages of creation. The world was created in two stages. First, there was an entirely spiritual creation which was produced by divine thought. Afterwards, a material creation came into existence through divine speech.

> It is known that our sages of blessed memory said concerning the verse, "*And God completed His work on the seventh day* . . . ,"[49] "What was the world lacking? *Menuhah.* When Shabbat came, *menuhah* came . . ." And I have found written in the name of the supreme saint, Rabbi Ber . . . , the meaning is in keeping with the truth of our faith that the creation of the worlds was for Israel. . . . The meaning is that it arose before Him in thought that the worlds should exist so that Israel would be created in their midst and would serve and cleave to Him. This ascent in thought was an actual immediate [act of] creating . . . except it was a very spiritual [kind] of creating in accord with the level of thought. . . . But the ultimate intention was a material creation, and later divine speech came and a chain of emanations from cause to cause until [the process] reached its completion in materiality . . .[50]

Meshullam Feibush is not concerned with Dov Ber's explication of the mystical connections between *Shabbat* and repentance, but only with his implied association of *Shabbat* with divine immanence. Thus, he brings the teaching in a passage that deals with the need to fill the world with additional illumination so that it may continue to exist. This is the case because the second, material stage of creation involved excessive contraction of the divine essence. When the work of creation was completed, the resulting material world needed to be infused with some of the divine energy which had been withheld within the primordial divine thought. This energy is a manifestation of the divine essence which is called "*menuhah*" (rest), because it issues from a level that is beyond time and space.[51]

> After everything was completed on the sixth day, if the world had remained in this condition, creation would not have been able to [continue to] exist because of the little energy that was in it. For the [divine] energy in corporeality is contracted. Consequently, after the completion of the work of creation, God manifested an illumination from the concealed [level] of creation, i.e., from that which was constituted in His thought, [as a] very spiritual entity. It is the actual divine essence. He caused His glorious splendor to shine forth from one end of the world to the other throughout all the work of creation. Above all, He radiated into man, His chosen creature, an illumination from his concealed root which is in God's thought. This is the meaning of "what was the world lacking? *menuhah.*" In other words, God is called *menuhah* because movement from place to place does not apply to Him, as is the case concerning [His] creatures.[52]

The notion of two stages of creation, thought and speech, are also typical of Dov Ber's thought.[53] The mere fact that Meshullam Feibush has chosen to elaborate on these ideas here does not in itself constitute a divergence
from Dov Ber's teachings. However, there does seem to be a significant difference in Meshullam Feibush's argument. Meshullam Feibush tends towards a more pessimistic appraisal of human spiritual potential than Dov
Ber. This is reflected here in the total emphasis on the need for divine aid
rather than human effort in order to maintain the world's existence. In
Meshullam Feibush's text only the idea of *Shabbat* as an additional manifestation of divine energy is brought out. Of course, in the larger context of
his thought, Meshullam Feibush also indicates that this manifestation of divine immanence constitutes a favorable opportunity for *devequt*. Nevertheless, the possibility of realizing this *devequt* is only due to the fact that God
has, so to speak, made Himself available.[54] In Dov Ber's text, on the other
hand, the issue of *Shabbat* is set within the context of repentance. Repentance is compared to *Shabbat* because it restores cosmic harmony. The
Maggid's emphasis is on the power of repentance which is a human action.
Thus, the entire thrust of Dov Ber's text is to underscore the vast potential
of human spiritual effort, while the aspect of divine grace is not emphasized
at all.[55]

A final example of Meshullam Feibush's tendency to adopt early Hasidic teachings, without being concerned with their original context, is his
use of the talmudic midrash concerning concealed light.

> I heard [the following] from the Rav, the Hasid, our teacher and master, Rabbi
> Gershon Lutzker,[56] a disciple of the divine R. Dov Ber of blessed memory. In the
> name of his master, he interpreted a teaching of our sages of blessed memory,[57]
> "the Holy One blessed be He saw that it was not proper to make use of the light
> and He concealed it for [the use of] *Zaddiqim* in the future."[58] He raised the
> question, "where did He conceal it?" I'll abbreviate his discussion, [presenting
> only] the essence of his interpretation of the words of our sages of blessed mem
> ory. The Torah is a great light, and at first this light was revealed. But later the
> Holy One, blessed be He, concealed it. Where did He conceal it? In the Torah. He
> concealed it so that the light is not revealed to fools and to people who are not
> whole. They do not grasp what is concealed. But the light is destined to reach the
> *Zaddiqim* who tremble for His word and seek God, searching for Him like a
> treasure. As the verse says, "*if you will seek me like silver . . .*"[59] And this is [the
> meaning of] He concealed it for the *Zaddiqim* of the future: in the future, the
> light will reach them through their seeking God by means of the Torah.[60]

Primordial light has been concealed in the Torah. This light is only seen by
the *Zaddiqim* who constantly seek God while they are studying. However,

those whose spiritual development is not complete fail to grasp this light. The light, of course, is the divine presence which is apprehended through the inner feelings of love and awe.

> For God is concealed and revealed. [He is] concealed from every eye, but revealed in the hearts and minds that diligently desire and constantly seek to cleave to Him by means of His Torah and His commandments. Through this, God, who is concealed in His Torah which is His name, reveals Himself in the hearts of His people and the heart feels His love and awe most intensely . . . In other words, [the Torah] reveals and shows them what is concealed, namely, God.[61]

Although Dov Ber does make use of this midrash in a number of places in his extant writings,[62] he never uses it merely to argue that God is revealed through Torah study. In general, the Maggid uses the midrash to deal with three issues: the need to reduce the divine illumination so that creation will be capable of receiving it, light as a symbol for *Hokhmah*, and as an explanation for how miracles can be effected by *Zaddiqim*. Since Meshullam Feibush reports that he heard this teaching of the Maggid from Gershon Lutzker, but is not bringing it in its entirety, it is not possible to determine exactly what, if anything, he chose to omit. It is clear, however, that his version reflects none of the interests that are found in texts attributed to Dov Ber. Most significant, perhaps, is Meshullam Feibush's lack of interest in the miraculous aspect of the midrash. Early Hasidic interest in this aspect goes back to the Ba'al Shem Tov and emphasizes the latter's ability to see clairvoyantly by gazing into *sefer ha-Zohar*.[63] Nevertheless, the issue does not seem to appear anywhere in Meshullam Feibush's extant writings.

Up to this point, we have been dealing with examples of Meshullam Feibush's use of Dov Ber's teachings that remain essentially faithful to the Maggid's thought. The most that can be said is that Meshullam Feibush's interests tend to be much narrower than those of Dov Ber. Where the latter concerns himself with a number of subtle issues and questions that arise in the course of presenting his interpretation of earlier, primarily, kabbalistic sources, Meshullam Feibush tends to focus on the one central issue of the mystical experience of *devequt* as apprehension of the divine presence and the moral and spiritual development which it implies. In removing Dov Ber's teachings from their original context, there is no implied criticism of or deviation from the Maggid's teachings. Rather, Meshullam Feibush has taken the position of an intermediary who selects and interprets those aspects of Dov Ber's teaching which he deems appropriate for his readers.[64] There are, however, a number of important cases in which Meshullam

Feibush does take a position that is different than the Maggid's. An analysis of these cases is crucial for the understanding of his contribution to early Hasidism.

The first case in which Meshullam Feibush takes a position that deviates from Dov Ber's involves the Maggid's analogy comparing Lurianic *kavvanot* to keys which open locks.[65] The analogy implies that the journey which a prayer makes on the way to its ultimate goal involves passing through many intermediate stations. Each of these can be entered by applying the appropriate *kavvanah* which functions like a key. However, there is another way to pass through all of these barriers. Through breaking one's heart, one, as it were, breaks all the locks like a thief who breaks in without using keys. The point of the analogy is to compare the efficacy of the *devequt* of prayer with the Lurianic *kavvanot*. However, in the version of this analogy which appears in the Maggid's writings,[66] a further step is taken. There it is emphasized that *devequt* is not only equal in efficacy to the Lurianic approach, but is indeed superior to it. For *devequt* immediately connects one with the "intellect that is beyond the worlds." In another passage, Dov Ber argues that the way of the *kavvanot* is limited, whereas *devequt*, by uniting man directly to God, is necessarily unlimited in its effect.[67] Dov Ber is advocating an alternative mystical approach to prayer which supercedes the way of *kavvanot*.[68]

> Whoever prays using all the *kavvanot* that are known to him can only use those [specific] *kavvanot* which he knows. But when one says [each] word [of his prayer] with great connection [to God], all of the *kavvanot* are immediately included in the entire word. For each and every letter is a whole world. When one says the word with great attachment, surely those supernal worlds[69] are aroused and he does great deeds through this. Therefore, a person should be sure to pray with great attachment and great enthusiasm[70] and he will certainly accomplish great acts in the supernal worlds. For every letter has an effect (*me'orer*) above.[71]

We have already seen that Meshullam Feibush by and large ascribes to Dov Ber's theory of prayer which emphasizes focusing on the letters.[72] Nevertheless, his use of the Maggid's analogy has a different purpose. Meshullam Feibush is not primarily interested in arguing that *devequt* is equivalent or superior to the Lurianic method. Rather, he wishes to emphasize the importance of "breaking the heart."

> The meaning is that for every concealed matter there is a key which is the *kavvanah* that applies to that matter. But the essence of the key is to be like a thief

who breaks everything, i.e., to thoroughly break the heart in great submission. Then the barrier which divides above will be broken . . .73

Meshullam Feibush is not arguing against the *kavvanot* as such. Nor is he taking the position that the *kavvanot* are outmoded. He is claiming that the key to the *kavvanot* is *devequt*. Only an inner state of genuine submission and attachment to God renders the *kavvanot* effective. His reason for not advocating use of the *kavvanot* is not because there is a better way, but because it is so difficult to fulfill even the most basic requirement for employing them. *Devequt* can only be achieved when one has purified himself of all corporeal desires and negative qualities. Then one would be able to practice the Lurianic *kavvanot*. However, since he addresses himself to those who cannot claim such a lofty spiritual achievement, he argues that it would be vanity to try to use the *kavvanot*.

> For the essence of the *kavvanah* is breaking the heart and love and awe. . . . If we would merit this, we could easily practice all the Lurianic *kavvanot*. For, in reality, they were only addressed to people like him, or [to those] on a slightly lower level, whose hearts are already pure of all contamination. . . . But we are tainted from head to foot . . . and are, consequently, far from God and unable to direct our minds to Him at all, even in the literal sense. So how can we employ *kavvanot* that stand at the summit of the world? Consequently, I have chosen to practice one *kavvanah*, to direct the heart to God as much as possible, concentrating on the words [of prayer] as much as possible.74

We see here a very different position concerning the Lurianic *kavvanot* from the one that Dov Ber takes. Meshullam Feibush does not advocate a new way of prayer that is superior to the Lurianic method. Indeed, he is not even recommending for general use, Dov Ber's intensely contemplative approach. His argument maintains that even *devequt* is beyond the capacity of people like himself.75 Meshullam Feibush's position regarding the *kavvanot* reflects that fundamental difference between his religious outlook and that of Dov Ber which we mentioned above. The Maggid's teachings are remarkably optimistic concerning the human potential for religious experience. His way is even more powerful than the awesome *kavvanot* that unlock the gates of supernal worlds. Dov Ber's method allows one to reach "the Intellect that is beyond the worlds, where even a great sinner is received in repentance."76 In contrast, Meshullam Feibush is decidedly more pessimistic. According to him, "we cannot even turn our minds to [God] in the literal sense." However, it is not so much that he denies Dov Ber's approach in theory, as that he reserves its application for Dov Ber and other great *Zaddiqim*, especially his own master, Yehiel Mikhel of Zlotchov. However, he is totally skeptical about his own ability and worthiness to follow such a way himself.[77]

The attitude that some of Dov Ber's teachings, at least, were appropriate only for a spiritual elite was also expressed in regard to another important issue. The question of how to deal with intrusive thoughts during prayer (*meheshevot zarot*) was one of the most important themes addressed in early Hasidic literature.[78] The issue held great interest for Meshullam Feibush who was concerned lest Dov Ber's solution to the problem be adopted for general use. In essence the issue reverted to an innovation of the Ba'al Shem Tov.[79] Earlier kabbalists, at least since the sixteenth-century, had been concerned with the problem of disturbing thoughts. However, their approach tended to advocate rejection of these thoughts through heightened concentration or through asceticism.[80] However, the Ba'al Shem Tov developed an approach which involved a psychological interpretation of the Lurianic doctrine concerning divine sparks which had fallen into the external shells as a result of the shattering of the vessels.[81] Combining his interpretation of this doctrine with a strong tendency towards pantheism, the Ba'al Shem Tov assumed that a divine spark is to be found in all thoughts. Consequently, thoughts which seem to be impure should not be rejected, but should be seen as an opportunity for releasing a divine spark from captivity in the external shells. In practice, this called for recognition of a thought's divine source in the world of the *sefirot*. For example, a lustful thought was assumed to be a spark that has fallen from the *sefirah*, *Hesed*. Through identifying the thought's divine source, one elevated it from the external shells.

At the root of the Ba'al Shem Tov's approach was a metaphysical assumption which had a wider application. Not only impure thoughts during prayer were to be viewed as shells containing divine sparks, but also neutral, nominally secular activities such as eating, drinking, and ordinary conversation came under the general rule that the divine was to be found everywhere. Thus, even activities which involve corporeal pleasure were to be treated as opportunities for releasing sparks (*avodah be-gashmiyut*). The Ba'al Shem Tov's radically "tantric" approach[82] was, in general, adapted by Dov Ber of Mezeritch.

The doctrines of elevating impure thoughts and *avodah be-gashmiyut* appear in all the collections of Dov Ber's teachings and were included in the manuscripts which reached Meshullam Feibush. This is true even in the case of *Liqqutim Yeqarim*.[83]

Since the teachings of the Ba'al Shem Tov, himself, were not in general circulation until the publication of *Toledot Ya'aqov Yosef* in 1780, the circulation

of Dov Ber's teachings in the 1770s marked the first widespread dissemination of these ideas.[84] Consequently, Meshullam Feibush felt compelled to
comment on them.

In order to illustrate the general approach, Meshullam Feibush cites a
text which compares the process of elevating impure thoughts to the rabbinic hermeneutical principle called *"qal ve-homer."*[85] The implication is
that if one feels a certain emotion in regard to a material entity, one should
realize how much more that feeling is aroused by the object's divine source
in the *sefirot.* Through this reflection the material object is transformed into
a means for cleaving to the divine. However, Meshullam Feibush has argued
that this argument is easier to apply in theory than in practice. As long as
one continues to enjoy or be affected by the feeling produced by the material object, the transformative argument has no real effect: one remains attached to corporeality. His position is, then, that only those who have developed spiritually to the extent that they indeed are detached from
corporeality can apply this teaching. This in effect restricts it for the use of a
very select spiritual elite.

> This should be your general rule, for certainly you even understand this your-
> self. Nevertheless [I feel compelled to comment], since these aforementioned
> writings of our master and teacher, the Rav Dov Ber, of blessed memory,
> have been revealed to many people. Yet few are they who may be compared to him
> and follow his practice, even in the least degree. But they see there that he fre-
> quently writes in the following manner. From an evil love which occurs to a
> person, he can grasp love of the Creator, through [applying the reasoning of]
> *qal ve-homer.* If my will inclines to love this foolishness which is [only residue
> that fell during the shattering of the vessels], then *qal ve-homer,* [it should in-
> cline to its root, love of the Creator. For from Him this love was taken.
>
> Similarly, in the case of an evil awe . . . [etc][86] Now those who lack intelli-
> gence think, when they see this, that it is an easy matter to apply this *qal ve-
> homer* argument, just as one reasons *qal ve homer* in the Gemara. But there it
> is [merely] an intellectual operation and here it is a matter of practice. For it is
> impossible to make use of this *qal ve-homer* unless one is detached from corpo-
> reality. For if one is attached to corporeality and desires and willfully receives
> pleasure from [such things], then he certainly knows nothing of love of the
> Creator and awe of Him and His splendor, etc. For he has not tasted it at all. But
> the verse says, *"taste and see that YHVH is good."*[87] God forbid, one may fall
> into a deep pit, if he is not very careful. So one must protect himself with all the
> protective measures *(herhaqim)* which are found in the ethical works. The rem-
> edy of extracting the precious from the worthless through applying the *qal ve-
> homer* may only be employed by one who is [already] detached from corporeal-
> ity. Even so, occasionally some evil love or evil awe [may be aroused in his
> heart]. For he is not yet completely purified and detached. The residue wishes to

seize him and to distract him. Thus he will be more greatly aroused with love of the Creator and awe of Him.[88]

It is important to note that Meshullam Feibush takes no issue with the general theory of *avodah be-gashmiut*. *Qal ve-homer* can be applied when feelings are aroused by material things. However, it may only be resorted to by those who are primarily free of desire for and attachment to such feelings. Indeed he goes on to present in detail a parable from Dov Ber's writings,[89] which teaches that all the emotions that are aroused in the normal course of material existence, whether of love or fear, are in actuality messengers from God. They are only meant to remind a person that the proper object towards which those emotions should be directed is God Himself.

> The parable concerns a person in whose heart awe and love of God constantly burn like a fire, but who is still not yet completely purified. [If] occasionally evil love or awe or splendor is aroused in him, he will know clearly that this was sent to him by God. For example, in the case of awe, one may see something that arouses fear, such as a gentile or a fearsome dog[!] When he becomes frightened by this thing, he will know that it was sent to him from heaven, because he has fallen off and slipped in his thought from awe of God. The King wishes to summon him to His awe. So he sends him this frightful messenger from the shattering [of the vessels] which is in this world. Now if he is alert (*nilbav*), he will remember and flee from this fear to awe of the King. For this thing came to summon him and to remind him to quickly approach the King. So why should he appease the messenger? Let him flee in his thought and soul to God.[90]

The only aspect of the interpretation that diverges somewhat from the original sources is the repeated emphasis that the entire issue applies to a person who is, more or less, constantly in a state of *devequt*. For Meshullam Feibush, this means one who constantly experiences awe and love of God. The explicit restriction is Meshullam Feibush's addition. However, like the Ba'al Shem Tov, Meshullam Feibush understands the process of *avodah be-gashmiyut* as a psycho-spiritual basis for elevating the fallen sparks.

> And it is similar in the case of transforming corporeal love. If some evil love is aroused in him because he fell from love of God and God wishes to arouse him and to delight him with His great love, [He] sends a residue of love which is this world's messenger for [divine] love. Then by means of [the process] that I explained in the parable, sparks from the broken vessels are elevated. For evil [experiences] of love, awe, and splendor, which are only drawn to materiality [as a means] for connecting to God, are the residue from the broken vessels which have not been purified (*nivreru*).[91]

Meshullam Feibush's treatment of the issues of *avodah be-gashmiyut* and elevation of impure thoughts is indicative of his general approach to the teachings of Dov Ber. He accepts in principle Dov Ber's theories and analogies, but does not advocate the general practice of the contemplative and "tantric" aspects.

> The Rav, R. Ber, may his memory be a blessing for life in the world to come, offered a fine analogy concerning this matter of impure thoughts that overwhelm us during prayer. One must make a great effort to drive them off, even though the impure distractions increase. For it is virtually impossible for a mortal to subdue them were it not for God's help. [Dov Ber] spoke many wonderful secrets concerning this. Some of them are contained in the writings that are in your possession. But these things are meant for the [spiritual] giants, while we know nothing of how to elevate impure thoughts to their root as is written there, just as I wrote in the first treatise.[92] But the analogy [itself][93] does apply to us.[94]

In Meshullam Feibush's version of the analogy, a father asks a learned guest to test his son in knowledge of the Torah. When the guest sees that the father takes pleasure in the son's answers, he increases the difficulty of the questions in order to increase the father's pleasure. As long as the son continues to make an effort to solve the problems, the father is proud. The point of the analogy is to show that the impure thoughts are sent by God as a test. Despite one's efforts, God increases the impure thoughts because of the pleasure He receives from the determined, if unsuccessful, efforts to overcome them.

However, there is a significant difference between Meshullam Feibush and Dov Ber's use of this analogy. In Dov Ber's version the son does succeed no matter how difficult the test becomes.[95] Moreover, Dov Ber does not relate this analogy to the specific problem of elevating wayward thoughts. It concerns the general problem of overcoming the evil urge. In Dov Ber's version, God helps the *Zaddiq* to overcome the evil urge because of His great love for His son. He cannot bear to see His son frustrated. Although the evil urge increases the difficulties that the son must confront so that God's pleasure will be increased, the son is able to meet the challenge because of the divine aid that he receives. Dov Ber uses the analogy to illustrate the extent of the divine love that a person merits when he has attained that lofty spiritual level called "son [of God]." At this level, the son's victory over the evil urge is paradoxical. God takes pleasure in the son's efforts despite the fact that the victory is, in reality, entirely the result of divine aid.

Meshullam Feibush, on the other hand, assumes that his readers are not capable of overcoming the evil urge. Thus, they have no hope of elevat-ing impure thoughts. In his version, although the son cannot possibly win, he is, nevertheless, rewarded for his efforts. Meshullam Feibush's version recalls a teaching of the Ba'al Shem Tov that makes use of a somewhat sim-ilar analogy.

> It may be compared to a young child who is very much loved by his father. When the child asks his father for something, even though he stutters and can-not speak properly, the father is very pleased. Consequently, when a person ut-ters words of Torah with love, God loves him very much and is not concerned whether he says them properly or not. As the sages said [concerning the verse], "'and his flag (diGLo) of love over me,'[96] God said, 'and his stammering (liGLuBo) of love over me.'"[97]

As in Meshullam Feibush's teaching, the Ba'al Shem Tov seems to be assert-ing that God's love overlooks the imperfections of those who sincerely serve Him. Nevertheless, Meshullam Feibush's context and meaning is consider-ably different. He specifically has in mind the impossibility of overcoming wayward thoughts and opposes the Ba'al Shem Tov's practice of elevating them. The Ba'al Shem Tov's analogy, as is clear from the context, is con-cerned with a very different phenomenon. He is addressing the problem of a person who, while cleaving to the spiritual lights contained in the letters of the Torah, fails to adhere to the cantillation. The Ba'al Shem Tov invokes the Midrash's analogy in order to justify his preference for the mystical practice of cleaving to the letters even when this results in inaccurate articulation of the words. Thus, the Ba'al Shem Tov's teaching is related to the Cordoverian conception of Torah study which emphasizes cleaving to the spiritual lights within the letters. This is pleasing to God even when the person does not understand what he is reading.[98]

One important point should be noted in Meshullam Feibush's use of the analogy. Unlike Dov Ber, he does not apply it specifically to the Zad-diqim who are "sons [of God]." For Meshullam Feibush, it becomes more of a general explanation for the human spiritual condition.

> Accordingly, we can draw an inference from [Dov Ber's] words. Although one cannot defeat the evil urge with its many stratagems for increasing the [im-pure] thoughts that surround us like hills around a field, nevertheless, let us do all that we can. God will still derive some pleasure, as in the analogy. If the youth is unable to succeed in arriving at the truth, but at least offers some basis for solving the problem (mepalpel kakh 'o kakh), although he does not arrive at the truth, his father still receives some pleasure from him. For he thinks, I see that at least he makes an effort. . . . This can be applied to many other matters

[regarding] subduing the evil urge. For this is required in every act and with every quality. It is true that above all subduing the evil urge apples to prayer. Nevertheless, whenever an evil quality arises in us, one must subdue [it] as much as possible. God will derive great pleasure from this. . . . For this is the reason that] He created us, even though we cannot finish the battle . . .[99]

Again we see Meshullam Feibush's emphasis on the limitations of human power. This emphasis, as we have indicated, distinguishes his religious orientation from that of Dov Ber. Although, it must be stressed that this is a matter of emphasis and not an absolute distinction, it seems fair to characterize Dov Ber's position as more optimistic concerning human power, since there is so much emphasis in his writings on contemplative experience and the miraculous powers which are acquired when *devequt* is complete. It is possible to find passages in which Dov Ber acknowledges the absolute power of God. However, even in such cases, one may find an ultimate emphasis on human effort.

> And the verse continues, "*great is YHVH and much praised [in the city of our God]*."[100] In other words, we should glorify and praise Him for all the good that He bestows upon us. But, He gives us the power to serve Him. For all the greatness and splendor that He derives from our worship is entirely "*in the city*" (*be-'iR*) which means through the arousal (*hit'oReRut*) "*of our God.*" For [it is] He [who] arouses us and gives us the power to serve Him and to overcome. As our rabbis, of blessed memory, said, "if the Holy One blessed be He did not help him, [one would not be able to prevail]."[101] Nevertheless, God derives pleasure and pride (*tif'eret*) and pays us a great reward as if we did it all ourselves. But in reality, the true service would have to be due to our arousal, for we are a portion of the divine above. So this is the meaning of "*in the city*:" through the arousal of the good urge [which is] the divine portion within us, this is the meaning of "*our God.*"[102]

The passage is remarkable, for within it Dov Ber virtually defines the divine aid that can overcome the evil urge as the positive tendency already present within the human soul. That is "*our God.*" According to Meshullam Feibush's analysis of the human predicament, human nature is generally too weak to be effective. Submission to God through recognition of one's helplessness sets the stage for divine aid. Nevertheless, Meshullam Feibush is not so extreme as to deny entirely the importance of human effort.

As we have seen, Meshullam Feibush is for the most part extremely faithful to Dov Ber's teachings, only he tends to present them within a context that is much less optimistic concerning an ordinary person's capacity to achieve *devequt* with God. This attitude leads directly to his reservations

concerning the attempt to follow Dov Ber's contemplative method of praying and the adaptation of the "tantric" practices of *avodah be-gashmiyut*
and elevation of impure thoughts.

The question which remains to be asked is whether this express tendency to restrict Dov Ber's practices to the exclusive use of a spiritual elite
itself constitutes a deviation from the Maggid of Mezeritch's teachings?[103]
Meshullam Feibush, himself, answers this question for us by citing a teaching that he found in the manuscripts that he has associated with Dov Ber.

> In these words you will have a great light for all circumstances, so that you may
> understand which way to follow. For very far from us is the true way. You
> should understand that the aforementioned writings speak entirely of a saintly
> person [who is] detached [from corporeality], as I wrote *above, and as the Rav,
> of blessed memory, wrote in the new writings that are in my possession*[104] con-
> cerning the mishnah, "children may go out [on *Shabbat*] with garlands (*qe-
> sharim*), and children of kings with bells, and every person [may act accord-
> ingly], except the sages spoke in terms of their own experience."[105] This means,
> that those who are called children [since they] possess the level of *neshamah* in
> addition to the levels of *nefesh* and *ruah*,[106] and [who] are connected (*meqush-
> arim*) in their thought to the blessed Creator, are permitted to go out occasion-
> ally to the market when necessary. Since they are very connected to the blessed
> Creator, the passersby will not interrupt their *devequt*. This is [the meaning of]
> "the children may go out with garlands (*QeSHaRim*)" [they are] connected *be-
> hitQaSHRut*) In their thought to the Creator. "And the children of kings" refers
> to those who have only a *nefesh* or even a *ruah*. [They] are called children of
> kings, [because the portion of their soul comes] from the side of the heavenly
> kingdom.[107] But [since] they have yet to acquire the portion of the *neshamah*,
> [they must] ""go out" with bells." They may not rely on the binding (*QiSHuR*)
> of their thought [to God], since they have not yet acquired the level of *ne-
> shamah*. Perhaps the bond will not be strong enough, and they will fall. So one
> should not go out idle, but rather like a bell that clangs, sounding its tone. Thus
> one should constantly sound his voice with words of Torah, prayer, and awe of
> God, and not depend on the *devequt* of his thought. For, since his *devequt* is
> weak, the passersby will distract him, God forbid. "And everyone [should act ac-
> cordingly]" means that everyone is equal in this and there is hardly anyone on
> the level of the children who may go out in garlands. The sages only mentioned
> [the level] of the children who may go out in garlands, because they were
> speaking in terms of their own experience. They were referring to themselves
> and not to others. Such were [Dov Ber's] words.[108]

Meshullam Feibush's version of Dov Ber's text makes a clear distinction between levels of spiritual attainment. The point is that only those of the
highest level who possess a *neshamah* can practice *avodah be-gashmiyut*
with impunity. They are free to involve themselves in areas of life that are

not directly connected to religious activity. This is possible for them because of their ability to remain connected to God in their minds. However, everyone else must rely on the presence of words of Torah and prayer in their minds in order to remain connected with God. Thus, ordinary people are not so free to involve themselves with the public. An attempt on their part to practice *avodah be-gashmiyut* could be dangerous for them. For it is likely that they would be distracted by the secular conversations of others and run the risk of losing the *devequt* they might otherwise have maintained had they remained connected to the Torah.

Dov Ber's text, which is meant to explain how a *Zaddiq* can remain in *devequt* even when circumstances compel him to abandon his studies and prayer, does indeed make this distinction.

> There are *Zaddiqim* for whom learning Torah is their trade. [Yet] such a one is compelled to neglect his learning and to go through the markets and streets in order to provide for his family. What does the *Zaddiq* do before venturing out to the marketplace? He prays and beseeches God and joins and unites his soul with holy thought in order not to be caught in the traps of the evil urge when he goes out. Now it is known that whoever has [attained] a *neshamah* which is from *Binah* is called "child" and there are those who have only managed [to attain] the portion of *nefesh* which is from *Malkhut*, such a one is called "child of the king." So this may be what is alluded to in the Mishnah, "the children," i.e., those that have a *neshamah*, are permitted to go out with garlands, i.e., [such a person] should connect his *neshamah* with its root which is called "thought" as is known,[109] and then he can go out . . .[110]

The reliance on the *devequt* of thought is only for *Zaddiqim* who have attained a *neshamah*, everyone else, as the text continues, must go out with "bells," the sound of words of Torah, just as Meshullam Feibush has indicated. Thus, a basis for distinguishing between practices that are appropriate only for a small spiritual elite and those that should be followed by ordinary people can be found in Dov Ber's authentic teachings.[111]

Meshullam Feibush's opposition to the unrestricted employment of contemplative and "tantric" practices that were advocated by the Ba'al Shem Tov and Dov Ber of Mezeritch is consistent with an attitude that is expressed in the latter's teachings. To this we might add that the other leading disciple of the Ba'al Shem Tov, Jacob Joseph of Polnoy, also acknowledged that the process of elevating impure thoughts, at least, is dangerous.[112] Moreover, in Jacob Joseph's writings a clear distinction between the spiritual leadership (*anshey zurah*) and the masses (*anshey homer*) is repeatedly stressed. Nevertheless, Meshullam Feibush does not seem to have been influenced in his early writings by Jacob Joseph whom he never mentions.[113] As for Dov Ber, while, as we have seen, the distinction is clearly made, it cannot be said that this issue receives much emphasis in his writings. Thus, Meshullam Feibush has taken a basically peripheral issue in Dov Ber's thought and placed it in the center. The question that must be answered is whether in doing so, Meshullam Feibush was expressing his own temperament or responding to historical circumstances. Earlier scholars have tended to emphasize only the first explanation.[114] However, regardless of whatever natural impulses may have contributed to the formulation of Meshullam Feibush's position, there is no doubt that historical circumstances required him to deal with the issue. Dov Ber's teachings emanate from a period in which no popular Hasidic movement as such yet existed. His teachings are invariably addressed to a spiritual elite whom he wished to influence and to persuade to follow his methods.

Meshullam Feibush, on the other hand, wrote when the Hasidic teachings were becoming more widely available through the circulation of manuscripts. At the same time, followers of both the Ba'al Shem Tov and Dov Ber had begun to function as religious leaders who represented their masters' teachings throughout a wide area of eastern Europe. At this point, two important developments had occurred. On the one hand, Hasidism as a popular movement was beginning to become a reality. On the other, organized opposition to the movement and criticism of its teachings had become a threat. Under such circumstances, the question of the *Zaddiq* could not remain theoretical. Nor could it be assumed that everyone that was attracted to the Hasidic teachings could become a *Zaddiq* or would want to become one. As Hasidism was transformed from an esoteric school involving an elite group of pneumatics to a popular movement that attracted a wider range of religious types, the need arose for Hasidic teachings that were addressed to the followers of the Hasidic leadership and not merely to its potential successors. This was the role that Meshullam Feibush's writings played. In general, Meshullam Feibush remained faithful to the teachings of Dov Ber. However, he presented them in a more popularized way that, based upon a more pessimistic and sober view of human spiritual potential, placed particular emphasis on the distinction between the *Zaddiqim* and the ordinary people. In making this important distinction, Meshullam Feibush's relationship to his own master, the *Zaddiq*, Yehiel Mikhel of Zlotchov, must certainly have been a deciding factor.

8
The Importance of *Zaddiqim*

As we have seen, a distinction between religious practices which are restricted to a spiritual elite and those which are appropriate for general use plays a fundamental role in Meshullam Feibush's thought. Moreover, while this distinction expresses reservations concerning certain aspects of Dov Ber's teachings, it nevertheless has at least some basis in the Maggid of Mezeritch's own writings. However, if Meshullam Feibush has not introduced an entirely foreign element into his interpretation of Dov Ber's teachings, it is certainly the case that he gives the distinction far greater emphasis than can be found in the extant writings of his teacher. This calls for some explanation.

It has already been suggested with justification that Dov Ber failed to stress that his teachings were directed specifically to a spiritual elite for two main reasons. First, as a teacher who was primarily imparting his path to disciples who did for the most part constitute a spiritual elite, he had no reason to state the obvious. Second, Dov Ber, a contemplative mystic by temperament, did not stress the social implications of his teachings, but was primarily concerned with developing a method for cultivating the inner aspects of mystical praxis which lead to immersion in divine immanence.[1] While it would be going too far to suggest that Dov Ber was entirely unconcerned with the spiritual needs of ordinary people, the spiritual virtuoso's relationship to the masses and social role are not important issues in his teachings. From the historical perspective, it should also be noted that the establishment of Dov Ber's disciples as leaders in various parts of eastern Europe occurred, for the most part, towards the end of his life, c. 1770.[2] Consequently, while the theological, metaphysical, and practical aspects of Dov Ber's theory of the spiritual virtuoso were particularly relevant at this time, the wider social context within which the Maggid's disciples would function had hardly begun to exist. Thus, issues of a more social nature were not nearly as relevant at this time.[3] When viewed within the historical context, Dov Ber appears primarily as a theoretician and teacher of a new type of Jewish mysticism which places particular stress on self-transcendence through union with divine immanence both within and beyond the traditional boundaries of religious life. However, the transformation of his teachings into the basis for a broad and popular religious movement was left for the most part for his disciples to accomplish, primarily after his death.

Meshullam Feibush's writings, with which we are directly concerned, were written precisely in the period following Dov Ber's death. At this time, a Hasidic leadership began to establish itself as religious leaders and spiritual guides who expressly identified themselves as followers of the way of the Ba'al Shem Tov and Dov Ber of Mezeritch. Consequently, it is in the Hasidic writings that were produced in this period that we should expect to find concern for those specific issues that emerged when Hasidism first began to become a bona fide social movement. Such writings, moreover, contained more than merely theoretical discussions of these issues. They reflected the real problems that were encountered when individuals began to be identified as exponents of Hasidic teachings and when these teachings themselves became available to wider audiences through their dissemination, first in manuscript, and a few years later in print.

Among the first questions that had to be addressed by Hasidic thinkers during this early stage of dissemination of the teachings of Dov Ber, concerned the status of the teachings themselves. Did they constitute norms to which all Jews should aspire? If so, given their extremely high standards regarding mystical experience and dedication to spiritual life, it can hardly be imagined that Hasidism could have become a popular movement. As Meshullam Feibush himself tells us in his few references to the difficulties that were commonly encountered during his age, the average Jew could not possibly have found the time that would be required to perfect the path outlined in early Hasidic teachings. A spiritual adept, already dedicated to a life dominated by religious concerns, might be persuaded to embrace the Hasidic way in lieu of the older, more ascetic Lurianic mystical praxis. But the teachings in the form attributed to Dov Ber would have had little to offer to the typical Jew in the villages of eastern Galicia who, indeed, may not have been sufficiently well versed in traditional mystical texts or temperamentally suited to fathom their meaning.

The success of Hasidism as a distinct religious movement depended directly on the articulation of a teaching that could unite ordinary Jews and the Hasidic spiritual masters.[4] In other words, the need existed for an interpretation of Hasidic teachings that was not primarily addressed to potential emulators of Dov Ber's practices, but rather to those who would look upon his followers, in the narrow sense, as the true spiritual leaders of the generation. What was required was a justification of the figure of the spiritual virtuoso who now became increasingly known as a *Zaddiq*.[5] Questions that had to be answered included: what criteria distinguished a *Zaddiq*? What practices were restricted to the *Zaddiq*? What was the basis of the *Zaddiq*'s powers? What benefits were to be gained through attachment to a *Zaddiq*? Who, in actuality, were the genuine *Zaddiqim* of the age? All of these questions were addressed in Meshullam Feibush's writings.

Yosher Divrey Emet is a rather comprehensive interpretation of Judaism from the Hasidic viewpoint. As we have seen, it discusses in some detail the place and nature of Torah study, prayer, and the holidays within religious life. It also places great emphasis on spiritual development, mystical experience, and faith in divine immanence. While all of these issues are treated in the teachings of earlier Hasidic figures, Meshullam Feibush's presentation is in some ways unique. His position tends towards a much more pessimistic assessment of human spiritual potential than is found in Dov Ber's writings and he has his own views concerning the use of Lurianic *kavvanot* and the best way to pray. However, what distinguishes his writings from earlier Hasidic teachings perhaps even more than the specific areas in which he differs is the particular viewpoint from which he interprets the implications of Hasidism.

Earlier Hasidic teachings, especially those attributed to Dov Ber, are primarily addressed to those who would aspire to practice the Hasidic approach to the fullest degree. Meshullam Feibush's writings are written from an entirely different perspective. Significantly, he does not identify himself as a master, but rather as one who has learned from and admires the masters. By taking this position, he immediately establishes a unique basis for relating Hasidic teachings to a class of followers who are fundamentally distinct from the movement's spiritual virtuosi. His interpretation of Hasidism is one of the earliest to justify and explain the teachings of Hasidic *Zaddiqim* like the Maggid of Mezeritch and Yehiel Mikhel of Zlotchov while strongly cautioning against unrestricted imitation of their personal practices. This admonition implies no veiled criticism of these figures, but rather the opposite—it underscores their uniqueness.

Instead of attempting to follow the practices of the *Zaddiqim*, Meshullam Feibush calls for a constant effort towards resisting the "evil urge" through cultivating the moral virtues, especially humility. While the average person cannot follow in the footsteps of the masters, he can nevertheless benefit from a spiritual relationship with them. In other words, the average person can be associated with Hasidism despite the fact that the more radical and pneumatic Hasidic practices are beyond his ability.

Meshullam Feibush's writings, then, can be seen as essentially a defense of the *Zaddiq*. Their intent in interpreting the teachings of Dov Ber is not to explain to his readers how the Maggid's practices can be perfected, but rather to portray them as beyond ordinary aspiration. The effect is a strong emphasis on the exalted level of spiritual *virtuosi*. This presentation of Hasidic teachings is meant to underscore the almost superhuman spiritual achievement of the *Zaddiqim* and thus to foster faith in them. Thus, *Yosher Divrey Emet* documents, an important phase in the transition of early Hasidic teachings, especially as they developed in Dov Ber's school, from an esoteric mysticism cultivated by an elite to the basis for a more popularly based religious movement. That Meshullam Feibush's perspective is indicative of a specific historical phase rather than merely a personal tendency is supported by the evidence of Zechariah Mendel of Jaroslav's letter in defense of his master, R. Elimelekh of Lizensk. The letter was written at about the same time as *Yosher Divrey Emet* and also emanates from an extremely important Galician school of Hasidism. Zechariah Mendel takes a position rather similar to that of Meshullam Feibush. He also identifies himself as a disciple of *Zaddiqim* rather than as a master, but is even more lavish and descriptive than Meshullam Feibush in his praise of *Zaddiqim*.[6]

Meshullam Feibush's argument for faith in *Zaddiqim* has four basic parts. First, he establishes the fundamental distinction between the *Zaddiq* and others. Second, he clarifies the qualities and nature of the *Zaddiq*. He must also indicate the benefits that accrue from association with *Zaddiqim*. Finally, he argues that the followers of the Ba'al Shem Tov are, in fact, the only true *Zaddiqim*. Ultimately, *Yosher Divrey Emet* is not merely a theoretical argument for faith in *Zaddiqim*, but rather a justification and defense of Hasidic leadership. Indeed, since Meshullam Feibush writes as a close follower of the *Zaddiq*, Yehiel Mikhel of Zlotchov, his arguments can be read as a defense and justification of that important Hasidic leader's position and activities. During the 1770s, Yehiel Mikhel was both at the height of his influence as a Hasidic leader and also the target against which much of the anti-Hasidic propoganda was directed in the Brody region.[7]

From several remarks that appear in the tractates, it is clear that Meshullam Feibush wrote at a time when Hasidic leaders were already attracting a following in eastern Galicia. However, their leadership and its charismatic mystical basis was not without controversy. The main source of opposition is apparent from the criteria Meshullam Feibush establishes for spiritual excellence from the very beginning of his work.

> Indeed, in this generation there are people who mock and deny the sages, just as there were such people in the time of Isaac Luria. . . . My heart has always been attached to these sages in faith. . . . Fortunate is he who has faith in them and their words, woe to the wicked who put off the yoke of Torah and fear of the

> Lord and pretend to be *Zaddiqim*. They slander God's angels with lies of their
> own invention. I know very well the extent of their wickedness. Some are guilty
> of adultery, God forbid. Some are full of pride and jealousy. Through their jeal-
> ousy they taint the holy ones with lies.[8]

Although Meshullam Feibush has always believed in the Hasidic leaders,
other religious scholars have been skeptical of them to the extent of insult-
ing them and tarnishing their reputations as holy men. This opposition is
composed of individuals who see themselves as *Zaddiqim* and who are essentially jealous of the Hasidic leaders' appeal. However, even if they are
great scholars and well versed in kabbalistic practices, they cannot truly be
considered as *Zaddiqim* because of their moral vices.[9] As we have seen, the
essential characteristic of spiritual perfection is *devequt*. This, however, can
only be attained by an individual who has perfected the moral virtues. In
particular, *devequt* demands the total eradication of pride.

In Meshullam Feibush's view, the despute over the criteria for religious
leadership pits those who claim proximity to God merely on the basis of
their accomplishments in Torah study against those who claim to be experientially aware of their adhesion to God as a result of moral perfection. Only
the latter truly achieve *devequt* while studying the Torah. *Yosher Divrey
Emet* is addressed to those who appreciate this distinction even if they cannot fully comprehend how this *devequt* is achieved.

> This matter really requires a thorough explanation, even though I am not
> speaking to the ears of a fool. . . . As Rabbenu Tam wrote in *Sefer ha-Yashar*; if
> all the wisdom of King Solomon were uttered before a fool, [the fool] would
> [only] scorn it, for iniquity swells his heart. . . . His heart is polluted with de-
> sires for wealth, food, and sex, jealousy, hate, competition, anger, and honor.
> True wisdom and morality will find no place to rest in his heart. For in his pride,
> he will scorn all this and consider it all as folly, just as he is, in reality, a fool. But
> I am only speaking to people like us who are familiar with and believe in the
> words of the sages of our age, the true sages, i. e., [those who] truly cleave to
> God. We believe all their words, [although] we really only partially understand
> them.[10]

The passage aids us in distinguishing the intended audience. They are individuals familiar enough with Hasidic teachings and masters to take them seriously. They understand Hasidic teachings enough to believe in them. Yet
they cannot fully comprehend and practice them. They are, then, not only to
be distinguished from the opponents of Hasidism, who scoff at the claims of
the Hasidim, but also, in a definitely qualitative sense, from the Hasidic
masters. As we have seen, this second distinction has important implications

in regard to the general adaptation of such basic early Hasidic practices as elevating disturbing thoughts and the technique of *qal ve-homer*. Such practices are entirely restricted to *Zaddiqim*.[11]

Particularly important is the attitude the text expresses in regard to the *Zaddiqim*. Meshullam Feibush and his audience believe in all of their teachings even though they cannot be completely comprehended. The *Zaddiq* occupies a spiritual level which is entirely beyond ordinary attainment. One may agree with Meshullam Feibush concerning the moral and spiritual criteria which are prerequisites for *devequt*, but the experience itself cannot be fully understood by one who has not experienced it. It remains *nistar* (concealed). The *Zaddiq*, according to Meshullam Feibush's conception, is an awe-inspiring figure. His awesomeness is due to extraordinary moral perfection and holiness that result from his direct connection to God.[12]

An important aspect of Meshullam Feibush's argument for faith in *Zaddiqim* is that the latter cannot be judged by ordinary standards. They are not subject to the same restraints that apply to the common Jew. Because of their superior spiritual station and mastery of certain esoteric techniques, they are able to involve themselves in a wider range of activities. Indeed, they can transform any situation into a religious experience. However, the ordinary person must be careful to avoid, as much as possible, idle conversations which are liable to arouse those natural tendencies that tend to seduce one from the religious path. The *Zaddiq*, however, may freely participate in all types of social interaction, for he finds the divine presence everywhere.

> [Dov Ber] also explained there[13] the meaning of the verse, "*Do not be confused by your mouth and let not your heart be in a hurry to utter a word before God. For God is in heaven and you are on the earth. Therefore, let your words be few.*"[14] In *Reishit Hokhmah*, Gate of Holiness, the author has difficulty explaining why the verse says, "*therefore, let your words be few.*" But [Dov Ber] of blessed memory wrote, according to his manner and holy way, that in reality, whoever properly cleaves to God through his faith that God's glory fills all of creation, constantly reflects on this without ceasing for a moment. As a result, he experiences fear and love and *devequt* with the blessed Creator. Thus he is truly able to speak many words. Since he is so thoroughly attached to holiness, he is able to elevate even secular words to holiness by means of the technique of permuting letters that was known to the divine saint, the Ba'al Shem Tov . . . and his disciples, who, inspired by the holy spirit, drank from his waters. Some are [now] in the true world, may their merit protect us. Others are alive in this world. May God grant them long life and may they and their children live as sages of Israel.[15]

Dov Ber has interpreted Kohelet's warning against idle speech as applying to ordinary states of consciousness. According to conventional experience and faith, God is transcendent in the heavens, while man is separated from God on the earth. Idle conversation only increases the distance between creation and God. According to Meshullam Feibush, this is the situation in which ordinary people like himself typically find themselves.

However, the experience of the *Zaddiq* is entirely of another order. Through his constant mental attachment to God, he does not become absorbed in what is occurring around him. For him, every thought and word is only a specific combination of the very same letters with which God created the world. Moreover, he knows the esoteric significance of these letters and thus, through his attention to them, even while seeming to indulge in idle talk, he can elevate ordinary conversation to the realm of holiness. This ability and esoteric technique is not, however, something new. According to Meshullam Feibush, it was possessed by the earliest rabbinic figures and is alluded to in talmudic literature.

> This is not surprising. For we must concede that such an esoteric technique exists. For do we not find in the Gemara several matters in *aggadot* that appear to be lacking religious import? But the tannaim possessed the holy spirit and had full mastery of the esoteric technique of permuting letters. They said everything with their holy spirit and [these matters] are secrets of the Torah. They managed all of this because of their great cleaving to supernal holiness through their righteousness and uprightness and their constant great awe and love for God.[16]

In Meshullam Feibush's view, ordinary people can attain some degree of *devequt* only through prayer, studying the Torah, and observing holidays, that is, through the conventional aspects of religious practice. They cannot employ the esoteric techniques that enable the religious *virtuosi* to extend the parameters of religious experience to include even those areas which are conventionally defined as secular. The reason is that the esoteric techniques are not conceived as having immediate magical efficacy. They are themselves conditioned by internal existential states of love and awe of God, the psychological coordinates of genuine *devequt*.

Since Meshullam Feibush recognizes that such genuine *devequt* is difficult to attain even with the divine aid that is present in the Torah and prayer, he considers it virtually precluded from extra-religious contexts. *Devequt* can only be extended to secular areas when its emotional and psychological components have become thoroughly established in an individual's consciousness. Since this is true only of a small group of spiritual *virtuosi*, ordinary people cannot spiritualize or "enliven" secular activities or conversations. For them, only words of Torah are full of life, since the Torah directly is energized by the divine immanence that is contained within it. The *Zaddiqim*, however, have internalized the connection to the source of divine energy that normally occurs only when one is directly involved with Torah. It remains with them at all times. Thus, through their esoteric techniques, they can bring divine energy to all of their activities.

> Why are ordinary conversations called idle? Because they lack [divine] vitality since they are not words of Torah. But whoever is attached to God can purify them and infuse them with [divine] energy through his supreme *devequt* and knowledge of esoteric techniques,[17] which is quite beyond our comprehension. For we have no experience of it at all. How can we know its place and worth? Only, through faith we believe that it is so. That is, through our faith in the sages, we believe that they possess this wisdom, which we noted in the Gemara, as indicated above.[18]

This spiritual ability which is attributed to the Hasidic leaders is indeed extraordinary. It is beyond ordinary comprehension. However, it is not foreign to Judaism, but was found among the great figures of the rabbinic period. Therefore, one should accept it in contemporary holy men, just as one believes the stories concerning the early sages. This attempt to equate the spiritual level of the Hasidic *Zaddiqim* with that of the rabbinic sages is not merely rhetorical. As we shall see, Meshullam Feibush uses this ploy not only to demonstrate the authenticity of the *Zaddiq's* practices, but also to maximize the importance and authority of Hasidic leadership.

By definition, the *Zaddiq* is a person who knows God directly. An awareness of God is always present in his mind. It is precisely this affective knowledge of God which eradicates the conventional boundaries between sacred and profane. For the *Zaddiq* has acquired a consciousness in which the presence of God is revealed everywhere. He need not rely on the Torah as conventionally understood for communion with God, since God is already established in his mind. Consequently, for him, the entire world is Torah. All of creation reveals for him the hidden reality of divine presence. Thus the *Zaddiq* is a kind of intermediary between the two poles that are so unalterably separate in ordinary consciousness. The *Zaddiq* is the link between God and creation. As such, the *Zaddiq* plays an integral role in maintaining the world's existence. It is through him that God's sustaining energy reaches creation.[19]

> He really sees that all of creation is full of God's glory. This is the meaning of the verse, "*the chambers are filled with Da'at.*"[20] Whoever possesses experiential knowledge of God (*Da'at*) sees that all the chambers of the world are full of

divine glory. He can learn divine wisdom from all that he sees. . . . Thus he connects the world with God and God with the world. The world rests upon him. For the world can only exist through God's enlivening energy. And who is it that draws it forth and establishes it? A person (*adam*) through this *devequt* and enlightenment. Such a person is called *Zaddiq*, because he possesses the attribute of joining together (*hitqashrut*). For he is connected to God while he is in this world. Thus he connects God with this world. He is called "covenant"[21] which connects the bestower with the receiver. And he is alluded to in the verse, "*for everything in heaven and earth*,"[22] which the Targum Yonaton renders, "who joins heaven and earth."[23] This is the human *Zaddiq* [24] who is connected to God who is called "heaven," while he is himself on the earth. . . . Thus before such a person, the entire world is full of God and full of Torah. Since the Torah, as its name implies, reveals what is hidden. Before such a person every creature reveals [divine] wisdom, how and why it was created. Our forefather Abraham, of blessed memory, attained this [wisdom] and wrote *Sefer Yezirah*. The tannaim and amoraim also possessed it.[25]

Again we see the identification of the Hasidic *Zaddiq*'s wisdom with early Jewish heroes. Although Meshullam Feibush makes use of some typical kabbalistic motifs in order to define the *Zaddiq*, the theosophical sources are not particularly emphasized or exploited. More important to Meshullam Feibush is the extraordinary nature of the *Zaddiq*'s consciousness which renders his experience so qualitatively different from that of the ordinary person. In effect, Meshullam Feibush is projecting the basis of his faith in contemporary *Zaddiqim* onto the major figures of earlier periods. Rather than viewing the talmudic rabbis as essentially religious scholars and experts in religious law, he sees them as holy men who possessed awareness of God's presence and understood the secrets of Creation. Nevertheless, this depiction of the past lends authority to the claims of the contemporary Hasidic *Zaddiqim*.

The existence of such *Zaddiqim* and faith in them has real consequences for the spiritual life of ordinary people. Within the framework of Meshullam Feibush's pessimistic view of human nature and spiritual capacity, the ordinary person has little hope of fulfilling God's will on his own efforts. God wishes man to find Him from the great distance of his fallen state in material creation. However, due to the extent to which the human soul is contaminated by pride and other moral vices and the tenacity of the evil urge which is inherent in human nature, only the *Zaddiqim* succeed in overcoming the barriers to *devequt*. The ordinary person's chances for success in religious life are very much enhanced through his establishing a spiritual bond with a *Zaddiq*.

In his discussion on prayer at the beginning of the second tractate,[26] Meshullam Feibush goes into considerable detail in explaining how spiritual bonding can occur. The relationship to the *Zaddiq* is analogous to any love relationship. Both partners possess the image of the other in their minds. Through love, this image of the other can be awakened at any time, even when the beloved is not physically present. Moreover, the mental image (*deyoqan*) is in reality the person's spiritual essence. For thoughts, being entirely spiritual in nature, are more real than corporeal objects which only seem real from the materialistic perspective of ordinary consciousness. Consequently, a person can form a spiritual bond with a *Zaddiq* by visualizing the *Zaddiq*'s image in his mind.[27] Spiritual bonding with a *Zaddiq* is particularly important during prayer.[28] Since an ordinary person can effectively employ neither the Lurianic *kavvanot* nor Dov Ber's method of praying in *devequt*, the efficacy of his worship is in question. However, Meshullam Feibush argues, as long as such a person makes a strong effort to apply his mind to the words he is uttering, his prayer will be imbued with at least some vitality. If, at the time of prayer, he also attaches himself to the *Zaddiqim* that he knows, they will make sure that his prayer reaches the intended destination. The influence of *Zaddiqim* is also necessary for success in Torah study. In essence, the care and detail which the rabbis brought to their discussions of all aspects of human experience should impress upon the student of Torah the importance of avoiding sin.[29] The great moral weight that is contained in the Torah would seem sufficient to instill fear of sin in a person. But because ordinary people are so tainted by pride and vanity, their Torah study does not accomplish its purpose.

> When a person sees in our holy Torah how [deeply] the tannaim searched for the truth concerning fulfilling the Torah, this will lead him to fear of sin and separate him from what is false. It is otherwise with us whose souls are polluted from our youth. For we learn without paying attention to all of this. How our hearts are inflated both while studying and afterwards! How immersed we are in the vanities of the world! All kinds of seduction hold fast to our souls like a dog, as the *Reishit Hokhmah* explained at length.[30] Whoever will inquire for himself will see that he has not arrived at the truth. We have failed to see and teach our hearts. We imagine that the light within [the Torah] will [be sufficient to] restore us to goodness. But all of this is false. For each of us knows, if he will only [admit it], that he has not yet gotten over all evil desires and vices and pride and all manner of falsehoods to which he has become accustomed till now.[31]

Only the *Zaddiqim* learn Torah in the proper manner, because their motivation is pure. They have no interest in enhancing their reputation as scholars, but are full of humility and fear of sin. Only through their relationship with the true *Zaddiqim*, others can learn to study Torah with the proper motivation so that their studies will instill in them fear of sin.

> But the truth is as the Maggid [of Zlotchov] wrote, if one's Torah study was not sufficient to guard him from sin before the fact, now that he has already sinned, how can it possibly keep him from evil, unless he also connects himself to the true *Zaddiqim*?[32]

Most of Meshullam Feibush's moral and spiritual directives are neither radical nor new. They are almost entirely drawn from the classical ethical literature like *Hovot ha-Levavot*, *Orhot Zaddiqim* and *Sefer ha-Yashar* which is attributed to Rabbenu Tam, as well as from the later kabbalistic ethical works like *Reishit Hokhmah* and *Sheney Luhot ha-Berit*. However, although these works were readily available in eastern Europe and even well known, their power to inspire their readers to follow in their spiritual paths is not nearly as great as teachings received directly from *Zaddiqim*. Receiving spiritual guidance from personages whom one believes to be divinely inspired and morally superior has a far more profound effect. Even when one is well-versed in the arguments and exhortations of the literature, faith in *Zaddiqim* may be required as a catalyst, before the moral teachings can be effectively followed. Here we find a motive which is typical of mystical traditions. Even though one may comprehend the various aspects of a spiritual path intellectually, the influence of an inspired and accomplished spiritual guide is required before one may actually make progress on the path.

> I have to thoroughly explain this to you, although I realize that you understand all of this without me. But I also understood all that I heard from my holy masters, whom I have mentioned, before I heard [these matters] from them. But, I could not benefit from these things, since it is written, *"do not rely on your [own] understanding,"*[33] until I heard them from their mouths and writings which we know were divinely inspired. Some of them experienced a revelation of Elijah, of blessed memory, like the Ba'al Shem Tov and his disciple, our teacher and master, Dov Ber, of blessed memory, and our teacher and master, Menahem Mendel [of Premishlan], of blessed memory. When I heard [the teachings] from them, they were joined to my heart as if I had received them from the sages of the Mishnah, of blessed memory. Everything that I am writing is entirely from their teachings.[34]

Meshullam Feibush was able to apply the moral teachings only when he received them from people whom he believed to be divinely inspired masters. This inspired source lends spiritual authority to Meshullam Feibush's own writings which are meant to faithfully transmit his masters' teachings.

Again we see the major themes of Meshullam Feibush's argument. Faith in
Zaddiqim is essential and effective. The contemporary *Zaddiqim* are divinely inspired and comparable to the sages of the Mishnah. These *Zaddiqim* are no other than the Hasidic leaders, the Ba'al Shem Tov and his disciples.[35] Since Meshullam Feibush's argument is intended to bolster the
authority of Hasidic masters, the exclusion of his current master, Yehiel
Mikhel of Zlotchov, may be intentional. Unlike the three *Zaddiqim* to
whom Meshullam Feibush attributes divine inspiration, Yehiel Mikhel was
still alive and active at the time the letter was written. It may be that
Meshullam Feibush hoped to shield Yehiel Mikhel in this way from further
attacks.[36]

Although much of the content of Meshullam Feibush's moral and religious directives is drawn from earlier sources which had a broad impact on
eastern European Judaism during the eighteenth century, his appeal for faith
in *Zaddiqim* distinguishes his writings from the large number of ethical and
homiletical works that were produced during that century under the general
influence of the post-Safedian kabbalistic ethical texts. Meshullam Feibush is
not merely another voice echoing the same mystical-ethical values and complaints against the corruption of the rabbinic elite that resound from the
pages composed by the preachers of the age. The path that he advocates is
not generic, but representative of a specific religious party and leadership.
His appeal for faith in *Zaddiqim* goes beyond merely theoretical arguments.
His remedy for the contemporary spiritual crisis is support for and spiritual
bonding with the Hasidic leaders. When, for example, he depicts the *Zaddiq*
as a holy man whose level of religiosity transcends the bounds of ordinary
comprehension, he has in mind the specific example of none other than his
own master, Rabbi Yehiel Mikhel, the Maggid of Zlotchov.

> For in our entire Torah, whether written or oral, there is not a single word or
> letter that has any purpose other than to [teach how] to serve God. . . . In other
> words, [all 613 *mizvot*] advise a person how to cleave to his Creator. All of this
> was revealed to me by the sages whom I have mentioned. And I heard so from
> the holy mouth of the Rav, the Maggid [of Zlotchov]. He said that, all his life,
> whenever he looked at a religious text, regardless of whether it was Gemara or
> Kabbalah, he only saw how to serve God. Indeed it is so. But this is true for him
> who is a *Zaddiq* and the son of a *Zaddiq*, the descendent of [a long line] of per-
> fected ones (*shelemim*). But it is beyond our comprehension. Only through
> faith, I believe this . . .[37]

The specific appeal for faith in the Hasidic *Zaddiqim* is based on one
central assumption. Although there are indeed others who may be regarded

as great *Zaddiqim* from the standpoint of excellence in religious scholarship and meticulousness in religious observance, nevertheless their religiosity is tainted by pride. This, as we have seen, makes them incapable of attaining real *devequt*. Thus, they cannot instruct the ordinary person in the true ways of divine service that depend on moral excellence nor can they enhance his limited efforts in this direction through mystical means. The disciples of the Ba'al Shem Tov are worthy of faith, since only they are free of the generation's greatest flaw, pride and egotism. Because of their genuine humility, they are true *Zaddiqim* who connect heaven and earth.

> Whoever wishes to be close to God has to exert great caution, even though he loathes pride. For this concerns the heart which constantly turns to desire, loving praise and hating scorn. In this generation, none are free of this, even the great *Zaddiqim*, except that spiritual elite that managed to receive instruction from the Ba'al Shem Tov, may his memory be a blessing for life in the world to come, and his disciples who held firm to their path. Other than them, all are caught in this trap. As we can see, because of the multitude of our sins, our generation is rife with contention and jealousy. May God have mercy upon us.[38]

We learn from Meshullam Feibush's writings that a power struggle took place in eastern Galicia when the disciples of the Ba'al Shem Tov began to acquire a reputation for their holiness and to attract a popular following. Contention seems to have begun at least by the 1760s when Menahem Mendel of Premishlan was still in eastern Galicia. Indeed, opposition to Menahem Mendel may have, in part, motivated his departure for the Land of Israel.[39]

Although Meshullam Feibush never identifies the specific source of this opposition, the intended target of his complaints may be fairly inferred from his description of the opposition's appearance. They appear as "*Zaddiqim*, rabbinic scholars, and *Hasidim* clothed in white."[40] The practice of donning white garments for Sabbaths and holidays was adopted by pre-Beshtian hasidim from the kabbalistic customs of Safed. Ironically, it is the followers of the Ba'al Shem Tov who were often ridiculed in early anti-Hasidic literature for adopting this custom.[41] However, the practice was not restricted to the Ba'al Shem Tov and his followers. In a proclamation that was issued at the Brody Fair in the spring of 1772, the wearing of white garments was expressly forbidden to all but a specific group of sages and kabbalists who met in the Brody *Kloyz*.[42] Since Brody was the most important religious center in Meshullam Feibush's area at that time and also the place where Yehiel Mikhel convened his followers, it is quite possible that it is the members of the Brody *Kloyz* whom he is identifying as the prime opponents of the Hasidic *Zaddiqim*.[43] Hasidic sources suggest that the Ba'al Shem Tov, himself, wanted to be accepted by this group, although he did not succeed in gaining their approval because of his relatively low standing as an authority on rabbinic law.[44]

According to this reading of Meshullam Feibush's account, the members of the *Kloyz*, which, in actuality, included some of the leading rabbinic authorities of eastern Europe,[45] were jealous of the popular appeal of the Hasidic *Zaddiqim* and were unable to acknowledge their spiritual preeminence because of stubborn pride.

> They become jealous when they see that in our age, these sages have become fa-
> mous and the pure among the masses are very much attached to them. It is only
> proper to be followers of the sages and true *Zaddiqim* and to rest in the dust of
> their feet. But none of [these false *Zaddiqim*] will turn to them. For they imag-
> ine that they are the greater *Zaddiqim*, *hasidim* and scholars. Consequently,
> they slander them and invent all kinds of unthinkable lies [about them].[46]

In Meshullam Feibush's view, the new Hasidic way which calls for faith in the true *Zaddiqim* who have attained genuine humility and *devequt* is the answer to the spiritual crisis. Everyone who truly desires to serve God should turn to the Hasidic *Zaddiqim*. That those particular scholars who oppose Hasidism are prevented from doing so only by their pride is indicated by the fact that other great scholars have indeed submitted to the authority of the Hasidic *Zaddiqim*. Anyone sincerely motivated by awe of God could not help but be impressed by the piety and sanctity of the Ba'al Shem Tov's disciples.

> If they themselves recognized the truth that they had not yet even begun to
> serve God ([and this must be the case] for if they managed even one moment of
> awe, not to mention the other levels, they would run after these *Zaddiqim* that
> they might teach them the way of God, just as, in fact, [some of the] great rab-
> binic authorities have recognized this. They bowed before these *Zaddiqim* like a
> slave before his master, because God touched their hearts and they desired to
> truly serve Him. In true submission, they wished to be a "tail to lions,"[47] for
> they realized that they did not yet know the beginning of how to serve Him.
> They found and learned from these sages who instructed them each receiving
> according to the merit of his soul.[48]

Although some distinguished rabbinic authorities were attracted to the Ba'al Shem Tov and his disciples, the leaders of the Brody *Kloyz* opposed Beshtian Hasidism in eastern Galicia. This opposition first was apparently directed against Menahem Mendel of Premishlan who, according to Meshullam Feibush, was himself accused of the sin of pride. After Menahem Mendel's departure, the same charge continued to be directed against Yehiel Mikhel of Zlotchov, who, by the 1770s, had become the leading exponent of Beshtian Hasidism in the Brody area.[49]

It is ironic that both sides of the conflict condemn the other for their pride. However, Meshullam Feibush finds a biblical precedent for this situation in the opposition of Korah and his party to Moses' leadership.

Although Moses, as a true *Zaddiq* was the humblest of men, in assuming the yoke of leadership, he had to act in a manner that seems like pride. However, Moses never sought to become a leader for his own advantage. He was selected by God and compelled to serve as leader precisely because of his great humility. Korah attacked him because he did not understand how a person without personal ambition could assume the role of leader. He could only imagine that Moses was motivated by pride and the desire for personal advantage. Korah's challenge and desire for leadership, on the other hand, was indeed based on pride, the only motivation that a person of his consciousness can comprehend. However, the Hasidic *Zaddiqim* are like Moses. They are too humble to consider themselves worthy of leadership. It is only that God compels them to take on this role since they alone are worthy to guide Israel in the true ways of Torah.[50]

Given the history of opposition to Beshtian Hasidism in the Brody area, *Yosher Divrey Emet* must be viewed, at least in part, as a propagandistic answer to that opposition. From this viewpoint, Meshullam Feibush's explicit restriction of the more radical spiritual aspects of Hasidic practice to the exclusive domain of the *Zaddiqim* may appear to be a concession to early anti-Hasidic criticism. Meshullam Feibush's version of Hasidism repeatedly discourages the ordinary believer from imagining that he has any hope of attaining genuine intimacy with God. The moral prerequisites for genuine *devequt* are simply too unattainable. Nevertheless, despite this decidedly sober interpretation of Hasidism, *Yosher Divrey Emet* remains a highly polemical document. It is highly likely that anti-Hasidic proclamations emanating from Brody were provoked by Yehiel Mikhel and his followers. Their existence as a separate, charismatically led, esoteric kabbalistic group may well have threatened the earlier group of pietistic kabbalists who were accepted and respected in Brody.

Moreover, the stringent conditions that exclude ordinary people from *devequt* also apply to the members of the Brody *Kloyz*. Despite the oft-repeated emphasis on humility, there is a certain arrogance in Meshullam Feibush's one-sided polemic. Individuals who are generally recognized as eminent scholars and mystics are disqualified by Meshullam Feibush's standards from the role of religious exemplars. The true spiritual leaders of the generation are only the disciples of the Ba'al Shem Tov. They, however, are paradoxically, like Moses, too humble to desire authority. For this very reason, God has chosen them and compelled them to lead.

9

Meshullam Feibush's
Place in Early Hasidism

Meshullam Feibush Heller's *Yosher Divrey Emet* occupies a unique place in the history of early Hasidic literature. Written in the late 1770s, Meshullam Feibush's writings were among the earliest to be produced. They were written during the period when organized persecution of Hasidism was rife in the Brody area of eastern Galicia. By this time, Hasidic leaders like Yehiel Mikhel of Zlotchov and Elimelekh of Lizhensk had succeeded in attracting significant followings in the region. Yet their recognition as leaders encountered opposition from other elements in the rabbinic world as well as from representatives of local authority.[1]

The new model of rabbinic leadership which the Hasidic *Zaddiqim* represented was initially successful in attracting many adherents from among the scholarly class. Later, the Hasidim were able to appeal to wider elements of the populace. As the popularity of Hasidic leaders grew, a real challenge to the authority of non-Hasidic leadership arose. However, the issue was not only political in nature. The rabbinic opponents to Hasidism were certainly motivated in part by the desire to retain authority. However, also at stake was the scale of values in Jewish life involving the relative importance of Torah study, prayer, and ethical-spiritual development. Hasidism, because of its emphasis on an emotional-contemplative concept of *devequt* as the supreme goal of religious life, tended to accentuate those non-intellectual components of Jewish religion which were most conducive to attaining the experience of *devequt*. In other words, prayer and the self-cultivation of ethical and spiritual qualities took on as a great an importance in the Hasidic scale of values as Torah study. While Torah study continued to be honored and practiced by the Hasidim, its importance was more conditioned by the extent to which the learner achieved *devequt* while studying than by comprehension of the subject material or exercise of the intellectual faculties per se.[2] In addition, greater attention was given to the study of ethical literature (*musar*).

On the other hand, while Hasidism's rabbinic opponents also valued prayer and ethical-spiritual development, or *yirat ha-Shem*, for them intellectual comprehension of the Torah in all its depth and breadth occupied pride of place in the scale of religious values. It must be added, however, that the opposition also saw *devequt*, or intimacy with God, as a fundamental condition of Torah study. However, here the intellectual act of studying Torah when performed by a scholar who had acquired *yirat ha-Shem*, was itself equated with *devequt*.[3] In essence, two competing interpretations of the classical concept of *devequt* collided. Where the Hasidim defined *devequt* primarily in emotional and contemplative terms, their opponents located *devequt* in the intellectual aspects of Torah study itself.

Much of *Yosher Divrey Emet* is intended as an explanation and justification of the Hasidic viewpoint. The opponents are decried for their immorality and general lack of ethical-spiritual development. Their primarily intellectual concept of *devequt* through Torah study is rejected. In its place a Hasidic definition of *devequt* is championed that is characterized by genuine experiences of love and awe of God while learning Torah. The rabbinic opponents are seen as lacking these essential experiences because of their attachment to pride in their learning.[4] Pride, moreover, is the fundamental flaw in human consciousness, since it prevents a person from apprehending the exclusive reality of God. Consequently, the practitioners of the intellectual approach to *devequt* are denied attainment of the hidden truth which Torah study is meant to reveal, direct knowledge of the divine presence.

On the other hand, the Hasidic leaders are primarily characterized by the absence of pride. As such, their intimacy with God may even reach *unio mystica*. As a result of their virtually complete detachment from the allures of this world, the Hasidic *Zaddiqim* can spiritualize even the most corporeal aspects of human life. Unlike their opponents, they have no need to protect their spirituality by isolating themselves within the prophylactic world of Torah study. They can contemplatively maintain their *devequt* even when participating in seemingly idle conversation. This is indeed one of the principal differences in the two approaches. For the Gaon of Vilna, *perishut* (separation from mundane society) was an essential part of the life of a *Hasid*. Torah study had the effect of protecting one's soul from sin.[5] However, the school of the Maggid of Mezeritch, following the personal example of the Ba'al Shem Tov, asserted that *devequt* could be attained under all conditions.[6] Thus, the Hasidic *Zaddiqim* are free to associate with the masses and can be of spiritual assistance to them.

If *Yosher Divrey Emet* had only addressed the issues which we have been recounting, it would have to be appreciated as a rather clearly argued and thorough presentation of a Hasidic religious approach that was meant to counter opposition to Hasidism in general and, specifically, the Hasidic leadership of Yehiel Mikhel of Zlotchov. However, such a characterization does not fully capture the uniqueness of Meshullam Feibush's writings. It is true that Meshullam Feibush deserves credit for producing epistles which both passionately and cogently presented the case for Hasidism. However, many of his arguments and positions are probably typical of the Hasidic defense during this period. What distinguishes Meshullam Feibush's epistles from other Hasidic writings of the time is their unique response to another historical development, the circulation of manuscripts containing records of the teachings of Dov Ber of Mezeritch.

To a certain extent, Meshullam Feibush's motivation in commenting on and qualifying the teachings attributed to Dov Ber must also have been inspired by the same general need he felt to defend Hasidism against the attacks of its opponents. Dov Ber's teachings contain a number of explicit spiritual directives which were based on a transformative psychology that blurs the classical ethical distinction between good and evil. Thoughts and ethical qualities that are conventionally considered evil or negative and which the classical ethicists would expect a religious person to reject were said to contain divine sparks. By concentrating on these sparks, or "the good within the evil," one could transform the "evil" thoughts and qualities into aspects of divine worship. However, this non-dual, transformative psychology was open to abuse. A person could resort to these teachings in order to justify the presence of character defects that really needed to be overcome in order to make spiritual progress. In short, such a psychology could become the justification for religious hypocrisy.

This criticism was, of course, not lost on Hasidism's opponents who seized it as a basis for viewing Hasidism as a continuation of the Sabbatean heresy.[7] Clearly, the dissemination of Dov Ber's teachings for the first time in manuscript must have provided Hasidism's opponents with hard evidence of the new movement's radical and potentially dangerous tendencies. Thus, Meshullam Feibush's interest in emphasizing the stringent preconditions required of those who would practice Dov Ber's approach must have been, at least, partially stimulated by the need he felt to defend Hasidism from its enemies.

It must be borne in mind, however, that *Yosher Divrey Emet* was not originally meant for publication or even widespread dissemination.[8] The epistles were written to a fellow admirer of Yehiel Mikhel of Zlotchov and were meant to provide guidance for other followers of Meshullam Feibush who were probably located at some distance from the Brody center.[9] Thus, while *Yosher Divrey Emet* may indeed be viewed as a defense of Hasidism that was to a certain extent influenced by external opposition, it was not intended to directly confront Hasidism's opponents. Its more immediate purpose was to strengthen the faith of Hasidic adherents by presenting them with a clarification of the essentials of Hasidism.[10] It is precisely within this clarification that Meshullam Feibush's unique position as an early Hasidic thinker is revealed. For *Yosher Divrey Emet* may be viewed, primarily, as an eastern Galician contribution to an intra-Hasidic dialogue concerning the teachings of Dov Ber of Mezeritch. Meshullam Feibush's views represented important elements typical of the spiritual outlook of his teacher, Yehiel Mikhel of Zlotchov.

The general problem that arose was due to two aspects of the material contained in the manuscripts. On the one hand, Dov Ber's teachings involved radical and potentially dangerous spiritual directives, as we have indicated. On the other hand, while the variants that appear in the manuscripts do indicate certain prerequisites for following the radical practices, the general impression created is that here is the way of the Maggid of Mezeritch and whoever wishes to follow his path may do so. Dov Ber, himself, was considerably more cautious. Recent research has proven that passages in which he expressed concern for the abuse that extremists might make of certain aspects of his teachings were deliberately expunged from some of the most widely disseminated manuscripts.[11] We have also indicated that at least one passage remains in which Dov Ber explicitly indicated that only the spiritual elite could safely remain contemplatively attached to God without the safeguard of words of Torah. Moreover, the general openness in which Dov Ber presented his teachings was appropriate, under the conditions in which he taught. He directed his teachings principally to members of the scholar class. Those initially attracted to the Maggid constituted an elite guard of spiritualists and contemplatives who were sometimes recruited for him by his closest disciples. Individuals who lacked the requisite background and development could easily have been excluded. There is no evidence that Dov Ber ever attempted to broadly circulate his teachings.[12]

After Dov Ber's death in 1772, the potential danger that his teachings might be unwisely applied or abused increased. Although many outstanding individuals were trained by Dov Ber, none could claim undisputed leadership of a united Hasidic movement. Hasidism spread widely throughout eastern Europe during the 1770s, primarily through the efforts of Dov Ber's direct disciples. Alliances, of course, existed between various Hasidic leaders who shared similar outlooks and backgrounds, or who were related through marriage. Thus, conditions conducive to mutual influencing and criticism existed which served as restraints against the danger of too great a measure of independence. However, in each region, local leaders reigned who functioned with a high degree of autonomy, since no single, central Hasidic authority existed.[13] Indeed Yehiel Mikhel can be viewed as one such leader, whose followers were centered in Brody. Thus a number of important regional centers were established, each presided over by its resident *Zaddiq*. These early *Zaddiqim* served as spiritual exemplars and authoritative representatives and interpreters of the teachings of the Ba'al Shem Tov and Dov Ber of Mezeritch upon which nearly all Hasidism was nominally based.[14] It is clear from even a cursory perusal of early Hasidic literature that a considerable range of interpretations of Dov Ber's teachings existed among his disciples.[15] It was virtually left to each leader to determine for himself and his followers how the Hasidic founders teachings were to be interpreted, which aspects should be emphasized, how the practices should be applied, and who should undertake them. Significant differences existed concerning the interpretation of *devequt*, the nature of Hasidic prayer, the question of uplifting disturbing thoughts, the status of Torah study, and the manner in which it should be pursued, not to mention the various views concerning the role of the *Zaddiq*, himself, and the nature of his powers.

Under such circumstances, the appearance of Dov Ber of Mezeritch's teachings in accessible manuscripts must have been a source of ferment in many Hasidic communities. It would seem that greater access to the manuscripts would have enabled many adherents of Hasidism, who may never have met the Maggid of Mezeritch, to encounter his teachings in a form that was relatively unmediated by the viewpoint of his disciples However, we now know that the order and content of these writings were greatly influenced by the teachings of Yehiel Mikhel and his followers.[16] Although, in many areas disciples of Dov Ber were themselves both the disseminators and interpreters of the often difficult teachings.

Nevertheless, it must have been the case that manuscripts also came into the hands of individuals who were not closely enough associated with Hasidic *Zaddiqim*. Here the danger of religious anarchy and the potential for abuse and irresponsible application of the teachings was very real. There would have been little to prevent such would-be Hasidim from learning the radical non-dual theology of these teachings. They could then appropriate the teachings concerning the uplifting of negative thoughts and qualities and the theory of spiritualizing corporeal acts and proclaim themselves as *Zaddiqim*.

It seems clear that Meshullam Feibush was responding to this phenomenon as well in *Yosher Divrey Emet*. His critique of false *Zaddiqim*, although often directed against Hasidism's rabbinic opposition, also evinced concern for the abusers of Dov Ber's teachings. His continued assertion that the radical aspects of Dov Ber's teachings can no longer be followed by his generation was, in large measure, a direct denial of the validity of independent would-be *Zaddiqim*, who were vulgarizing Hasidic teachings. Thus, he repeatedly stressed that such teachings only applied to individuals of an exalted level; no longer was this to be found among the members of his own age. In essence, he was excluding the possibility that the teachings themselves constituted a means of attaining the spiritual rung occupied by Dov Ber and his disciples. Possession of the manuscripts and the assertion that one follows the spiritual path therein described does not make one a *Zaddiq*.

However, there is an even more important explanation for Meshullam Feibush's unique response to the problem created by the dissemination of Dov Ber's manuscripts. Meshullam Feibush wrote from the viewpoint of one who was initiated into the Hasidic outlook by Menahem Mendel of Premishlan who left eastern Europe for the Land of Israel in 1764. Thus, much of Meshullam Feibush's formative development in Hasidism may have taken place before Dov Ber and his teachings came into prominence. By the time *Yosher Divrey Emet* was written, Meshullam Feibush had become an ardent disciple of Yehiel Mikhel of Zlotchov. The latter was himself an associate and friend of Meshullam Feibush's first master, Menahem Mendel of Premishlan.[17] Moreover, while Yehiel Mikhel may have accepted Dov Ber as the Ba'al Shem Tov's successor, he must be viewed as more of an associate of the Maggid of Mezeritch than as a disciple, per se. Like Menahem Mendel of Premishlan, Yehiel Mikhel's association with Hasidism went back to the Ba'al Shem Tov. Although he is said to have visited Dov Ber on several occasions, there is little reason to suppose that Yehiel Mikhel's spiritual approach was significantly altered by his relationship with the Maggid of Mezeritch. He was already a mature figure by the time of Menahem Mendel's emigration. At any rate, it is clear that teachings in Yehiel Mikhel's name reveal some significant differences from the spiritual outlook of Dov Ber of Mezeritch.[18]

One of the most striking differences between Yehiel Mikhel's teachings and those of the Maggid of Mezeritch was the former's apparently total lack of interest in the practice of elevating disturbing thoughts and negative qualities.[19] It has been suggested that opposition to the Ba'al Shem Tov's teaching concerning the elevation of negative thoughts goes back to Menahem Mendel of Premishlan himself.[20] Consequently, it would seem that Meshullam Feibush's strong reservations concerning this matter were in accord with the spiritual outlook of his teachers. Since at the time that Dov Ber's teachings were being circulated, Yehiel Mikhel was the foremost Hasidic figure in the Brody region, Dov Ber's teachings in the manuscripts must have had a particularly critical effect among the Hasidic milieu of that region. Some of the followers of Yehiel Mikhel, may only have encountered these authentic teachings of the Maggid of Mezeritch for the first time in the circulating manuscripts.

It is highly likely that the circulating manuscripts both aroused interest in the radical teachings of Dov Ber and created confusion among the Hasidim of the Brody area who were primarily acquainted with the religious outlook of Yehiel Mikhel of Zlotchov and Menahem Mendel of Premishlan. As noted, Yehiel Mikhel had accepted the leadership of Dov Ber after the death of the Ba'al Shem Tov. Thus, there is no doubt that the Maggid of Mezeritch's prestige among the Hasidim of eastern Galicia was very great. Meshullam Feibush, himself, had visited Dov Ber on at least one occasion. Nevertheless, the dominant influence in the area was Yehiel Mikhel of Zlotchov. Thus the conflict between the two approaches was in acute need of resolution. Meshullam Feibush's interest in resolving this problem was probably one of the most important factors motivating his writing of *Yosher Divrey Emet*. For he very much shared the more classical ethical outlook of his principal teachers, Menahem Mendel and Yehiel Mikhel. Yet he was too much an admirer of Dov Ber of Mezeritch to reject his (and the Ba'al Shem Tov's) authentic teachings out of hand.[21] Moreover, such rejection would have been tantamount to deserting the Hasidic camp, since the teachings bore the authority of Hasidism's founders.

Meshullam Feibush's solution to the problem took form in his articulation of the doctrine of faith in *Zaddiqim*. The radical teachings were indeed valid, but were not meant for general use. Their presence in the manuscripts only provided evidence of the extraordinary level which the Ba'al Shem Tov, Dov Ber of Mezeritch, and their direct disciples had reached. They had been able to follow such practices because of their qualitatively superior degree of spiritual attainment, which was comparable to that of the greatest religious figures in Jewish history. Such a level was conditioned by criteria which no one in Meshullam Feibush's generation could honestly claim to meet. Since the ability to follow the radical practices, involving the transformation of evil into good, was itself evidence of *devequt* and closeness to God, the Hasidic *Zaddiqim* deserved adulation. They should be seen as the generation's true spiritual leaders. Because of their experience of *devequt*, they alone were in a position to lead people back from the mire of materiality to their divine root. Within Meshullam Feibush's bleaker view of his generation's spiritual potential, faith in *Zaddiqim* provided a ray of optimism. Although an individual's independent spiritual efforts might seem inadequate, through association with *Zaddiqim*, his prayers could be elevated and rendered effective. The existence of *Zaddiqim* in the world, like the sacred calendar, is a kind of concession to the otherwise virtually hopeless predicament of human life with its separation from the divine source. Because of such expressions of divine mercy, even the modest spiritual efforts of ordinary people are enabled to participate in the grand process of fulfilling God's will through the return of creation to its divine root.

At the heart of Meshullam Feibush's position regarding the restriction of practices involving the transformation of evil to an exclusive spiritual elite was the assertion of a definite criterion for the attainment of *devequt*. The Ba'al Shem Tov's emphasis and interpretation of *devequt* had been based on an enthusiastic proclamation of divine immanence. Because God was present everywhere, a person who had true faith in divine immanence would have to view even his negative thoughts as containing a spark of the divine. Thus, the need to uplift negative thoughts rather than rejecting them was established by the very nature of faith in divine immanence.[22] Rejecting thoughts could be compared to the cardinal Jewish sin of idol worship: it was tantamount to rejecting a spark of the divine presence.

In the teachings of the Maggid of Mezeritch, this fundamental faith in divine immanence was retained. However, Dov Ber's teachings tended to emphasize contemplative practices through which the divine presence was realized as one progressively overcomes all sense of independent self-awareness. These exercises were primarily practiced during prayer. However, once one had become expert in realizing the state of *Ayin* or extinction of the sense of independent existence, it became possible to maintain some degree of this state through mentally cleaving to God (*devequt*), even under the most mundane conditions of life. To be sure, the Maggid of Mezeritch's teachings were not exclusively contemplative. They were very much based in classical ethical literature and constituted a spiritual path that combined contemplative-mystical experience with traditional ethical values, especially humility, love, and fear of God. Moreover, as we have noted, Dov Ber taught a relatively limited number of disciples whose characters he could have measured. Thus, the potential for abuse of his teachings was considerably reduced as long as he was alive. Nevertheless shortly before Dov Ber's death, at least one of his disciples, Abraham Kalisker, established a Hasidic group in the area of Shklov that was accused of spiritual arrogance and offensive behavior. It may be that as a direct result of this group's activity, opposition to Hasidism became intense, particularly in Lithuania, White Russia, and the Brody region.[23] If so, apparently even direct disciples of Dov Ber were sometimes capable of following his teachings in ways that provoked serious opposition. Moreover, while Dov Ber was himself disturbed by the potential abuses that extremists among his students might commit, the recorded versions of his teachings generally do not express this concern.[24]

Classical ethical values, indeed, form an essential part of Dov Ber's thought, but they do not contribute much to its distinctiveness. What gives the Maggid's teachings their unique flavor is their author's ingenious ability to interpret well-known biblical verses and rabbinic sayings as references to the conditions of mystical intimacy and even union with God.

Meshullam Feibush, apparently like his teachers, held a far less optimistic view of human nature than that expressed in the teachings of the Ba'al Shem Tov and Dov Ber. True, he did articulate an extreme version of the teaching of divine immanence that was expressed in terms of an acosmic cosmology. Only God was real and man's purpose was to discover this concealed truth from within the camouflage of material existence. Yet knowledge of this condition or mere faith in its implications was not sufficient for realizing the goal of returning to the divine root. A person had to train himself over a long period of time through constantly remembering God, before an immediate awareness of the divine presence could become established in his consciousness. Such apprehension of the divine was required if authentic emotions of love and awe of God, the experiential components of *devequt* were to manifest.

However, realizing the spiritual goal of *devequt* was not merely a matter of transforming one's consciousness. From Meshullam Feibush's viewpoint, human nature was too fundamentally corrupt to permit such a transformation of consciousness as long as the natural human tendencies towards self-importance and self-gratification were not uprooted. For the character defects that result from these natural tendencies were themselves the barriers to apprehension of the divine reality. Consequently, Meshullam Feibush did not condone the general practice of uplifting negative thoughts. Such a practice may be theoretically implied by faith in divine immanence, but it was only justifiable when such faith had become genuine experiential apprehension. Then one could, indeed, locate the "good in the evil" because one was fundamentally established in the condition of cleaving to God (*devequt*). However, this condition can only be met by someone who had succeeded in overcoming the centrifugal force of corrupt human nature. As we have seen, Meshullam Feibush repeatedly stressed that the battle to overcome the "evil urge" is one that was virtually impossible to win. Even great *Zaddiqim* did not manage to defeat it entirely. As for ordinary people, they can only hope to make constant efforts to overcome the corruption of their natures, knowing full well that, although they cannot prevail, God delights in their struggles.

Meshullam Feibush's view of human nature was diametrically opposed to that assumed in the teachings of the Ba'al Shem Tov and the Maggid of Mezeritch. Consequently, he could only affirm a spiritual path that the founders of Hasidism had, in a certain sense, gone beyond. Although Meshullam Feibush never seemed to have indulged in extreme ascetic penitential acts, his spiritual outlook recalled pre-Beshtian religious psychology. Man's soul was in constant danger of being seduced by a wily "evil urge." Religious merit was gained through human resistance and rejection of evil. This outlook was not strictly based on a negative judgment of his generation's worth, but was rooted in Meshullam Feibush's own personal religious struggle. The few Hasidic anecdotes concerning him revealed a character that was uncommonly zealous to serve the Lord, but deeply suspicious of his own motivations.[25] He carefully examined his motivations before undertaking any diversion from established norms, even when his initial impulse seemed to be positive. He seemed to be particularly suspicious of religious enthusiasm that occurred outside the framework of conventional religious practice. Such excess emotions, although directed towards divine worship, were condemned as wiles of the evil urge. Genuine enthusiasm and ecstasy in the service of God occurred he believed, during the fulfillment of the divine commandments in the manner mandated by tradition. If greater degrees of these emotions arose under other circumstances they must be viewed as temptations to be rejected.

Such a personality was fundamentally unreceptive to the teaching of elevating negative thoughts and qualities. Meshullam Feibush's inner life was characterized by a classical struggle between good and evil that had become unusually subtle. Evil was not primarily an external shell that concealed good within it. It was more of a cunning force that presented itself as good and thus had to be exposed and entirely rejected. Meshullam Feibush judged himself favorably for the deliberate scrutiny he applied to all of his motivations.[26] Since Meshullam Feibush was himself so psychologically unsuited to the practices involving the transformation of evil, he could only view those who advocated them in one of two ways. Either they were hypocrites and misguided individuals who were victims of the subtlety of their "evil urge," or they were individuals of so vastly superior a spiritual level that they were in no danger of being deceived. Individuals of the first type, which included virtually everyone in Meshullam Feibush's generation who was interested in following the radical teachings found in the Dov Ber manuscripts, were in need of rebuke and spiritual guidance. The second type was worthy of the greatest admiration because of their awesome spiritual superiority over everyone else. This latter category, of course, was particularly exemplified by Yehiel Mikhel of Zlotchov and included only the greatest Hasidic *Zaddiqim*.

At this point, it will be worth our while to consider another question.

How did a personality like Meshullam Feibush, who seems so unlike the Ba'al Shem Tov and the Maggid of Mezeritch, become attracted to Hasidism? One possible answer is that Meshullam Feibush was drawn to Hasidism by the example of his first master, Menahem Mendel of Premishlan. This master, himself, although an ardent follower of the Ba'al Shem Tov and a close associate of Nahman of Horodenka, seems to have been unreceptive to the teaching of uplifting wayward thoughts. Menahem Mendel seems to have been firmly committed to the classical ethical position that disturbing thoughts had to be rejected. This position was normative in sixteenth-century Safed and the one advocated by Isaiah Horowitz's influential *Sheney Luhot ha-Berit*.[27]

In Menahem Mendel, Meshullam Feibush must have found a religious personality that he could admire. This master's intensely serious personality must have reflected the basic concerns of Meshullam Feibush's own inner struggle. We may recall that, according to *Shivehey ha-BeSHT*, Menahem Mendel had practiced silence for many years, communicating only through writing, until he visited Jacob Joseph of Polnoy, before departing for the Land of Israel.[28] Clearly, his was not a personality of the wildly enthusiastic type. Although Menahem Mendel asserted the possibility of total immersion in the divine, he viewed this as a possibility that could only occur after great spiritual development. Meshullam Feibush's other master, Yehiel Mikhel of Zlotchov, was also a personality of an extreme type. According to one account, after his marriage, he isolated himself for a thousand days, devoting all of his time to *devequt*. The intensity of his solitary meditation and extraordinary death became legend in Hasidic sources.[29] At the time of writing the letters, Meshullam Feibush was an ardent follower of Yehiel Mikhel and the member of an important group of Hasidim in the Brody area who considered the Maggid of Zlotchov to be a divinely inspired *Zaddiq*. In all likelihood, Meshullam Feibush was attracted to Hasidism by the living examples of his masters, whose extreme behavior he viewed as indications of spiritual perfection. Their extraordinary exertions as well as their teachings impressed him greatly. At any rate, Hasidism came to mean for Meshullam Feibush, a serious emphasis on spiritual perfection through self-control and overcoming the vain attractions of this world. Acknowledgment of divine immanence and *devequt* did not constitute the beginning point of Hasidism, but rather its ideal. This ideal was represented by the extraordinary *Zaddiqim* who had managed to attain it.

For Meshullam Feibush, the fundamental prerequisites for *devequt* are detachment from corporeality (*hitpashtut ha-gashmiyut*) and humility. A person must become indifferent to natural corporeal desires in order to be drawn to the divine element that is concealed within Creation. In addition one's natural sense of self-importance must be replaced by effacement before God, the only Being that truly exists. According to Meshullam Feibush's view, these qualities are absolute prerequisites for all of Dov Ber's radical practices. They are, moreover, essential for fulfilling the Lurianic task of refining out holy sparks from their captivity in the shells of materiality. Nevertheless, while these qualities are essential for fulfilling the Hasidic religious ideals, they are extremely difficult to attain. Few can honestly claim to possess them. Indeed, for Meshullam Feibush, detachment from corporeality and humility are the distinguishing marks of the Hasidic *Zaddiqim* and the basis of their extraordinary state of *devequt*. It is these qualities that enable the *Zaddiqim* to assume positions of authority, even when such positions are accompanied by the external trappings of worldly splendor. The *Zaddiqim* have been chosen by God for these positions of advantage, precisely because of their humility and indifference to power and corporeality.[30]

All those who sincerely seek to serve God should accept the authority of the Hasidic *Zaddiqim* as exemplars and teachers of the true way to return to God. However, since even the sincere seeker cannot claim to have achieved detachment from corporeality and true humility, his religious life should conform to the restrictive guidelines of classical ethical literature that lead a person to the realization of the spiritual ideals. Only the *Zaddiqim* can safely follow a way that erases to some extent the conventional boundaries between religious and profane life.

Meshullam Feibush's response to issues raised by the spread of Dov Ber's teachings and increased external opposition to Hasidism is essentially sober and conservative. Tendencies towards undisciplined expressions of ecstasy and deviant behavior that were sometimes evident during the spread of early Hasidism are effectively squelched by Meshullam Feibush's directives. The question of ecstatic prayer that is so central to much of early Hasidic thought is hardly addressed in *Yosher Divrey Emet*. One should pray in a state of sincerity, characterized by the union of thought and utterance. Genuine emotions of love and awe are aspects of *devequt*. Even without them, sincere prayer can be accepted and elevated by attachment to *Zaddiqim*.

The Hasidic *Zaddiqim* might act in ways that would conventionally be judged as extreme. However, they constituted an extremely exclusive spiritual elite. Certain deviations from established norms were, after all, permitted to another elite in the Brody region, the kabbalists who gathered at the Brody *Kloyz*.[31] Moreover, definite criteria, which were in accord with the ideals of classical ethical literature, established a basis for the authority of the *Zaddiqim*. Although Meshullam Feibush's interpretation of Hasidism effectively proscribed many of the abuses that aroused the contempt of early Hasidism's opponents, he remained true to certain basic tendencies that distinguished the religious outlook of the Hasidim from their rivals.

First of all, his emphasis on ethical qualities rather than erudition, establishes a more spiritual standard whereby a greater range of the community can receive approval for their spiritual efforts. The fundamental arena for serving God is in the inner struggle against the "evil urge." True, learning Torah is one of the principal means of overcoming evil. However, God's delight is the result of the spiritual effort made and not conditioned by the amount of Torah learned. This struggle should occur at all times. The greater the effort to resist evil, the more God is pleased. Consequently, even those who have achieved only a modest degree of expertise in the study of Torah can view their spiritual efforts as significant causes of divine pleasure. It should be stressed, however, that while Meshullam Feibush's outlook reaches beyond the narrow world of those who specialized in Torah study, his view cannot be described as entirely democratic. His spiritual hierarchy not only recognizes the superiority of the *Zaddiqim*, but also includes a category of individuals who occupy a rung below that of his readers. This is clear from remarks he makes concerning fasting. Here he disparages an approach to fasting that does not emphasize repentance. People of his level should not believe that fasting alone is effective. It must be accompanied by the inner cultivation of contrition. Nevertheless, he speculates that the external act itself may be effective for those who do not know any better.

Another distinguishing feature is that the ethical criteria that characterize the *Zaddiqim* enable them to have more contact with the larger Jewish community than would criteria that primarily emphasize scholarship. Because of the purity of the *Zaddiq's* thought, he can maintain an inner adhesion to God under all circumstances. Thus, he is freer to involve himself with the community than scholars whose spiritual level depends more on constant immersion in study and prayer. Moreover, the Torah that the Hasidic *Zaddiqim* teach concerns spiritual matters that are of common interest and not primarily innovations in the interpretation of rabbinic texts that could be appreciated mainly by experts and specialists.

Although Meshullam Feibush's interpretation of Hasidism was articulated as a response to specific historical conditions and problems, some of his positions were adopted by later Hasidic leaders and became normative aspects of later Hasidism. This is particularly the case regarding the restriction of elevating wayward thoughts to the prerogative of *Zaddiqim*. By the beginning of the nineteenth century, most Hasidic practice followed Meshullam Feibush's view.[32] Although unique in many respects, Shneur Zalman of

Liadi's *Tanya,* written some ten years after *Yosher Divrey Emet,* echoes
Meshullam Feibush's fundamental distinction between *Zaddiqim* and the
average adherent of Hasidism. *Zaddiqim* occupy a virtually unattainable,
morally superior rung. The average person *(benoniy)*is called upon to overcome his naturally evil tendencies through rejecting evil and redirecting his
impulses towards positive spiritual ends.[33] To the extent that such views became normative, Meshullam Feibush's work must be viewed as a watershed
in early Hasidic thought.[34]

The epistles of Meshullam Feibush Heller constituted one of the earliest comprehensive attempts to systematize the teachings of early Hasidism.
Heller's approach essentially harmonized two somewhat conflicting schools
of early Hasidic thought: that of his local eastern Galician masters, Menahem Mendel of Premishlan and Yehiel Mikhel of Zlotchov and the increasingly influential Hasidism based on the teachings of Dov Ber of Mezeritch.
This harmonization directed adherents of Hasidism to follow the classical
ethical path of spiritual development advocated by the Galician masters and
to view Dov Ber's more radical approach as evidence of the awesome spiritual superiority of Dov Ber and the Hasidic *Zaddiqim.* As such, Meshullam
Feibush presented an early version of Hasidism, meant primarily for followers of the *Zaddiqim,* that called upon them to humbly accept their own inherent limitations and to have faith in the extraordinary powers of spiritual
exemplars. Moreover, this model, which would soon become virtually normative for Hasidism, was consistant with a text found among Dov Ber's own
writings which indeed made a restrictive hierarchical distinction concerning
spiritual levels of development and the practices that are appropriate to
them.

Notes

1. In fact, at least two important comprehensive historical studies have been published. Simon Dubnow's early work, *History of Hasidism* (Hebrew) (reprint, Tel Aviv: Devir, 1984), makes outdated historical assumptions. Raphael Mahler's, *Hasidism and the Jewish Enlightenment: Their Confrontation in Galicia and Poland in the First Half of the Nineteenth Century* (Philadelphia: Jewish Publiciation Society, 1985), does not chronicle the beginnings of Hasidism and is colored by too Marxist an outlook. On the Ba'al Shem Tov, see Moshe Rosman, *Founder of Hasidism: A Quest for the Historical Ba'al Shem Tov* (Berkeley: University of California, 1996). For a bibliography of works dealing with Hasidism, see Roman A. Foxbrunner, *HABAD: The Hasidism of R. Shneur Zalman of Lyady* (Tuscaloosa: University of Alabama, 1992), pp. 203–206.

2. Gershom Scholem's most important studies on Hasidism include the concluding chapter to his *Major Trends in Jewish Mysticism* (New York: reprint, Schocken, 1967), essays on the neutralization of Messianism in early Hasidism and on *devequt* (communion with God), included in his *The Messianic Idea in Judaism* (New York: Schocken, 1971), and an article on the historical Ba'al Shem Tov [Hebrew] in *Devarim be-Go* (Tel Aviv: Am Oved, 1976).

3. Many of Joseph Weiss's English essays on Hasidism are collected in *Studies in Eastern European Jewish Mysticism* (Oxford: Oxford University Press, 1985). Rivka Schatz Uffenheimer's classic work only recently appeared in English, see *Hasidism as Mysticism* (Princeton: Princeton University Press, 1993). Isaiah Tishby and Joseph Dan's Hebrew article on Hasidism is found in the *Hebrew Encyclopedia*, vol. 17 (1988), cols. 769–822. Also see Joseph Dan's introduction to his *The Teachings of Hasidism* (New York: Behrman, 1983).

4. For a thorough discussion of earlier approaches to the study of Hasidism and the current state of research, see Immanuel Etkes, "The Study of Hasidism: Past Trends and New Directions," in *Hasidism Reappraised* (London: Littman, 1996), pp. 447–464.

5. See Moshe Idel, *Hasidism: Between Ecstasy and Magic* (Albany: State University of New York, 1995).

6. Abraham Joshua Heschel's Yiddish articles have been translated and collected by Samuel Dresner in *The Circle of the Ba'al Shem Tov* (Chicago: University of Chicago Press, 1985). On HaBaD Hasidism, see Rachel Elior, *The Paradoxical Ascent to God: The Kabbalistic Theosophy of Habad Hasidism* (Albany: State University of New York, 1993); Roman A. Foxbrunner, *HABAD: The Hasidism of R. Shneur Zalman of Lyady* (Tuscaloosa: University of Alabama, 1992); and Naftali Lowenthal,

Communicating the Infinite: The Emergence of the Habad School (Chicago: University of Chicago Press, 1990). On Bratslav, see Arthur Green, *Tormented Master: A Life of Rabbi Nahman of Bratslav* (New York: Schocken, 1981); Mendel Piekarz, *Studies in Bratslav Hasidism*, 2nd ed. (Jerusalem: Mosad Bialik, 1995); Yehudah Liebes, "*Ha-Tikkun Ha-Kelali* of Rabbi Nahman of Bratslav and Its Sabbatean Links" in his *Studies in Jewish Myth and Jewish Messianism* (Albany: State University of New York, 1993). Rachel Elior's "Between *Yesh* and *Ayin*: The Doctrine of the Zaddik in the Works of Jacob Isaac, the Seer of Lublin," in *Jewish History: Essays in Honour of Chimen Abramsky* (London: Halban, 1988), pp. 393–445, is also a notable exception.

7. On R. Yehiel Mikhel of Zlotchov's prophetic activities as a prototype of the later Hasidic *Zaddiq*, see Dr. Mor Altshuler's dissertation, *Rabbi Meshullam Feibush Heller and His Place in Early Hasidism* [Hebrew] (Tel Aviv: Hebrew University, 1994).

8. See Ada Rapoport-Albert, "Hasidism after 1772: Structural Continuity and Change," in *Hasidism Reappraised* (London: Littman, 1996), pp. 94–109.

9. On the publication of this and other early Hasidic texts, see Zev Gries, *The Book in Early Hasidism: Genres, Authors, Scribes, Managing Editors and Its Review by Their Contemporaries and Scholars* [Hebrew] (Israel: Hakibbutz Hameuchad, 1992).

10. See Altshuler, *Rabbi Meshulam Feibush Heller*, pp. 19–29.

11. See the selections from Solomon Maimon's autobiography in Gershon Hundert, ed. *Essential Papers on Hasidism* (New York: New York University Press 1991).

12. See Rapoport-Albert, *Hasidism Reappraised*, pp. 76–141.

13. See especially Immanuel Etkes' articles, "The Rise of R. Shneur Zalman of Liadi to a Position of Leadership," [Hebrew] *Tarbiz* 54 (1985): 429–39; and "R. Shneur Zalman of Liadi's Way as a Leader of Hasidim," [Hebrew] *Zion* 50 (1985): 321–54. Also see the sources on HaBaD in note 5 above.

14. See Mordecai Wilensky, *Hasidim and Mitnagdim: A Study of the Controversy Between Them in the years 1772–1815* [Hebrew] (Jerusalem: Bialik, 1970).

15. On the publication of Hasidic and Kabbalistic texts in this region, see Zev Gries, *Book in Early Hasidism*.

16. See Altshuler *Rabbi Meshulam Feibush Heller*, pp. 61–66.

17. See Moshe Halamish, "The Teachings of R. Menachem Mendel of Vitebsk," in *Hasidism Reappraised*, pp. 268–287.

18. For example, R. Elimelekh of Lizhensk's *Sefer Noam Elimelekh*.

19. The importance of the ethical dimension in R. Meshullam Feibush's thought was already recognized by Rivka Schatz-Uffenheimer in the original Hebrew edition of *Hasidism as Mysticism*. However, it is Mendel Piekarz who has argued most strongly that the ethical dimension may be even more important than the mystical. See Mendel Piekarz, *Between Ideology and Reality: Humility, Ayin, Self-Negation and Devequt in the Hasidic Thought* [Hebrew] (Jerusalem: Bialik, 1994). Also see Piekarz's English article, "Hasidism as a Socio-religious Movement on the

Evidence of *Devekut,*" in Ada Rapoport-Albert, ed., *Hasidism Reappraised,* pp. 225–248.

20. The problem of pleasure in spiritual practice deserves a broader study. For the present, cf. Thich Nhat Hanh, *Thundering Silence: Sutra on Knowing the Better Way to Catch a Snake* (Berkeley: University of California, 1993).

21. On the conflict between these two kabbalistic approaches, see Idel, *Hasidism.*

22. See Arthur Green, "Early Hasidism: Some Old/New Questions," in *Hasidism Reappraised,* pp. 441–446.

1. Meshullam Feibush Heller and His Circle in Eastern Galicia

1. While no complete biography or systematic study of the Ba'al Shem Tov's teachings currently exists, Moshe Rosman's, *Founder of Hasidism: A Quest for the Historical Ba'al Shem Tov* (Berkeley: University of California, 1996) is an important contribution to our understanding of what can be known about the Ba'al Shem Tov and the sources attributed to him. Simon Menahem Mendel of Gowarczow's, *Sefer Ba'al Shem Tov* (Jerusalem: Lodz, 1938 reprint, 1992), remains a useful if not critical collection of teachings ascribed to the Ba'al Shem Tov. Dan Ben-Amos and Jerome R. Mintz have published an English translation of an early collection of legends concerning the founder of Hasidism. See *In Praise of the Baal* [sic] *Shem Tov* [*Shivhei ha-BeSHT*] (Bloomington, Ind.: Indiana University Press, 1970). Also see Gershom Scholem, "Demuto ha-Historit shel R. Israel Ba'al Shem Tov," in *Devarim be-Go* (Tel Aviv: Am Oved, 1982), pp. 287–324; and Simon Dubnov, *Toledot ha-Hasidut* (Tel Aviv: Devir, 1975), pp. 41–75.

2. On Dov Ber, see Dubnov, *Toledot,* pp. 76–92. Also see the article on Dov Ber in *Encyclopedia le-Hasidut: Ishim* (Jerusalem, 1986), v. 1, col. 419–441. A popular biography of Dov Ber was written by Jacob I. Schochet, *The Great Maggid* (Brooklyn: Kenot, 1978). Important aspects of Dov Ber's teachings are discussed by Rivka-Schatz Uffenheimer in *Hasidism as Mysticism: Quietistic Elements in Eighteenth Century Hasidic Thought* (Princeton: Princeton University Press, 1993); "Contemplative Prayer in Hasidism," in *Studies in Mysticism and Religion Presented to G. Scholem* (Jerusalem: 1962); "*Anti-Spiritualism be-Hasidut,*" *Molad* 20 (1963); and by Joseph Weiss in *Studies in Eastern European Jewish Mysticism* (Oxford: Oxford University Press, 1986). Also see Isaiah Tishby and Joseph Dan,"*Torat ha-Hasidut ve-Sifrutah,*" in *Studies in Hasidism* [Hebrew] (Jerusalem: 1977). Rivka Schatz-Uffenheimer has also prepared an essential critical edition of an early collection of Dov Ber's teachings, *Maggid Devarav le-Ya'aqov le-Maggid Dov Ber mi-Mezeritch,* 2nd ed. (Jerusalem: Magnes, 1976, 1990). Important points concerning the editing and dissemination of Dov Ber's spiritual directives (*hanhagot*) have been clarified by Zev Gries. *The Book in Early Hasidism* [Hebrew] (Israel: Hakkibutz Hameuchad, 1992), and *Conduct Literature (Regimen Vitae): Its History and Place in the Life of Beshtian Hasidism* [Hebrew] (Jerusalem: Bialik, 1989). Also see Gries' articles

"Arikhat Zava'at ha-RYVaSH," *Kiryat Sefer 52,* and *"Sifrut ha-Hanhagot ha-Ha-sidit,"* *Zion 46.* Also see Ada Rapoport-Albert, "Hasidism after 1772: Structural Continuity and Change" in *Hasidism Reappraised* (London: Littman, 1996), pp. 76–140.

3. Kohelet 12:10.

4. I have omitted the epithet, "may his memory be a blessing for life in the world to come," which is appended to the names of the Ba'al Shem Tov, Menahem Mendel, and Dov Ber, all of whom were deceased by 1777 when Meshullam Feibush began writing the tract.

5. It is not entirely clear from the Hebrew whether the reference is to words of the Ba'al Shem Tov or of Dov Ber. See Mor Altshuler's dissertation, "Rabbi Meshullam Feibush Heller and His Place in Early Hasidism" [Hebrew] (Tel Aviv: Hebrew University, 1994), pp. 61–62.

6. *Liqqutim Yeqarim,* 110a (YDE, sect. 1).

7. See note 25, the discussion of Menahem Mendel of Premishlan.

8. See Rivka Schatz-Uffenheimer's introduction to her critical edition of *Maggid Devarav le-Ya'aqov* [Hebrew] (Jerusalem: Magnes, 1976), and Zev Gries, "The Editing of *Zava'at ha-RYVaSH,"* [Hebrew] *Kiryat Sefer* 52: 187–209. Mor Altshuler has shown that a major role in the dissemination of these writings was played by disciples of Meshullam Feibush's master, R. Yehiel Mikhel of Zlotchov. See Mor Altshuler, *Rabbi Meshullam Feibush* and His Place in Early Hasidism (Tel Aviv: Hebrew University, 1994), p. 82.

9. *Liqqutim Yeqarim,* 114b (YDE, sect. 10).

10. Leviticus Rabbah, 23:1. This teaching is discussed in detail in the chapter, "Meshullam Feibush and the Maggid of Mezeritch."

11. An eyewitness account of Dov Ber's practice appears in Solomon Maimon, *An Autobiography* (New York: Schocken, 1967). An excerpt from the diary can be foumd in Gerhon David Hundert, *Essential Papers on Hasidism* (New York: New York University, 1991), pp. 11–24. See Joseph Weiss, *"Via Passiva* in Early Hasidism," in *Studies in East European Jewish Mysticism* (Oxford: Oxford University Press, 1985), pp. 78–82. Also see Rivka Schatz-Uffenheimer, *Hasidism as Mysticism: Quietistic Elements in Eighteenth-Century Hasidic Thought* [Hebrew] (Jerusalem: Bialik, 1980 and Princeton: Princeton University Press, 1993), pp. 110–121.

12. Mor Altshuler has shown that the second epistle was written shortly after Yehiel Mikhel's death. See Altshuler, *Rabbi Meshulam Feibush Heller,* pp. 21–22.

13. See *Liqqutim Yeqarim,* 116b, 117a (YDE, sects. 13, 14).

14. Altshuler's dissertation documents much of the Maggid of Zlotchov's influence.

15. See page 19 ff.

16. Meshullam Feibush did, however, make reference to the important Hasidic emigration to the Land of Israel, which was led by Menahem Mendel of Vitebsk in 1777. Thus, he clearly was aware of Hasidic leaders from beyond eastern Galicia and looked upon them as important *Zaddiqim,* although he did not mention them by name. See *Liqqutim Yeqarim,* 131a (YDE, sect. 36).

17. See Isaac Halevy Biladi's biographical introduction in Samuel Shmelke's, *Sifrey ha-Rav ha-Qadosh ha-Rebbe Rebbe Shmelke mi-Nikolsberg* (Jerusalem: Mosodot Boston, 1988), p. 43. R. Shmelke died in the spring of 1778.

18. On Elimelekh of Lizhensk, see the introduction to Gedalyah Nigal, *Introduction to the Critical Edition* of *No'am Elimelekh* [Hebrew] (Jerusalem: Mosad Harav Kook, 1978).

19. See Nigal, *No'am Elimelekh*, and Louis Jacobs, *Jewish Mystical Testimonies* (New York: Schocken, 1977), pp. 208–214. We shall have more to say about this letter in the chapter, "The Importance of *Zaddiqim*."

20. See note 17. Also see Aaron Zev Eshkoli, "*Ha-Hasidut be-Folin*," *Beyt Yisrael be-Folin: Mi-Yamim Rishonim ve-ad li-Yemot ha-Horban*, vol. 2, edited by Israel Haleprin (Jerusalem, 1947); and Rachel Elior, "Between *Yesh and Ayin*: The Doctrine of the Zaddik in the Works of Jacob Isaac, the Seer of Lublin," in *Jewish History: Essays in Honor of Chimen Abramsky*, edited by Ada Rapoport-Albert (London, 1988), pp. 393–455.

21. Mor Altshuler has called attention to the connections between Levi Isaac of Berdichev, Elimelekh of Lizhensk, and Israel of Kozhenitz, and the Maggid of Zlotchov. Further research will be required before the membership of R. Yehiel Mikhel's inner circle can be determined with certainty.

22. See, e.g., Mor Altshuler's remarks concerning Lev Isaac of Berditchev, Altshuler, *Rabbi Meshullam Feibush Heller*, p. 328–329

23. See Mordecai Wilensky, *Hasidim and Mitnaggedim: A Study of Controversy Between Them in the Years 1772–1815*, 2nd ed. [Hebrew] (Jerusalem: Bialik, 1970). Also see Altshuler, *Rabbi Meshulam Feibush Heller*, p. 43, on the possible relationship of this opposition to R. Yehiel Mikhel and his circle.

24. As Rivka Schatz-Uffenheimer and Zev Gries have established, the posthumously published *Darkhey Yesharim*, although attributed to Menahem Mendel, is primarily a collection of teachings from Dov Ber of Mezeritch. Whether anything included in this work was actually written by Menahem Mendel or whether he was even responsible for the collection, selection, and arrangement of the teachings is difficult to determine.

25. The most complete collection of Menahem Mendel's teachings can be found in Menahem Mendel Vizhnitzer's *Torat ha-Hasidim ha-Rishonim* (Israel: Bnai Brak, 1981). This volume includes an edition of *Darkhey Yesharim* and a section of teachings collected from various sources. See pp. 272–289. Although the selection includes several sources of doubtful authenticity, it consituties a useful tool for the investigation of Menahem Mendel's thought. A chapter devoted to Menahem Mendel of Premishlan appears in Yehiel Granatstein, *Talmidey ha-Ba'al Shem Tov be-Erez Yisrael* [Hebrew] (Tel Aviv: Maor, 1982), pp. 101–122. Several important discussions of Menahem Mendel's teachings can be found in Joseph Weiss, *Studies in Eastern European Mysticism*, see index. An article by Abraham Rubenstein, "*Shevah' mi-Shivhey ha-BeSHT?*," in *Tarbiz* 35 (1966): 174–191, deals specifically with a recently discovered source concerning an event in Menahem Mendel's life.

26. The name Menahem Mendel ben Eliezer appears in the signature to two authentic letters sent from the Land of Israel and in a *Haskamah* written for Barukh of Kosov's *Nehmad ve-Na'im, Yesod ha-Avodah* (Israel: Bnai Brak, 1988). The text of Menahem Mendel's letters can be found in Ya'acov Barnai, *Hasidic Letters from Eretz-Israel: From the Second Half of the 18th-Century and Beginning of the 19th-Century* [Hebrew] (Jerusalem: Ben Zvi, 1980), pp. 52-56. The name Menahem Mendel ben Batsheva appears only in a letter originally published in the late collection, *Midrash RYVaSH Tov* While the authenticity of this source has been challenged, a photograph of the manuscript of the letter appears in Vizhnitzer's *Torat ha-Hasidim ha-Rishonim*, p. 290.

27. One of the two authentic letters from the Land of Israel was addressed to "my brother . . . Zvi, who is commonly known as R. Zvi the Hasid of Zlotchov." See Altshuler, *Rabbi Meshullam Feibush Heller*, pp. 333–338.

28. Mentioned in the writings of R. Mordecai of Slonim. See Vizhnitzer, *Torat ha-Hasidim ha-Rishonim*, p. 288.

29. See the English translation by Dan Ben-Amos and Jerome R. Mintz, eds., *In Praise of the Baal Shem Tov* [Shivhei ha-BeSHT] (Bloomington: Indiana University Press, 1970), p. 155. Concerning the difficulties relying on this nineteenth-century text as a reliable source for earlier Hasidic history, see Moshe Rosman, *Founder of Hasidism: A Quest for the Historical Ba'al Shem Tov* (Berkeley: University of California, 1966), pp. 143–158.

30. See Rubinstein, "*Shevah'*," pp. 180–182.

31. This interpretation is suggested by Menahem Vizhnitzer in *Torat ha-Hasidim ha-Rishonim*. See section *Milley de-Avot*, pp. 190–191, 198.

32. Amos and Mintz, *In Praise of the Baal Shem Tov*, p. 153. The text as written is garbled and seems to indicate that the incident occurred around the time of R. Nahman's death. However, the sequence of events is out of order. R. Nahman died the following year in the Land of Israel. Menahem Mendel must have received this teaching from Nahman of Horodenka in Nemerov, during the summer of 1764, before they departed for the Land of Israel. See Rubenstein's reconstruction, "*Shevah'*," p. 189.

33. See below our discussion of Menahem Mendel's teachings. Also see the discussion of Meshullam Feibush's position regarding the elevation of wayward thoughts.

34. Amos and Mintz, *In Praise of the Baal Shem Tov*, p. 155.

35. See Arthur Green, *Tormented Master: A Life of Rabbi Nahman of Bratslav* (Montogomery: University of Alabama, 1979).

36. For an account of the journey, see Vizhnitzer, *Torat ha-Hasidim ha-Rishonim*, pp. 217–221. R. Fridel is mentioned in *Shivhey ha-BeSHT*.

37. The reference appears in *Birkey Yosef, Yoreh De'ah*, sect. 299. See Granatstein, *Talmidey ha-Ba'al Shem Tov*, p. 101.

38. *Sefer Yosef Tehilot*, 30b. The text appears in Granatstein, *Talmidey ha-Ba'al Shem Tov*, p. 119. The interpretation to Ps. 32:2, which Abraham Azulai cites in the

name of Menahem Mendel is a well-known Hasidic teaching that Menahem Mendel probably learned from his teachers and repeated in the Land of Israel. It also appears in *Degel Mahaneh Efraim, Balak,* attributed to the Ba'al Shem Tov and in *Toledot Ya'akov Yosef,* attributed to R. Menahem Mendel of Bar.

39. The will was published in *Sefer Darkhey Zion* (Bartfeld, 1909). See Rubenstein, "*Shevah,*" p. 186.

40. See Barnai, *Hasidic Letters from the Land of Israel,* pp. 54–56.

41. See Yitzhak Alfasi, *Ha-Hasidut* (Tel Aviv: Maariv, 1974), p. 52. The date also appears in Viznitzer, *Torat ha-Hasidim ha-Rishonim,* p. 291. According to Piekarz, Menahem Mendel died in 1770. See Mendel Piekarz, *Between Ideology and Reality: Humility, Ayin, Self-Negation and Devekut in the Hasidic Thought* [Hebrew] (Jerusalem: Bialik, 1994), p. 25.

42. The year has been erased from the stone and is disputed. See Granatstein, *Talmidey ha-Ba'al Shem Tov,* p. 105. Abraham Rubenstein questions the authenticity of the date on the stone. See Rubenstein "*Shevah,*" p. 186. At any rate, Menahem Mendel was certainly deceased by the winter of 1776–1777, since Meshullam Feibush refers to him as such in his writings of spring 1777.

43. However, see Moshe Rosman's comments in *Founder of Hasidism,* p. 131.

44. See *Liqqutim Yeqarim,* 131a YDE: , sect. 36. Concerning the early Hasidic emigration to the Land of Israel, see Israel Halperin, *Ha-Aliyot ha-Rishonot shel ha-Hasidim* (Jerusalem: le-Erez Yisrael, 1947). On the relationship between Hasidism and messianism, see Ben Zion Dinur, *Be-Mifne ha-Dorot* (Jerusalem: Bialik, 1955), pp. 181–227; Isaiah Tishby, "The Messianic Idea and Messianic Trends in the Growth of Hasidism" [Hebrew], *Zion* 32 (1967); and Gershom Scholem, "The Neutralization of Messianism in Early Hasidism," in *The Messianic Idea in Judaism and Other Essays* (New York: Schocken, 1971). On the role of messianism in the circle of R. Yehiel Mikhel of Zlotchov, see Altshuler, *Rabbi Meshullam Feibush Heller,* pp. 285–289.

45. See Mordecai Wilensky, *Hasidim and Mitnaggdim.*

46. See *Liqqutim Yeqarim,* 125b YDE: sect. 29).

47. See Rubenstein, "*Shevah,*" pp. 177–180.

48. While Ada Rapoport-Albert has shown that no contest for succession could have taken place at this time, it is still possible that a figure like Menahem Mendel of Premishlan could have vied with the Maggid for influence. See Rapoport-Albert, "Hasidism after 1772," in *Hasidism Reappraised* (London: Littman, 1996).

49. The anecdote is recounted in *Qehal Hasidim he-Hadash*: sect. 36. See Vizhnitzer, *Torat ha-Hasidim ha-Rishonim,* pp. 281–282.

50. Gen. 27:33.

51. See below pp. 21–23.

52. See note 24.

53. See *Liqqutim Yeqarim,* 129b, YDE: sect. 34. On R. Solomon Vilner's connection to eastern Galician Hasidic leaders and his activities in behalf of the Hasidic community in Israel, see Altshuler, *Rabbi Meshullam Feibush Heller,* pp. 23–25, 334.

54. The story appears in a manuscript of R. Joseph of Brisk, the author of *Minhat Yosef*. See Granatstein, *Talmidy ha-Ba'al Shem Tov*, p. 113.

55. This is disputed by Altshuler, *Rabbi Meshullam Feibush Heller*, p. 335, n. 209. However, see below, p. 38, n. 63, 64, for sources concerning Yehiel Mikhel's respect for Menahem Mendel.

56. Amos and Mintz, *In Praise of the Baal Shem Tov*, p. 155.

57. This is discussed in greater detail in ch. 8, "The Importance of *Zaddiqim*."

58. Reported in *Liqqutim Yeqarim* of R. Aaron Joseph Luria and in *Kitvey R. Yosef SHuV*. See Vizhnitzer, *Torat ha-Hasidim ha-Rishonim*, p. 280.

59. On the Lurianic *kavvanot* of eating, see Ronit Meroz, "Selections from Ephraim Penzieri: Luria's Sermon in Jerusalem and the *Kavvanah* in Taking Food," [Hebrew] in *Jerusalem Studies in Jewish Thought*, vol. 10, edited by Rachel Elior and Yehuda Liebes (Jerusalem, 1992), pp. 211–257.

60. See *Liqqutim Yeqarim*, 119B, YDE: sect. 18.

61. Menahem Mendel's practice of immersing in a *Mikvah* before eating is reported in *Pe'er li-Yesharim*, 15, sect. 154. See Vizhnitzer, *Torat-Hasidim ha-Rishonim*, p. 179. This is but one of several teachings attributed to Menahem Mendel brought by Vizhnitzer that place special emphasis on the sanctity of eating. For a discussion of the spiritual nature of eating in Hasidism, see Louis Jacobs, "Eating as an Act of Worship in Hasidic Thought," in *Studies in Jewish Religious and Intellectual History* (Alabama: University of Alabama, 1979), pp. 157–166. A late Hasidic work dealing with the sanctity of eating is Rabbi Aharon (Reb Arele) Roth's *Shulhan ha-Tahor* (Satu-Mare, 1933).

62. See Vizhnitzer, *Torat ha-Hasidim ha-Rishonim*, p. 286. Sources are listed on page 289. The somewhat obscure Hebrew text reads as follows: *she-hafsaqah ahat hayah mafsiq be-sihah le-shaber zot ha-midah, ve hafsaqah ahat be-re'iah, u-ve-'eleh rabot.*

63. See Amos and Mintz, *In Praise of the Baal Shem Tov*, p. 154.

64. For a Jewish example, see Hyman Enelow's edition of Al-Nakawah's *Menorat ha-Maor*, v. 4: p. 367ff. For a discussion of the importance of silence in Kabbalah and Hasidism, see Moshe Hallamish, "Al ha-Shetiqah ve-Kabbalah u-ve-Hasidut, Da'at ve-Safah" (1982), 79–89.

65. The text of the document appears in Granatstein, *Talmidey ha-Ba'al Shem Tov*, p. 121. It is discussed in detail by Rubinstein in *"Shevah."*

66. See Avraham Greenbaum, *The Sweetest Hour: Tikkun Chatzot* (Jerusalem: Breslov Research Institute, 1993), which offers an account of this practice in the tradition of the Hasidim of Bratzlav.

67. The Hebrew reads: *"she-hithilu li-nesoa' elav la-'asok be-asaqim."* That is, they began to visit him because of their business interests. See Rubinstein's discussion of the meaning of this phrase in *"Shevah',"* p. 177.

68. Recorded in Benjamin of Zalozitz's *Turey Zahav*, 105c. See Vizhnitzer, *Torat ha-Hasidim ha-Rishonim*, p. 272.

69. Amos and Mintz, *In Praise of the Baal Shem Tov*, p. 155. "They" includes

R. Fridel of Brody who had led the prayers in Nemerov before Menahem Mendel's arrival.

70. Recorded in *Kitvey R. Mordecai mi-Slonim.* See Vizhnitzer, *Torat ha-Hasidim ha-Rishonim,* p. 284.

71. Recorded in *Kitvey R. Yosef SHuV.* See Viznitzer, Ibid.

72. *Ahavat Dodim,* 144b–145a. See Viznitzer, Ibid., p. 276.

73. Recorded in *Yesod ha-Avodah* (Slonim), 148d. See Vizhnitzer, Ibid., p. 275.

74. See Mendel Piekarz, *The Beginning of Hasidism: Idelogical Trends in Derush and Musar Literature* (Jerusalem: Bialik, 1978), pp. 209–218. Also see my introduction to Miles Krassen, *Isaiah Horowitz: the Generations of Adam* (Mahwah, N.J., Paulist, 1996), p. 33.

75. Recorded in *Pe'er le-Yesharim* and *Imrey Pinhas.* See Vizhnitzer, *Torat ha-Hasidim ha-Rishonim,* p. 281. Compare Meshullam Feibush's attitude toward fasting, *Liqqutim Yeqarim,* 133a–134a YDE: sects. 40–41.

76. Recorded in *Hibat ha-Arez,* p. 18, sect. 122. See Vizhnitzer, *Torat ha-Hasidim ha-Rishonim,* p. 285. Vizhnitzer lists the source as *Hovat ha-arez,* which is probably a printer's error. I have not been able to examine the source.

77. Reported in a letter to his friend, R. Meir of Premishlan, a fellow disciple of the Ba'al Shem Tov. See Vizhnitzer, Ibid., p. 284.

78. Reported in *Or ha-Galil.* See Vizhnitzer, Ibid.

79. Dov Ber's complex and varied approach to the problem of wayward thoughts still awaits thorough study. However, the fundamental difference between his approach and that of Menahem Mendel is apparent in Rivka Schatz-Uffenheimer, *Maggid Devarav le-Ya'aqov,* sect. 41: 61–63.

80. Menahem Mendel's general theory concerning the cause of wayward thoughts is brought in *Nozer Hesed,* p. 120, ch. 6, *ahdut,* where it is quoted from a manuscript attributed to Menahem Mendel. See Vizhnitzer, *Torat ha-Hasidim ha-Rishonim,* p. 278–279.

81. See *Degel Mahaneh Efraim, be-ha'alotekhah,* towards the end. See Vizhnitzer, Ibid, p. 274 for the section quoted in the name of Menahem Mendel.

82. Although a full account of early Hasidic approaches to this issue has yet to be written a useful introduction to the subject can be found in Louis Jacobs, *Hasidic Prayer* (Philadelphia: Jewish Publication Society, 1973), pp. 104–120.

83. Recorded in *Orah le-Hayyim,* 287a, 292b, 294b. See Vizhnitzer, *Torat ha-Hasidim ha-Rishonim,* p. 273.

84. See *Liqqutim Yeqarim,* 122a, YDE: sect. 22. Also compare the important remarks of Moshe Idel on this passage in *Kabbalah: New Perspectives* (New Haven, 1988), p. 58. Also see Idel, *Hasidism: Between Ecstasy and Magic* (Albany: State University of New York, 1995), p. 37.

85. See the list of sources in Vizhnitzer, *Torat ha-Hasidim ha-Rishonim,* pp. 288–289.

86. The most thorough appraisal of Yehiel Mikhel and his role in early Hasidism is to be found in Altshuler, *Rabbi Meshullam Feibush Heller.* Also see Simon

Dubnov, *History of Hasidism* [Hebrew] (4th ed., Tel Aviv: Devir, 1975), pp. 188–191. Also see Isaac Matityahu Tanenbaum's biography of Yehiel Mikhel, his ancestors and sons, *To'afot Harim: Beyt Zlotchov* (Jerusalem: Zekher Naftali, 1986). Anecdotes concerning Yehiel Mikhel along with his spiritual practices and fragments of his teachings have been collected in Nathan Nata Doner's *Mayim Rabbim* (Warsaw, 1899) and in Moshe Hayyim Kleinman's collection, *Zikaron la-Rishonim* (Pietrekov, 1912). A more recent collection of Yehiel Mikhel's teachings is *Yeshu'ot Malko* (Jerusalem: Mosad Levin, 1974).

87. See Abraham Joshua Heschel, *The Circle of the Baal Shem Tov: Studies in Hasidim* (Chicago: University of Chicago, 1985), pp. 153–154.

88. On transcending pain during martyrdom by means of mystical practices, see Nehemia Polen, "Ecstasy and Sanctification," in *Kabbalah* (1988): v. 3, n. 1. Also see Michael Fishbane, *The Kiss of God: Spiritual and Mystical Death in Judaism* (Seattle: University of Washinton Press, 1994), pp. 51–86.

89. See Heschel, *Circle of Ba'al Shem Tov*, pp. 154–155.

90. See Tanenbaum, *To'afat Harim*, p. 49. Dates for his death range from 1742–1768.

91. On Rabbi Joseph Yospe of Ostrog, see *Mizkeret le-Gedoley Ostrog*, p. 148: sect. 194.

92. On Brody, see N. M. Gelber, *History of the Jews of Brody* [Hebrew] (Jerusalem: Mosad Havau Kuk, 1955).

93. See Tanenbaum, *To'afat Harim*, pp. 31–32. Also consider note 3 on p. 32, which describes the various conflicting accounts of the tale. Altshuler proves that this incident could only have occurred in Horochov, before Isaac Hamburger became Head of the Rabbinical Court in Brody in 1760. See Altshuler, *Rabbi Meshullam Feibush Heller*, p. 35, n.29.

94. Reported in *Mevasser Zedeq, Korah*. See Tanenbaum, *To'afat Harim*, p. 43.

95. See Heschel, *Circle of Ba'al Shem Tov*, p. 152.

96. See Altshuler, *Rabbi Meshullam Feibush Heller*, p. 39.

97. Legends concerning R. Isaac and the Ba'al Shem Tov appear in *Shivhey ha-BeSHT*, see the index to the English edition. On one well-known legend concerning R. Isaac's opposition to the BeSHT's use of amulets, see Abraham Heschel, *Circle of the Ba'al Shem Tov*, pp. 167–170. Also see Idel, *Hasidism: Between Ecstasy and Magic*, pp. 76–77.

98. Heschel, *Circle of Ba'al Shem Tov*, p. 172.

99. See Amos and Mintz, *In Praise of the Baal Shem Tov*, pp. 87–89. He appears there as "Isaac Drobziner." A chapter on Isaac of Drohobitch can also be found in Kleinman's *Zikaron la-Rishonim*.

100. See Heschel, *Cicrcle of Ba'al Shem Tov*, p. 174. Additional sources are listed in Tanenbaum, *To'afat Harim*, p. 63. See below notes 101, 102. Also see Altshuler, *Rabbi Meshullam Feibush Heller*, p. 33 and 45. Based on family traditions, Altshuler calculates Yehiel Mikhel's year of birth as 1726.

101. See Heschel, *Circle of Ba'al Shem Tov*, p. 175. An interpretation of this

bizzare tale is offered by Samuel Dresner, the editor of the English edition of Heschel's article. See p. 175f., n. 86.

102. See Tanenbaum, *To'afat Harim,* pp. 63–64.

103. See Heschel, *Circle of Ba'al Shem Tov,* p. 179. The tradition concerning Yehiel Mikhel's instruction to his sons is found in *Mayim Rabbim,* p. 95.

104. The story is recounted in *Qehal Hasidim he-Hadash,* sect. 41. See Tanenbaum, *To'afat Harim,* p. 30.

105. The exact year is not indicated in available sources.

106. See Tanenbaum, *To'afat Harim,* p. 64.

107. Ibid.

108. Heschel, *Circle of Ba'al Shem Tov,* p. 175. The text appears in *The Geneology of Chernobyl and Ruzhin* [Hebrew], p. 103.

109. See Altshuler, *Rabbi Meshullam Feibush Heller,* discussion of R. Yehiel Mikhel's role in popularizing this Hasidic custom, pp. 269–278.

110. See Tanenbaum, *To'afat Harim,* pp. 68–69.

111. A detailed analysis of this sermon is found in Altshuler, *Rabbi Meshullam Feibush Heller,* pp. 83–177.

112. Altshuler has suggested that Yehiel Mikhel's presence in so modest a post may have been the result of opposition. See Altshuler, Ibid. pp. 43–44.

113. See Altshuler, Ibid. pp. 322–323.

114. See Altshuler, Ibid., pp. 297–302.

115. Reported by Rabbi Israel Hofstein of Kozhenitz in *Avodat Yisrael, Avot.* See Tanenbaum, *To'afat Harim,* p. 89. This charismatic ability was attributed to a number of Kabbalists, including Isaac Luria of Safed. See Lawrence Fine, "The Art of Metoposcopy: A Study in Isaac Luria's Charismatic Knowledge," in *Essential Papers on Kabbalah* (New York: New York University Press, 1995), pp. 315–337, originally published in *AJS Review* 11 (1986): pp. 79–101. Altshuler brings sources that indicate that this was an ability also attributed to Yehiel Mikhel's father, R. Isaac. See Altshuler, *Rabbi Meshullam Feibush Heller,* pp. 37–39.

116. See Tanenbaum, *To'afat Harim,* p. 84.

117. Ibid., p. 79.

118. Ibid., p. 80. Aspects of the material contained in the late sources for this incident are problematic. David Tevele's letter refers to "disciples of the Ba'al Shem Tov and disciples of the Maggid of Mezeritch." Since Ezekiel Landau left Yampol in 1755, the incident would have had to occur before that time. However, it is doubtful if Dov Ber of Mezeritch would have been linked with the Ba'al Shem Tov as early as the early 1750s. Nor is there evidence that Yehiel Mikhel was associated with Dov Ber before the death of the Ba'al Shem Tov. As for Ezekiel Landau, evidence does exist that he was strongly opposed to certain aspects of Hasidic practice, particularly the custom of reciting the kabbalistic formula "for the sake of uniting the Holy One, blessed be He and His *Shekhinah,* etc." before performing *mizvot.* Yehiel Mikhel's disciple, Hayyim of Tchernovitz would later write a famous defense of the Hasidic practice (see Jacobs, *Hasidic Prayer,* pp. 140–153). However, Landau's written

objection to this practice was composed in the late 1770s. If Yehiel Mikhel indeed arrived in Yampol during the time that Landau served there, it is possible that tension could have existed between them. However, the sources adduced by Tanenbaum seem anachronistic. Perhaps they date from a later time, when Landau was agitating against the Hasidim.

119. See Tanenbaum, *To'afat Harim*, pp. 134–135. This is the date indicated in *Mayim Rabbim*. It also appears on the tombstone in Yampol.

120. Thus, he would have been born in 1726.

121. Uziel Meisels, *Tiferet Uziel, Tavo*. On Uziel Meisels and his relationship to Yehiel Mikhel, see Altshuler, *Rabbi Meshullam Feibush Heller*, pp. 330–333.

122. The story of Yehiel Mikhel's death appears in *Netiv Mizvotekha*. See Tanenbaum, *To'afat Harim*, p. 134. The declaration of unity, or "*Shema*," Deuteronomy 6:4, is supposed to be uttered by a Jew at the moment of death.

123. Amos and Mintz, *In Praise of the Baal Shem Tov*, p. 185.

124. See Tanenbaum, *To'afat Harim*, pp. 138–142.

125. The story appears in some editions of *Shivhey ha-BeSHT*. See Tanenbaum, *To'afat Harim*, pp. 139–140. It was characteristic of early Hasidic teachings to discourage excessive preoccupation with sins already committed. See Schatz-Uffenheimer, *Hasidism as Mysticism*, pp. 93–111.

126. See Tanenbaum, *To'afat Harim*, pp. 147–148.

127. Others were Menahem Nahum of Chernobyl and Menahem Mendel of Vitebsk.

128. See Tanenbaum, *To'afat Harim*, p. 149. A visitation by Elijah was considered an indication of the highest spiritual attainment.

129. See Tanenbaum, *To'afat Harim*, pp. 151–152.

130. Ibid., p. 162.

131. Ibid., p. 159.

132. See Rosman's discussion of HaBaD's use of legendary Hasidic material in *Founder of Hasidism*, pp. 187–211. Also see Ada Rapoport-Albert, "Hagiography with Footnotes: Edifying Tales and the Writing of History in Hasidism," in *History and Theory, Beiheft 27: Essays in Jewish Historiography*, 1988.

133. See Tanenbaum, *To'afat Harim*, pp. 157–158. On Rabbi Pinhas, see Heschel, *Circle of the Ba'al Shem Tov* pp. 1–43. Also see, Altshuler, *Rabbi Meshulam Feibush Heller*, pp. 258–268.

134. On the importance of ritual slaughter in early Hasidism, see Chone Shmeruk, "The Social Meaning of Hasidic Ritual Slaughter" [Hebrew] in *Zion* 20 (1956): pp. 47–72; also see Aaron Wertheim, *Law and Custom in Hasidism* (Hoboken: Ktvar, 1992), pp. 302–315.

135. This entire issue has been considerably clarified by Altshuler. See Altshuler, *Rabbi Meshullam Feibush Heller*, pp. 258–269.

136. See Tanenbaum, *To'afat Harim*, p. 145–146.

137. Ibid., pp. 144–145.

138. See Amos and Mintz, *In Praise of the Baal Shem Tov*, pp. 260–261. I have

included this story mainly for the light it sheds on Yehiel Mikhel's priorities. How-ever, the account, itself, contains details of doubtful historicity. Jacob Joseph's writ-ings were burned in Brody in 1780. By that time, Joseph of Yampol was already in his mid-twenties. Even Yehiel Mikhel's youngest son, Mordecai of Kremenitz would have been about sixteen at the time, probably too old to have been the "boy" referred to in the story. Moreover, Yehiel Mikhel himself died within a year, if we accept the date of his death as 1781.

139. For a more detailed discussion of Yehiel Mikhel's disciples and associates, see Altshuler, *Rabbi Meshullam Feibush Heller*, especially pp. 293–344. Also see Tanenbaum, *To'afat Harim*, pp. 165–195.

140. Mordecai of Neshkiz's teachings are collected in *Rishpey Esh*. Also see Martin Buber, *Tales of the Hasidim: The Early Masters* (New York: Schocken, 1947), pp. 163–166.

141. He was the author of the kabbalistic work, *Berit Kehunat Olam*. See Alt-shuler, *Rabbi Meshullam Feibush Heller*, pp. 318–319. Also see Aaron Walden, *Shem ha-Gedolim he-Hadash* (Warsaw, 1880), sect. 2 (*ma'arekhet ha-sefarim*), p. 15.

142. Isaac of Radvil was the author of the work, *Or Yizhaq*. Several of his teachings are discussed by Altshuler. Also see Schatz-Uffenheimer in *Hasidism as Mysticism*.

143. On Yehiel Mikhel's sons, see Tanenbaum, *To'afat Harim*, pp. 201–298.

144. See Amos and Mintz, *In Praise of the Baal Shem Tov*, pp. 204–206.

145. On Yom Tov Lipman Heller, see Joseph Davis, *R. Yom Tov Lipman Heller, Joseph b. Isaac haLevi, and Rationalism in Ashkenazic Jewish Culture, 1550–1650*, Ph.D. diss. Harvard University, 1990.

146. On Brezhin, see Zvi Ha-Levi Ish Horowitz, *Toledot ha-Qehillot be-Folin* (Jerusalem: Mosad Harva Kook, 1978), pp. 151–153.

147. The geneology in *Zerizuta de-Avraham* lists his name as Moshe Aaron. However, the name appears as Aaron Moshe in the Munkacz geneology and in Meshullam Feibush's signatures.

148. See the geneology of the Heller family, prepared by a descendent of Abra-ham Noah, which appears in the latter's *Zerizuta de-Avraham* (New York, 1952).

149. According to a note written by Meshullam Feibush's great-grandson, Samson Ha-Levi Heller of Kolymyja, which accompanies the family geneology that is included in the Munkacz edition of *Yosher Divrey Emet* (1905), the Ba'al Shem Tov visited Rabbi Meir, Meshullam Feibush's grandfather. However, I have not been able to locate any other reference that would confirm the veracity of this statement.

150. See the geneology in *Zerizuta de-Avraham*. The cognomen, "The Hasid," does not in itself suggest any connection to Hasidism. The appellation was rather commonly applied to pietists in eastern Europe. Moreover, according to Samson Ha-Levi Heller's note to the geneology in *Yosher Divrey Emet*, Meshullam Feibush's mother was descended from the Kabbalist, Judah the Hasid, who led a group of fol-lowers to the Land of Israel at the turn of the eighteenth century. Meshullam Feibush's brother might have been named after his better-known ancestor.

151. See Rappaport's approbation, written in 1768, which appears in the New York edition of *Zerizuta de-Avraham*.

152. Details concerning the scope of his writings and the fire appear in the approbations published in *Zerizuta de-Avraham*.

153. Abraham Noah Heller, *Zerizuta de Avraham* (New York, 1952). According to the title page, the homilies on Genesis and Exodus were already printed in 1900. The title page also lists the author's name as Abraham Noah. However, in the geneology that appears in a few pages later, he is consistently called Noah Abraham.

154. Yitzhak Alfasi, in his entry for Meshullam Feibush in *Ha-Hasidut* (Tel Aviv: Maariv, 1974), p. 85, claims that Abraham of Dolina was also a disciple of Dov Ber of Mezeritch. However, Alfasi offers no evidence to support his assertion.

155. Altshuler suggests that he was born in or before 1742. See Altshuler, *Rabbi Meshullam Feibush Heller*, p. 1. While this date is certainly reasonable in itself, her position is based on the ban against studying Lurianic Kabbalah before the age of forty. However, there is little reason to preclude Meshullam Feibush's having begun to study Lurianic kabbalah before the ban was imposed in 1772 and well before his fortieth birthday. In fact, he states explicitly that he "studied some [Lurianic] *kavvanot* in my youth." See *Liqqutim Yeqarim*, 135 b, YDE: 43.

156. See below our discussion of Torah study.

157. See *Sidduro shel Shabbat*, part 2, third homily, section 3.

158. Perhaps she was a descendent of the famous kabbalist, Rabbi Samson of Ostropol. Samson Ha-Levi Heller's note to the geneology in *Yosher Divrey Emet* indicates that Meshullam Feibush was a grandson of Samson of Ostropol and the author of *Zon Qodashim*. However, the latter was in fact the father of Meshullam Feibush's second wife. Since the name of Samson of Ostropol does not appear in the ancestry of either of Meshullam Feibush's parents, perhaps he was an ancestor of the first wife. Having died in 1648, Samson of Ostropol could not possibly have been Meshullam Feibush's father-in-law.

159. Perhaps his name was Aaron Moses, see note 105. Presumably, the first son was named after Meshullam Feibush's father who must have been deceased by the time of the birth. Knowledge of the date of the father' death could aid us in estimating the year of Meshullam Feibush's birth, since we may suppose that the first child was born when Meshullam Feibush was between the ages of 15–20. Unfortunately, this information is not presently available.

160. See the geneology of the Heller dynasty in Alfasi, *Ha-Hasidut*, pp. 85–86.

161. See *Toledot ha-Qehillot be-Folin*, p. 298.

162. He is identified in the beginning of *Yosher Divrey Emet* as his brother-in-law, Rabbi Joel.

163. Altshuler has suggested that the letter was sent to the Hasidic community in the Land of Israel. See Altshuler, *Rabbi Meshullam Feibush Heller*, pp. 19–29.

164. Indeed, the text contains a lengthy homily that Meshullam Feibush had heard at Yehiel Mikhel's court on the holiday of Shavuot, 1777, shortly before he wrote the first part of *Yosher Divrey Emet*. Thus, he was still visiting his master during

the festivals. According to Altshuler, the esoteric meaning and circumstances surrounding this homily form the principal motivation for Meshullam Feibush's writing the epistle.

165. The letters appear in the Munkacz edition of *Yosher Divrey Emet*, pp. 37c–39d. Neither the dates nor the intended recipients of the letters are indicated.

166. For a discussion of the history of the publication of Meshullam Feibush's writings, see below, pp. 38–42.

167. Simon Dubnov first suggested the role of Meshullam Feibush in the editing of *Liqqutim Yeqarim* in *Toledot ha-Hasidut* 4th ed. (Tel Aviv, 1975), pp. 323–324, n.5, Joseph Weiss went even further in identifying Meshullam Feibush as sole editor. See "The Kavvanoth of Prayer in Early Hasidism" in *Studies in Eastern European Jewish Mysticism* (Oxford: Oxford University Press, 1985), pp. 122–124, n. 57. Rivka Schatz-Uffenheimer has more recently argued that Meshullam Feibush should also be considered the editor of the work attributed to Menahem Mendel of Premishlan, *Darkhey Yesharim*. See pages 17–18 of the introduction to her critical edition of *Maggid Devarav le-Ya'aqov* (Jerusalem: Magnes, 1976) and especially the footnote on page 18.

168. The anecdote appears in the Munkacz edition of *Yosher Divrey Emet*, p. 38b. There it is brought from *Sefer Qevuzat Ya'aqov*. Also see *Qehal Hasidim he-Hadash* (Warsaw, 1900), p. 38d, sect. 160. The anecdote was recorded by the grandson of the Rabbi of Zalishtik.

169. Hasidic historiography attributes weakened health as a result of asceticism to several of its early leaders, including Dov Ber of Mezeritch and Jacob Joseph of Polnoy. The Ba'al Shem Tov was very much against the ascetic approach and vigorously opposed such tendencies among his disciples. See, e.g., Amos and Mintz, *In Praise of the Baal Shem Tov*, pp. 64–65. Nevertheless, austerities continued to be practiced by some of the earlier Hasidic masters. Meshullam Feibush would have been aware of such practices among the *Zaddiqim* in his area like Elimelekh of Lizhensk and his own master Yehiel Mikhel of Zlotchov. And see below, the story concerning Meshullam Feibush's decision not to fast.

170. The anecdote is section 161 in *Qehal Hasidim he-Hadash*. According to his disciple, Rabbi Hayyim of Volozhin, Rabbi Elijah, the Gaon of Vilna, Hasidism's arch-enemy, rejected similar temptations. See Louis Jacobs, *Jewish Mystical Testimonies* (New York: Schocken), p. 172.

171. The story appears in the Munkacz edition of *Yosher Divrey Emet*, pp. 9d–10a.

172. See *Qehal Hasidim he-Hadash*, sect. 162.

173. See the Munkacz edition of *Yosher Divrey Emet*, p. 9d.

174. See *Liqqutim Yeqarim*, 136a YDE: sect. 44. A story concerning Rabbi David of Mikolajov appears in *Shivhey ha-BeSHT*, see Amos and Mintz, *In Praise of the Baal Shem Tov*, pp. 197–198. Additional teachings in his name can be found in *Hesed le-Avraham, Lekh Lekha*, and also at the end of the *sefer*.

175. See our chapter on Meshullam Feibush and Dov Ber of Mezeritch.

176. See Altshuler, *Rabbi Meshullam Feibush Heller*, esp. pp. 61–82, 191–278.

177. See *Liqqutim Yeqarim*, p. 122b, YDE: sect. 22.

178. See *Liqqutim Yeqarim*, p. 129b. YDE: sect. 34. And see Altshuler, *Rabbi Meshullam Feibush Heller*, p. 334, n. 206.

179. See Barnai, *Hasidic Letters from Eretz-Israel*, p. 54..

180. See *Liqqutim Yeqarim*, p. 130, YDE: sect. 34. The text indicates that he was deceased at the time of writing. However, see Altshuler, *Rabbi Meshullam Feibush Heller*, pp. 13–14, 322–323. He is also mentioned on p. 123, YDE: sect. 23. There, he is simply quoted in the name of "his teacher." It is not clear from the context if the reference is implictly to Menahem Mendel or to Dov Ber of Mezeritch. Altshuler suggests that the indication that he was deceased at the time of writing is a printer's error.

181. On Rabbi Ze'ev Wolf of Charny-Ostrog, see Menahem Mendel Vizhnitzer, *Taqifa de-Ar'a Yisrael* (Israel: B'nei Brak, 1986). He was later associated with Rabbi Nahman of Bratzlav. See Arthur Green, *Tormented Master*, pp. 69, 71, 110, and Aryeh Kaplan, *Until the Mashiach: Rabbi Nachman's Biography: An Annotated Chronology* (Jerusalem, Brooklyn, Breslov Research Institute, 1985), pp. 235–236. The town, Charny-Ostrog, is mentioned once in *Liqqutim Yeqarim*, p. 136, YDE: sect. 44. There Meshullam Feibush indicates that he met Rabbi David of Mikolajov in Charny-Ostrog while visiting his in-law. However, there is no evidence that Meshullam Feibush and Ze'ev Wolf were related by marriage.

182. On Pinhas of Koretz, see Heschel, *Circle of the Baal Shem Tov*, pp. 1–43. Heschel's view that R. Pinhas's opposition to "the Maggid" was addressed to Dov Ber of Mezeritch has now to be corrected. Altshuler has shown that "the Maggid" in question was most likely Yehiel Mikhel. See Altshuler, *Rabbi Meshullam Feibush Heller*, pp. 258–269.

183. See *Taqifa de-Ar'a Yisrael*, pp. 70–71. Pinhas of Koretz is not mentioned in *Yosher Divrey Emet*. Altshuler has suggested that R. Pinhas may have been bitter about the loss of some of his disciples to the Maggid of Zlotchov. Nevertheless, it is possible that Meshullam Feibush could have visited him in the 1780s, after *Yosher Divrey Emet* was written.

184. See note 158.

185. See *Taqifa de'Ar'a Yisrael*, pp. 75–76, n. 3.

186. For example, Louis Jacobs consistently refers to Meshullam Feibush's first text as *Derekh Emet* in his book, *Hasidic Prayer*.

187. See, e.g., in Dubnov, *Toledot ha-Hasidut*, pp. 323–324. Dubnov was aware that the material was later published separately as *Derekh Emet* (Tchernovitz, 1815).

188. For a detailed discussion of the printing history, see Altshuler, *Rabbi Meshullam Feibush Heller*, pp. 8–18.

189. See Altshuler, Ibid., pp. 25-28. Also see Miles Krassen, *'Devequt' and Faith in 'Zaddiqim': The Religious Tracts of Meshullam Feibush Heller of Zbrarazh* (Ph.D. dis. University of Pennsylvania, 1990), p. 70, n. 165, and Weiss, *Studies in Eastern European Jewish Mysticism*, pp. 122–123, n. 57.

190. On the content of the censored material, see our discussion in the chapter, "The Place of Meshullam Feibush in Early Hasidism."

191. *Liqqutim Yeqarim* (Zholkva, 1780), title page.

192. See Krassen *'Devequt' and Faith* (1990), p. 71, n. 176. Also see Altshuler, *Rabbi Meshullam Feibush Heller*, pp. 8–18.

193. *Liqqutim Yeqarim* (Zholkva, 1780), 21b–22d.

194. See Altshuler, *Rabbi Meshullam Feibush Heller*, pp. 8-18.

195. According to Friedberg, *Bet Eqed Sefarim*, the very same year a work by this title was printed in Zhitomer. However, I have not been able to examine this edition and do not know what it contains. Friedberg indicates that it consisted of twenty-four columns. Assuming that there were four columns per sheet, the text would seem to be too short to have included all of *Yosher Divrey Emet*. On the other hand, the shorter *Derekh Emet* typically requires twelve columns and three sheets. It seems likely that the Zhitomer edition contained only the shorter text, printed on six small sheets, each containing four columns.

196. This volume is part of the Scholem Collection at the National Library of the Hebrew University in Jerusalem. The title page contains neither date nor place of publication. However, it is classified as the edition Friedberg called 1830 Lemberg.

197. Yehiel Mikhel of Zlotchov is consistently referred to in the text as already deceased. Since his death is believed to have occurred in late summer of 1781, *Derekh Emet* could not have been written until sometime thereafter. Had Yehiel Mikhel died close to the time of writing, chances are that Meshullam Feibush would have made note of it. The text merely makes use of a conventional formula for referring to a deceased *Zaddiq*.

198. At the end of the first letter, the subjects that will be discussed in the second letter are listed.

199. Menahem Mendel Vizhnitzer has indicated that a work entitled *Yosher Divrey Emet ha-Shalem* will appear in his series, *Torat ha-Hasidim ha-Rishonim*. Presumably, Vizhnitzer will include material not contained in the Munkacz edition. However, the work has yet to appear.

200. *Yosher Divrey Emet* (Munkacz, 1905), pp. 1a–10a.

201. Ibid, p. 40a–d. The prayer is basically a *kavvanah* to be recited before performing a *mizvah*. The editor indicates that it was found in a manuscript written by Meshullam Feibush. The *kavvanah* is composed in a style influenced by Lurianic Kabbalah, somewhat similar to the prayers in Nathan Nata of Hanover's *Sha'arey Zion*.

202. Ibid, 10a–b.

203. Ibid, pp. 38a–39d. See above.

204. Ibid. The letter appears among the unnumbered pages at the beginning of the book.

205. Ibid, pp. 41–51d.

206. Ibid, pp. 51a–58b. The author was the son of Rabbi Meshullam Feibush of Brezhin, the son of Rabbi Barukh Itzik.

207. Ibid. The introduction appears in the unnumbered section, on the first side of the sheet that contains the *Hevra Mishnayot* document.

208. Ibid. Dov Ber is mentioned on 5b and 9b. Menahem Mendel is mentioned on 8c and 9b.

209. The dating of the material in this section is fraught with difficulties. It is quite possible that various sections were written at different times. The introduction is clearly dated 1775 and seems to refer to the beginning of the writing. However, some of the material appears to have been written at a later date. For example, on page 4, beginning at the bottom of column a, Meshullam Feibush writes, "due to our many sins, the Kaiser has now issued a decree obligating the children to polute themselves through also learning the German language." Galicia became part of Austro-Hungary in 1772. However, the first edict of Kaiser Josef II was decreed in 1782. (See Dubnov, *Toledot ha-Hasidut*, pp. 175–176). Therefore, unless evidence of an earlier decree can be discovered, this passage could not have been written before 1782.

210. Another possibility, which Altshuler proposes in other contexts, is that a degree of secrecy was employed by Yehiel Mikhel's disciples to cover over the Maggid's teachings.

211. He also published an independent edition of *Yosher Divrey Emet*.

2. Sources of Devequt in Early Hasidism

1. Gershom Scholem, "Hasidism: the Latest Phase," in *Major Trends in Jewish Mysticism* (New York: Schocken, 1954), pp. 341–343. Scholem's position was articulated in greater detail in "Devekut, or Communion with God," in *The Messianic Idea in Judaism and Other Essays* (New York: Schocken, 1971), p. 203.

2. Ibid., p. 209.

3. The most serious challenge to Scholem's approach is presented by Mendel Piekarz in *Between Ideology and Reality: Humility, Ayin, Self-Negation and Devekut in the Hasidic Thought* [Hebrew] (Jerusalem: Bialik, 1994). Piekarz argues that the mystical elements in early Hasidism have been exaggerated and that ethical and social aspects were at least equally important. Also see Piekarz's English essay, "Hasidism as a Socio-religious Movement on the Evidence of *Devekut*," in Rapoport-Albert, ed., *Hasidism Reappraised*, pp. 225–248.

4. Major contributions to our understanding of *devequt* have been made by Moshe Idel, Mendel Peikarz, Mordecai Pechter, Rivka Schatz-Uffenheimer, Isaiah Tishby, Gedalyah Nigal, and others. Specific references will be noted where appropriate.

5. A useful, if incomplete, summary can be found in Morris M. Faierstein, "Gershom Scholem and Hasidism," *JJS* 38, 2 (1986): pp. 228–230. Also see Byron Sherwin, *Mystical Theology and Social Descent: the Life and Works of Judah Loew of Prague* (London and Toronto: Fairleigh Dickerson University Press, 1982), pp. 124–141. Also see Idel, *Hasidism: Between Ecstasy and Magic*, pp. 86–95.

6. E.g., Deut. 4:4, 11:22, and 13:5.

7. See sources in Abraham Joshua Heschel, *Theology of Ancient Judaism* [Hebrew] (London: Soncino, 1962) 1: pp. 153–155. It is Heschel's theory that this line of interpretation constitutes the "school of Rabbi Ishmael" while the mystical interpretations are the product of the "school of Rabbi Akiva."

8. See discussion in Mosha Idel, *Kabbalah: New Perspectives* (New Haven: Yale University Press, 1988), pp. 38f.

9. Sanhedrin 64a.

10. Sanhedrin 65b.

11. God is likened to a consuming fire in Deut. 4:24, and 9:3.

12. Sifre, *Eqev*, 49.

13. See note 7.

14. See Idel, *Kabbalah*, ch. 3. These phenomenological models are further applied to Hasidism by Idel in *Hasidism: Between Ecstasy and Magic*.

15. For a fuller discussion of these models, see Idel, *Hasidism: Between Ecstasy and Magic*, pp. 45–102.

16. For a full discussion of this subject, see Seth Brody, "Human Hands Dwell in Heavenly Heights: contmeplative Ascent and Theurgic Power in Thirteenth Century Kabbalah" in *Mystics of the Book*, ed. by R. A. Heresa (Lang, 1993).

17. See Idel, *Kabbalah*, pp. 52f. Also see Idel, *Hasidism: Between Ecstasy and Magic*, pp. 189–207.

18. On Abulafia and Ecstatic kabbalah see Moshe Idel, *The Mystical Experience in Abraham Abulafia* (Albany: State University of New York, 1988), and Idel, *Studies in Ecstatic Kabbalah* (New York: State University of New York, 1984), pp. 119–155, and Gershom Scholem, *Ha-kabbalah shel Sefer ha Temunah ve-shel Avraham Abulafia* (Jerusalem, 1965).

19. See Idel, *The Mystical Experience*, p. 125.

20. Texts describing some of these practices can be found in Aryeh Kaplan, *Meditation and Kabbalah* (Weiser, 1982), pp. 83–106.

21. Abulafia's *Or ha-Sekhel* (Light of the Intellect) is quoted by Moses Cordovero in *Pardes Rimmonim* (Jerusalem, 1962), Gate 21, chapter 1. However, it is identified there as an anonymously composed, *Sefer ha-Niqqud*. Excerpts from Abulafia's *Hayyey Olam ha-Ba* (Life of the World to Come) can be found in the fourth part of Hayyim Vital's *Safer Sha'arey Qedushah*. However, this part only circulated in manuscript and remained unprinted until 1988. See Vital's *Ketavim Hadashim le-Rabbenu Hayyim Vital* (Jerusalem, 1988), Vital, *Sefer Sha'arey Qedushah*, part 4, pp. 24ff.

22. The precise nature of Abulafian influence on Hasidic conceptions of *devequt* still requires clarification. See Idel's comments in *Hasidism: Between Ecstasy and Magic*, pp. 53–65, especially, p. 55, n.44.

23. Although Gershom Scholem was intensely interested in and wrote about the Kabbalah of Abulafia, he interpreted Abulafian texts where mystical experience is described in explicit unitive language as something less that *unio mystica*. See,

e.g., Gershom, *Major Trends in Jewish Mysticism*, p. 141. The first scholar to take issue with Scholem's view that *devequt* did not involve total mystical union was Isaiah Tishby. See, e.g., Isaiah Tishby, *Wisdom of the Zohar* (Oxford: Oxford University Press, 1989), 3: 985–987.

24. See Idel, *Kabbalah*, pp. 60–72.

25. See for example the texts collected and discussed by Arthur Green, "Hasidism: Discovery and Retreat," in *The Other Side of God: Polarity in World Religions*. Edited by Peter L. Berger (New York: Anchor, 1981), pp. 104–130. Also see Idel's view in *Hasidism: Between Ecstasy and Magic*, pp. 222–223, 225. On the other hand, see Mendel Piekarz, *Between Ideology and Reality: Humility, Ayin, Self-Negation and Devekut in Hasidic Thought* [Hebrew] (Jerusalem: Bialik, 1994), esp. pp. 77–79. Piekarz argues that the use of such bold language, although suggesting *unio mystica*, is really only hyperbole.

26. Gershom Scholem, *Devequt in Messianic Idea*, p. 226.

27. On Azulai's influence on early Hasidism, see Bracha Sack, "Iyyun be-Hashpa'at R. Moses Cordovero al ha-Hasidut," *Eshel Be'er Shev'a* 3 (1986): pp. 229–246.

28. On *Reshit Hokhmah* see Bracha Sack, "The Influence of *Reishit Hokhmah* on the Teachings of the Maggid of Mezhirech," in Rapoport-Albert, ed., *Hasidism Reappraised*, pp. 251–257; Mordecai Pechter, "The Concept of Devequt in the Homiletical Ethical Writings of 16th Century Safed," in *Studies in Medieval Jewish History and Literature*, edited by I. Twersky (Cambridge, Mass.: Harvard University Press, 1984), pp. 171–230; Mordecai Pechter, *Ikvot Hashpa'ato shel Sefer Reshit Hokhmah le-R. Eliahu de Vidas be-khitvey R. Ya'aqov Yosef mi-Polnoy,"* in *Studies in Jewish Mysticism, Philosophy and Ethical Literature Presented to Isaiah Tishby on his Seventy-Fifth Birthday* (Jerusalem: Magnes, 1986), pp. 569–592. On *Sheney Luhot ha-Berit*, see especially Mendel Piekarz, "Hasidism as a Socio-religious Movement on the Evidence of *Devekut*," in Rapoport-Albert, ed., *Hasidism Reappraised*, pp. 234–237 and Piekarz, *Between Ideology and Reality, passim* also see Mendel Piekarz, *"The Beginning of Hasidism: Ideological Trends in Derush and Musar Literature* [Hebrew] (Jerusalem: Bialik, 1978), *passim*. Also see Miles Krassen, *Isaiah Horowitz: Generations of Adam* (Mahwah: Paulist, 1996). On the concept of *devequt* in Safed also see Zvi Werblowsky, *Joseph Karo, Lawyer and Mystic* (Philadelphia: Jewish Publication Society, 1977), pp. 38–83.

29. This idea which is so typical of early Hasidism apparently does not yet appear in its pseudo-Zoharic form in the Safedian literature. See Tishby, *"Qudsha Berik Hu Orayta ve-Yisrael Kula Had,"* *Kiryat Sefer* 50: 480–492; and Bracha Sack, *"'Od le-Gilgulah shel ha-Imrah Qudsha Berik Hu Orayta ve-Visrael Kula Had,"* *Kiryat Sefer* 57: 179–184.

30. Gershom Scholem identified this as a characteristic of Hasidic *devequt*. See *"Devequt,"* p. 211. Also see Elliot R. Wolfson, "Walking as a Sacred Duty: Theological Transformation of a Social Reality in Early Hasidism," in *Along the Path: Studies in Kabbalistic Myth, Symbolism, and Hermeneutics* by Elliot R. Wolfson (Albany: State University of New York, 1995), pp. 89–109.

31. See Elliot R. Wolfson, "Spiritual Ascent in Sixteenth-Century Jewish Mysticism," in *Death, Ecstasy, and Other Worldly Journeys* edited by Daniel Collins and Michael Fishbane (Albany: State University of New York, 1995), pp. 207–247.

32. See Mordechai Pechter, ed., *Miley de-Shemaya'* [Hebrew] (Jerusalem: Bialik, 1991).

33. For an account of the Lurianic practice of *yihudim*, see Lawrence Fine, "The Contemplative Practice of *Yihudim* in Lurianic Kabbalah," in *Jewish Spirituality: From the Sixteenth-Century to the Present*, edited by Arthur Green (New York: Crossroad, 1987), 2: 64–98.

34. See Mordechai Pechter, "Concept of Devequt," pp. 202–209.

35. On the history of this meaning of the term *hitbodedut* see Moshe Idel, "*Hitbodedut* as Concentration in Ecstatic Kabbalah," in *Jewish Spirituality*, edited by Arthur Green, v. 1: 405–438.

36. Pechter still describes it as "close to *unio mystica*." See Pechter, "Concept of Devequt," p. 224.

37. Mendel Piekarz has already noted that contrary to Joseph Weiss's theory, alien thoughts were of concern to mystics before Hasidism. See Piekarz, "Beginning of Hasidism," pp. 271f.

38. See Pechter, ibid, pp. 210–224.

39. See Pechter, ibid, pp. 227f.

40. See Idel's comments regarding the importance of the *SHeLaH* in *Hasidism: Between Ecstasy and Magic*, esp. pp. 341–342, n. 73. Also see Piekarz, *Between Ideology and Reality*, see index, idem, *Beginning of Hasidism*, index, and idem, "Hasidism as a Socio-religious Movement on the Evidence of *Devekut*," in Rapoport-Albert, ed., *Hasidism Reappraised*.

41. These deal with both the concept of *devequt* and the *Zaddiq*. The influence of the *SHeLaH* on the Hasidic concept of the *Zaddiq* will be discussed in chapter 4. See Piekarz, "Hasidism as a Socio-religious Movement on the Evidence of *Devekut*," in Rapoport-Albert, ed., *Hasidism Reappraised*, and Krassen, *Isaiah Horowitz: Generations of Adam*.

42. As quoted in Piekarz, *Beginning of Hasidism*, p. 354f. This source will be considered in more detail in our discussion of *devequt* and learning in early Hasidism. See below.

43. See Piekarz, *Beginning of Hasidism*, pp. 210–212.

44. Indeed early polemics against Hasidism often charged the Hasidim with innovating deviations which were in fact explicitly proposed in works like *Sheney Luhot ha-Berit*. See Piekarz, *Beginning of Hasidism*, especially pp. 387–390. On the early polemics, see Mordecai Wilensky, *Hasidim and Mitnaggedim: A Study of Controversy Between Them in the Years 1772–1815*, 2nd. ed. [Hebrew] (Jerusalem: Bialik, 1970).

45. See Idel, *Hasidism: Between Ecstasy and Magic*, pp. 60–64.

46. Gershom Scholem considered this to be the most important innovation of early Hasidism's attitude toward *devequt*. See Idel, *Kabbalah*, ibid, pp. 49f. For an

analysis of Isaac of Acre's conception of *devequt*, see Efraim Gottlieb, "He'arot, Devequt, u-Nevuah be-Sefer 'Ozar he-Hayyim le-fi Yizhaq di-me-'Ako," in Gottlieb
Studies in the Kabbala Literature [Hebrew] (Tel Aviv: Tel Aviv University, 1976), pp.
231–247. Also see Idel, Hitbodedut," pp. 414–420.

47. However, it seems that Idel was not entirely correct in identifying Isaac of
Acre's concept of *devequt* with the very beginning of the path. In fact, R. Isaac makes
devequt conditional on prior ethical development. See *Ketavim Hadashim le-
Rabbenu Hayyim Vital* (Jerusalem, 1988), *Sefer Sha'arey Qedushah*, part 4, p. 10.

48. On the question of to what extent *devequt* constituted an initial spiritual
stage in early Hasidim, see Piekarz, "Conceptural and Historical Lessons from a Hasidic Book," [Hebrew], in *Daat* 14 (1985): 83–98. Also see Piekarz "Hasidism as a
Socio-religious Movement on the Evidence of *Devekut*," in Rapoport-Albert, ed.,
Hasidism Reappraised. We will have more to say on this theme below.

49. See Israel Jacob Dienstag, "Ha-Moreh Nevukhim ve-Sefer ha-Mad'a be-
Sifrut ha-Hasidut," in *The Abraham Weiss Jubilee Volume* (New York, 1964), pp.
307–330.

50. Concerning this panoramic approach, see Idel, *Hasidism: Between Ecstasy
and Magic*, pp. 1–30.

51. On the relationship of Hasidic attitudes to those in contemporary homiletical and ethical literature, see Piekarz, *The Beginning of Hasidism*.

52. For the most part our remarks are confined to generalizations concerning
the second generation of Hasidism, especially in the writings of R. Jacob Joseph of
Polnoy and R. Dov Ber of Mezeritch. A definitive statement concerning the Baal
Shem Tov's conception of *devequt* awaits the construction of a sound methodological
basis for distinguishing the authentic from the spurious in the corpus of teachings
attributed to him. A definitive treatment of *devequt* in the second generation itself,
would require several monographs devoted to each of the sources.

53. This is one of several essential points of Piekarz', *The Beginning of Hasidism*.

54. Both Gershom Scholem and Martin Buber saw Hasidism as essentially a
reaction to Lurianic Kabbalah, although each understood this reaction in a different
way. See, e.g., Gershom Scholem, "The Neutralization of Messianism in Early Hasidism," in *The Messianic Idea in Judaism* (New York: Schocken, 1971), pp. 176–202.
Also see Martin Buber, *Origin and Meaning of Hasidism* (New York: Horizon,
1960). More recently, Moshe Idel and Bracha Sack have emphasized the Cordoverian
influence. See Sack, "The Influence of R. Moshe Cordovero on Hasidism," [Hebrew]
in *Eshel Be'er Sheva* 3 (1986): 229–246. Idel makes the case for the importance of
Cordoverian influence in *Hasidism: Between Ecstasy and Magic*, passim. Also see
Idel, "Martin Buber and Gershom Scholem on Hasidism: A Critical Appraisal," in
Rapoport-Albert, *Hasidism Reappraised*, pp. 389–403.

55. Translated from Isaiah of Dinovitz, *Zava'at ha-RYVaSH* (Brooklyn: Kehot,
1982), p. 50. (Unless otherwise noted all translations are by the author).

56. Isaiah of Dinovitz, *Zava'at ha-RYVaSH* , pp. 30f. The Baal Shem Tov's analogy seems to be based on a passage in *Reishit Hokhmah*, Gate of Love, 4. There, a

parable appears that is attributed to R. Isaac of Acre. The parable emphasizes abandonment of the sensuous in order to cleave to the intelligibles. Idel has noted a similarity between Isaac of Acre's parable and a passage in Plato's Symposium and also speculates that Rabbi Isaac may have received the parable through Sufi sources. See Moshe Idel, "Ha-Hitbodedut ke-Rikkuz ba-Kabbalah ha-Ekstatit ve-Gilgulaha," *Da'at* 14 (1985): 53–54. Also see the English version of this article, Idel, *Hitbodedut as Concentration,*" in *Jewish Spirituality*, v. 1: 417–420. Also see Idel's discussion of this parable in *Hasidism: Between Ecstasy and Magic*, pp. 61–63, and in *Studies in Ecstatic Kabbalah*, pp. 115–118.

57. Isaiah of Dinovitz, *Zava'at ha-RYVaSH*, p. 31.

58. For an analysis of the pantheistic, acosmic, and panentheistic aspects of Habad theology, see Rachel Elior, *The Paradoxical Ascent to God: The Kabbalistic Theosophy of Habad Hasidism* (Albany: State University of New York, 1993), ibid; *HaBaD: the Contemplative Ascent to God,* in Green, ed., *Jewish Spirituality*, v. 2:157–205. Also see Racel Elior, *Torat ha-Elohut ba-Dor ha-Sheniy shel Hasidut Habad* (Jerusalem: Magnes, 1982).

59. Emanationist theology in Judaism is, of course, as old as Neo-Platonic and Kabbalistic sources. However, whereas Kabbalists usually distinguished however subtly, between what was emanated and the divine essence itself, early Hasidic sources before HaBaD often avoid such distinctions.

60. *Ben Porat Yosef*, 23b. Cited in Pechter, *"Ikvot Reishit Hokhmah,"* pp. 578f.

61. See Pechter, ibid, p. 580.

62. Maimonides, *Guide of the Perplexed*, 111:49.

63. Deut. 10:20.

64. Micah 2:13.

65. Elijah De Vidas, *Reshit Hokhmah*, Gate of Love, ch. 11.

66. *Ben Porat Yosef*, 49a, cited in Pechter, *"Ikvot Reishit Hokhnah,"* p. 589.

67. The passivity implicit in certain aspects of early Hasidic mysticism was noted by Joseph Weiss. See *"Via Passiva* in Early Hasidism," in *Studies in Eastern European Jewish Mysticism* (Oxford: Oxford University Press, 1985), pp. 69–94. Also see Rivka Schatz-Uffenheimer, *Hasidism as Mysticism*.

68. Ps. 48:2.

69. B.T. Sukkah 52b.

70. *Zava'at ha-RYVaSH*, p. 52.

71. See our discussion of contexts of *devequt* below.

72. This is but the simplest of a number of spiritual practices that involve visualization of various combinations of letters associated with sacred names. See Idel, *Hasidism: Between Ecstasy and Magic*, pp. 56–60.

73. For a discussion of *unio mystica* in Judaism, see Idel, *Kabbalah: New Perspectives*, pp. 58–73. Cf. Scholem, *"Devekut,"* passim. And see Idel's comments in *Hasidism: Between Ecstasy and Magic*, pp. 222–225.

74. Ps. 73:28.

75. Deut. 32:15.

76. *Leshon Hasidim* (Jerusalem: Ben Adam, 1978), 40b. The passage is quoted from *Toledot Ya'aqov Yosef, va-yigash.*

77. See Lawrence Fine, *Safed Spirituality* (New York: Paulist Press, 1984).

78. A very likely source for the connection between *devequt* and aceticism in Hasidism may be found in the writings of Moshe Hayyim Luzzatto. To my knowledge, this connection, denied emphatically by Scholem in his article on *devequt*, has been suggested only by Isaiah Tishby. See note 90 below.

79. B.T. Menahot 43b.

80. Gen. 3:6.

81. *Zava'at ha-RYVaSH*, p. 2, sect. 5.

82. Ibid, p. 4, sect. 11.

83. Isa. 55:8.

84. Deut. 11:16. *Zava'at ha-RYVaSH* p. 24, sect. 76. The equation of separation from *devequt* to *avodah zarah* is not unique to the Baal Shem Tov. See Piekarz, *Beginning of Hasidism*, pp. 18f.

85. Ps. 16:8.

86. Equanimity as an ethical ideal was already emphasized by German Pietists who flourished from about 1150–1250. See Scholem, *Major Trends*, pp. 96–97. For a discussion of its importance in Ecstatic Kabbalah, see Idel, *Hasidism: Between Mysticism and Magic*, pp. 60–62. Also see Idel, *Studies in Ecstatic Kabbalah*, pp. 133, 148, n. 41.

87. *Zava'at ha-RYVaSH*, p. 1, sect. 2.

88. Ibid, p. 3, sect. 10.

89. See Idel, *Hasidism: Between Ecstasy and Magic*, pp. 59–64.

90. Another possible source, although categorically denied by Scholem, is R. Moses Hayyim Luzzatto. This is particularly likely where *devequt* is associated with a transformation of the body into a state of holiness. Luzzatto's writings were known in eastern Europe and highly praised. However, they are rarely if ever cited. This may be due to the author's controversial association with Sabbateanism. See Isaiah Tishby, "Iqvot R. Moshe Hayyim Luzzato be-Mishnat ha-Hasidut," *Zion* 43 (1978): 201-234, ibid, Isaiah Tishby, *Hiqrey Kabbalah u-Sheluhoteha*, vol. 3 (Jerusalem: Magnes, 1993). Also see Elisheva Carlebach, *Pursuit of Heresy: Rabbi Moses Hagiz and the Sabbatian Controversies* (New York: Columbia University Press, 1990).

91. See Piekarz, *Between Ideology and Reality*, pp. 47–54.

92. The divine is present in every thought in the form of the ten *sefirot*. Thus, every thought has the power to profoundly affect the divine realm itself.

93. Prov. 16:5. *Zava'at ha-RYVaSH*, p. 32, sect. 92.

94. Ps. 22:7.

95. *Zava'at ha-RYVaSH*, p. 4, sect. 12.

96. See Piekarz, *The Beginning of Hasidism*, pp. 377–383.

97. On *Ayin*, see Daniel C. Matt, "Ayin: The Concept of Nothingness in Jewish Mysticism," in *The Problem of Pure Consciousness: Mysticism and Philosophy*, edited by Robert K. C. Forman (New York: Oxford University Press, 1990), pp. 121–159.

98. *Shevirah* is a Lurianic Kabbalistic term referring to a cosmogonic stage called the "shattering of the vessels." As a result of this cataclysm a mixture of primordial dross and holy sparks descended to ultimately become lower worlds. The purer lights ascended to their divine source. Since human souls are primarily a product of this stage, Dov Ber recommends remembering it as an antidote to pride. For an outline and discussion of Lurianic cosmogony see Scholem, *Major Trends*, Scholem, *Sabbatai Zevi: the Mystical Messiah* (Princeton: Bollingen, 1973); Lawrence Fine, "The Contemplative Practice of *Yihudim* in Lurianic Kabbalah," in Green, ed. *Jewish Spirituality*, vol. 2: 64–98; Louis Jacobs, "The Uplifting of Sparks in Later Jewish Mysticism," in Green, ed. *Jewish Spirituality*, vol. 2: 99–126.

99. Jer. 9:22, 23.

100. Gen. 4:25.

101. *Maggid Devarav le-Ya'aqov*, pp. 187f, sect. 114.

102. On the importance of humility in pre-Hasidic kabbalistic texts, see Idel, *Hasidism: Between Ecstasy and Magic*, pp. 108–111. Also see Piekarz, *Ideology and Reality*, pp. 29–46.

103. Ps. 16:8.

104. Lev. 6:6.

105. *Keter Shem Tov*, p. 22a, sect. 84.

106. See Pechter, "Concept of *Devekut*," and "*Hayyav ve'-Ishiuto shel R. Eleazar Azikri bi-Re'i Yomano ha-Mistiy ve-Sefer Haredim*" *Shalem* 3 (1981): 127–147.

107. The term *yihudim* has a wide range of references in Hasidic sources. See Idel, *Hasidism: Between Mysticism and Magic*, pp. 184-186, 275, n. 53; Idel, *Studies in Ecstatic Kabbalah*, p. 114. Also see Mark Verman, "The Development of *Yihudim* in Spanish Kabbalah," in *The Age of the Zohar*, edited by Joseph Dan (Jerusalem, 1989), pp. 25–42. On the practice of *yihudim* in Lurianic Kabbalah, see Fine, "The Contemplative Practice" in Green, ed., *Jewish Spirituality*, vol. 2: 64–98.

108. *Zava'at ha-RYVaSH*, p. 1, sect. 3. And compare *Liqqutum Yeqarim*, sect. 180.

109. See the following example for a more generic use of the term "unification" that does not involve linguistic elements.

110. See Piekarz, "Beginning of Hasidism," p. 24.

111. *Zava'at ha-RYVaSH*, p. 4, sect. 22.

112. See Louis Jacobs, "Eating as an Act of Worship in Hasidic Thought" in *Studies in Jewish Religious and Intellectual History Presented to Alexander Altmann on the Occasion of His Seventieth Birthday*, edited by Siegfried Stein and Raphael Loewe (London: University of Alabama, 1979), pp. 157–166.

113. *Zava'at ha-RYVaSH*, p. 38, sect. 109.

114. According to Lurianic Kabbalah, as a result of a cosmic cataclysm (*Shevirat ha-kelim*) holy sparks fell and became lodged in the lower worlds. It is the religious task to release those sparks and to restore them to their proper location. See Louis Jacobs, "The Uplifting of Sparks," in Green, ed. *Jewish Spirituality*, vol. 2: 99–126.

115. *Zava'at ha-RYVaSH*, p. 38, sect. 109.

116. I have corrected the text to read *'al beney adam* instead of *'im beney adam* in accordance with the wording in the parallel found in *Liqqutim Yeqarim*, sect. 177.

117. *Zava'at ha-RYVaSH*, p. 38, sect. 109.

118. *Zava'at ha-RYVaSH*, p. 10, sect. 31.

119. For a discussion of the history of the term *"hitbodedut"* as mental concentration, see Idel, "Hitbodedut as Concentration" in Green, ed., *Jewish Spirituality*.

120. *Keter Shem Tov*, p. 55, sect. 216.

121. *Zava'at ha-RYVaSH*, p. 20, sect. 63.

122. See Tanenbaum *To'afot Harim* (Jerusalem: Zecher Naftali, 1986), p. 133f.

123. Kiddushin, 39b.

124. *Keter Shem Tov*, p. 7, sect. 17.

125. The holiness of the *mizvah* and the holiness of God are united.

126. *Keter Shem Tov*, p. 74b.

127. The theory of *ruhaniyut* is also important for understanding the Hasidic attitude toward Torah study and prayer. See Idel, *Hasidism: Between Mysticism and Magic*, pp. 66–67. Also see Moshe Idel, "Perceptions of Kabbalah in the Second Half of the Eighteenth Century." *Journal of Jewish Thought and Philosophy* 1 (1990): 53–114. And see below.

128. See Rivka Schatz-Uffenheimer, *Quietistic Elements in Eighteenth-Century Hasidic Thought* [Hebrew] (Jerusalem: Magnes, 1980) p. 65.

129. See Piekarz *"Beginning of Hasidism,"* pp. 346–360. Also see Lawrence Fine, "The Study of Torah as a Rite of Theurgical Contemplation in Lurianic Kabbalah," in *Approaches to Judaism in Medieval Times*, v. 3 edited by David Blumenthal (Atlanta: Scholars Press, 1988), pp. 29–40. Also see Idel, *Hasidism: Between Ecstasy and Magic*, pp. 171–188.

130. Quoted by Piekarz, *Beginning of Hasidism*, p. 355.

131 In fact Luria's attitude concerning Torah study is more complex than the *SheLaH* indicates here. See Fine, "Study of Torah as a Rite of Theurgical Contemplation" in Blumenthal, ed., *Approaches to Judaism in Medieval Times*, v. 3: 29–40. Luria does emphasize that Torah study and *devequt* can occur simultaneously, in other passages cited by Tishby. See *"Iqvot RaMHaL,"* p. 226, n.61. Tishby also proves, on the basis of authentic traditions in *Yosher Divrey Emet*, that Piekarz, *Beginning of Hasidism*, was incorrect in attributing to Menahem Mendel of Premishlan the view that Torah study and *devequt* are incompatible. Piekarz's remarks assume that the teachings of R. Dov Ber in *Darkhey Yesharim* were written by Menahem Mendel. See our discussion in the following chapter.

132. See Krassen, *Isaiah Horowitz*, pp. 137–138,148–155. Also see Idel, *Hasidism: Between Ecstasy and Magic*, pp. 215–218.

133. See Piekarz, *Beginning of Hasidism*, p. 355.

134. *Keter Shem Tov*, p. 125, sect. 426.

135. See Piekarz, *Beginning of Hasidism*, pp. 351–354.

136. B.T. Berakhot 8a.

137. Job 19:26.

138. A reference to the immanent, female aspect of the divine.

139. That is, to the Torah's spiritual essence and not to its "matter."

140. *Toledot Ya'aqov Yosef*, 131b. Quoted by Piekarz, *Beginning of Hasidism*, p. 350. A possible source for Jacob Joseph's use of erotic images as a metaphor for Torah study is Solomon Alkabetz, *Ayelet Ahavim*. Alkabetz interprets all of the Song of Songs as an allegory concerning the Torah and her lover, the student.

141. The lowest of the divine *Sefirot*.

142. He has raised the lower *sefirah* to the higher *sefirah* of understanding. *Toledot Ya'aqov Yosef*, 144b. And compare *Keter Shem Tov*, sections 405, 410, and 423. On the Ba'al Shem Tov's method of study, see Weiss, *Studies in East European Jewish Mysticism*, pp. 56–68. Also see Schatz-Uffenheimer's chapter on the problem of Torah study in early Hasidism, *Hasidism as Mysticism*, pp. 310–325 (pp. 157–167 in the Hebrew edition). See also Idel's "Perceptions of Kabbalah" which emphasizes the aural aspects of the Besht's method. And see his more thorough discussion of this issue in *Hasidism: Between Ecstasy and Magic*, pp. 171–188.

143. See for example *Keter Shem Tov*, sect. 423.

144. See Schatz-Uffenheimer, *Hasidism as Mysticism*, p. 159.

145. B.T. Hagigah 9b.

146. *Degel Mahaneh Efraim* (Yozefof, 1883), 45c. Quoted in Schatz-Uffenheimer, *Hasisdism as Mysticism*, p. 159.

147. I have accepted the reading proposed by R. Abraham Isaac Kahn. See *Liqqutim Yeqarim*, 10a, sect. 51, n. 30.

148. Prov. 3:18.

149. *Liqqutim Yeqarim*, ibid. Cf. *Zava'at ha-RYVaSH*, p. 9, sect. 30.

150. Avot 1:17.

151. *Zava'at ha-RYVaSH*, p. 49, sect. 133. On the issue of silence and mystical study, see Wolfson, "Spiritual Ascent in Sixteenth-Century Jewish Mysticism," pp. 216ff. Also compare Idel, *Hasidism: Between Ecstasy and Magic*, pp. 116–125.

152. See above, p. 63.

153. Reading *bo* instead of *bahem*.

154. From manuscript 1467 in the National Library in Jerusalem. Quoted in Schatz–Uffenheimer, *Hasidism as Mysticism*, p. 314 (p. 161f in Hebrew edition). This manuscript which belonged to R. Shmelke of Nikolsburg contains the complete text of this teaching of R. Dov Ber which was published in *Darkhey Yesharim* in an edited version that distorts the Maggid's intention. See Schatz-Uffenheimer, *Hasidism as Mysticism*, pp. 316ff (pp. 159–163 in Hebrew edition).

155. The truncated version in *Darkhey Yesharim*, which is falsely attributed to Menahem Mendel of Premishlan, gives the impression that its author was speaking against excessive learning. See previous note. Also see Schatz-Uffenheimer, introduction to the critical edition of *Maggid Devarav le-Ya'aqov* (Jerusalem: Magnes, 1976) p. 18, n. 1. And compare Altshuler's discussion of the possible source for this

text in the school of the Maggid of Zlotchov in Altshuler, *Rabbi Meshullam Feibush Heller*, pp. 235–252.

156. Avot 2:5. See note 154.

157. See the continuation of our text which is quoted in full by Schatz-Uffenheimer, *Hasidism as Mysticism*, pp. 316–317 (p. 161 in Hebrew edition).

158. Hasidic prayer has already been studied in considerable depth. See Idel, *Hasidism: Between Ecstasy and Magic*, pp. 149–170; Joseph Weiss, "The *Kavvanoth* of Prayer in Early Hasidism," in *Studies in Eastern European Jewish Mysticism*, pp. 95–125, and ibid, "Petitionary Prayer in Early Hasidism, pp. 126–131. Also see Schatz-Uffenheimer, *Hasidism as Mysticism*, chapters 6–7, and Louis Jacobs, *Hasidic Prayer*; and see Altshuler, *Rabbi Meshullam Feibush Heller*, pp. 253–257, 269–278.

159. The complexities of Lurianic prayer have yet to be studied in detail. Menahem Kallus is currently completing a dissertation on this subject at Hebrew University. Primary sources include various redactions of Hayyim Vital's writings, especially *Sha'ar ha-Kavvanot* and *Peri Ez Hayyim*, as well as the various editions of the Lurianic prayerbook. A recent work that makes some of this material comprehensible is Gamaliel HaKohen Rabinowitz's *Tiv ha-Kavvanot al Sha'ar ha-Kavvanot* (Jerusalem: Sha'arey Ziv, 1996). Also see Yehiel Abraham Barlev's two volume text, *Yedid Nefesh: Kavvanot ha-Ari z'l al ha-Tefillah* (Petah Tikvah, 1988).

160. On Lurianic *kavvanot* of prayer and early Hasidism, see Idel, *Hasidism: Between Ecstasy and Magic*, pp. 149–154.

161. That is, the Ba'al Shem Tov.

162. Ps. 109:4. The verse is interpreted as referring to the *Shekhinah* in several places in the Zohar. See, e.g., part 1: 24a; part 3: 49b.

163. Lam. 1:14.

164. *Zafnat Paneah*, 1b.

165. This issue is discussed in detail by Schatz-Uffenheimer in chapter 6 of *Hasidism as Mysticism*.

166. According to Hasidic tradition, the Ba'al Shem Tov's teacher was Ahijah the Shilonite, a biblical prophet who also taught King David.

167. A term applied to kabbalists because they separate the *Shekhinah* or the *sefirah*, *Malkhut*, from the external forces of evil. *Malkhut* is called the "apple field."

168. As in the root MLL.

169. As in the root MUL.

170. *Keter Shem Tov*, 5b–5c, sect. 28.

171. The interplay between mystical, magical, and theurgic interests in early Hasidism is treated at length by Idel in *Hasidism: Between Ecstasy and Magic*. A close study of Lurianic influences, whether messianic or theurgic, is an urgent desideratum.

172. Ps. 102:1.

173. *Keter Shem Tov*, sect. 97.

174. See Schatz-Uffenheimer, *Hasidism as Mysticism*, ch. 6.

175. This issue is discussed in detail in Weiss's article, "The *Kavvanoth* of prayer in Early Hasidism." In an unpublished paper, Menahem Kallus has recently shown that Lurianic *kavvanot* were far more important in early Hasidism than Weiss maintains, at least in the case of the Ba'al Shem Tov's practices and teachings.

176. On the meaning of this classical kabbalistic term in early Hasidism, see Idel, *Hasidism: Between Ecstasy and Magic*, pp. 132–140.

177. Jerusalem Talmud, Blessings, 1:1; Midrash Numbers Rabbah, 15:12.

178. Lev. 12:2. *Keter Shem Tov*, 35a–b, sect. 259.

179. Compare *Sefer Ba'al Shem Tov al ha-Torah*, Noah, sect. 65 and the commentary *Meqor Mayim Hayyim*, on this passage, n. 66.

180. Joseph Weiss termed this meditative technique "attachment of oneself to the letters" or atomization of the letters. See his article, "*Kavvanoth of Prayer* in Early Hasidism," pp. 103–105.

181. That is, to focus on the Lurianic *kavvanot* through calling to mind the appropriate letters or Divine Name and locus in the upper worlds.

182. That is, the Ba'al Shem Tov had been unable to enter the state of *gadlut*.

183. That is, the lowest level.

184. *Ketonet Passim*, p. 43a–b, quoted in *Sefer Ba'al Shem Tov*, p. 133. Also compare Weiss's translation, "*Kavvanoth of Prayer* in Early Hasidism," p. 103.

185. See Idel, *Hasidism: Between Ecstasy and Magic*, pp. 56–60; Idel, *The Mystical Experience in Abraham Abulafia* (Albany: State University of New York, 1988). See also Elliot R. Wolfson, "Letter Symbolism and Merkavah Imagery in the *Zohar*," in *'Alei Shefer: Studies in the Literature of Jewish Thought Presented to Rabbi Dr. Alexandre Safran*, edited by Moshe Hallamish (Ramat Gan, 1990), pp. 195–236.

186. Ps. 97:12.

187. Zohar, v. 2, 85b; v. 3, 73a.

188. This equation, which Hasidic texts frequently falsely attribute to the *Zohar*, does not seem to have appeared before the sixteenth century. See Bracha Sack, "'Od le-Gilgulah shel ha-'Imra Qudsha Berikh Hu Oraita ve-Yisrael Kula Had," in *Kiryat Sefer* 57 (1982):179–184, and Isaiah Tishby, "Qudsha Berikh Hu Oraita ve-Yisrael Kula Had," *Kiryat Sefer* 50: 480–492.

189. *Keter Shem Tov*, 37a, sect. 284.

190. The visual aspects of Hasidic prayer have been noted and emphasized by both Weiss and Schatz-Uffenheimer. More recently, Moshe Idel has emphasized the aural aspects of the experience. See Idel, *Hasidism: Between Ecstasy and Magic*, pp. 147–148, 160–170. Also see Idel, "*Perceptions of Kabbalah in the Second Half of the Eighteenth Century*," a paper delivered at a symposium on Jewish thought in the eighteenth century at Harvard University in 1984.

191. Other strategies include vigorous physical movements to release the soul from the bonds of corporeality, praying in a loud voice, and reciting psalms before beginning the prayer service.

192. See Idel, "Perceptions of Kabbalah."

193. Clarification of the relative influences of Lurianic and Cordoverian Kabbalah on early Hasidism deserves additional attention. See Idel, *Hasidism: Between Ecstasy and Magic*, pp. 13–15, 41–43, 86–88, 159–162. Also see Bracha Sack, "The Influence of R. Moshe Cordovero on Hasidism," [Hebrew] in *'Eshel Be'er Sheva'* 3 (1986): 229–246. Also see Rachel Elior, "*Ha-Ziqah she-veyn Kabbalah le-Hasidut: Rezifut u-Temorah*, in *Proceedings of the World Congress of Jewish Thought* 3 (1986):107–114.

194. Isa. 6:3.

195. *Tiqquney Zohar, Tiqqun* 57.

196. Since each thought contains an emanation of the divine, the entire sefiratic structure is present within it.

197. *Keter Shem Tov*, 6d, sect. 39.

198. B. T., *Berakhot*, 58a. The saying also appears in number of other Talmudic and midrashic sources. *Keter Shem Tov*, ibid.

199. Compare Joseph Weiss's discussion of the genesis of the practice of elevating extraneous thoughts in his article, "*Reishit Zemihatah shel ha-Derekh ha-Hasidit*," in Abraham Rubenstein, ed., *Peraqim be-Torat ha-Hasidut ve-Toledotehah*, pp. 164–179. Weiss views the practice as, essentially, an extension and further development of Sabbatian tendencies.

200. The writings of Jacob Joseph of Polnoy already acknowledged the potential for abusing the practice, if undertaken by individuals who lack sufficient spiritual development. See, e.g., *Ben Porat Yosef*, 43a.

201. See our detailed discussion of the issue in chapter seven on "Meshullam Feibush and the Maggid of Mezeritch" and chapter nine "Meshullam Feibush's Place in Early Hasidism."

202. Although the authentic teachings in the name of the Ba'al Shem Tov do not tend to emphasize mystical extinction in confronting the divine reality, the notion may be at least latent in his thought. Consider, for example, the Ba'al Shem Tov's likening of genuine prayer to death, *Keter Shem Tov*, 21d, sect. 168. However, this teaching cannot yet be conclusively attributed to the Ba'al Shem Tov.

203. *Keter Shem Tov*, 56a–b, sect. 387. Although appended to a teaching in the name of the Ba'al Shem Tov, this passage is in all likelihood an example of Dov Ber's thought. Its source can be located in Schatz-Uffenheimer's critical edition of *Maggid Devarav le-Ya'aqov*, pp. 85–86, sect. 57.

204. The use of this concept in the teachings of Dov Ber and his disciples is discussed in detail in the opening chapters of Schatz-Uffenheimer's *Hasidism as Mysticism*. Also see Daniel C. Matt's "Ayin: The Concept of Nothingness in Jewish Mysticism," in *Essential Papers on Kabbalah*, edited by Lawrence Fine (New York: New York University Press, 1995), pp. 85–93.

205. Gen. 28:11.

206. Dov Ber's commentary assumes the rabbinic notion that the world was created by a series of divine utterances. Divine speech like human utterance is composed of words which are themselves combinations of letters. In *Sefer Yezirah*, ch. 4,

mishnah 12, the letters are called "stones," suggesting that they are the fundamental building blocks of creation.

207. Dov Ber regularly uses the terms "world of thought" and "world of speech" to refer to specific *sefirot* or divine powers active in various stages of creation. "World of speech" refers to *Malkhut* or the *Shekhinah*. "World of thought" indicate the higher *sefirot*, *Binah* or *Hokhmah*. See chapter 9 of Schatz-Uffenheimer's *Hasidism as Mysticism*.

208. That is, the *Zaddiq* has no personal interest in the petitionary content of the words of prayer. He does not pray in order to have his own needs fulfilled, but only for the sake of the pleasure God derives when the divine emanation s inherent in the letters are returned to their root.

209. Schatz-Uffenheimer, *Maggid Devarav le-Ya'aqov* (Jerusalem: Magnes, 1976), pp. 94–95, sect. 60.

210. Ps. 51:17.

211. Schatz-Uffenheimer, *Maggid Devarav le-Ya'aqov*, p. 184, sect. 106.

212. On this important issue, see especially Ada Rapoport-Albert, "God and the Zaddik as the Two Focal Points of Hasidic Worship," in *History of Religions* 18 (1979): 296–325.

213. This issue is clarified in the introduction to Gedalyah Nigal's Critical Edition of *Zafnat Paneah* [Hebrew] (Jerusalem: Institute for the Study of Hasidic Literature, 1989), 21–30.

214. For a discussion of some approaches to *devequt* in the thought of Hasidism's opponents, see Immanuel Etkes, *Rabbi Israel Salanter and the Beginning of the Musar Movement* [Hebrew] (Jerusalem: Magnes, 1984), p. 27–57. Also see Norman Lamm, *Torah Lishmah, Torah for the Torah's Sake in the Works of Rabbi Hayyim of Volozhin and His Contemporaries* (New York: Ktav, 1989). A detailed comparison of the two approaches would be a valuable contribution to understanding the theoretical nature of the conflict.

3. Cosmological Bases for Meshullam Feibush's Concept of Devequt

1. On the confrontation between Lurianic and Cordoverian schools of Kabbalah, see Isaiah Tishby, *Studies in Kabbalah and its Branches* [Hebrew] (Jerusalem: Magnes, 1982), pp. 177–268.

2. To a certain extent, Lurianic influence was already challenged in the seventeenth century by the dessemination of such works as *Sheney Luhot ha-Berit and Reishit Hokhmah*. On the question of Lurianic influence on *Sheney Luhot ha-Berit*, see Elliot Wolfson, "The Influence of Luria on the *Shelah*," [Hebrew] in *Jerusalem Studies in Jewish Thought*, vol. 10, Lurianic Kabbalah (Jerusalem, 1992), and Krassen, *Isaiah Horowitz*.

3. This issue is discussed in detail in Moshe Idel's article, "Perceptions of Kabbalah," pp. 53–114. Also see Idel, *Hasidism: Between Ecstasy and Magic*, pp. 33–43.

4. See Idel, *Hasidism: Between Ecstasy and Magic.*

5. On the influence of these works, see our discussion in the preceding chapter.

6. This is particularly true in regard to Meshullam Feibush's mystical theory of prayer. See our discussion of prayer in the chapter six, "The Remedy: Prayer, Torah, Sacred Calendar." In this chapter, we are primarily concerned with the practical mystical implications of Cordoverian and Lurianic approaches.

7. The position that Lurianic kavvanot, while not suitable for use, were still valuable to be learned, was also held by the contemporary anti-Sabbatian, R. Jacob Emden. See Idel, *Hasidism: Between Ecstasy and Magic*, p. 150.

8. On the problem of pantheism and Kabbalah, see Gershom Scholem, *Kabbalah* (New York: Quadrangle, 1974), pp. 144–152. In actuality, there were two major schools of interpretation of Lurianic Kabbalah in Europe, The school of Hai Ricchi tended to interpret Lurianic concepts literally. However, the school of Joseph Ergas argued that Lurianic Kabbalah should be understood metaphorically. Proponents of the latter school neutralized to some extent the implications of divine withdrawal. For a discussion of this debate involving Hasidic and non-Hasidic views, see Tamar Ross, "Rav Hayyim of Volozhin and Rav Shneur Zalman of Liadi: Two Interpretations of the Doctrine of *Zimzum*," [Hebrew] in *Jerusalem Studies in Jewish Thought* (1982): 153–169.

9. For a discussion of Cordoverian theology, see Bracha Sack, *The Kabbalah of Rabbi Moshe Cordovero* [Hebrew] (Israel: Ben Gurion University, 1995). Also see Joseph Ben-Shlomo, *The Mystical Theology of Moses Cordovero* [Hebrew] (Jerusalem: Bialik, 1965).

10. The concept of *zimzum* in Cordoverian Kabbalah is discussed by Sack, *Kabbalah of Rabbi Moshe Cordovero*, pp. 57–82. According to her research, Cordovero's theory of *zimzum* is much closer to the Lurianic view than had previously been realized. Thus Cordovero's concept of *zimzum*, like so many other aspects of his thought, could have served as the source for Luria's innovations. However, even if Cordovero's complete system did contain a similar conception of *zimzum*, Cordovero's treatment of the subject appears primarily in his commentary on the Zohar, *Or Yaqar*. This work had not yet appeared in print during the eighteenth century and probably did not influence the Hasidic perception of Cordoverian Kabbalah that was primarily drawn from *Pardes Rimmonim* and the three secondary sources mentioned above. Also see Ben-Shlomo, *Mystical Theology*, pp. 98–100. However, Ben-Shlomo also noted the similarity of the Cordoverian concept of *Or Hozer* (retracted light) and Lurianic *zimzum*. See, Ibid., pp. 207–272.

11. Cordovero's classification of levels of studying Torah appears in *Pardes Rimmonim*, 37,1. On the concept of drawing down *ruhaniyut* in Cordovero, see Idel, *Hasidism: Between Ecstasy and Mysticism*, pp. 66–71. On the history of *ruhaniyut*, see Shlomo Pines, "On the Term *Ruhaniyyut* and its Souces and on Judah Halevi's Doctrine," [Hebrew] in *Tarbiz* 57 (1988): 511–540. On Cordovero's conception of the Torah, see Sack, *Kabbalah of Rabbi Moshe Cordovero*, pp. 113–192.

12. Compare Mendel Piekarz's discussion of this Cordoverian view, especially

as expressed in *Sheney Luhot ha-Berit,* in Mendel Piekarz's, *The Beginning of Hasidism: Ideological Trends in Derush and Musar Literature* [Hebrew] (Jerusalem: Bialik, 1978), pp. 354–359.

13. This is essentially Moshe Idel's theory.

14. See Sack, *Kabbalah of Rabbi Moshe Cordovero* [Hebrew], pp. 103–109.

15. See Bracha Sack, "The Influence of *Reishit hokhmah* on the Teachings of the Maggid of Mezhirech," in Rapoport-Albert, ed, *Hasidism Reappraised,* pp. 251–257. Also see Mordechai Pechter's article, "*Iqvot Hashpa'ato shel Sefer Reishit Hokhmah le-R. Eliyahu De Vidas be-Khitvey R. Ya'aqov Yosef mi-Polonoy,*" in *Studies in Jewish Mysticism, Philosophy, and Ethical Literature Presented to Isaiah Tishby on his Seventy-Fifth Birthday* [Hebrew], pp. 569–592. On the influence of *Sheney Luhot ha-Berit,* see Mendel Piekarz, "Hasidism as a Socio-religious Movement," in Rapoport-Albert, ed., *Hasidism Reappraised,* pp. 232–237.

16. *Liqqutim Yeqarim,* 119b (YDE, sect. 18)

17. See our discussion at the end of the preceding chapter. Also see Schatz-Uffenheimer's opening chapters of *Hasidism as Mysticism.*

18. *Liqqutim Yeqarim,* ibid. On the *kavvanot* of eating in Lurianic Kabbalah, see Ronit Meroz, "Selections from Ephraim Penzieri: Luria's Sermon in Jerusalem and the *Kavvanah* in Taking Food," [Hebrew], *Jerusalem Studies in Jewish Thought,* vol. 10, Lurianic Kabbalah (Jerusalem, 1992), pp. 211–257.

19. Three orders of heavenly beings mentioned in the *qedushah* section of the liturgy.

20. *Liqqutim Yeqarim,* 119 a–b (YDE, sect. 18).

21. The notion that *devequt* precludes evil is fundamental to Meshullam Feibush's ethics. This will be discussed in subsequent chapters dealing with the ethical basis of Meshullam Feibush's theory of *devequt.*

22. This moralistic account of the Lurianic Kabbalah recalls Moses Hayyim Luzzatto's formulation of Lurianic Kabbalah. See, for example, the beginning of *Derekh ha-Shem.* The influence of Luzzatto on early Hasidic thought has generally not received sufficient recognition. See Isaiah Tishby's important article, "*Iqvot Rabbi Moshe Hayyim Luzzatto be-Mishnat ha-Hasidut,*" in Tishby, *Studies in Kabbalah and Its Branches: Researches and Sources,* vol. 3, pp. 961–994. Although particularly emphasized by Luzzatto, the moralistic explanation for the *shevirah* already formed a part of Hayyim Vital's record of the Lurianic teachings. See Isaiah Tishby, *The Doctrine of Evil and the 'Kelippah' in Lurianic Kabbalism* [Hebrew] (Jerusalem: Magnes, 1984).

23. This is discussed in detail in the following chapters.

24. Meshullam Feibush does, however, discuss *zimzum* in the context of the cosmic events that occur on New Year's Day. See our discussion in the chapter six, "The Remedy: Prayer, Torah, and the Sacred Calendar." However, even in that context, his discussion is significantly informed by Cordoverian concepts.

25. Dov Ber of Mezeritch had already developed a Hasidic interpretation of *zimzum* which had virtually the opposite meaning of the Lurianic concept. Dov Ber

used the term metaphorically to indicate the diminution of the divine mind that took place so that the human mind of *Zaddiqim* would be able to apprehend divinity. See, e.g., Schatz-Uffenheimer, *Maggid Devarav le-Ya'aqov*, p. 9, sect. 1. On two types of *zimzum* in Hasidism, see Idel, *Hasidism: Between Ecstasy and Magic*, pp. 89–95.

26. For a comprehensive discussion of acosmism in HaBaD Hasidism, see Rachel Elior, *The Paradoxical Ascent to God : The Kabbalistic Theosophy of Habad Hasidism* (Albany: State University of New York, 1993). Also see Elior, *The Theory of Divinity of Hasidut HaBaD*, and Elior, "HaBaD: The Contemplative Ascent to God," in Green, ed., *Jewish Spirituality*, v. 2: 157–205. Also see Louis Jacobs, *Seeker of Unity: The Life and Works of Aaron Straosselje* (New York: Basic Books, 1966).

27. See Isaiah Horowitz, *Sheney Luhot ha-Berit* (Amsterdam, 1698), tractate *Shavuot*, 189b.

28. Deut. 4:39.

29. *Liqqutim Yeqarim*, 115b (YDE, sect. 11). The passage in *Sheney Luhot ha-Berit* was also a major source for R. Shneur Zalman of Liadi's *Sha'ar ha-Yihud ve-ha-Emunah*, the second part of his *Liqqutim Amarim* (*Tanya*).

30. The issue of Horowitz's relationship to Lurianic Kabbalah was addressed directly by Wolfson in "The Influence of Luria on the Shelah," [Hebrew] in *Jerusalem Studies in Jewish Thought*, vol. 10, Lurianic Kabbalah, pp. 423–448. Also see the introduction to Krassen, *Isaiah Horowitz: The Generations of Adam*.

31. Meshullam Feibush frequently refers to Yehiel Mikhel of Zlotchov as "the Maggid." However, Dov Ber, the Maggid of Mezeritch, is always referred to by name.

32. Job 32:8. Compare Altshuler's comments on this teaching, see Altshuler, *Rabbi Meshullam Feibush Heller*, pp. 96–102.

33. B.T., *Hagigah*, 12a.

34. Prov. 25:25.

35. B.T. *Berakhot*, 6b.

36. *Liqqutim Yeqarim*, 116b (YDE, sect. 13).

37. Ps. 16:8.

38. Isa. 6:3.

39. *Tiqquney Zohar*, *Tiqqun* 57.

40. *Liqqutim Yeqarim*, 115a–b (YDE, sect. 11).

41. On the ethical sense of humility and *Ayin* in early Hasidism, see Piekarz, *Between Ideology and Reality* [Hebrew], passim.

42. Meshullam Feibush here supports his statement by referring to the commandments of faith, love, awe, and unity which should be practiced at all times.

43. *Liqqutim Yeqarim*, 115b (YDE, sect. 12).

44. Neh. 9:6.

45. *Liqqutim Yeqarim*, 115b (YDE, sect. 12).

46. *Liqqutim Yeqarim*, 116a (YDE, sect. 12).

47. Ibid.

48. On *unio mystica* in early Hasidism, see Idel, *Hasidism: Between Ecstasy*

and Magic, pp. 222–223. But compare Piekarz, *Between Ideology and Reality* [Hebrew], pp. 55–81, esp. p. 78.

49. Literally, "the Infinite." In early kabbalistic literature, the term was applied to the ultimate transcendent degree of divinity, the *deus absconditus*. However, in early Hasidic thought, with its emphasis on divine immanence, the term is frequently used with less precision.

50. *Liqqutim Yeqarim*, 117b (YDE, sect. 14).

51. On the *Shekhinah*, see Gershom Scholem, *On the Mystical Shape of the Godhead* (New York, 1991), pp. 140–196. Also see Wolfson, *Through a Speculum that Shines: Vision and Imagination in Medieval Jewish Mysticism* (Princeton, N.J.: Princeton University, 1994), pp. 306–317.

52. In a later passage, Meshullam Feibush does discuss the union of these two aspects that occurs on the Sabbath. See *Liqqutim Yeqarim*, 138a (YDE, sect. 47).

53. *Liqqutim Yeqarim*, 137b (YDE, sect. 47)

54. This type of mystical experience, along with its cosmological basis, contains elements that are common to the mysticism of many of the world's religions. See W. T. Stace, *Mysticism and Philosophy* (Los Angeles: Tarcher, 1987), esp. pp. 41–133. However, in the light of more recent research, Stace's characterization of Jewish mysticism as an exception to the general rule requires revision.

55. The return of the soul to its root is a typical neo-Platonic motif. For an early Jewish version, see Idel, *Kabbalah: New Perspectives*, p. 306, n. 62.

56. See Idel's discussion of this motif, *Kabbalah: New Perspectives*, pp. 67–70. This metaphor has an Aristotelian source and is also found in Muslim and Christian mystical texts. See references cited by Idel, Ibid. p. 306, n. 64.

57. On the cosmic tree in early Kabbalah, see Elliot R. Wolfson, "The Tree that is All: Jewish-Christian Roots of a Kabbalistic Symbol in *Sefer ha-Bahir*," in *Journal of Jewish Thought and Philosophy* 3: 31–76.

58. Contrast Piekarz's interpretation in *Between Ideology and Reality* [Hebrew], p. 78.

59. Compare Idel's discussion of our text, *Kabbalah: New Perspectives*, pp. 68f.

60. See Krassen, *'Devequt' and Faith* (1990). The exception is Altshuler whose theory of esotericism in the school of the Maggid of Zlotchov is a bit different.

61. See Dubnov, *History of Hasidism* [Hebrew] 4th ed., p. 323, n. 5.

62. See Weiss, *Studies in Eastern European Jewish Mysticism*, p. 123, n. 57.

63. See Idel, *Kabbalah: New Perspectives*, p. 307, n. 84.

4. The Barrier to Divine Aid

1. See chapter one, "Meshullam Feibush and His Circle in Eastern Galicia."

2. Literally, Samael.

3. See note 2.

4. Or, "as a front."

5. *Liqqutim Yeqarim* 110b (YDE, sect. 1).

6. Elsewhere, Meshullam Feibush presents this problem in a doctrine of Original Sin. See below, p. 152.

7. A variant of this analogy, attributed to Meshullam Feibush's teacher, Yehiel Mikhel of Zlotchov, appears in *Yeshu'ot Malko* (Jerusalem: Levin, 1974), p. 123. The text is transcribed from a manuscript called *Liqqutim Yeqarim*. No further information concerning the provenance of this manuscript is provided. The text may be translated as follows:

A person who thinks to himself that the urge of pride has passed him by (*pasah alav*) may be likened to one who was born on a high mountain and never in his life seen the valley. He never considers that his feet are trampling on a lofty mountain.

8. *Liqqutim Yeqarim*, 110b (YDE, sect. 2).

9. Ibid., 110b–111a (YDE, sect. 2).

10. Ibid., 111a (YDE, sect. 2).

11. Ibid.

12. Prov. 16:5.

13. *Liqqutim Yeqarim*, 112a (YDE, sect. 6).

14. Avot 2:16.

15. *Liqqutim Yeqarim*, 112a (YDE, sect. 6).

16. When speaking of humility, Meshullam Feibush uses the Hebrew words, *shiflut* (lowliness) and *anavah* (humility) interchangebly. However, whenever the context seems to warrant it, I use the word "effacement," especially to translate *shiflut*.

17. Avot 6:1.

18. Ibid., 6:6.

19. *Liqqutim Yeqarim*, 112a–112b (YDE, sect. 7).

20. The *musar* works that Meshullam Feibush specifically mentions are *Hovot ha-Levavot*, *Sefer Yashar le-Rabbenu Tam*, *Orhot Zaddiqim*, and *Reishit Hokhmah*. For a description of these works, see Joseph Dan, *Hebrew Ethical and Homiletical Literature* [Hebrew] (Jerusalem, 1975).

21. Lev. 26:16.

22. *Liqqutim Yeqarim*, 148a (*Derekh Emet*, sect. 6).

23. For Meshullam Feibush, the psyche contains two parts. One is drawn after materiality and its desires. The other is an immortal divine portion which "desires what God desires."

24. Mishnah, *Nega'im*, 2:5.

25. *Liqqutim Yeqarim*, 149b (DE, sect. 8).

26. Prov. 16:5.

27. B.T., *Sotah* 5a.

28. B.T., *Yoma* 38b.

29. *Liqqutim Yeqarim*, 149a (DE, sect. 7).

30. See the chapter eight, on "The Importance of *Zaddiqim*."

31. Ps. 34:15, 37:27.

32. B.T., *Berakhot* 35b.

33. *Liqqutim Yeqarim*, 128b (YDE, sect. 33).

34. And see the following chapter, "The Problem of Corporeality, Conditions for *Devequt*" especially the discussion concerning how the invincibility of the *yezer ha-ra* serves God's desire for delight.

35. These are discussed elsewhere. See especially the chapters on detachment from corporeality, prayer, and the importance of *Zaddiqim*.

36. See, for example, *Zava'at ha-RYVaSH*, p. 9a, sect. 55 and p. 23a sect., 126.

37. Prov. 16:5.

38. *Liqqutim Yeqarim*, 123b–124a (YDE, sect. 25).

39. Ibid., 124a (YDE, sect. 25).

40. 2 Chron. 17:6.

41. B.T., Sanhedrin 37a.

42. B.T., Kedushin 40b.

43. *Liqqutim Yeqarim*, 124b–125a (YDE, sect. 27).

44. Kohelet 7:14.

45. Prov. 21:8.

46. Isa. 5:20.

47. This argument is obviously at least partially polemical. On the propagandistic aspect of the argument, see my discussion in chapter eight, on "The Importance of *Zaddiqim*."

48. *Liqqutim Yeqarim*, 125a–125b (YDE, sect. 28).

49. Ibid., 125a (YDE, sect. 27).

50. See the chapter eight, on "The Importance of *Zaddiqim*."

51. Meshullam Feibush's attitude is generally consistant with the teachings of Dov Ber of Mezeritch. The aspect of passivity in Dov Ber's teachings was interpreted in a variety of ways by his many desciples. For a general discussion of this problem, see texts cited by Joseph Weiss, "*Via Passiva* in Early Hasidism," *Studies in East European Jewish Mysticism*, pp. 69–94. Weiss, however, underestimated the place of *unio mystica* in early Hasidism. See also Schatz-Uffenheimer's discussion in *Quietistic Elements in Eighteenth-Century Hasidic Thought* [Hebrew], pp. 111–119. From the texts cited in these studies, it would appear that Meshullam Feibush and Abraham Hayyim of Zlotchov held particularly extreme views concerning the exclusivity of divine agency. Since both were influenced by Yehiel Mikhel of Zlotchov, this would seem to lend weight to Weiss's assertion that the latter was a more thoroughgoing pantheist than Dov Ber of Mezeritch. See Weiss, op. cit., pp. 73, 88–89.

52. Ps. 37:39.

53. *Liqqutim Yeqarim*, 150a (DE, sect. 8).

54. See note 52.

55. *Liqqutim Yeqarim*, 150a (DE, sect. 8).

5. The Problem of Corporeality

1. Esther Rabbah, 10:3.

2. literally, "heart."

3. Lam. 3:41.

4. *Liqqutim Yeqarim*, 150a (*Derekh Emet*, sect. 8).

5. Avot 6:6 lists forty means of acquiring Torah.

6. *Liqqutim Yeqarim*, 111b (YDE, sect. 4).

7. Avot 6:6.

8. B.T., *Pesahim* 25b.

9. The rabbis interpreted Exod. 21:10 to mean that a husband is obligated to provide his wife with sexual relations. See B.T., *Ketubot* 47b. The frequency of such relations generally depends on a person's profession. Those involved with the study of Torah, e.g., are only obligated to perform their sexual duty on Sabbath eves. A complete account of the laws regarding obligatory sex appears in Maimonides' *Mishnah Torah, Nashim*, Laws concering Marriage, chapter 14. On sex as a commandment, see Rachel Biale, *Women and Jewish Law* (New York: Schocken, 1984) and David Biale, *Eros and the Jews* (New York: Basic Books, 1992).

10. *Liqqutim Yeqarim*, 11b (YDE, sect. 4)

11. Judg. 13:25.

12. *Liqqutim Yeqarim*, 115a (YDE, sect. 11).

13. The notion that the human soul is subject to two opposing forces is rooted in rabbinic thought. See Solomon Schechter, "The Evil Yezer: The Source of Rebellion" in Solomon Schecter, *Aspects of Rabbinic Theology* (New York: Schocken, 1961), pp. 242–263. This general notion of psychological conflict is retained in *Sefer ha-Zohar*. However, in the Zohar the psychological situation reflects a cosmic dualism. The evil urge in man is conceived as the actual representative of *sitra ahara*, the evil force that opposes holiness. See Isaiah Tishby, *Wisdom of the Zohar*, vol. 2: 447–475, 509–512. However, the fully crystalized notion of two distinct opposing souls seems to be based in Lurianic dualism. See *Ez Hayyim*, Gate 50, ch. 2 and *Sha'arey Qedushah*. Also compare the later, more systematic, *HaBaD* Hasidic presentation in *Sefer Liqqutey Amarim Tanya*, ch. 1, 5b.

14. That is, in no sense material. In Meshullam Feibush's writings, *ruhani*, refers to the nonmaterial reality which pervades existence. See below.

15. *Liqqutim Yeqarim*, 115a (YDE, sect. 11).

16. See chapter three, "Cosmological Bases of Meshullam Feibush's Concept of Devequt."

17. Zohar, vol. 2, 42b.

18. *Liqqutim Yeqarim*, 117b (YDE, sect. 15).

19. That is, there is no *devequt*. A sense of awe in the presence of God is the beginning of intimacy.

20. Ps. 118:20.

21. The lowest of the ten *sefirot*. *Liqqutim Yeqarim*, 117b–118a (YDE, sect. 15).

22. Laws of Prayer, sect. 98. *Liqqutim Yeqarim*, ibid.

23. The process of inner awareness is discussed more fully in *Derekh Emet*. See the discussion in the preceding chapter. Here, again, is an attitude that suggests the possible influence of Luzzatto's path of mystical-ethical development in *Mesillat Yesharim*.

24. *Liqqutim Yeqarim*, 113a (YDE, sect. 8).

25. Meshullam Feibush here quotes a long passage from *Mishneh Torah*, Laws of Repentance, 10:3. *Liqqutim Yeqarim*, ibid.

26. B.T., *Shabbat* 13a.

27. In *Avot de-Rabbi Natan*, ch. 2, Ulla expressly forbids all physical contact.

28. *Liqqutim Yeqarim*, 118a (YDE, sect. 16).

29. Compare the discussion in Schatz-Uffenheimer, *Hasidism as Mysticism*, p. 109. (See pp. 52–53 in the Hebrew edition.) She notes that the notion of a bifurcated consciousness during *devequt* was already attributed to the Ba'al Shem Tov by Jacob Joseph of Polnoy in *Toldot Ya'aqov Yosef*, 26b, *Va-Yishlah*. Joseph Weiss also discussed Hasidic *devequt* in terms of a divided consciousness in his essay, "*Reshit Zemihatah shel ha-Derekh ha-Hasidit*," *Zion* 16 (1951): 63 and see the comments of Ada Rapoport-Albert, "God and the Zaddiq as the two Focal Points of Hasidic Worship," *History of Religions* 18 (1979): 297.

30. "*U-falaga dideih a-dideih*" Literally, "and his [position here]diverges from his [position there]." This is an expression that is commonly used in talmudic literature to indentify an apparent contradiction when two conflicting opinions are ascribed to the same source. Meshullam Feibush novelly ascribes a psychological-mystical meaning to the expression which both justifies the bizzare behavior of the Babylonian Amora, Ulla (c. 320) and illustrates the psychological basis of detachment from corporeality.

31. *Liqqutim Yeqarim*, 118a–118b (YDE, sect. 16).

32. Gen. 1:28.

33. Cf. the discussion above in the chapter three, "Cosmological Bases of Meshullam Feibush's Concept of *Devequt*." God's purpose in creating the world was to create conditions from which humankind would extricate himself/herself through spiritually returning to his/her divine origin.

34. *Liqqutim Yeqarim*,120b–121a (YDE, sect. 20).

35. This entire discussion of upright and bent posture is based upon a comment of Rashi on the verse, "*and I will cause you to be fruitful and to be great*," (Lev. 26:9). There Rashi says that the second verb means "with an upright body." See *Liqqutim Yeqarim*, 117 a (YDE, sect 14) where Yehiel Mikhel's interpretation begins. And see below, p. 113.

36. See note 17.

37. *Liqqutim Yeqarim*, 121a (YDE, sect. 20).

38. For Meshullam Feibush, spiritual ideas in the mind are objectively real. This idealism validates mystical experience. A more fully developed presentation of his position appears in the second part of *Yosher Divrey Emet*, sect. 34 in *Liqqutim Yeqarim*, 129a–130a. This will be discussed below in the chapter eight, "The Importance of *Zaddiqim*." Here, one should note that a similar position concerning the objective reality of alternative states of consciousness and the reliability of spiritual conceptions within the mind is found in the early Hasidic anthologies without attribution to any particular figure. Cf., e.g., *Liqqutim Yeqarim*, 3b–4a (sect. 19).

When one is greatly attached to the *Shekhinah* in the lower state of consciousness (*qatnut*), later, then, just as soon as he thinks of the supernal worlds, immediately he *is* in the supernal worlds. For in whatever place a person's mind is, there he is (indeed). If he were not in the supernal world, he would not be thinking of it at all.

39. Ibid. 121a (YDE, sect. 20).

40. In *Derekh Emet*, Meshullam Feibush identifies sexual incontinence as the root of all vices. See *Liqqutim Yeqarim*, 145a (DE, sect. 1). In addition, throughout *Yosher Divrey Emet*, he repeatedly attributes sexual incontinence to the enemies of the true *Zaddiqim*, as we shall see.

41. Lev. 26:9.

42. Ibid.

43. *Liqqutim Yeqarim*, 121a (YDE, sect 20).

44. See the chapter three, "Cosmological Bases of Meshullam Feibush's Concept of *Devequt*."

45. *Liqqutim Yeqarim*, 119b (YDE, sect. 18).

46. Ibid.

47. Or "experiential knowledge of God." See below, p. 115f.

48. See below, p. 115.

49. Zohar, vol. 2, 254b.

50. *Liqqutim Yeqarim*, 119b (YDE, sect. 18).

51. See chapter three, "Cosmological Bases of Meshullam Feibush's Concept of *Devequt*."

52. On the Lurianic *kavvanot* of eating see Ronit Meroz, "Selections from Ephraim Penzieri" [Hebrew] in *Jerusalem Studies in Jewish Thought*, vol. 10: 211–258.

53. Menahem Mendel's comment is a word play on the familiar talmudic dictum, *mittokh she-lo li-shemah ba li-shemah*" (through performing a *mizvah* for an ulterior motive one eventually comes to performing it for its own sake). See, e.g., B.T., *Pesahim* 50b.

54. *Liqqutim Yeqarim*, 119b (YDE, sect. 18).

55. See the chapter three, "Cosmological Bases of Meshullam Feibush's Concept of *Devequt*."

56. *Liqqutim Yeqarim*, 122a (YDE, sect. 21). In this passage, Meshullam Feibush has presented what later will become the HaBaD contemplative practice known as *hitbonenut*. On the development of this contemplative practice in early Hasidism, see Naftali Loewenthal, "Habad Approaches to Contemplative Prayer," in Rapoport-Albert, *Hasidism Reappraised*, pp. 288–300.

57. B.T., Sanhedrin 92a.

58. 1 Chron. 28:9.

59. Or, "recognition," See below, p. 118.

60. *Liqqutim Yeqarim*, ibid. 122a (YDE, sect. 21).

61. Traditional rabbinic curriculum, is conventionally divided into two areas of

study, exoteric and esoteric, or revealed teachings and concealed teachings. The latter includes all the literature of the Kabbalah, especially the Zohar and Safedian texts from the schools of Moses Cordovero and Isaac Luria. Revealed Torah refers primarily to Talmudic literature and rabbinic codes.

62. B.T., *Hagigah* 14b.

63. *Mishneh Torah*, Laws Concerning the Fundamentals of Torah, end of ch. 4. *Liqqutim Yeqarim*, 122a (YDE, sect. 22). See Idel, *Hasidism: Between Ecstasy and Magic*, pp. 173–176. Also Compare Moshe Idel's translation and important comments regarding this text in *Kabbalah: New Perspectives*, p. 58.

64. Or, perhaps, "without awareness of Him."

65. Or, "awareness."

66. *Liqqutim Yeqarim*, 122b (YDE, sect. 22).

67. B.T., *Nedarim* 32a.

68. Prov. 24:4.

69. Ibid. 3:6.

70. *Liqqutim Yeqarim*, 122b–123a (YDE, sect. 23).

71. See p. 89.

72. Job 35:11.

73. *Liqqutim Yeqarim*, ibid.

74. And see Idel's remarks, *Kabbalah: New Perspectives*, p. 58.

75. The *sefirah* Yesod, which connects the upper *sefirot* to *Malkhut*, is frequently referred to as *Zaddiq*. Here, in typical Hasidic fashion, the anthropomorphic symbolism that early Kabbalah used to describe theosophical matters is restored to the anthropological realm.

76. In the Kabbalistic symbolism of *hieros gamos*, Yesod represents the phallus which is called "covenant" because of the association with circumcision. Thus Yesod as phallus joins male and female in the sexual act. On the centrality of this sexually nuanced symbolism in Spanish Kabbalah, see Wolfson, *Through a Speculum that Shines*, q.v. phallus.

77. 1 Chron. 29:11.

78. This "targum" actually appears in the *Zohar*, v. 1, 31a. Also see our discussion in chapter eight "The Importance of *Zaddiqim*."

79. *Liqqutim Yeqarim*, 123a (YDE, sect. 23). See Elliot R. Wolfson's comments on the connection of the zoharic kabbalists to Yesod, as divine phallus containing "all," in *Through a Speculum that Shines*, pp. 388–390.

80. Ps. 103:19.

81. *Liqqutim Yeqarim*, 123a (YDE, sect. 23).

82. Indeed *Yosher Divrey Emet* is full of admonitions against those who would attempt to apply the specific mystical means of divine service which can only be employed by those who have attained *devequt* in the sense of detachment and *Da'at*. This entire issue is discussed in detail in the chapter eight, "The Importance of *Zaddiqim*."

6. The Remedy

1. To a lesser degree, Meshullam Feibush also discusses the performance of *mizvot*. He deals specifically only with fasting, ritual immersion, and the general use of Lurianic *kavvanot* while performing *mizvot*. On the lack of extensive treatment of the *mizvot* in Hasidic homilies, see Schatz Uffenheimer, *Hasidism as Mysticism*, pp. 111–143.

2. Meshullam Feibush's conception of love for God is based on the famous passage in Maimonides' *Mishneh Torah, Hilkhot Teshuvah*, 10:3, which he cites. See *Liqqutim Yeqarim*, 113a (YDE, sect. 8).

3. Literally, "Torah for its own sake." Meshullam Feibush's mystical understanding of this rabbinic concept is discussed in the following section. On this concept in another important early Hasidic source, see Roland Goetschel, "*Torah lishmah* as a Central Concept in the *Degel Mahaneh Efrayim* of Moses Hayyim Ephraim of Sudylkow," in Rapoport-Albert, *Hasidism Reappraised*, pp. 258–267.

4. This text is part of a longer critique of the behavior of scholars whose spirituality is more rooted in study than in prayer. The attack against dry scholarship is a common complaint in the ethical and homiletical literature of the eighteenth century. While it was in no sense initiated by the Hasidic leaders, it was certainly embraced by them. This is discussed in detail by Piekarz in *The Begining of Hasidism*.

5. *Liqqutim Yeqarim*, 115a (YDE, sect. 8).

6. See *Liqqutim Yeqarim*, 128b (YDE, sect. 33). The passage is discussed in the chapter four, "Barrier to Divine Aid."

7. A kabbalistic reference to the *Shekhinah*.

8. *Liqqutim Yeqarim*, 118a (YDE, sect. 15).

9. On contemplative prayer in Hasidism, see Schatz-Uffenheimer, *Hasidism as Mysticism*, ch. 6, ibid, and Schatz-Uffenheimer in "Contemplative Prayer in Hasidism," *Studies in Mysticism and Religion Presented to G. Scholem*, edited by Rivka Schatz-Uffenheimer (Jerusalem, 1967), pp. 209–226. Also see Jacobs, *Hasidic Prayer*, ch. 6, 7. Also see Idel's discussion of mystical and magical prayer in Hasidism in *Hasidism: Between Ecstasy and Magic*, pp. 149–170; and see Naftali Loewenthal, "Habad Approaches to Contemplative Prayer, 1790–1920," in Rapoport-Albert, ed., *Hasidism Reappraised*, pp. 288–300.

10. This teaching of Menahem Mendel suggests that the ideal of contemplative prayer as involving complete detachment from corporeality was not an innovation of Dov Ber of Mezeritch. Since little evidence presently exists which would connect Menahem Mendel and Dov Ber, the likelihood that the latter influenced the former is not great.

11. B.T., Berakhot 28b.

12. Menahem Mendel's interpretation depends on a pun. "Donkey" (*HaMoR*) has the same letters as "matter" (*HoMeR*).

13. *Liqqutim Yeqarim*, 118a (YDE, sect. 15). Compare Piekarz's discussion of this text in *Ideology and Reality* [Hebrew], p. 105.

14. *Liqqutim Yeqarim,* 129a (YDE, sect. 33).

15. In the morning liturgy, the declaration of unity ("the *Shema*') and its blessing are preceded by two preliminary sections. The first involves biblical and rabbinic passages dealing with the Temple and sacrifices. The second primarily contains selections from the Psalms and other verses of praise.

16. In Hebrew, the number 248 is represented by the letters $r = 200$, $m = 40$, $h = 8$. These letters spell *romah,* "spear."

17. *Liqqutim Yeqarim,* 129a (YDE, sect. 53).

18. This is in keeping with the Lurianic conception of stages of prayer. The initial stages involve rectification of the lowest of the cosmic worlds. Only at such levels are the worlds vulnerable to attack from the forces of evil. However, Meshullam Feibush's conception of the stages is more typical of Hasidic prayer. He is not concerned so much with ascending through the worlds as with increasing the degree of concentration. For an account of the various stages of Lurianic prayer and their kabbalistic significance, see Yehiel Abraham Barlev, *Yedid Nefesh: Kavvanot ha-Ari z'l al ha-Tefillah* (Petah Tikvah, 1988). A possible bridge between the two conceptions of prayer may be seen in Jacob Emden's prayer book, *Beyt Ya'aqov.* Here stages of the service are compared to succeedingly inner courts of the Temple.

19. Meshullam Feibush's primary interest in prayer is markedly different from the theurgic interest that is implied in the use of Lurianic *Kavvanot.* More will be said concerning this below.

20. *Liqqutim Yeqarim,* 129a (YDE, sect. 53).

21. See *Liqqutim Yeqarim,* 85a (sect. 166). Dov Ber's version of the analogy differs in several important aspects. See the following note.

22. Meshullam Feibush's use of the analogy leads to a way of dealing with the problem of disturbing thoughts which diverges from that taught by Dov Ber. See chapter seven, "Meshullam Feibush and the Maggid of Mezeritch."

23. *Liqqutim Yeqarim,* 130b (YDE, sect. 35).

24. Compare this motif of evil ultimately serving good with Yehiel Mikhel's explanation of the divine name, *Shaddai* in "Cosmological Bases of Meshullam Feibush's Concept of *Devequt.*" A teaching which argues that disturbing thoughts are a sign of favor is attributed to the Ba'al Shem Tov by Meshullam Feibush of Brezhin in *Sefat Emet, va-era.* See *Sefer Ba'al Shem Tov, Noah,* sect. 105. An English translation of this text appears in Green and Holtz, *Your Word is Fire: The Hasidic Masters on Contemplative Prayer* (New York: Paulist, 1977), p. 90.

25. *Liqqutim Yeqarim,* 130b (YDE, sect. 35).

26. *Liqqutim Yeqarim,* 130b–131a (YDE, sect. 35).

27. In advocating subduing rather than sublimating negative thoughts and qualities Meshullam Feibush takes a position which is at variance with a central teaching of Dov Ber of Mezeritch. See the discussion in chapter seven, "Meshullam Feibush and the Maggid of Mezeritch."

28. *Liqqutim Yeqarim,* 130b–131a (YDE, sect. 35).

29. At present, no complete study of the nature and usage of Lurianic *kavvanot*

exists, although important work in this area is being done by Menahem Kallus. In the meantime, see Scholem, *Kabbalah*, pp. 176–182; 369–370. Also see Weiss, *Studies in Eastern European Jewish Mysticism*, pp. 95–126. On the early Hasidic attitude toward Lurianic *kavvanot*, see also Jacobs, *Hasidic Prayer*, pp. 70–81. And see Idel, *Hasidism: Between Ecstasy and Magic*, pp. 149–154. Also see Ronit Meroz, "Selections from Ephraim Penzieri: Luria's Sermon in Jerusalem and the *Kavvanot* in Taking Food," [Hebrew] in *Jerusalem Studies in Jewish Thought*, vol. 10: 211–257.

30. See *Liqqutim Yeqarim*, 134a–135a (YDE, sect. 42).

31. *Liqqutim Yeqarim*, 135a (YDE, sect. 42).

32. See below the discussion on the metaphysical basis of prayer, p. 130f.

33. This virtuosity is a distinctive feature of Komarna Hasidism. See, e.g., R. Yizhaq Isaac Yehudah Yehiel Safran of Komarna, *Netiv Mizvotekha*. Even without the Hasidic emphasis on *devequt*, mastery of Lurianic *praxis* demands exceptional dedication and ability. Mastery of the full system of Lurianic cosmology is itself an impressive prerequisite for practice of the *kavvanot*. According to a recent biography of the one of the last masters of this contemplative practice in Jerusalem, even after the material in Hayyim Vital's *Ez Hayyim* had been studied for ten years, an additional six years were required in order to master the *kavvanot* themselves. See Ben Zion Muzafi, *Olomo shel Zaddiq: Hayyav u-Foalo shel ha-Mequbbal ha-Zaddiq R Salman Muzafi* (Jerusalem, 1976).

34. Compare Rivka Shatz-Uffenheimer's remarks in *Hasidism as Mysticism*, pp. 217–218 (p. 130 in Hebrew edition).

35. The analogy between *Kavvanot* and opening locks makes use of a pun. The verb *kavven* can bear both the meanings of turning and directing the mind.

36. *Liqqutim Yeqarim*, 135a–135b (YDE, sect. 42).

37. *Liqqutim Yeqarim*, 135b (YDE, sect. 43).

38. For other examples of this aspect of Meshullam Feibush's thought, see, for example, his discussion on fasting and repentance. And see below, on the binding of one's prayer to the prayer of *Zaddiqim*, p. 131f.

39. Isa. 1:5.

40. *Liqqutim Yeqarim*, 135b (YDE, sect. 43).

41. Ps. 90:17.

42. Zohar, v. 2, 93b.

43. *Liqqutim Yeqarim*, 135b (YDE, sect. 43).

44. Here again, Meshullam Feibush's outlook prefigures the practice developed by R. Shneur Zalman of Liadi, whose *Sefer ha-Beynoni*, the first part of the famous *Tanya*, more fully develops a spiritual path that is specifically intended for those who are not *Zaddiqim*.

45. Lev. 19:18. The Lurianic prayer books recommend making this affirmation when one enters the prayer house. According to Altshuler, this intention was made by Yehiel Mikhel's disciples before the *Shema'*. See Altshuler, *Rabbi Meshullam Feibush Heller*, p. 92.

46. *Liqqutim Yeqarim*, 129a (YDE, sect. 33).

47. Compare, for example, the Tibetan Buddhist practice of envisioning oneself in the presence of an assembly of great Buddha's and bodhisattvas at the beginning of meditation sessions. Also the practice of meditating on the form of Buddha or a deity is common in Indian and Chinese religion.

48. *Hesed le-Avraham* (Amsterdam, 1685) *Ma'ayan* 2, *Eyn ha-Qore, Nahar* 33, p. 18a. The passage is cited by Ada Rapoport-Albert in "God and the Zaddik as the Two Focal Points of Hasidic Worship," *History of Religions* 18 (1979), p. 321. See our discussion in chapter eight "The Importance of *Zaddiqim*." Although not mentioned by Azulai, an early rabbinic saying may have influenced later visualization practices. See Palestinian Talmud, *Shabbat*, ch. 1 *Halakhah* 2: "R. Gidel said: '[when quoting a teaching], a person should always envision the sage who originated the saying as standing before him.'" This teaching is cited at least twice by Moshe Hayyim Efraim of Sudilkov in *Degel Mahaneh Efraim*. See *Va-yera* and *Hayyey Sarah*. Here the rabbinic saying is used to support the notion that Torah sages achieve immortality. Thus, a sage's eternal spiritual form (*zelem*) may be visualized by subsequent generations that preserve his teachings. However, the Azulai practice that Meshullam Feibush adopts is meant to enhance the efficacy of an ordinary person's spiritual efforts. Thus, it may closely be related to the Lurianic practice of prostrating on graves of *Zaddiqim*. See Pinhas Giller, "Recovering the Sanctity of the Galilee, The Veneration of Sacred Relics in Classical Kabbalah," in *The Journal of Jewish Thought and Philosophy*, vol. 4, pp. 147–169. Also see Krassen "Visiting Graves" in *Kabbalah*, v. 3, n. 1. Nevertheless, it seems that here, Meshullam Feibush primarily has in mind spiritual bonding with living *Zaddiqim*. In fact Altshuler understands this passage as referring specifically to an act of spiritual binding involving Yehiel Mikel of Zlotchov and his disciples. See Altshuler, *Rabbi Meshullam Feibush Heller*, pp. 87–95, 181–190. On the broader issue of the visual element in Jewish mysticism, see Elliot R. Wolfson, *Through a Speculum that Shines*.

49. *Liqqutim Yeqarim*, 129a (YDE, sect. 33).

50. *Sefer Peri Hayyim*, 39b (Lemberg, 1833), a commentary on Avot. The author, Abraham Hayyim of Zlotchov (1750–1816), was an important Hasidic leader and author in Galicia. See Altshuler, *Rabbi Meshullam Feibush Heller*, pp. 297–302. He was the son in law of R. Pinhas Horowitz of Frankfort and later of R. Issachar Ber of Zlotchov. Both of the fathers-in-law were associated with Dov Ber, the Maggid of Mezeritch, who is frequently quoted in Abraham Hayyim's writings. A direct connection between Abraham Hayyim and Yehiel Mikhel of Zlotchov is also indicated by explicit references to the latter in *Peri Hayyim*, 11d, and in *Orah le-Hayyim*, on the portion Noah. See *Mayim Rabbim*, p. 57.

51. See the important discussion of this issue in Altshuler, *Rabbi Meshullam Feibush Heller*, pp. 87–95, 181–190.

52. *Liqqutim Yeqarim*, 129a-129b (YDE, sect. 34). The final sentence is a direct quote from the passage in *Hesed le-Avraham*. See note 48.

53. On this fundamental paradox in early Hasidic thought, see Rachel Elior, "*Yesh* and *'Ayin* as Fundamental Paradigms in Hasidic Thought," [Hebrew] in

Massu'ot, edited by A. Goldreich and M. Oron (Jerusalem, 1994), pp. 53–76. An English version of this essay appears as "The Paradigms of *Yesh* and *Ayin* in Hasidic Thought," in Ada Rapoport-Albert, ed., *Hasidism Reappraised* (London, 1996), pp. 168–179.

54. *Liqqutim Yeqarim,* 129a–129b (YDE, sect. 34).

55. Compare the importance of knowing the face of *Zaddiqim* with the emphasis on awareness *(hakarah)* of the divine presence. See chapter eight, "The Importance of *Zaddiqim.*"

56. According to the principle of *gematria* (esoteric numerology), words whose consonants are equal in numerical value may bear an esoteric connection. In this case, love is *'aHaVaH,* i.e., 1+5+2+5=13. One is *'eHaD,* i.e. 1+8+4=13. Therefore love implies union.

57. *Liqqutim Yeqarim,* 130a (YDE, sect. 34).

58. That is, he does not have more esoteric *kavvanot* in mind when he prays.

59. On the importance of the letters, see below, pp. 135f.

60. This level of prayer is insignificant compared to ones in which the mind is full of awe and love and supernal *kavvanot.*

61. Ps.115:17. *Liqqutim Yeqarim,* 130a (YDE, sect. 34).

62. The analogy is quoted in the name of "the late *Zaddiq,* our Teacher and Master, Issachar Ber, of blessed memory, of our community, who said [it] in the name of his teacher, R. Mendel." In all probability he is Issachar Ber of Zlotchov, the father-in-law of Abraham Hayyim of Zlotchov (see note 50) and author of *Sefer Mevasser Zadeq,* who died in the Land of Israel. See Altshuler, *Rabbi Meshullam Feibush Heller,* pp. 13–14, 322–323.

63. *Liqqutim Yeqarim,* 130a (YDE, sect. 34).

64. See, e.g., Zohar, v. 3, 124a, *Ra'aya Maheymna.* Also see Hayyim Vital's annotations on Zohar, v. 2, 121b.

65. Another possible translation: "even if it is something not permissable."

66. *Liqqutim Yeqarim,* 130a (YDE, sect. 34).

67. See chapter three, "Cosmological Bases of Meshullam Feibush's Concept of *Devequt.*"

68. The idea that creation occurred through divine speech by means of ten utterances is rabbinic. It was adopted by the Kabbalists and became an important symbolic basis for representing the process of emanation in the World of *Sefirot.*

69. See *Sefer Yezirah,* ch. 2, *mishnah* 3.

70. Song of Songs 5:6.

71. Meshullam Feibush seems to have chapter 10 of the Gate of Holiness in mind. However, the passage which follows is not a direct quotation.

72. On the letters of the Tetragrammaton, see Idel, *Hasidism: Between Ecstasy and Magic,* pp. 59 and 278, n. 73.

73. *Liqqutim Yeqarim,* 131b (YDE, sect. 37).

74. See Zohar, v. 2, 93b.

75. *Liqqutim Yeqarim,* 131b (YDE, sect. 37).

76. *Liqqutim Yeqarim*, 131b–132a (YDE, sect. 37). Also see Idel, *Hasidism: Between Ecstasy and Magic*, pp. 159–160. Idel cites another Hasidic text from R. Jacob Joseph of Polnoy which also compares the body to the form of the letters. Idel derives this idea from sixteenth-century kabbalist, Solomon Alkabetz. See Idel, Ibid., p. 345, n. 90.

77. Ibid. A very similar passage is found in a sixteenth-century text written by the Safedian kabbalist, Solomon Alkabetz. See Ms. Oxford Neubauer 1663 fol. 169b, quoted by Idel, "Perceptions of Kabbalah in the Second Half of the Eighteenth Century."

78. Meshullam Feibush borrows the theory of *ruhaniyut* of the letters of prayer and Torah from the Kabbalah of Moses Cordovero, which he knows from Cordovero's *Pardes Rimmonim*, Gate of the Letters and Isaiah Horowitz's commentary on the prayer book, *Sha'ar ha-Shamayim*. However, the theory is much older and probably originated in Sabian Arabic Texts. It was an important feature of the school of Abraham Abulafia since the thirteenth century. In the Kabbalah of Safed, it was emphasized in Cordovero's school. However, it is also found in texts of Cordovero's teacher, Solomon Alkabetz. For a discussion of this issue, see Moshe Idel, *Hasidism: Between Ecstasy and Magic*, pp. 156–160. Also see Shlomo Pines, "On the Term *Ruhaniyyut* and Its Sources and on Judah Halevi's Doctrine," in *Tarbiz* 57 (1988): 511–540.

79. Or, perhaps, "with a sincere thought." The meaning is, at any rate, that the mind has to be concentrating on the words of the prayer.

80. *Liqqutim Yeqarim*, 134a (YDE, sect. 37).

81. See chapter seven, "Meshullam Feibush and the Maggid of Mezeritch."

82. *Liqqutim Yeqarim*, 134a (YDE, sect. 41).

83. The symbolism seems to refer to a transformation that occurs to the *parzuf, Ze'ir Anpin*, during prayer. This *parzuf*, although formed primarily from the six *sefirot* from *Hesed* to *Yesod*, takes on three higher *sefirot, Hokhmah, Binah*, and *Da'at*, which are called the three brains. However, to the best of my knowledge, the term *reshimu* or "impression" only occurs in the cosmogonic context of the *zimzum* and *shevirat ha-kelim* in the Lurianic writings. Since Meshullam Feibush brings this passage in the name of Dov Ber, the appropriation of this term in order to describe a state of mind after prayer may be an innovation of the Maggid of Mezeritch. However, I have yet to locate the source in his writings. It should also be noted, that the term *roshem* is associated with prayer in the kabbalistic writings of Moshe Cordovero which may indeed have influenced Meshullam Feibush in this context more than the Lurianic material. See Bracha Sack, "Prayer in the Teachings of R. Moshe Cordovero" [Hebrew], *Da'at* 9, pp. 5–12.

84. *Liqqutim Yeqarim*, 134a (YDE, sect. 41).

85. Ibid.

86. See Idel, *Hasidism: Between Ecstasy and Magic*, pp. 171–188. Also see Weiss, "Torah Study in Early Hasidism," in *Studies in East European Jewish Mysticism*, pp. 56–68. Weiss's article is seriously flawed by conclusions based on

his attribution of the pamphlet, *Darkhey Yesharim* to Menahem Mendel of Premishlan. See Rivka Schatz-Uffenheimer's chapter, "The Problem of Torah Study in
Hasidism" in *Hasidism as Mysticism*, pp. 310-325 (pp. 157-167 in the Hebrew edition). Also see Altshuler, *Rabbi Meshullam Feibush Heller*, pp. 231–252.

87. *Liqqutim Yeqarim*, 133a (YDE, sect. 39).

88. See chapter two, "Sources of *Devequt* in Early Hasidism."

89. Meshullam Feibush does not specifically identify these kabbalists. The
question of their identity is taken up in the chapter eight, "The Importance of
Zaddiqim."

90. Ps. 19:8.

91. *Liqqutim Yeqarim*, 112b–113a (YDE, sect. 8).

92. Isa. 5:21.

93. *Tiqquney Zohar, Tiqqun 6*, 22a.

94. *Liqqutim Yeqarim*, 113a (YDE, sect. 8).

95. Leviticus Rabbah, 27:1

96. Literally, "for its own sake," See pp. 142–143 below for a discussion of the
various meanings that Meshullam Feibush applies to this early rabbinic concept.

97. Josh. 1:8.

98. The literal meaning of the verse is "upon it," i.e. upon the Torah. However,
since Hebrew has no specific form for the neuter, the word *bo* "upon it," can also be
read "upon him," i.e. upon the divinity, itself.

99. *Liqqutim Yeqarim*, 114b (YDE, sect. 10).

100. See note 95.

101. B. T., *Nazir*, 34b.

102. Ps. 45:14.

103. Ibid.

104. Ibid.

105. Prov. 16:5.

106. Ibid., 3:34.

107. *Liqqutim Yeqarim*, 114b (YDE, sect. 10).

108. See chapter four, "The Barrier to Divine Aid." Also see Altshuler, *Rabbi
Meshullam Feibush Heller*, pp. 219–224. Altshuler cites a legend concerning Yehiel
Mikhel of Zlotchov in which the latter is depicted as fulfilling Meshullam Feibush's
teaching cited above.

109. This position is virtually the same as the one expoused by Hasidism's arch-
rival, Elijah, the Gaon of Vilna. See Immanuel Etkes, *Rabbi Israel Salanter and the
Beginning of the 'Musar' Movement* [Hebrew] (Jerusalem: Magnes, 1984), pp. 31ff.

110. Avot, 6:1.

111. Ibid, 6:6.

112. An idolatrous practice.

113. Prov. 26:8. B. T., *Hulin*, 133a. Meshullam Feibush slightly misquotes the text.

114. Mishnah, Sanhedrin, ch. 7, mishnah 6.

115. See note 110.

116. *Liqqutim Yeqarim*, 112b (YDE, sect. 7).

117. Zohar, v. 3, 53b.

118. The notion that the letters of the Torah constitute the name of God is an early kabbalistic idea. This notion was also sometimes combined with the idea that God and His name were identical. And thus the Torah can be identified with God as in the Zohar. See Gershom Scholem, "The Meaning of the Torah in Jewish Mysticism," in *On the Kabbalah and its Symbolism* (New York: Schocken, 1965), pp. 37–44. Also see Krassen, *Isaiah Horowitz*, pp. 64–98.

119. *Liqqutim Yeqarim*, 111a (YDE, sect. 3).

120. Prov. 7:4.

121. Ibid, 31:10.

122. *Liqqutim Yeqarim*, 113b (YDE, sect. 9).

123. Prov. 2:6.

124. *Liqqutim Yeqarim*, 113b (YDE, sect. 9).

125. Ibid.

126. See Mishnah Gittin, 3:1.

127. *Orah Hayyim*, 1:1.

128. Ps. 16:8.

129. *Liqqutim Yeqarim*, 113b (YDE, sect. 9).

130. See *Liqqutim Yeqarim*, 114a. In maintaining that Torah study *she-lo lishemah* is indeed a transgression, Meshullam Feibush follows the position stated in *Sheney Luhot ha-Berit*, tractate Shavuot.

131. Prov. 30:5.

132. *Liqqutim Yeqarim*, 113b (YDE, sect. 9).

133. The Bible is conventionally referred to as the written Torah. The Talmud and other rabbinic writings are designated as "oral Torah," even though they exist in written form.

134. Palestinian Talmud, *Peah*, ch. 1, *halakhah* 1.

135. Zohar, v. 2, 82b.

136. *Liqqutim Yeqarim* 123b (YDE, sect. 24).

137. Ibid.

138. A rabbinic term for esoteric studies based on the vision of the throne in the first chapter of Ezekiel.

139. B. T., *Sukkah* 28a.

140. Isa. 40:6. Gate of Love, end of chapter 8.

141. *Liqqutim Yeqarim*, 113a–113b (YDE, sect. 8).

142. Or, perhaps, "and does not pertain to God."

143. *Liqqutim Yeqarim*, 113b (YDE, sect. 8).

144. Two important texts by R. Joseph Gikatilla. *Sha'arey Orah* is based on the Kabbalah of the *sefirot* and is similar in method to the Zohar. See Avi Weinstein's English translation, R. Joseph Gikatilla, *Gates of Light* (San Francisco: Harper, 1994). *Ginat Egoz* was written earlier when Gikatilla was under the influence of Abraham Abulafia. See Efraim Gottlieb, "The Kabbalah in the Writings of R. Joseph

Gikatilla and in *Sefer Ma'arekhet ha-Elohut*," [Hebrew] in *Studies in the Kabbala* [sic] *Literature* (Tel Aviv: Tel Aviv University Press, 1976), pp. 257–343.

145. *Liqqutim Yeqarim*, 132b (YDE, sect. 39).

146. The concluding prayer.

147. *Liqqutim Yeqarim*, 112b (YDE, sect. 38).

148. For a discussion concerning the polemic against this Hasidic practice, see Jacobs, *Hasidic Prayer*, pp. 140–153.

149. *Liqqutim Yeqarim*, 132b (YDE, sect. 39).

150. Ibid (YDE, sect. 38).

151. See chapter two, "Barriers to Divine Aid."

152. That is, to study *li-shemah*. See above, pp. 142–144.

153. *Liqqutim Yeqarim*, 133a (YDE, sect. 39).

154. Although Meshullam Feibush asserts that all of the holy days and festivals present unique opportunities for *devequt*, his discussion is limited to the Sabbath, Days of Awe, and Sukkot. See *Liqqutim Yeqarim*, 144b (YDE, sect. 57).

155. See *Liqqutim Yeqarim*, 136a–136b (YDE, sect. 45).

156. The notion that creation involved a diminution of the divine light is typical of both Lurianic and Cordoverian Kabbalah. According to the Lurianic system, creation required an initial act of divine contraction, *zimzum*. The divine essence and light was withdrawn in order to make room for creation. See Scholem, "The Doctrine of Creation in Lurianic Kabbalah," in *Kabbalah*, pp. 128–135. Cordovero's less dualistic system emphasizes a continuity between the creator and creation that extends to all levels. However, creation occurs paradoxically. Every act of revelation involves concealment. The divine light is progressively revealed to lower levels of creation by increasingly dense "garments." See Ben-Shlomo, *The Mystical Theology of Moses Cordovero* [Hebrew], pp. 95–100. For a more comprehensive discussion of *zimzum* in Cordovero's thought, see Sack, *The Kabbalah of Rabbi Moshe Cordovero* [Hebrew], pp. 57–82. The Hasidic Interpretation of *zimzum* is expressed anthropologically. God, as it were, reduces the divine intellect so that it can exist within the minds of human *Zaddiqim*. See, e.g., Schatz-Uffenheimer's critical edition of *Maggid Devarav le-Ya'aqov*, sect. 1, p. 9.

157. *Liqqutim Yeqarim*, 137a (YDE, sect. 45).

158. In the Lurianic system a ray of divine light is projected into the vacated space after the *zimzum*. However, this event is not necessarily associated with *Shabbat*. In the Zohar, *Shabbat* is governed by the divine *sefirot*, whereas the days of the week depend on a lower source, the angel Metatron. See Tishby, *Wisdom of the Zohar*, v. 3: 1226. Meshullam Feibush may have in mind a Zoharic myth that justifies beginning the eve of the Sabbath early. According to the *Zohar*, vol. 1: 14a, the demons were created on the eve of the Sabbath. Had their creation been completed, the world would not have been able to remain in existence. So God began the first Sabbath early, before the demons could find bodies. Consequently, the Sabbath saved the world from destruction. See Tishby, *Wisdom of Zohar*, pp. 1227–1228. Also see Elliot K. Ginsburg, *Sod Ha-Shabbat (The Mystery of the Sabbath)* (Albany: State

University of New York, 1989), pp. 23–24, and Ginsburg, *The Sabbath in the Classical Kabbalah* (Albany: State University of New York, 1989), p. 95. Another possible Zoharic source is *Tiqquney Zohar, haqdamah,* 11a. Here the additional Sabbath soul (see below) restores the divine splendor lost to man through Adam's sin. See Tishby, *Wisdom of Zohar,* pp. 1230–1233.

159. Meshullam Feibush's hasidic conception of *Shabbat* emphasizes the increased opportunity for *devequt* rather than specific kabbalistic transformations that occur in the upper worlds.

160. *Liqqutim Yeqarim,* 137a (YDE, sect. 45).

161. Prayer book. From the blessings before the *shema'.*

162. *Liqqutim Yeqarim,* 138b (YDE, sect. 48).

163. See Ginsburg, *The Sabbath in the Classical Kabbalah,* pp. 78–101.

164. On *Shabbat* as sacred time, see Arthur Green, "Sabbath as Temple: Some Thoughts on Space and Time in Judaism," in *Go and Study: Essays and Studies in Honor of A. Jospe,* edited by S. Fishman and R. Jospe (Washington, D.C.: B'nai Brith Hillel Foundations, 1980), pp. 287–305.

165. That is, the name *Shabbat* is derived from the root *shuv* which means "to return."

166. Most of these ideas are typical of Medieval Jewish Philosophy. See, e.g., Maimonides, *Mishneh Torah, Hilkhot Yesodey Torah,* ch. 1.

167. *Liqqutim Yeqarim,* 137b (YDE, sect. 46).

168. This recalls the Lurianic concept of *zimzum* (withdrawal or contraction) followed by *hitpashtut* (emanation). A ray of the divine must be returned to the locus from which it has been removed, so that creation will not be entirely separated from the divine source. However, Meshullam Feibush interprets the concepts anthropologically.

169. That is, they exist because they are cleaving to God who is eternal existence and because they are fulfilling His will.

170. *Liqqutim Yeqarim,* 137b (YDE, sect. 46).

171. Zohar, v. 2., 135a. The passage is included in the Hasidic version of the Sefardi liturgy which is recited before the Friday evening prayers.

172. Isa. 66:1.

173. *Liqqutim Yeqarim,* 137b–138a (YDE, sect. 47).

174. See Tishby, *Wisdom of the Zohar,* vol. 3: 1223–1226. Also see Ginsburg, *The Sabbath in the Classical Kabbalah,* pp. 101–121.

175. Meshullam Feibush interprets literally an expression that means "eternal covenant."

176. Zohar, v. 2., 137b.

177. *Tiqqun* 6, 21a.

178. *Liqqutim Yeqarim,* 138a (YDE, sect. 47).

179. On the association of the "canopy of peace" and Shabbat, see Ginsburg, *The Sabbath in the Classical Kabbalah,* pp. 33, 129, 131, 169, 171, 185, 214, 230. The "Canopy of peace" (*sukkat shalom*) is associated with the *Shekhinah* in the

Zohar. Meshullam Feibush's etymological interpretation, which emphasizes the possibility of *devequt*, does not appear in any of the earlier kabbalistic examples cited by Ginsburg.

180. *Liqqutim Yeqarim*, 138b (YDE, sect. 48).

181. This notion already appears in Zohar, v. 3, 242b (*Ra'aya Meheymna*). See Tishby, *Wisdom of the Zohar*, vol. 3: 1231. Also see Ginsburg, *The Sabbath in the Classical Kabbalah*, p. 128.

182. B. T., *Beyzah*, 16a and repeated verbatim in *Ta'anit* 27b. Although the additional Sabbath-soul is mentioned only once in rabbinic literature, it became an important kabbalistic motif in the works of Moshe de Leon and the Zoharic writings. However, its usage does not seem to have become widespread until the dissemination of the Zohar. See Ginsburg, Ibid., pp. 121–126, esp. p. 125.

183. *Liqqutim Yeqarim*, 140a (YDE, sect. 52).

184. Ibid.

185. In *Sefer Sheney Luhot Ha-Berit*, Isaiah Horowitz warns that overindulgence in the physical pleasures of *Shabbat* can interfere with *devequt*. However, he emphasizes Torah study rather than prayer as essential. See *Sheney Luhot Ha-Berit, Massekhet Shabbat* (Warsaw, 1862), 97d–98a.

186. Zohar, v. 2, 205a. Meshullam Feibush slightly misquotes the text.

187. Isaiah Horowitz notes in his commentary on the prayer book, *Sha'ar Ha-Shamayim*, that according to the Lurianic *kavvanot*, "one should intend to receive the additional *nefesh* when Shabbat enters, i.e., when one says 'Come, O Bride,' the additional *ruah* during the '*borekhu*,' and the additional *neshamah* when [one says] 'spread the canopy of peace over us.'"

188. *Liqqutim Yeqarim*, 140a (YDE, sect. 52).

189. Ps. 36:10.

190. *Liqqutim Yeqarim*, 139b (YDE, sect. 51).

191. See chapter five, "The Problem of Corporeality: Conditions for *Devequt*."

192. *Liqqutim Yeqarim*, 139b-140a (YDE, sect. 51).

193. Ps. 118:24.

194. Zohar, v. 3, 105a. *Liqqutim Yeqarim*, 140a (YDE, sect. 51).

195. Most of these ideas already appear in the *Zohar*. See Tishby's discussion of the High Holy Days in *Wisdom of the Zohar*, pp. 1238–1248. In the zoharic passages where the sacred calendar is related to the *sefirot*, New Year's Day is invariably associated with the divine attribute, *Gevurah*. See, e.g., Zohar, v. 1: 226b; *Tiqquney Zohar, Tiqqun* 6, 22a, *Tiqqun* 21, 54b. *Gevurah* is characteristically associated with divine judgment in the *Zohar*. The rabbinic notion that the High Holy days are occasions of divine judgment and call for *teshuvah* (repentance) is echoed in the *Zohar*. See Zohar, v. 3: 95a. The *Zohar* explains the association of judgment and the New Year on the basis of several earlier rabbinic *midrashim*. According to one of these, Adam was created, judged, and repented on New Year's Day. See Zohar, v. 3: 100b. (Compare Tishby, *Wisdom of the Zohar*, pp. 1243–1246.) The reduction of divine light that occurs during New Year's Day is related in Zohar, v. 3: 100b, to the fact that

New Year's Day coincides with the New Moon. The *Zohar's* discussion is based on a rabbinic midrash in B. T., *Beyzah*, 16a. The notion that the world is full of fear at this time is also explained in the *Zohar*. The entire period of "the days of repentance, " i.e., from New Year's to the Day of Atonement, is conceived as the time when the male and female aspects of God prepare for a *hieros gamos* that is consummated at the end of the *Sukkot* festival. On each day, a stage of this process occurs. On New Year's Day, the divine male's left arm beckons to the female. In the zoharic symbolism, the left arm is associated with judgment and the *sefirah, Gevurah*. Humans respond with fear when the divine left arm is aroused. See Zohar, v. 3: 214b. (Compare Tishby, *Wisdom of Zohar*, p. 1241). The association of New Year's Day with judgment and *Gevurah* is also prominent in the Lurianic *kavvanot*. According to the Lurianic myth, which is itself based on the zoharic *hieros gamos* myth, the period from New Year's to the Day of Atonement chiefly involves the building of the female *parzuf, Nuqba*. On New Year's Day, the cosmos returns to its original state. At that time the female first emerged from the "side of *Gevurah*" and was joined to her male consort, back-to-back. This mode of union is associated with judgment. See *Sha'ar Ha-Kavvanot*, 89d.

196. See *Liqqutim Yeqarim*, 140a (YDE, sect. 52).

197. The distinction between two types of *yir'ah* is typical of Jewish ethical literature, since the Middle Ages. The first to make this distinction was, apparently, Bahya Ibn Pekudah in *Sefer Hovot Ha-Levavot*. In the last chapter of that work, the Gate of Love of God, Bahya distinguished between *yir'ah* as fear of punishment and as awe before the divine majesty. The latter is considered the higher level. See Tishby's discussion of fear, love, and *devequt, Wisdom of the Zohar*, v. 2: 974–998. For a more comprehensive discussion of fear and love in medieval Jewish thought, see G. Vajda, *L'Amour de Dieu dans la theologie juive du moyen age* (Paris, 1957), pp. 73–140.

198. Compare, Mircea Eliade, *The Myth of the Eternal Return or, Cosmos and History* (Princeton: Bollinger, 1971).

199. The name "*Elohim*" is understood in rabbinic thought to indicate a manifestation of divine judgment. In Kabbalistic thought this attribute is associated with restriction. See below.

200. Gen. 1:1.

201. *Liqqutim Yeqarim*, 140b (YDE, sect. 53).

202. On *zimzum* in Cordoverian Kabbalah, see Ben-Shlomo, *The Mystical Theology of Moses Cordovero* [Hebrew], pp. 98–100. Ben-Shlomo notes on p. 100, that in the context of the beginning of creation, Cordovero's usage of the term *zimzum* is diametrically opposed to that of Isaac Luria. However, see Sack's more definitive discussion in *The Kabbalah of Rabbi Moshe Cordovero* [Hebrew], pp. 57–82. See also, Scholem, *Sabbatai Sevi*, pp. 28–32 and ibid, *Kabbalah*, pp. 129–135. However, a usage of the term in Cordovero's Kabbalah that is similar to Luria's does appear in the context of the *Or Hozer* (returning light). This is indeed the context with which Meshullam Feibush is concerned. See below. Also see, Idel, *Hasidism: Between Ecstasy and Magic*, pp. 89–95.

203. *Reishit Hokhmah*, v. 1: 59, Gate of Awe, ch. 2, sect. 15.

204. Ps. 48:5–7.

205. See Moses Cordovero, *Tefillah le-Moshe* (Premishl, 1892), 150b–152a, Gate 7, sect. 5.

206. *Liqqutim Yeqarim*, 140b (YDE, sect. 53).

207. See Zohar, v. 1., 15a. On *Bozina de-qardinuta*, see Yehudah Liebes, *Sections of the Zohar Lexicon* [Hebrew] (Jerusalem: Hebrew University, 1976), pp. 145–151, 161–164. Elliot R. Wolfson has also discussed gender aspects of this concept in several places, See Wolfson, *Through a Speculum that Shines*, p. 382, n. 204.

208. Cordovero discusses the *Or Hozer* in *Pardes Rimmonim* Gate 15: "From Below to Above." For a discussion of *Or Hozer* in the Kabbalah of Cordovero and its similarity to the concept of *zimzum* in the Kabbalah of Isaac Luria, see Ben-Shlomo, *Mystical Theology of Moses Cordovera*, pp. 270–272. The *Or Hozer*, which is a weakened reflection of the direct light (*Or Yashar*) of emanation is necessary for completing creation since the direct light is too powerful for the created vessels to bear. On the association of *Or Hozer* and judgment, see Ben-Shlomo, Ibid., pp. 272–274. Also see Sack, *The Kabbalah of Rabbi Moshe Cordovero* [Hebrew], pp. 143ff.

209. Ps. 48:6.

210. *Liqqutim Yeqarim*, 140b (YDE, sect. 53).

211. *Liqqutim Yeqarim*, 141a (YDE, sect. 53).

212. Zohar, v. 1, 15a. on the "black spark" (*bozina' de-qardinuta'*) see note 207 above.

213. *Liqqutim Yeqarim*, 141a (YDE, sect. 53).

214. The use of human pregnancy as an analogy for cosmic processes and transformations is very typical of Lurianic Kabbalah.

215. This expression appears in the liturgy of the *Musaf* (additional) *Amidah* for New Year's.

216. The tradition that the world was created on the first of Tishri is attributed to Rabbi Eliezer in B.T., *Rosh Ha-Shanah*, 11a. However, in the *Midrash Rabbah*, *Va-Yiqra*, ch. 29, 1, R. Eliezer states that creation actually began on the 25th of Elul. Consequently, creation was completed on the sixth day, the first of Tishri, when Adam was created. (See Rabbi David Luria's note on the beginning of *Pirqey de-Rabbi Eliezer*, ch. 8.) R. Meir Ibn Gabbai refers to these traditions in his commentary on the secrets of the New Year's liturgy. He states that on this day "the pregnancy of the world was completed." See *Tola'at Ya'aqov, Sod Tefillat Rosh Ha-Shanah*, 36d:

> On the 25th of Elul the world was created. On the sixth day, which corresponds to New Year's the first man was created. On that very day he was judged and he emerged free from sin (on the second day of New Year's). Consequently, this day has been established as a day of judgment for all generations.

Isaiah Horowitz essentially repeats Ibn Gabbai's remarks on "this is the day the world was born" in his commentary on the prayer book, *Sha'ar Ha-Shamayim*, 296a.

However, the explicit analogy of physical pregnancy, which Meshullam Feibush employs, is closer to Lurianic conceptions. See, e.g., Shabbetai of Rashkov's *Siddur Ha-Ari*, pt. 3, 75a: "The term *harat* (birth of) is related to *herayon* (pregnancy) . . . on Tishri, the *ibbur* (formation of the embryo) occurred . . ."

217. *Liqqutim Yeqarim*, 141a (YDE, sect. 53).

218. Ibid.

219. The New Year's liturgy includes the request, "inscribe us for life in the book of life."

220. *Liqqutim Yeqarim*, 141b (YDE, sect. 54).

221. Deut. 32:15. *Liqqutim Yeqarim*, ibid.

222. Although *zimzum* involves a contraction or withholding of divine mercy, the very act of contraction is really an expression of mercy since it reduces judgment to a measure that can be tolerated.

223. *Liqqutim Yeqarim*, 141b–142a (YDE, sect. 55).

224. Ibid.

225. Early Hasidic teachings strongly caution against excessive sadness. See Schatz-Uffenheimer, *Hasidism as Mysticism*, pp. 93–111 (pp. 41–53 in the Hebrew edition). Nevertheless, the idea that God can only enter and redeem a "broken heart" is also typical. See, e.g., the text from *Degel Mahaneh Efraim, Va-ethanan*, that is translated by Joseph Dan in *The Teachings of Hasidism* (New York: Behrman, 1983), p. 55.

226. Literally the other side," a kabbalistic term for the forces of evil which are opposite to the side of holiness. See Tishby, *Wisdom of the Zohar*, pp. 447–546.

227. *Liqqutim Yeqarim*, 142a (YDE, sect. 55).

228. See Zohar, v. 3: 122a in the *Ra'aya Meheymna*. The *Zohar* associates the Day of Atonement with the *sefirah, Binah*. See sources concerning the sacred calendar and the *sefirot* that are mentioned in note 194. Although *Din* (judgment) is generally associated with the *sefirah, Gevurah*, its roots are in *Binah* which is also located on the left side of the sefirotic tree, the side of judgment. On the Day of Atonement, judgments are sweetened. As a result, cosmic harmony is restored and all the *sefirot* return to their proper places. When this process is complete, *Binah*, the source from which all the lower *sefirot* emerge, also returns to its place. Thus *Binah* is called "*teshuvah shelemah*" (complete return). See *Zohar*, v. 3: 55b. *Binah* is also compared in the zoharic writings to Noah's ark. It is the place where all *ba'aley teshuvah* take refuge. See *Tiqquney Zohar*, 6, 22a; 21, 54b, 60a. For a summary of the Day of Atonement in the zoharic writings, see Tishby, *Wisdom of the Zohar*, v. 3: 1246–1248. The centrality of *Binah, Din*, and *teshuvah* also appears in Meir Ibn Gabbai's *Tola'at Ya'aqov*. See, e.g., *Sitrey Yom Ha-Kippurim*, 39a. "The Day of Atonement is the day when the supernal light from which all other lights shine is revealed. It is the mystery of the 'world-to-come.'" (The 'world-to-come' is a common image associated with the *sefirah, Binah*, in the Zohar). On this day, the forces of judgment, represented by the sins, which might otherwise be expected to testify against Israel, are converted into advocates, by means of the scapegoat. "But only a

person whose soul is clean can enter this world. Accordingly, Israel has to clean their souls on the day that is like a day of souls. Cleanliness of soul means to return in *teshuvah shelemah* (perfect repentance). . . . The efficacy of the Day of Atonement prayers depends on *teshuvah*.

229. *Liqqutim Yeqarim*, 142a (YDE, sect. 55).

230. *Liqqutim Yeqarim*, 142b (YDE, sect. 55).

231. Ibid., 143a (YDE, sect. 56).

232. Ibid.

7. Meshullam Feibush and the Maggid of Mezeritch

1. *Liqqutim Yeqarim*, 134a (YDE, sect. 41).

2. See index to Schatz-Uffenheimer's critical edition of *Maggid Devarav le-Ya'aqov*, p. 382. This may be evidence to support Altshuler's view that the manuscripts reflect Yehiel Mikhel's teachings and that the attribution to Dov Ber in some cases is only camouflage. See Altshuler, *Rabbi Meshullam Feibush Heller*, pp. 67–82. Another interesting use of the term is found in the writings of Dov Ber's disciple, Hayyim Haikel of Amdur. See Schatz-Uffenheimer, *Hasidism as Mysticism*, pp. 20–211 (pp. 125–126 in Hebrew edition).

3. See, for example, Schatz-Uffenheimer, *Maggid Devarav le-Ya'aqov*, sect. 161.

4. Ps. 145:9.

5. *Liqqutim Yeqarim*, 124a (YDE, sect. 25).

6. Schatz-Uffenheimer, *Maggid Devarav le-Ya'aqov*, sect. 102: 181.

7. See pp. 166–168 below.

8. See the discussion of this midrash in the preceding chapter six.

9. *Liqqutim Yeqarim*, 114b (YDE, sect. 10).

10. Prov. 13:16.

11. Gen. 4:1.

12. 1 Chron. 28:9.

13. Schatz-Uffenheimer, *Maggid Devarav le-Ya'aqov*, sect. 181: 281–282.

14. *Liqqutim Yeqarim*, 124b (YDE, sect. 26).

15. Ps. 118:20.

16. *Liqqutim Yeqarim*, 117b–118a (YDE, sect. 15).

17. The problem of how to distinguish genuine from inauthentic religious emotion especially concerned the leaders of Habad Hasidism. See Louis Jacobs, *On Ecstasy: A Tract by Dobh Baer of Lubavitch* (New York: Rossel, 1983). Also see Elior, *The Paradoxical Ascent*.

18. Literally: "red bile."

19. Literally, "female waters," a Lurianic term for a spiritual process that ascends from below. In general, it also refers to a spiritual arousal that is initiated by humanity rather than by God. Here the meaning is that God must be the source of the awe. It must be a case of *Mayyin Dukhrin* (male waters), i.e., from above to

below. For Cordovero's account of *Mayyin Dukhrin* and *Mayyin Nuqbin*, see *Pardes Rimmonim*, Gate 8, chapter 19.

20. *Liqqutim Yeqarim*, 71–7b, sect. 42.

21. Awe is here associated with *Malkhut* which is considered female, while *YHVH*, which is associated with love, is the male. Thus, the meaning is that if the female divine presence (*Shekhinah*) is manifested through awe, her male consort, or love, can be counted on to follow after her.

22. Schatz-Uffenheimer, *Maggid Devarav le-Ya'aqov*, pp. 97–98 (sect. 61).

23. It is important to note that Meshullam Feibush does not rely exclusively on Dov Ber's teachings concerning annihilation and detachment from the body. He also cites Yehiel Mikhel of Zlotchov (*Liqqutim Yeqarim*, 117b, YDE, sect. 14), and Menachem Mendel of Premishlan (*Liqqutim Yeqarim*, 118a, YDE, sect. 14) as sources of these ideas. In fact, it seems to be the case that their somewhat more extreme approach has influenced him decisively here.

24. A kabbalistic designation for the *Shekhinah* (divine presence). See *Reishit Hokhmah ha-Shalem*, Gate of Love, ch. 4, p. 408. "For Leah, the supernal mother gave birth to six sons and one daughter. And this daughter is the *Shekhinah*."

25. *Liqqutim Yeqarim*, 118a (YDE, sect. 15).

26. See B.T., *Temurah*, 31a.

27. Ps. 104:24.

28. Kohelet 3:20.

29. Ibid.

30. Avot, 6:1. *Liqqutim Yeqarim*, 116a–117a (YDE, sect. 13).

31. See, for example, Schatz-Uffenheimer, *Maggid Devarav le-Ya'aqov*, sects. 56, 60, 78, 178, 180.

32. See, for example, ibid, p. 91, sect. 60.

33. Ibid. Nor is he interested in the Maggid's identification of *Hyle* with the primordial intellect (*qadmut ha-sekhel*), see ibid, sect. 180.

34. Ps. 104:24.

35. Schatz-Uffenheimer, *Maggid Devarav la-Ya'aqov*, p. 134, sect. 78.

36. See *Liqqutim Yeqarim*, 137a–138a (YDE, sect. 47).

37. Mishnah, *Avot*, 6:1.

38. Two passages in which Dov Ber interprets this mishnah appear in *Or Torah*, p. 240b, sect. 419 and p. 217a, sect. 453. And compare *Liqqutim Yeqarim*, 14b, sect 76 and p. 61a, sect. 201. In both cases the meaning is that when one reaches the level of learning Torah *li-shemah*, he is constantly filled with words of Torah.

39. See Schatz-Uffenheimer, *Maggid Devarav le-Ya'aqov*, p. 209, sect. 123.

40. See *Liqqutim Yeqarim*, 120b (YDE, sect. 19).

41. In addition to his more explicit explanation of the Gemara and addition of Kohelet 3:20 as a proof text, he adds the term, *Tohu*, as a symbol for *Hyle*. This does not appear in any of the Maggid's texts.

42. *Liqqutim Yeqarim*, 117a (YDE, sect. 13).

43. Schatz-Uffenheimer, *Maggid Devarav le-Ya'aqov*, sect. 24, pp. 38–39.

44. See chapter three, "Cosmological Bases for Meshullam Feibush's Theory of *Devequt.*"

45. The passage cited appears in a context that also contains important teachings from Yehiel Mikhel of Zlotchov, Menahem Mendel of Premishian, and *Sefer Sheney Luhot ha-Berit.* For a discussion of these texts, see chapter three "Cosmological Bases for Meshullam Feibush's Theory of *Devequt.*"

46. See Rashi's comment on Gen. 2:2. The midrash is also cited in his commentary on B.T., *Megillah*, 9a. And compare *Bereishit Rabbah* 10:9. The Hasidic interpretation is also brought in the name of Dov Ber by Abraham Hayyim of Zlotchov in yet another context. See *Orah le-Hayyim*, *Va-Yehi*, 92b–93a, in the comment on "*Issachar is a stong-boned ass.*" Since the exact content of the manuscripts which were in Meshullam Feibush's possession has not yet been determined, it is conceivable that his text may not have contained the Maggid's teaching within the context published in *Maggid Devarav le-Ya'aqov.*" However, Rivka Schatz-Uffenheimer's critical edition makes no mention of the existence of such a variant within the extant manuscripts.

47. B.T., *Shabbat*, 118b.

48. Schatz-Uffenheimer, *Maggid Devarav le-Ya'aqov*, p. 156, sect. 90.

49. Gen. 2:2.

50. *Liqqutim Yeqarim*, 116b (YDE, sect. 45).

51. See our discussion of *Shabbat* in "The Remedy," pp. 149–154.

52. *Liqqutim Yeqarim*, 137a (YDE, sect. 45).

53. Indeed these ideas are typical of early Kabbalah and are developed in the Zohar. What is typical of Dov Ber's thought is the use of these terms to indicate psychological dimensions which are experienced during contemplative prayer. See Schatz-Uffenheimer, *Hasidism as Mysticism*, pp. 204–214 (pp. 121–128 in Hebrew version). Also see, Idel, *Hasidism: Between Ecstasy and Magic*, pp. 227–238.

54. See note 51.

55. See Schatz-Uffenheimer, *Maggid Devarav le-Ya'aqov*, pp. 155–158, sect. 90.

56. On Gershon of Lutzk (d. 1788), see Isaac Alfasi, *Encyclopedia le-Hasidut, Ishim* vol. 1, col. 405.

57. See B.T., *Hagigah*, 12a. the passage from the Gemara is not quoted literally.

58. The midrash in *Hagigah*, 12a states:

R. Eleazar said: [with] the light that the Holy One, blessed be He, created on the first day, Adam used to see from one end of the world to the other. When the Holy One, blessed be He [fore]saw the generation of the flood and the generation of Babel and saw their twisted deeds, He went and concealed it from them. . . . And for whom did He conceal it? For the *Zaddiqim* of the future . . .

59. Prov. 2:4.

60. *Liqqutim Yeqarim*, 111a (YDE, sect. 3).

61. Ibid.

62. See, for example, Schatz-Uffenheimer, *Maggid Devarav le-Ya'aqov*, p. 24, sect. 8 and pp. 67–68, sect. 45. Also see Israel Klapholtz, *Torat ha-Maggid*, v. 1, pp. 61a–66a.

63. See Simon Mendel of Gowarczow, *Sefer Ba'al Shem Tov*, v. 1: 43–44. Also see *Keter Shem Tov*, p. 21a, sect. 84 and p. 105b, sect. 355. These texts, however, do not deal with the issue of clairvoyance. The text in sect. 84 explains that the concealed light refers to the secrets which are hidden in the Torah's narratives. The second text, which comes from *Toledot Ya'aqov Yosef*, explains that God is not concealed from *Zaddiqim*, but does not emphasize Torah study per se.

64. Meshullam Feibush's viewpoint will be more fully discussed in the following chapter eight, "The Importance of *Zaddiqim*."

65. See *Liqqutim Yeqarim*, 135a–135b (YDE, sect. 42). A translation of this text and a discussion concerning Meshullam Feibush's position regarding Lurianic *kavvanot* can be found in the preceding chapter. See p. 129.

66. See *Or ha-Emet*, 14b. Also see Schatz-Uffenheimer's discussion in *Hasidism as Mysticism*, pp. 215–241 (pp. 129–147 in Hebrew edition).

67. See Schatz-Uffenheimer, Ibid., p. 218 (p. 131 in Hebrew edition).

68. Compare Weiss, "The Kavvanoth of Prayer in Early Hasidism," *Studies in Eastern European Jewish Mysticism*, esp. pp. 105–108. On the issue of *kavvanot* in Hasidic prayer, see Idel, *Hasidism: Between Ecstasy and Magic*, pp. 149–154.

69. According to the Lurianic system, these supernal worlds are only effected by the concentration on the appropriate *kavvanot*.

70. The term *hitlahavut* may mean more than mere enthusiasm. For a discussion of some early Hasidic connotations of this term, see Bezalel Safran, "Maharal and Early Hasidism," in *Hasidism: Continuity or Change?* (Cambridge: Harvard University Press, 1988), p. 83 and n. 66.

71. *Or ha-Emet*, 77b. Cited in Schatz-Uffenheimer, *Hasidism as Mysticism*, p. 218 (p. 131 in Hebrew edition). The text is also found in *Liqqutim Yeqarim*, 67a, sect. 227.

72. See our discussion in the preceding chapter, pp. 135–138.

73. *Liqqutim Yeqarim*, 135b (YDE, sect. 42).

74. Ibid. (YDE, sect. 43).

75. Compare Schatz-Uffenheimer, *Hasidism as Mysticism*, p. 228 (p. 138 in Hebrew edition).

76. *Or ha-Emet*, 14b.

77. This is indeed an extreme position in early Hasidism. Compare, for example, the position of Kalonymus Kalman Epstein of Cracow, a disciple Elimelekh of Lizhensk, which is cited by Jacobs, *Hasidic Prayer*, pp. 80–81. Kalonymus Kalman holds that Dov Ber's approach is the appropriate method for people of his generation.

78. See Joseph Weiss, "*Reishit Zemihatah shel ha-Derekh ha-Hasidit*," *Zion* 16 (1951):46–105; I. Tishby and J. Dan, "*Torat ha-Hasidut ve-Sifrutah*," in *Encyclopedia ha-Ivrit*, vol. 117, col. 784–791; Louis Jacobs, *Hasidic Prayer*, pp. 104–120. All of these scholars assumed that the source of the Hasidic approach is to be found in Sabbatianism. Piekarz, however, has shown that much of the theoretical basis could

have been adapted directly from *Sheney Luhot ha-Berit*. See his *Bi-Yemey Zemihat ha-Hasidut*. The possibility remains, however, that influence may have been drawn from both sources. For another view of the relationship between Hasidism and Sabbatianism, see Rachel Elior, "Hasidism— Historical Continuity and Spiritual Change," in *Gershom Scholem's Major Trends in Jewish Mysticism: Fifty Years After*, edited by Peter Schäfer and Joseph Dan (Tübingen: J. C. S. Mohr , 1993), pp. 303–324.

79. See Joseph Weiss, "*Reshit Zemihatah*," pp. 88–102. Weiss's article contains valuable philogical and psychological insights, but somewhat overemphasises the role of Sabbatianism as a source for early Hasidic thought and practice. See Piekarz's critique in *Bi-Yemey Zemihat ha-Hasidut*.

80. Both of these approaches were current among the Ba'al Shem Tov's associates. See Weiss, "*Reishit Zemihatah*," pp. 88–90. Weiss refers to a passage in *Shivehey ha-Besht* which indicates that Nahman Horodenker unsuccessfully tried to rid himself of obtrusive thoughts by immersions in icy streams. Weiss also cites a text from *Degel Mahaneh Efraim* in which Menahem Mendel of Premishlan advocates contemplative concentration on the Tetragrammaton in order to banish undesirable thoughts.

81. See Louis Jacobs, "The Uplifting of Sparks in Later Jewish Mysticism," in *Jewish Spirituality*, v. 2: 99–126.

82. I use the term "tantric" to refer to the religious attitude that sees conventionally neutral or even impure objects, emotions, and activities as particularly favorable means for achieving one's spiritual goals.

83. See Krassen, '*Devequt*' *and Faith*, p. 356, n. 95. Also see, A. Foxbruner, *Habad: the Hasidism of Rabbi Shneur Zalman* pp. 208–209.

84. Joseph Weiss asserted that no manuscripts of Jacob Joseph of Polnoy's writings circulated before the publication of his first book in 1780. See Weiss, *Mehkarim be-Hasidut Breslav* (Jerusalem: Bialik, 1974), pp. 105–107. This position has been challenged by Rivka Schatz-Uffenheimer who has determined that a manuscript containing teachings of Jacob Joseph, although dated 1789, was in fact written before 1780. See Schatz-Uffenhermer, *Hasidism as Mysticism*, pp. 351–354, originally published in Hebrew as, "*Perusho shel ha-BeSHT le-Mizmor 107*," *Tarbiz* 42 (1973): 160–162. Also see her remarks in the introduction to her critical edition of *Maggid Devarav le-Ya'aqov*, p. 20. Although Zev Gries is not certain that the manuscript in question is as old as Schatz-Uffenheimer claimed, he considers it highly unlikely that no manuscripts containing Jacob Joseph's teachings were in circulation before the publication of *Toledot Ya'aqov Yosef*. See "*Arikhat Zavva'at ha-RYVaSH*," *Kiryat Sefer* 52: 189–191. Also see Rosman, *Founder of Hasidism*, pp. 137–141.

85. The term literally means from the minor to the major. The meaning is that if a legal inference applies to a less stringent case, it certainly applies to a more stringent one.

86. That is, any experience of fear provoked by anything other than God. Meshullam Feibush goes on to include the other archtypical emotions under this general rule. Compare *Liqqutim Yeqarim*, 59a, sect. 194.

87. Ps. 34:9.

88. *Liqqutim Yeqarim*, 118b (YDE, sect. 17).

89. See *Liqqutim Yeqarim*, 18b, sect. 98. The text also appears in Schatz-Uffenheimer, *Maggid Devarav le-Ya'aqov*, pp. 260–261, sect. 161.

90. *Liqqutim Yeqarim*, 119a (YDE, sect. 17)

91. Ibid.

92. See note 88.

93. The source of the analogy appears in *Liqqutim Yeqarim*, 85b, sect. 266.

94. *Liqqutim Yeqarim*, 130b (YDE, sect. 35).

95. See *Liqqutim Yeqarim*, 85b, sect. 266.

96. Song of Songs 2:4.

97. Midrash Rabbah, Song of Songs, ch. 2.

98. The Cordoverian position was popularized through *Sheney Luhot ha-Berit*. See Piekarz, *The Beginning of Hasidism* [Hebrew], pp. 356–359. Piekarz discusses the Ba'al Shem Tov text on page 358. In the tales of later Hasidism, the Ba'al Shem Tov's use of the analogy seems to have been separated from its mystical context. It thus became a basis for praising the sincere prayers and religious efforts of the unlearned. Nevertheless, no evidence of this usage could be located among the theoretical teachings that are collected in *Sefer Ba'al Shem Tov*.

99. *Liqqutim Yeqarim*, 130b–131a (YDE, sect. 35).

100. Ps. 48:2.

101. B. T., *Kiddushin*, 30b.

102. *Liqqutim Yeqarim*, 85b–86a, sect. 266.

103. Weiss speculated that Meshullam Feibush's opposition to these practices may have been due to the influence of his master, Menahem Mendel of Premishlan. See Weiss, "The Kavvanoth of Prayer in Early Hasidism," p. 123f, n. 57. Tishby-Dan, following Weiss's lead, go so far as to assert that "the entire body of ideas that border on the sanctity of sin was foreign to Meshullam Feibush's temperament and wherever he was able to avoid a direct collision with the words of the Besht and 'the Maggid,' he openly deviated from their course." (Tishby-Dan, "*Torat ha-Hasidut ve-Sifrutah*," col. 788).

104. My emphasis.

105. Mishnah, *Shabbat*, 6:10.

106. According to Zohar, v. 2, 94b, these are three primary levels in the process of the soul's development. The higher levels are acquired as one progresses spiritually.

107. That is, from the lowest *sefirah* which is called "kingdom" (*Malkhut*).

108. *Liqqutim Yeqarim*, 120a (YDE, sect. 19).

109. See *Tiqquney Zohar, tiqqun* 22, 68b.

110. *Liqqutim Yeqarim*, 22b, sect. 113.

111. It is curious that this teaching from Dov Ber of Mezeritch does not appear in *Maggid Devarav le-Ya'aqov*. A critical study of the later collections of Dov Ber's teachings which, in actuality, were based on early, sometimes more complete manuscripts could aid us in establishing the authenticity of this source. At present, the only other reference attributing this teaching of the Maggid of Mezeritch, that I

have located, is in Hayyim of Tchernovitz's *Be'er Mayyim Hayyim, Noah*, 59a. (Jerusalem, 1992). R. Hayyim Tirer of Tchernovitz was also a disciple of R. Yehiel Mikhel of Zlotchov. On R. Hayyim, see Altshuler, pp. 314–316.

112. See Jacobs, *Hasidic Prayer*, p. 107.

113. The only reference to Jacob Joseph of Polnoy which I have located among the extant writings of Meshullam Feibush appears in an undated letter to an anonymous follower. The letter is printed on page 208 of Kahn's edition of *Liqqutim Yeqarim*. This letter would seem to have been written sometime after the publication of Jacob Joseph's writings in the 1780s.

114. See p. 277, note 103.

8. The Importance of Zaddiqim

1. These points are made in Rapoport-Albert's "God and the Zaddik as the Two Focal Points of Hasidic Worship," pp. 296–325. See, especially, pp. 319–320.

2. I am referring to the establishment of Hasidic courts such as they existed at that time. See Joseph Dan's introduction to *Teachings of Hasidism*, p. 2. Dan indicates that the Maggid's disciples began establishing Hasidic centers shortly after his death in 1772. However, figures like Shmelke of Nikolsburg and Levi Isaac of Berdichev were already active as rabbinic leaders before becoming associated with Dov Ber. In addition, the major Hasidic center of Aaron of Karlin was already functioning in the late 1760s. See Wolf Rabinowitsch, *Lithuanian Hassidism* [Hebrew] (Jerusalem, 1961), pp. 9–11. There is also evidence that Hayyim Haikel of Amdur, a student of the Maggid, had an independent group during the Maggid's life, as did Abraham of Kalisk.

3. There were, of course, exceptions. See Shmuel Ettinger, "Hasidism and the *Kahal* in Eastern Europe," in Rapoport-Albert, ed., *Hasidism Reappraised*, pp. 63–75.

4. Such an approach is, of course, to be found in the writings of Jacob Joseph of Polnoy. See Dresner, *The Zaddik: The Doctrine of the Zaddik According to the Writings of Rabbi Yaakov Yosof of Polnoy* (New York: Schocken, 1960). While much of these teachings were written and, in part at least, preached even before the advent of Dov Ber's school, they were not published until the 1780s. During the period under discussion, they do not appear to have had much influence on Dov Ber's disciples. But, see Gries, "The Editing of *Zava'at ha-RYVaSH*," *Kiryat Sefer* 52 (1977): 190. Meshullam Feibush does not make reference to Jacob Joseph even once in *Yosher Divrey Emet*. Thus, it seems that his response to our problem developed independently of Jacob Joseph's influence. On the other hand, early Hasidic teachings often spread orally. Thus, one cannot entirely rule out oral tradition as a source of influence. See Zev Gries, *The Book in Early Hasidism* [Hebrew] (Jerusalem: Hakibbutz Hameuchad, 1992), pp. 64–65.

5. For a list of some of the many terms that were applied to the spiritual virtuoso in earlier Hasidic teachings, see the discussion in Rappoport-Albert, *Hasidism*

Reappraised, pp. 305–308. Also see Arthur Green, "Typologies of Leadership and the Hasidic *Zaddiq*, in "*Jewish Spirituality*, v. 2 (New York: Crossroad, 1987), pp. 127–156.

6 The letter appears in many editions of *Noam Elimelekh*. For an English translation see Jacobs, *Jewish Mystical Testimonies*, pp. 208–214.

7. The relationship between Meshullam Feibush's letters and Yehiel Mikhel of Zlotchov's activities as a *Zaddiq* is treated in detail in Altshuler, *Rabbi Meshullam Feibush Heller*.

8. *Liqqutim Yeqarim*, 110a (YDE, sect. 1)

9. This accusation was a standard one and was frequently directed in both directions. See Wilensky, *Hasidim and Mitnaggdim* [Hebrew].

10. *Liqqutim Yeqarim*, 114b–115a (YDE, sect. 11)

11. See the discussion in the preceeding chapter seven.

12. For a discussion of the role of the *Zaddiq* as responsible for the material well-being of his followers, see Elior, "Between *Yesh* and *Ayin*: pp. 393–445.

13. The text appears in Schatz-Uffenheimer's, *Maggid Devarav le-Ya'aqov*, sect. 146, p. 247.

14. Kohelet 5:1.

15. *Liqqutim Yeqarim*, 120a–120b (YDE, sect. 19).

16. Ibid.

17. The text says, "*ve-hokhmato ha-elyonah*," literally, "through his supreme wisdom." However, from the context, it is clear that Meshullam Feibush has in mind letter permutation which he has already called "*hokhmah*" and which he particularly associates with the Ba'al Shem Tov and his disciples. See above. On letter permutation and Hasidic masters, see Idel, *Hasidism: Between Ecstasy and Magic*, pp. 56–60. Also see Rosman, *Founder of Hasidism*.

18. *Liqqutim Yeqarim*, 120a-120b (YDE, sect. 19).

19. These qualities suggest parallels to the Taoist sage. See Livia Kohn, *Early Chinese Mysticism: Philosophy and Soteriology in the Taoist Tradition* (Princeton: Princeton University Press, 1992), pp. 50–52.

20. Prov. 24:4.

21. The terms *Zaddiq* and *berit* (covenant) are adapted from early kabbalistic symbolism associated with the ninth *sefirah*, *Yesod*. This *sefirah* characteristically joins the bestowing male principle, *Tiferet*, with the recipient of descending divine energy in the sefirotic world, the female principle, *Malkhut*. See Wolfson, *Through a Speculum that Shines*, pp. 336–340. It is typical of early Hasidic literature to apply the sefirotic symbolism associated with *Yesod* to the figure of the human *Zaddiq*. See Scholem, "*Ha-Zaddiq*," in *Pirqey Yesod be-Havanat ha-Kabbalah u-Semalehah* (Jerusalem, 1980), p. 242. Also see Arthur Green, "The Zaddiq as *Axis Mundi* in Later Judaism," *JAAR* 45 (1977): 327–347. Although Meshullam Feibush does not mention it here, the most common proof text is "*the righteous (zaddiq) is the foundation (yesod) of the world.*" (Prov. 10:25).

22. 1 Chron. 29:11.

23. This *"Targum"* is actually offered by the Zohar, v. 1, 31a. There is no *Targum Yonaton* on Chronicles.

24. As opposed to the sefirotic *Zaddiq, Yesod.*

25. *Liqqutim Yeqarim,* 123a. (YDE, sect. 23).

26. See ibid, 129a–130a (YDE, sect. 34).

27. This is treated in greater detail in our discussion of prayer. According to Altshuler, this visualization practice was part of a ritual performed by Yehiel Mikhel and his followers in order to effect a *tiqqun* of the *parzuf, 'Arikh 'Anpin* during Shavuot, 1777. See Altshuler, *Rabbi Meshullam Feibush Heller,* p. 111.

28. See above, our discussion on prayer in chapter six.

29. See *Liqqutim Yeqarim,* 146a–146b (*Derekh Emet,* sect. 3).

30. Gate of Awe, chapter 8. The discussion mainly concerns itself with the symbolism of the dog which stands for the evil seductress, Lilith.

31. *Liqqutim Yeqarim,* 146b (*Derekh Emet,* sect. 3).

32. Ibid.

33. Prov. 3:5.

34. *Liqqutim Yeqarim,* 124b (YDE, sect. 26).

35. The specific mention of the somewhat obscure Menahem Mendel of Premishlan as comparable to the two most generally acknowledged leaders of Hasidism would seem to have two causes. First, he had an especially profound and personal influence on Meshullam Feibush's development. Second, he must have attained a significant local reputation as a Hasidic leader allied to the Ba'al Shem Tov, before he emigrated ot the Land of Israel in 1764. His establishment in the Holy Land probably only enhanced his stature which he continued to assert in Galicia through his letters. See chapter one, "Meshullam Feibush and His Circle in Eastern Galicia."

36. This esoteric characteristic of references to the Maggid of Zlotchov and his teachings is discussed in detail by Altshuler. See Altshuler, *Rabbi Meshullam Feibush Heller,* ch. 4.

37. *Liqqutim Yeqarim,* 123b (YDE, sect. 24).

38. Ibid, 136a (YDE, sect. 44).

39. See our discussion in chapter one, "Meshullam Feibush and His Circle in Eastern Galicia."

40. *Liqqutim Yeqarim,* 125b (YDE, sect. 29).

41. See Wilensky, *Hasidim and Mitnaggedim* [Hebrew]. References can be located in the index, v. 2, p 375, under *"levush."*

42. See Wilensky, ibid., v. 1: 48.

43. A passage in *Degel Mahaneh Efraim,* Noah, associates false (hasidic) *Zaddiqim* and white garments. The reference there may be to a Hasidic element that inclined towards extreme behavior and as a result, were responsible for arousing general opposition to the Hasidic movement. See Schatz-Uffenheimer, *Quietistic Elements,* p. 165, n. 30. It is also a possibity that the *Degel* may be refering to Yehiel Mikhel's circle. However, from the context, it is likely that Meshullam Feibush has some of Hasidism's rabbinic opponents in mind.

44. On the Ba'al Shem Tov's standing as a rabbinic authority, see Moshe Rosman, *Founder of Hasidism . . .*, pp. 116–119, 178. On Brody, see N. M. Gelber, *The History of the Jews in Brody* (1584–1943) [Hebrew] (Jerusalem: Mosad Harav Kook, 1955), pp. 109–110.

45. Among the most prominent members of the Brody *Kloyz* who opposed Beshtian Hasidism were Ezekiel Landau, author of *Noda bi-Yehudah*, and Hayyim Sanzer (to be distinguished from the later Hayyim Halberstam of Sanz, author of the important Hasidic work, *Divrey Hayyim*).

46. *Liqqutim Yeqarim*, 125b (YDE, sect. 29).

47. Avot 4:15.

48. *Liqqutim Yeqarim*, ibid.

49. Ibid.

50. See *Liqqutim Yeqarim*, 126a (YDE, sect. 30).

9. Meshullam Feibush's Place in Early Hasidism

1. For a discussion of the social basis of opposition to early Hasidism, see Chone Shmeruk, "*Mashma'utah ha-Hevratit shel ha-Shehitah ha-Hasidit, Zion*" 20: pp. 47–72 and Mendel Piekarz, *Bi-Yemey Zemihat ha-Hasidut* (Jerusalem: Bialik, 1978), pp. 377–392. The entire history of opposition to early Hasidism during the years 1772–1815 is treated in Mordecai Wilensky's, *Hasidim u-Mitnaggedim*. Also see Immanuel Etkes, "Hasidism as a Movement: The First Stage," in *Hasidism: Continuity or Innovation?* edited by Bezalel Safran (Cambridge: Harvard, 1988), pp. 1–26, and Shmuel Ettinger, "Hasidism and the *Kahal* in Eastern Europe," pp. 63–75

2. See Altshuler, *Rabbi Meshullam Feibush Heller*, pp. 235–244, for a discussion of the influence of Yehiel Mikhel's views on Torah study in early Hasidism.

3. For a discussion of the importance of *devequt* and *yir'at ha-Shem* (ethical-spiritual development) for Torah study in the teachings of early Hasidism's arch-rival, Elijah, the Gaon of Vilna, see Immanuel Etkes, *Rabbi Israel Salanter and the Musar Movement: Seeking the Torah of Truth* (Philadelphia: Jewish Publication Society, 1993). Also see Norman Lamm, *Torah Lishmah*.

4. According to Etkes, the Gaon of Vilna was as critical of pride associated with Torah study as were the Hasidim. See the GRA's extreme rejection of *Torah she-lo li-shemah* on p. 36. It seems clear that while real differences in methods and approaches to Torah study separated the two camps, the mutual recriminations that characterized the polemic literature of the period were exaggerated by both sides and in many cases, patently false.

5. See Etkes.

6. See our discussion of Dov Ber's interpretation of the Mishnah, "the sons of kings (may) go out in ribbons. " at the end of chapter seven on Meshullam Feibush and the Maggid of Mezeritch.

7. On Sabbatianism and Hasidism see Isaiah Tishby, *Netivey Emunah u-Minut*

(Jerusalem: Magnes, 1982), pp. 204–227; Abraham Rubenstein, *"Beyn Hasidut le-Shabta'ut,"* in *Peraqim be-Torat ha-Hasidut u-ve-Toledoteha* edited by Rubenstein (Jerusalem: Historical Society of Israel, 1977), pp. 182–197; Joseph Weiss, *"Reishit Zemihatah shel ha-Derekh ha-Hasidit"* pp. 122–181. Also see Gershom Scholem's articles, "Redemption through Sin" and "the Neutralization of the Messianic Element in Early Hasidism" in his *The Messianic Idea in Judaism* (New York: Schocken, 1974). Also see Piekarz's chapter, *"Maheshavot Zarot ve-Ra'ot,"* in Piekarz, *Bi-Yemey Zemihat ha-Hasidut*, pp. 269–279. But compare, Yehuda Liebes, *"Ha-Tikkun Ha-Kelali* of R. Nahman of Bratslav and Its Sabbatean Links," in his *Studies in Jewish Myth and Jewish Messianism* (Albany: State University of New York Press, 1993), pp. 115–150.

8. It only appeared in print more than ten years later as part of the first edition of the anthology, *Liqqutim Yeqarim*, Lemberg 1792. See above our discussion concerning the history of publication of Meshullam Feibush's works in chapter one, "Meshullam Feibush and His Circle."

9. Altshuler has suggested that the letters were intended for Yehiel Mikhel's followers in the Land of Israel. See Altshuler, *Rabbi Meshullam Feibush Heller*, pp. 19–29.

10. Altshuler, ibid, has proposed a more esoteric purpose.

11. See especially the articles by Zev Gries on the editing of *Zavva'at ha-RY-VaSH* and on the *hanhagot* literature in early Hasidism.

12. As Shlomo of Lutsk makes clear in his introduction to *Maggid Devarav le-Ya'aqov*, the Maggid did want him to collect existing manuscripts. Thus, he must have been concerned for the survival of his teachings in a more or less authoritive form. However, during Dov Ber's life, his teachings were for the most part transmitted orally. Moreover, as long as he was alive, he would have been able to assert a measure of control over the dissemination of such manuscripts as may have existed. Compare Gries, *The Book in Hasidism* [Hebrew].

13. See Ada Rapoport-Albert, "Hasidism after 1772: Structural Continuity and Change," in Rapoport-Albert, *Hasidism Reappraised*, pp. 76–140.

14. All members of the movement considered themselves followers of the Ba'al Shem Tov. By the 1770s most Hasidim had accepted Dov Ber as the founder's successor. However, most of the early direct disciples of the Ba'al Shem Tov are not known to have supported the leadership of the Maggid of Mezeritch. At present, scholars have paid insufficient attention to the fate of disciples of the Ba'al Shem Tov who did not follow Dov Ber's path.

15. A certain measure of the range of Hasidic views concerning key issues in early Hasidism can be gauged from the pages of Rivka Schatz-Uffenheimer's *Hasidism as Mysticism*. Louis Jacobs, *Hasidic Prayer* gathers and analyzes a variety of representative Hasidic views regarding issues related to prayer.

16. See Altshuler, *Rabbi Meshullam Feibush Heller*, pp. 191–257. While Schatz-Uffenheimer and Gries's work, had already established that these manuscripts often contained tendentious forms of Dov Ber's teachings, Altshuler has demonstrated the presence of Yehiel Mikhel's influence in specific cases.

17. In addition to a Hasidic tradition, which claims that when Menahem Mendel set out for the Land of Israel he asked Yehiel Mikhel to guide Meshullam Feibush, hard evidence of the friendship between these two early masters exists in the form of a letter that Menahem Mendel sent from the Holy Land to his brother in Zlotchov. That letter specifically refers to Yehiel Mikhel and his son. See Jacob Barnai: *Hasidic Letters from the Land of Israel: From the Second Half of the Eighteenth Century and Beginning of the Nineteenth Century.* [Hebrew]. (Jerusalem: Ben Zvi, 1980), pp. 52–54. Also see chapter one, "Meshullam Feibush and His Circle in Eastern Galicia."

18. This has already been noted by Joseph Weiss in "*Via Passiva* in Early Hasidism." See *Studies in Eastern European Jewish Mysticism* (Oxford: Oxford University Press, 1985), pp. 88–89. And see our discussion below. However, see Altshuler, *Rabbi Meshullam Feibush Heller*, for a more specific analysis of Yehiel Mikhel's teachings.

19. No teaching concerning *ha'ala'at maheshevot zarot* is attributed to Yehiel Mikhel in *Sefer Mayim Rabbim*, an anthology containing many examples of his teachings.

20. See, e.g., Tishby and Dan's Hebrew Encyclopedia article, "*Torat ha-Hasidut ve-Sifrutah*," in *Peraqim be-Torat ha-Hasidut u-ve-Toledoteha* edited by Rubenstein, p. 274. Menahem Mendel of Premishlan was cited by the author of *Degel Mahaneh Efraim* as an exponent of an older method of dealing with negative thoughts. See chapter one, "Meshullam Feibush and His Circle."

21. It must be kept in mind that the teaching of uplifting wayward thoughts was initiated by the Ba'al Shem Tov. It is referred to frequently in such reliable sources of the master's teachings as the works of Jacob Joseph of Polnoy and *Sefer Degel Mahaneh Efraim*, written by the Ba'al Shem Tov's grandson, Moses Hayyim Efraim of Sudilkov. Nevertheless, it is clear that it was possible to be a follower of the Ba'al Shem Tov without ascribing to this practice. It may even be the case that the Ba'al Shem Tov only recommended the practice in specific cases. Clearly, much work remains to be done in the study of this issue. For the present, the English reader can gain a general sense of the history of this practice in early Hasidism from Louis Jacob's discussion in *Hasidic Prayer.*

22. Of course, the teaching of elevating negative thoughts was also related to Lurianic Kabbalah's emphasis on releasing divine sparks from the *kelippot.* However, as Weiss already observed in "*Reishit Zemihatah shel ha-Derekh ha-Hasidit*," the Hasidic teaching does not require the Lurianic idea. It can also emerge as a necessary consequence of carrying the more Cordoverian emphasis on divine immanence to its extreme.

23. See Wilensky, *Hasidim u-Mitnagedim* [Hebrew]. The view that Abraham Kalisker and his group were primarily responsible for the development of organized opposition to Hasidism in Lithuania is reported mainly in Habad sources. See Wilensky, v.2: 361–362. But compare Zev Gries, "*Mi-Mitos le-Etos: Kavim li-Demuto shel R. Avraham mi-Kalisk*" in *Umah ve-Toldoteyhah* (Jerusalem, 1984). The opposition

that began in Shklov was soon supported in both Vilna and Brody region. A ban against the Hasidim was already issued in Brody in the spring of 1772. See Wilensky, Ibid., v. 1: 28, 44–49. The opposition in Brody may have been directed against Yehiel Mikhel and his group.

24. The one exception is the full version of his spiritual directive in favor of Torah study which was deleted from the many manuscripts and did not appear in its entirety in any of the early printed versions. See Schatz-Uffenheimer's critical edition to *Maggid Devarav le-Ya'aqov* and Gries's articles on the editing of *Zavva'at ha-RYVaSH* and on Hasidic *hanhagot* literature. Ironically, Meshullam Feibush, himself, may have been responsible for the spread of some of these censored editions.

25. See the anecdotes in chapter one, "Meshullam Feibush and His Circle."

26. This analysis of Meshullam Feibush's psychology is based not only on the anecdotes told about him, but also on his own teachings concerning self-awareness which appear at the end of his tractate, *Derekh Emet*.

27. See Piekarz' discussion of *maheshevot zarot* in *Bi-Zemihat ha-Hasidut*.

28. See *In Praise of the Baal Shem Tov*, pp. 153–155. Also see above, "Meshullam Feibush and His Circle in Eastern Galicia."

29. See above, "Meshullam Feibush and his Circle in Eastern Galicia."

30. While this Hasidic argument may appear self-serving and disingenuous, it should be pointed out that figures like Yehiel Mikhel and Elimelekh of Lizhensk, both of whom became powerful Hasidic leaders, spent most of their lives in extreme poverty. Both of these *Zaddiqim* inclined towards asceticism and evinced little interest in either power or wealth before becoming popular leaders. Yehiel Mikhel, moreover, was a victim of persecution throughout much of his life. As a result, he was repeatedly forced to change his residence. See chapter one, "Meshullam Feibush and His Circle in Eastern Galicia."

31. See the exemptions permitted to the members of the Brody *Kloyz* in the anti-Hasidic Brody proclamation of 1772. The text appears in Wilensky, op. cit., pp. 44–49.

32. See Louis Jacob's survey of positions regarding the elevation of *maheshavot zarot* in *Hasidic Prayer*.

33. Joseph Weiss already noticed a similarity between Meshullam Feibush's text and HaBaD Hasidism, especially in regard to its acosmic/panentheistic aspects. However, Weiss wondered whether Meshullam Feibush might have been influenced by HaBaD. This seems unlikely, since *Yosher Divrey Emet*, although not printed before 1792, was written considerably earlier than the *Tanya*. A fuller discussion of ways in which Shneur Zalman may have been influenced by Meshullam Feibush is a desideratum.

34. As has already been noted by Tishby and Dan, op. cit., p. 274.

Bibliography

Hasidic and Pre-Modern Works

Abraham ben Dov Ber of Mezeritch and Abraham Kalisker. *Hesed le-Avraham*. Jerusalem: Lewin-Epstein, 1973.

Abraham Hayyim ben Gedalyah of Zlotchov. *Orah le-Hayyim*. Jerusalem, 1960.

———. *Peri Hayyim*. Lemberg, 1833.

Abraham of Slonim. *Yesod ha-Avodah*. Jerusalem: Yeshivat Bet Avraham-Slonin, 1989.

Azikri, Eleazar. *Milley De-Shemaya* edited by Mordecai Pechter, Jerusalem: Bialik, 1991.

———. *Sefer Haredim*. Jerusalem, 1981.

Azulai, Abraham. *Hesed le-Avraham*. Bnai Brak, 1986.

Barukh of Kosov. *Nehmad ve-Na'im, Yesod ha-Avodah*. Bnei Brak, 1988.

Benjamin of Zalozitz. *Ahavat Dodim*. Brooklyn, 1978.

———. *Turey Zahav*. Jerusalem, 1989.

Bodek, Menaham Mendel. *Seder ha-Dorot he-Hadash*. Lemberg, 1865.

Cordovero, Moses. *Pardes Rimmonim*. Jerusalem, 1962.

———. *Tefillah le-Moshe*. Premishl, 1892.

De Vidas, Elijah. *Reishit Hokhmah ha-Shalem*. Jerusalem: Or Ha-Musar, 1984.

Dov Ber ben Avraham of Mezeritch. *Maggid Devarav le-Ya'aqov*. Jerusalem: Toledot Aharon, 1971.

———. *Maggid Devarav le-Ya'aqov* (Critical Ed.). Jerusalem: Magnes, 1976.

———. *Maggid Devarav le-Ya'aqov ve-Hu Liqqutey Amarim*. Brooklyn: Kehot, 1979.

———. *Or ha-Emet*. Brooklyn, 1960.

———. *Or Torah*. Brooklyn, 1979.

Elimelekh of Lizhensk. *Noam Elimelekh* (Critical Ed.). Jerusalem: Mosad Harav Kook, 1978.

Emden, Jacob. *Beyt Ya'aqov.*

Gikatilla, Joseph. *Ginat Egoz.* Jerusalem, 1989.

———. *Sha'arey Orah.* Warsaw, 1883.

——— *Gates of Light.* San Francisco: Harper, 1993.

Hannover, Nathan. *Sha'arey Zion.* Prague. 1662.

Heller, Abraham Noah. *Zerizuta de-Avraham.* New York, 1952.

Heller, Meshullam Feibush of Zbarazh. *Derekh Emet.* Tchernovitz, 1855.

———. *Derekh Emet.* Jerusalem: Toledot Aharon, 1974.

———. *Yosher Divrey Emet.* Munkatch, 1905.

———. *Yosher Divrey Emet.* Jerusalem: Toledot Aharon, 1974.

Hofstein, Israel of Kozhenitz. *Avodat Yisrael ha-Shalem.* Jerusalem, 1988.

Horowitz, Isaiah. *Sha'ar ha-Shamayim.* Jerusalem, 1987.

———. *Sheney Luhot ha-Berit.* Amsterdam, 1698.

———. *Sheney Luhot ha-Berit.* Warsaw, 1862.

———. *Sheney Luhot ha-Berit.* Jerusalem: Sha'arey Ziv, 1993.

Ibn Gabbai, Meir. *Avodat ha-Qodesh.* Jerusalem, 1992.

———. *Tola'at Ya'aqov.* Jerusalem: Sheviley Orhot he-Hayyim, 1996.

Isaac of Radvil. *Or Yizhaq.* Jerusalem, 1961.

Isaiah of Dinovitz. *Zavva'at ha-RYVaSH.* Brooklyn: Kehot, 1982.

Issachar Ber of Zlotchov. *Mevasser Zedeq.* New Square, N.D.

Jacob Joseph of Polnoy. *Zafnat Pa'aneah* (Critical Ed.). Jerusalem: Institute for the Study of Hasidic Literature, 1989.

———. *Ketonet Passim.* (Critical Ed.). Jerusalem: Peri Ha-Arez, 1985.

———. *Toledot Ya'aqov Yosef.* Jerusalem, 1973.

Keter Shem Tov. Brooklyn: Kehot, 1972.

Kleinman, Moses Hayyim. *Zikaron le-Rishonim.* Pietrekov: 1912 Rpt. Jerusalem, 1977.

Klepholtz, Israel. *Torat ha-Maggid.* Bnai Brak, 1976.

Levi Isaac of Berdichev. *Qedushat Levi ha-Shalem.* Jerusalem, 1958.

————. *Shemuah Tovah*. Warsaw, 1938.

Liqqutim Yeqarim. Lemberg, 1792.

————. Mezirov, 1794.

————. Zholkva, 1800.

————. Lemberg, 1850.

————. Lemberg, 1863.

————. Lemberg, 1887.

————. Jerusalem, 1974.

Luzzato, Moses Hayyim. *Adir ba-Marom*. Jerusalem, 1995.

Maimonides. *Guide of the Perplexed*. Jerusalem 1960.

Meiseles, Uziel. *Tiferet Uziel*. Jerusalem, 1962.

Menahem Mendel of Premishlan (attributed), *Darkhey Yesharim*. Bnei Brak, 1981.

Mordecai of Nezkhiz. *Rishpey Esh ha-Shalem*. Jerusalem, 1986.

Moses Hayyim Ephraim of Sudilkov. *Degel Mahaneh Efraim*. Jerusalem, 1986.

Nahman of Tcheryn. *Leshon Hasidim*. Jerusalem, 1978.

Nathan Nata of Hanover. *Sha'arey Zion*. Vienna, 1809.

Orhot Zaddiqim. Jerusalem, 1976.

Pinhas of Koretz. *Imrey Pinhas ha-Shalem*. Bnei Brak, 1988.

Roth, Aharon. *Shulhan ha-Tahor*. Sata Mare, 1933.

Safrin, Yizhaq Isaac Yehudah Yehiel of Komarna. *Netiiv Mizvotekha*. Jerusalem, 1983.

————. *Nozer Hesed*. Jerusalem, 1982.

Samuel Shmelke of Nikolsburg. *Sifrey ha-Rav ha-Qadosh he-Rebbe Rebbe Shmelke mi-Nikolsburg*. Jerusalem, 1988.

Sefer ha-Yashar ha-Miyuhas le-Rabbenu Tam. Jerusalem, 1978.

Shabbetai of Rashkov. *Seder Tifillah mi-Kol ha-Shanah im Kavvanat ha-Ari*. Israel, N. D.

Shneur Zalman ben Barukh of Liadi. *Liqqutey Amarim (Tanya)*. Brooklyn: Kehot, 1981.

Simon Menahem Mendel of Gowarczow. *Sefer Ba'al Shem Tov*. 2 vol. Jerusalem, 1992.

Tirer, Hayyim of Tchernovitz. *Be'er Mayim Hayyim*. 4 vol. Jerusalem, 1992.

————. *Siddoro shel Shabbat*. Jerusalem, 1960.

Torat ha-Hasidut ha-Rishonim. Bnai Brak: Nahalat Zevi, 1981.

Twerski, Aaron David. *Sefer ha-Yahas mi-Chernobyl ve-Ruzhin*. Lublin, 1938.

Viznitzer, Menahem Mendel. *Taqifa de-Ar'a Yisrael*. Bnai Brak: Nahalat Zevi, 1986.

Vital, Hayyim. *Ez Hayyim*. Jerusalem, 1930.

————. *Ketavim Hadashim*. Jerusalem 1988.

————. *Peri Ez Hayyim*. Dubrovna, 1798.

————. *Peri Ez Hayyim*. Jerusalem, 1980.

————. *Sha'ar ha-Kavvanot*. Jerusalem, 1902.

————. Sefer Sha'arey Qedushash.

Walden, Aaron. *Shem ha-Gedolim he-Hadash*. Warsaw, 1880.

Yehiel Mikhel of Zlotchov. *Mayim Rabbim*. edited by Nathan Nata Ha-Kohen. Warsaw, 1899.

————. *Yeshu'ot Malko*. Jerusalem: Mosad Lewin, 1974.

Zev Wolf of Zbarazh. *Razin de-Oraita*. Warsaw, 1903.

Secondary and Modern Works

Alfasi, Isaac. *Encyclopedia le-Hasidut: Ishim*. Jerusalem: Mosad Harav Kook, 1986.

————. *Ha-Hasidut*. Tel Aviv: Maariv, 1974.

Altschuler, Mor. *Rabbi Meshullam Feibush Heller and His Place in Early Hasidism*. Tel Aviv: Hebrew University, 1994.

Barlev, Yehiel Abraham. *Yedid Nefesh: Kavvanot ha-Ari z'l al ha-Tefillah*. Petah Tikvah, 1988.

Barnai, Jacob. *Hasidic Letters from the Land of Israel: From the Second Half of the Eighteenth Century and Beginning of the Nineteenth Century*. [Hebrew]. Jerusalem: Ben Zvi, 1980.

Ben Amos, Dan and Jerome Mintz, ed. *In Prase of the Baal Shem Tov [Shivhei ha-BeSHT]*. Bloomington, Ind.: Indiana University Press, 1970.

Ben-Shlomo, Joseph. *The Mystical Theology of Moses Cordovero*. [Hebrew]. Jerusalem: Bialik, 1965.

Biale, David. *Eros and the Jews*. New York: Basic Books, 1992.

Biale, Rachel. *Women and Jewish Law*. New York: Schocken, 1984.

Brody, Seth. "Human Hands Dwell in Heavenly Heights: Contemplative Ascent and Theurgic Power in Thirteenth-Century Kabbalah," in *Mystics of the Book*. Edited by R. A. Herera. Lang, 1993.

———. *Human Hands in Heavenly Heights*. (Dissertation) University of Pennsylvania, 1991.

Buber, Martin. *Tales of the Hasidim: The Early Masters*. New York: Schocken, 1947.

———. *Origin and Meaning of Hasidism*. New York: Horizon, 1960.

Carlebach, Elisheva. *Pursuit of Heresy: Rabbi Moses Hagiz and the Sabbatian Controversies*. New York: Columbia University Press, 1990.

Dan, Joseph. *Hebrew Ethical and Homiletical Literature*. [Hebrew]. Jerusalem: Keter, 1975.

———. *Jewish Mysticism and Jewish Ethics*. Seattle: University of Washington, 1986.

———. *Teachings of Hasidism*. New York: Behrman, 1983.

Davis, Joseph. "R. Yom Tov Lipman Heller, Joseph b. Isaac haLevi, and Rationalism in Ashkenazic Jewish Culture, 1550–1660." Ph.D diss., Harvard University, 1990.

Dienstag, Israel Jacob. "Ha-Moreh Nevukhim ve Sefer ha-Mada' be-Sifrut ha-Hasidut," in *The Abraham Weiss Jubilee Volume*. New York, 1964.

Dinur, Ben Zion. *Be-Mifne ha-Dorot*. Jerusalem: Bialik, 1972.

Dresner, Samuel. *The Zaddik: The Doctrine of the Zaddik According to the Writings of Rabbi Yaakov Yosef of Polnoy*. New York: Schocken, 1960.

Dubnov, Simon. *History of Hasidism*. [Hebrew]. Tel Aviv: Devir, 1975. Reprint, 1984.

Elbaum, Jacob. "Aspects of Hebrew Ethical Literature in Sixteenth Century Poland," in *Jewish Thought in the Sixteenth Century*. Cambridge: Harvard University Press, 1983.

Eliade, Mircea. *The Myth of the Eternal Return or, Cosmos and History*. Princeton: Bollingen, 1971.

Elior, Rachel. "Between *Yesh* and *Ayin:* The Doctrine of the Zaddik in the Works of Jacob Isaac, the Seer of Lublin," in *Jewish History: Essays in Honor of Chimen Abramsky*. London, 1988.

———. "HaBaD: The Contemplative Ascent to God," in *Jewish Spirituality: From the Sixteenth Century Revival to the Present*. Edited by Arthur Green. New York: Crossroad, 1987.

——. "Hasidism's Connection to Kabbalah: Continuity and Change" [Hebrew]. *Proceedings of the World Congress of Jewish Thought* 9, no. 3 (1986): 107–114.

——. *The Paradoxical Ascent to God: The Kabbalistic Theosophy of Habad Hasidism.* Albany: State University of New York Press, 1993.

——. *The Theory of Divinity of Hasidut HaBaD: Second Generation.* [Hebrew]. Jerusalem: Magnes, 1982.

——. "Yesh and 'ayin as Fundamental Paradigms in Hasidic Thought." In *Massu'ot.* Edited by A. Goldreich and M. Oron. Jerusalem, 1994.

Etkes, Immanuel. "Hasidism as a Movement, the First Stage." In *Hasidism: Continuity or Change?* Edited by Bezalel Safran. Cambridge: Harvard University Press, 1988. pp. 1–26.

——. *Rabbi Israel Salanter and the Beginning of the Musar Movement.* [Hebrew]. Jerusalem: Magnes, 1984. English translation Philadelphia: Jewish Publication Society of America, 1993.

——. *The Study of Hasidism: Past Trends and New Directions.* In *Hasidism Reappraised,* 447–464. London: Littman, 1996.

Ettinger, Shmuel. "Hasidism and the *Kahal* in Eastern Europe," in *Hasidism Reappraised.* Edited by Ada Rapoport-Albert. London: Littman, 1996.

Faierstein, Morris M. "Gershom Scholem and Hasidism," *JJS* 38, 2 (1987), pp. 221–233.

Fine, Lawrence. "The Art of Metoposcopy; A Study in Isaac Luria's Charismatic Knowledge." In *Essential Papers on the Kabbalah.* New York: New York University Press, 1995. pp. 315–337. Originally published in *AJS Review* (1986): 79–101.

——. "The Contemplative Practice of *Yihudim* in Lurianic Kabbalah," in *Jewish Spirituality: From the Sixteenth Century to the Present.* Edited by Arthur Green. New York: Crossroad, 1987.

——. "Maggidic Revelation in the Teachings of Isaac Luria," in *Mystics, Philosophers, and Politicans: Essays in Jewish Intellectual History in Honor of Alexander Altmann.* Durham, N.C.: Duke University Press, 1982.

——. "Recitation of Mishnah as a Vehicle for Mystical Inspiration: A Contemplative Technique Taught by Hayyim Vital." *Revue des Etudes Juives* 141, no. I–2 (1982).

——. *Safed Spirituality.* New York: Paulist, 1984.

——. "The Study of Torah as a Rite of Theurgical Contemplation in Lurianic Kabbalah," in *Approaches to Judaism in Medieval Times.* Vol. 3. Edited by David Blumenthal. Atlanta, Ga.: Scholars Press, 1988.

Fishbane, Michael. *The Kiss of God: Spiritual and Mystical Death in Judaism.* Seattle, Wash.: University of Washington Press, 1994.

Foxbrunner, Roman A. HABAD: *The Hasidism of R. Shneur Zalman of Lyady.* Tuscaloosa, 1992.

Friedberg, Ch. B. *Beyt Eqed Sefarim.* 4 vols. Israel, N.D.

Gelber, N. M. *History of the Jews of Brody (1584–1943).* [Hebrew]. Jerusalem: Mosad Harav Kook, 1956.

Giller, Pinchas. "Recovering the Sanctity of the Galilee the Veneration of Sacred Relics in Classical Kabbalah." In *The Journal of Jewish Thought and Philosophy.* vol. 4, pp. 147–169.

Ginsburg, Elliot K. *The Sabbath in the Classic Kabbalah.* Albany: State University of New York Press, 1989.

————. *Sod ha-Shabbat (The Mystery of the Sabbath): From the Tola'at Ya'aqov of R. Meir Ibn Gabbai.* Albany: State University of New York, 1989.

Goetschel, Roland. "Torah lishmah as a Central Concept in the Degel mahanah Efrayim of Moses Hayyim Ephraim of Sudylkow." In *Hasidism Reappraised,* edited by Ada Rapoport-Albert. London: Littman, 1996.

Gottlieb, Ephraim. *Studies in the Kabbalah Literature.* [Hebrew]. Tel Aviv: Tel Aviv University Press, 1976.

Granatstein, Yehiel. *Talmidey ha-Ba'al Shem Tov be-Erez Yisrael.* Tel Aviv: Maor, 1982.

Green, Arthur, ed. *Jewish Spirituality: From the Bible through the Middle Ages.* New York: Crossroad, 1986.

————, ed. *Jewish Spirituality: From the Sixteenth-Century Revival to the Present.* New York: Crossroad, 1987.

————. "Hasidism: Discovery and Retreat," in *The Other Side of God: A Polarity in World Religions.* New York: Anchor, 1981.

————. "Sabbath as Temple: Some Thoughts on Space and Time in Judaism," in *Go and Study: Essays and Studies in Honor of A. Jospe.* Washington, D.C.: Bnai Brith Hillel Foundations. 1980., 1982.

————. *Tormented Master: A Life of Rabbi Nahman of Bratslav.* Montgomery: University of Alabama Press, 1979.

————. "Typologies of Leadership and the Hasidic Zaddiq," in *Jewish Spirituality: From the Sixteenth-Century Revival to the Present.* New York: Crossroad, 1987.

————. "The Zaddiq as *Axis Mundi* in Later Judaism." *JAAR* 45 (1977): 3.

Green, Arthur and Barry W. Holtz, eds. *Your Word is Fire: The Hasidic Masters on Contemplative Prayer*. New York: Paulist, 1977.

Greenbaum, Avraham. *The Sweetest Hour: Tikkun Chatzot*. Jerusalem: Breslov Research Institute, 1993.

Gries, Zev. *The Book in Early Hasidism: Genres, Authors, Scribes, Managing Editors and its Review by Their Contemporaries and Scholars*. [Hebrew] Israel: Hakibbutz Hameuchad, 1992.

————. *Conduct Literature (Regimen Vitae): Its History and Place in the Life of Beshtian Hasidism* [Hebrew]. Jerusalem: Bialik, 1989.

————. "The Editing of *Zavva'at ha-RYVaSH*," [Hebrew]. *Kiryat Sefer* 52 (1977).

————. "Hasidic Conduct-Directive Literature" [Hebrew]. *Zion* 46 (1981).

Halamish, Moshe. "Silence in Kabbalah and Hasidism" [Hebrew]. *Da'at ve-Safah* (1982): 79–89.

Halperin Israel. *Ha-Aliyot ha-Rishonot shel ha-Hasidim la-Erez Yisrael* [Hebrew]. Jerusalem: Schocken, 1947.

————. *Beyt Yisrael be-Folin: Mi-Yamim Rishonim ve-ad li-Yemot ha-Horban*. Vol. 1. 2. Jerusalem, 1947.

Hann, Thich Nhat, *Thundering Silence: Sutra on Knowing the Better Way to Catch a Snake*. Berkeley: University of California, 1993.

Heschel, Abraham Joshua. *The Circle of the Baal Shem Tov: Studies in Hasidism*. Trans. Samuel Dresner. Chicago: University of Chicago Press, 1985.

————. *Theology of Ancient Judaism*. [Hebrew]. London: Soncino, 1962.

————. "Unknown Hasidic Documents." [Yiddish]. *Yivo Bletter*, 36.

Horodetzky, S. A. *History of Hasidim and Hasidism*. [Hebrew]. Tel Aviv, 1953.

Horowitz, Zvi Halevy. *Toledot ha-Qehillot be-Folin*. Jerusalem: Mosad Harav Kook, 1978.

Hundert, Gershon. *Essential Papers on Hasidism*. New York: New York University Press, 1991.

Idel, Moshe. "*Ha-Hitbodedut ke-Rikkuz ba-Kabbalah ha-Ekstatit ve-Gilguleha*." *Da'at* 14 (1985).

————. *Hasidism: Between Ecstasy and Magic*. Albany: State University of New York Press, 1995.

————. "Hitbodedut as Concentration in Ecstatic Kabbalah," in *Jewish Spirituality: From the Bible Through the Middle Ages*. New York: Crossroad, 1986.

————. *Kabbalah: New Perspectives*. New Haven: Yale University Press, 1988.

————. "The Land of Israel and the Kabbalah in the Thirteenth Century." [Hebrew]. *Shalem* 3 (1981).

————. *The Mystical Experience in Abraham Abulafia*. Albany: State University of New York, 1988.

————. "Perceptions of Kabbalah in the Second Half of the Eighteenth Century." A paper delivered at the symposium on Jewish Thought in the Eighteenth Century at Harvard University, 1984. *Journal of Jewish Thought and Philosophy* I (1990): 53–114.

————. *Rabbi Abraham Abulafia's Works and Thought*. [Hebrew]. Ph.D diss., Hebrew University, Jerusalem, 1976.

Jacobs, Louis. "Eating as an Act of Worship in Hasidic Thought," in *Studies in Jewish Intellectual History: Presented to Alexander Altmann on the Occasion of His Seventieth Birthday*. London: University of Alabama Press, 1979.

————. *Hasidic Prayer*. Philadelphia: Jewish Publication Society, 1972.

————. *Jewish Mystical Testimonies*. New York: Schocken, 1977.

————. *Seeker of Unity: The Life and Works of Aaron of Starosselje*. New York: Basic Books, 1966.

————. "The Uplifting of Sparks in Later Jewish Mysticism," in *Jewish Spirituality: From the Sixteenth-Century Revival to the Present*. New York: Crossroad, 1987.

————. *On Ecstasy: A Tract by Dobh Baer of Lubavitch*. New York: Rossel, 1983.

Kaplan, Aryeh. *Until the Meshiach: Rabbi Nachman's Biography: An Annotated Chronology*. Jerusalem: Breslov Research Institute, 1985.

————. *Meditation and Kabbalah*. Weiser, 1982.

Katz, Jacob. *Tradition and Change*. [Hebrew]. Jerusalem: Bialik, 1958.

Kohn, Livia. *Early Chinese Mysticism: Philosophy and Soteriology in the Taoist Tradition*. Princeton: Princeton University Press, 1992.

Krassen, Miles. *'Devequt' and Faith in 'Zaddiqim': The Religious Tracts of Meshullam Feibush Heller of Zbarazh*. University of Pennsylvania, 1990.

————. *Isaiah Horowitz: The Generations of Adam*. Mahweh: Paulist, 1996.

Lamm, Norman. *Torah Lishman, Torah for the Torah's Sake in the Works of Rabbi Hayyim of Volozhin and His Contemporaries.* New York: Ktav, 1989.

Liebes, Yehudah. "The Messiah of the Zohar—R. Simeon bar Yohai as Messianic Figure," [Hebrew] in *Ha-Ra'ayon ha-Meshihi be-Yisrael.* Jerusalem: Israel National Academy of Sciences, 1982.

———. *Sections of the Zohar Lexicon.* Ph.D. diss. [Hebrew]. Jerusalem: Hebrew University, 1976.

———. *Studies in Jewish Myth and Jewish Messianism.* Albany: State University of New York, 1993.

Lowenthal, Naftali. *Communicating the Infinite: The Emergence of the Habad School.* Chicago: University of Chicago Press, 1990.

Mahler, Raphael. *Hasidism and the Jewish Enlightenment: Their Comfrontation in Galicia and Poland in the First Half of the Nineteenth Century* (Philadelphia, 1984).

Maimon, Solomon. *An Autobiography.* New York: Schocken, 1967.

Malter, Henry. *The Treatise Ta'anit of the Babylonian Talmud.* Philadelphia Jewish Publication Society, 1967.

Matt, Daniel C. "Ayin: The Concept of Nothingness in Jewish Mysticism." In *The Problem of Pure Consciousness: Mysticism and Philosophy,* 121–159. Edited by Robert K. C. Forman. Oxford: Oxford University Press, 1990.

Meroz, Ronit. "Selections from Ephraim Penzieri: Luria's Sermon in Jerusalem and the *Kavvanah* in Taking Food." [Hebrew]. In *Jerusalem Studies in Jewish Thought.* Vol. 10. Lurianic Kabbalah (Jerusalem, 1992).

Muzafi, Ben Zion. *Olamo shel Zaddiq: Hayyav u-Foalo shel ha-Mequbbal ha-Zaddiq R. Salmon Muzafi.* Jerusalem, 1976.

Nigal, Gedalyah. *Critical Edition of No'am Elimelekh.* [Hebrew]. Jerusalem: Mosad Harav Kook, 1978.

———. *Critical Edition of Zofnath Panneah.* [Hebrew]. Jerusalem: Institute for the Study of Hasidic Literature, 1989.

———. "The Sources for *Devequt* in Early Hasidic Literature." [Hebrew]. *Kiryat Sefer* 46 (1971).

Pechter, Mordecai. "The Concept of *Devequt* in The Homiletical Ethical Writings of Sixteenth Century Safed," in *Studies in Medieval Jewish History and Literature.* Edited by Isadore Twersky. Cambridge: Harvard, 1984, pp. 171–230.

Pechter, Mordecai. "*Devequt* in the Sixteenth Century Homiletical and Ethical Literature of Safed," [Hebrew]. *Jerusalem Studies in Jewish Thought,* vol. 1, n.3 (1982).

———. *From Safed's Hidden Treasures: Studies and Texts Concerning the History of Safed and Its Sages in the Sixteenth Century.* Jerusalem: Merkaz Zalman Shazar le-Toledot Yisrael, 1994.

———. "*Ikvot Hashpa'ato shel Sefer Reishit Hokhmah* le-R. Eliahu de Vidas be-Khitvey R. Ya'aqov Yosef mi-Polnoy," in *Studies in Jewish Mysticism, Philosophy and Ethical Literature Presented to Isaiah Tishby on his Seventy-fifth Birthday.* Jerusalem: Magnes, 1986, pp. 569–592.

———. "The Life and Personality of R. Eleazar Azikri as Reflected in his Mystical Diary and in *Sefer Haredim,*" [Hebrew]. *Shalem* 3 (1981).

———. "*Reshit Hokhmah* of R. Elijah De Vidas and Its Abridgements," [Hebrew]. *Kiryat Sefer* 47 (1972).

Piekarz, Mendel. *The Beginning of Hasidism: Idelogical Trends in Derush and Musar Literature.* [Hebrew]. Jerusalem: Bialik, 1978.

———. *Between Ideology and Reality: Humility, Ayin, Self-Negation and Devekut in the Hasidic Thought.* Jerusalem: Bialik, 1994.

———. "Conceptual and Historical Lessons from a Hasidic Book." [Hebrew]. *Daat* 14 (1985).

———. "Religious Radicalism During the Spread of Hasidism," [Hebrew]. *Molad* 6 (1975).

———. *Studies in Bratslav Hasidism.* 2nd. rev. ed. Jerusalem: Bialik, 1995.

Pines, Sholomo. "On the Term *Ruhaniyyut* and its Sources and on Judah Halevi's Doctrine. [Hebrew]. *Tarbiz* 57 (1988): 511–540.

Polen, Nehemia. "Ecstasy and Sanctification," in *Kabbalah* (1988): vol. 3, n.1.

Rabinowitsch, Wolf. *Lithuanian Hasidism.* [Hebrew]. Jerusalem: Bialik, 1961.

Rabinowitz, Gamaliel Hakohen. *Tiv ha-Kavvanot al Sha'ar ha-Kavvanot.* Jerusalem: Sha'arey Ziv. 1996.

Rapoport-Albert, Ada. "God and the Zaddik as the Two Focal Points of Hasidic Worship." *History of Religions* 18 (1979): 296–325.

———, ed. *Hasidism Reappraised.* London: Littman, 1996.

——— and Steven Zipperstein, eds., *Jewish History: Essays in Honor of Chimen Abramsky.* London, 1988.

———. "Hagiography with Footnotes: Edifying Tales and the Writings of History in Hasidism." In *History and Theory Beiheft 271: Essays in Jewish Historiography.*

Rosman, Moshe. *Founder of Hasidism: A Quest for the Historical Ba'al Shem Tov.* Berkeley: University of California, 1996.

Ross, Tamar. "Rav Hayyim of Volozhin and Rav Shneur Zalman of Liadi: Two Interpretations of the Doctrine of *Zimzum,*" [Hebrew]. In *Jerusalem Studies in Jewish Thought.*

Rubenstein, Abraham. "*Beyn Hasidut le-Shabta'ut,*" in *Studies in Hasidism.* Jerusalem: Historical Society of Israel, 1977.

———. "*Shevah mi-Shivehey ha-BeSHT?*" *Tarbitz* 35 (1966).

———, ed. *Studies in Hasidism.* [Hebrew]. Jerusalem: Historical Society of Israel, 1977.

Sack, Bracha. "*Iyyun be-Hashpa'at R. Moses Cordovero al ha-Hasidut.*" In *Eshel Be'er Shev'a* 3 (1986): 229–246.

———. *The Kabbalah of Rabbi Moshe Cordovero.* Israel: Ben Gurion University, 1992

———. "Prayer in the Teachings of R. Moses Cordovero," [Hebrew]. *Daat* 9.

———."*Od le-Gilgulah shel ha-Imrah Qudsha Berikh Hu Orayta ve-Yisrael Kula Had.*" *Kiryat Sefer* 57:179, 184.

Safran, Bezalel. "Maharal and Early Hasidism," in *Hasidism: Continuity or Change?* Cambridge, Mass.: Harvard University Press, 1988.

Schecter, Solomon. *Aspects of Rabbinic Theology.* New York: Schocken, 1961.

Schochet, Jacob I. *The Great Maggid.* Brooklyn: Kehot, 1978.

Scholem, Gershom. "The Baal Shem Tov as a Historical Figure," [Hebrew] in *Devarim be-Go.* Tel Aviv: Am Oved, 1982.

———. "*Devekuth* or Communion with God," in *The Messianic Idea in Judaism and Other Essays.* New York: Schocken, 1971.

———. *Elements of the Kabbalah and Its Symbolism.* [Hebrew]. Jerusalem: Bialik, 1970.

———. *Kabbalah.* New York: Quadrangle, 1974.

———. *Kabbalah of Sefer Temunah and of Abraham Abulafia.* [Hebrew]. Jerusalem: Akademon, 1987.

———. *Major Trends in Jewish Mysticism.* 3rd rev. ed. New York: Schocken, 1954.

———. "The Meaning of the Torah in Jewish Mysticism" in *On the Kabbalah and its Symbolism.* New York, Schocken, 1965.

———. "The Neutralization of Messianism in Early Hasidism," in *The Messianic Idea in Judaism and Other Essays*. New York: Schocken, 1971.

———. *Origins of the Kabbalah*. Philadelphia: Jewish Publication Society, 1987.

———. *Sabbetai Zevi: The Mystical Messiah*. Princeton: Bollingen, 1973.

———."Ha-Zaddiq." In *Pirqey Yesod be-Havanat ha-Kabbalah u-Semalehah*. Jerusalem. 1980.

———. *Studies and Texts Concerning the History of Sabbetianism and Its Metamorphoses*. [Hebrew]. Jerusalem: Bialik, 1982.

———. "The Sub-Conscious and the *Qadmuth ha-Sekhel*." [Hebrew] in *Devarim be-Go*. Tel Aviv: Am Oved, 1982.

———.*On the Mystical Shape of the Godhead*. New York: Schocken, 1991.

Schatz-Uffenheimer, Rivka. "Anti-Spiritualism in Hasidism—Studies in the Thought of R. Shneur Zalman of Liadi." [Hebrew]. *Molad* 171–172 (1963).

———. "Contemplative Prayer in Hasidism," in *Studies in Mysticism and Religion Presented to G. Scholem*. Jerusalem, 1967.

———. *Hasidism as Mysticism: Quietistic Elements in Eighteenth-Century Hasidic Thought*. Princeton: Princeton University Press, 1993.

———. *Introduction to the Critical Edition of Maggid Devarav le-Ya'aqov le-Maggid Dov Ber mi-Mezeritch*. [Hebrew]. Jerusalem: Magnes, 1976.

———. *Quietistic Elements in Eighteenth-Century Hasidic Thought*. [Hebrew]. Jerusalem: Magnes, 1980.

———. "The *Zaddiq* in the Teachings of R. Elimelekh of Lizhensk." [Hebrew]. *Molad* 144–145 (1960).

Sherwin, Byron. *Mystical Theology and Social Descent: The Life and Works of Judah Loew of Prague*. London and Toronto: Fairleigh Dickenson University Press, 1982.

Shmeruk, Chone. "*Mashma'utah ha-Hevratit shel ha-Shehitah ha-Hasidit*." *Zion* 20.

Shochat, E. "On Joy in Hasidism." [Hebrew]. *Zion* (1951).

Stace, W. T. *Mysticism and Philosophy*. Los Angeles: Tarcher, 1987.

Tanenbaum, Yizhaq Matityahu. *To'afot Harim: Beyt Zlotchov*. Jerusalem: Zecher Naftali, 1986.

Tishby, Isaiah. *The Doctrine of Evil and the 'Kelippah' in Lurianic Kabbalism*. [Hebrew]. Jerusalem: Magnes, 1984.

———. "Hasidism," [Hebrew] in *Encyclopedia ha-Ivrit*.

———.*Hiqrey Kabbalah u-Sheluhoteha*, Jerusalem: Magnes 1993.

———. "*Iqvot R. Moses Hayyim Luzzato be-Mishnat ha-Hasidut.*" *Zion* 43 (1978).

———. "The Messianic Idea and Messianic Trends in the Growth of Hasidism" [Hebrew]. *Zion* 32 (1967): 1–45.

———. *Mishnat ha-Zohar.* Jerusalem: Bialik, 1971.

———. *Netivey Emunah u-Minut.* Jerusalem: Magnus, 1982.

———. "*Qudsha Berikh Hu Orayta ve-Yisrael Kula Had.*" *Kiryat Sefer* 50.

———. *Studies in Kabbalah and its Branches.* [Hebrew]. Jerusalem: Magnes, 1982.

———. *Wisdom of the Zohar.* Oxford: Oxford University Press, 1989.

Tishby, Isaiah and Joseph Dan. "Torat ha-Hasidut ve-Sifrutah." In *Studies in Hasidism* [Hebrew]. Jerusalem, 1977.

Vajda, G. *L'Amour de Dieu dans la thologie juives du moyen age.* Paris, 1957.

Verman, Mark. "The Development of *Yihudim* in Spanish Kabbalah. In *The Age of the Zohar,* 25–42. Edited by Joseph Dan. Jerusalem, 1989.

Vizhnitzer, Menahem Mendel. *Torat ha-Hasidut ha-Rishonim.* Israel: Bnai Brak, 1981.

Weiss, Joseph."Reshit Zemihatah Shel ha-Derekh ha- Hasidit," *Zion* 16 (1951).

———. *Studies in Bratzlav Hasidism.* [Hebrew]. Jerusalem: Bialik, 1974.

———. *Studies in Eastern European Jewish Mysticism.* Oxford: Oxford University Press, 1985.

———. "The Study of the Torah according to the Method of R. Israel Baal Shem Tov." [Hebrew] In *Essays Presented to Chief Rabbi Israel Bradie.* London, 1970.

Werblowsky, R. Z. Zvi. *Joseph Karo: Lawyer and Mystic.* Philadelphia: Jewish Publication Society, 1977.

Wertheim, Aaron. *Law and Custom in Hasidim.* Hoboken: Ktav, 1992.

Wilensky, Mordecai. *Hasidim and Mitnaggedim: A Study of the Controversy Between Them in the Years 1772–1815.* 2nd ed. enlarged and revised. [Hebrew]. Jerusalem: Bialik, 1990.

Wolfson, Elliot R. *Through a Speculum That Shines: Vision and Imagination in Medieval Jewish Mysticism.* Princeton: Princeton University, 1994.

———. "Walking as Sacred Duty: Theological Transformation of Social Reality in

Early Hasidism." In *Along the Path: Studies in Kabbalistic Myth, Symbolism, and Hermeneutics.* Albany: State University of New York, 1994.

———."Spiritual Ascent in the Sixteenth Century Jewish Mysticism." In *Death, Ecstasy, and Other Worldy Journeys.* Edited by Daniel Collins and Michael Fishbane. Albany: State University of New York, 1995.

———."Letter Symbolism and Merkavah Imagery in the Zohar." In *Alei Shefer: Studies in the Literature of Jewish Thought Presented to Rabbi Dr. Alexandre Safran.* Edited by Moshe Hallamish. Ramat Gan, 1990.

———."The Influence of Luria on the *Shelah*," [Hebrew]. In *Jerusalem Studies in Jewish Thought.* vol. 10 Lurianic Kabbalah. Jerusalem 1992.

———."The Tree That Is All: Jewish-Christian Roots of a Kabbalistic Symbol in *Sefer ha-Bahir.*" In *Journal of Jewish Thought and Philosophy* 3 (1993): 31–76.

Index

Aaron of Karlin, 278n
Abbaye, 145
Abraham David of Buczacz, 24
Abraham Hayyim of Zlotchov, 23, 26, 29,
    30, 132. *See also orah le-hayyim*
Abraham Mordecai of Pintshov, 31
Abulafia, Abraham, 235n
    and Ecstatic Kabbalah, 45–46, 48, 50
    and *ruhaniyut*, 263n
aggadot, 193
Akiva, 43
Alkabetz, Solomon, 46, 243n, 263n
Alsheich, Moses, 46–47
Altshuler, Mor, 8, 230n
    and Yehiel Mikhel of Zlotchov, 221n,
        227n, 232n, 234n, 272n, 280n
Amud ha-Avodah 23
anshey homer, 185
anshey zurah, 185
Arvey Nahal, 33
asceticism. *See under* corporeality
asifat ha-mahashevah, 47
assiyah, 71–72
avodah be-gashmiyut, 30, 178, 180–81,
    184–85
avodah zarah, 56
Avot, 32, 171
Ayin
    and ascent to *Hokhmah*, 77–78, 84,
        114, 210
    barriers to, 95
    ecstatic state of, 58, 240n
    as primordial matter (*Hyle*), 169–72
    and true humility, 88–91
Azikri, Eleazar, 46–49, 59. *See also Sefer
    Haredim*
Azulai, Avraham, 46–81

Azulai, Hayyim Joseph David 14

Ba'al Pe'or, 141
Ba'al Shem Tov. *See* Israel ben Eliezer
Barukh of Kossov, 23
Barukh of Mezbuzh, 31
behirut, 171
Benjamin of Zalozitz, 23, 24
Beri'ah. See under creation
berur
    and detachment from corporeality,
        83–84, 113–15, 120
    as a messianic process, 82, 93, 129,
        241n
    as purification, 138, 172, 180
Binah, 247n, 263n
    and *devequt*, 65, 116, 185
    and repentance, 159–60, 271n
Bloch, Joseph, 24
Brody
    Brody Kehillah, 4
    Brody *Kloyz*, 31, 32, 199–201, 215,
        281n, 284n
    Hasidic leadership in, 2, 4, 17, 24–26,
        205, 207–9, 213–14, 226n, 281n
    opposition to Hasidism in, 13, 15,
        190, 201, 203, 210, 284n
Buber, Martin, 238n

Cordoverian Kabbalah. *See* Cordovero,
    Moses
Cordovero, Moses
    cosmology, 81–93, 266n
        zimzum, 155, 248n, 269–70n
    and *devequt*, 54, 115, 248n
    and divine immanence, 68, 74
    Ecstatic Kabbalah, 45–46, 235n

Cordovero, Moses (*continued*)
  influence on early Hasidism, 7–8, 51,
    246–47n, 263n
  and Torah study, 63–64, 182, 248n,
    263n
  See also Pardes Rimmonim
corporeality
  and asceticism, 18, 30, 35, 48, 55, 108,
    111, 120, 178, 231n, 240n, 284n
  and *berur*, 178–80, 184
  concealment in, 135, 173
  detachment from, 18, 71, 255n, 273n
    and awe, 166–68
    and *Ayin*, 77, 83–84
    and *devequt*, 22, 73, 172
    and prayer, 124–25, 129, 245n,
     258n
    as a quality of *Zaddiqim*, 6, 163,
     204, 213–14
    and *shiflut*, 97, 213–14
  and *devequt*, 55, 59, 87, 107–21, 135,
    143, 157–58
  physicality (*gufaniyut*), 150
  and reality, 133, 196
  and Shabbat, 151–52
creation
  Beri'ah, 77, 155
  cosmological models of, 82, 266n
  and *devequt*, 86–89, 143, 161
  and divine speech, 136, 262n
  and divine unity, 91–93, 113
  and divine energy, 195, 174–75
  and divine will, 148–51, 255n
  menuhah, 172–73
  and the New Year, 155–56, 270n
  and *zimzum*, 266n, 269n

Da'at, 114–21, 156, 165, 194, 257n, 263n
  Da'ato rehavah, 118–19
  See also hakarah
Dan, Joseph, 1, 217n, 277n
Darkhey Yesharim, 16–17, 40, 221n,
  231n, 243n

David of Mikolajov, 37
Degel Mahaneh Efraim, 22
Derekh Emet, 38–42, 232–33n
devequt, 2, 5–7, 203–4, 207, 213–14,
  217n, 238n, 247n, 281n
  barriers to, 54–59, 97–105, 160–61,
    195, 249n. *See also* pride
  basis of, 50–54, 81–93
  contexts of, 59–79, 242n
  and Da'at, 257n
  and Dov Ber of Mezeritch, 163–65,
    168, 170–72, 174–75, 183
  in early Hasidism, 43–79
  and holidays, 123, 147–61, 174–75,
    266–67n
  and Menachem Mendel of Premish-
    lan, 18, 22–23
  preconditions for, 35, 107–21, 180,
    192, 210–11
  in Safedian texts, 43–50, 81–93
  and Torah study, 164–65, 242n
  and Yehiel Mikhel of Zlotchov, 2, 25,
    27
  and *Zaddiqim*, 185, 191–96, 199–201,
    209, 213–14
deviqah, 48
deyoqan, 196
divine aid
  barriers to, 95–105, 123
  and creation, 174
  and evil urge, 181, 183
  and prayer, 125, 131, 193
  and salvation, 121, 158–61
  and Torah study, 147, 193
divine energy. *See Hiyyut*
divine grace. *See Hesed*
divine judgment, 154–60, 268–69n,
  271n
divine mercy. *See Hesed*
Dov Ber of Hordikov, 37
Dov Ber of Mezeritch, 2–4, 6, 15–17,
  219n, 227n, 246–47n, 253n,
  277–78n, 282n

and *devequt*, 53–54, 58, 79, 84, 225n, 259n
and Meshullam Feibush Heller, 9–13, 21–23, 33–34, 37–38, 41–42, 163–86
and prayer, 70, 76–78, 124, 126, 137
and Safedian Kabbalah, 46, 127–29, 250n
and Shabbat, 151
and Torah study, 65–67, 140, 273n
and *unio mystica*, 92
and Yehiel Mikhel of Zlotchov, 28–29
and *Zaddiqim*, 187–92, 196–97, 204–14, 216
Dubnov, Simon, 92, 217n, 231n, 232n

Eliezer Mendel, 13
Elijah ha-Kohen of Smyrna, 74
Elijah de Vidas, 46, 48, 81, 83
Elijah ben Zalman of Vilna, 204, 264n, 281n
Elimelekh of Lizhensk
biographical, 11–12, 284n
and Yehiel Mikhel of Zlotchov, 26, 29, 203, 221n
and Zekhariah Mendel, 190
Epstein, Kalonymus Kalman, of Cracow, 30
Eybeshutz, David Solomon, of Soroka, 33
Eyn Sof
and creation, 82, 91
and *devequt*, 58, 62, 64
and unification of the *sefirot*, 48, 109
Ez Hayyim, 92

faith
and *Da'at*, 116
and *devequt*, 55–56, 129
in divine immanence, 51–52, 74–75, 78, 88–89, 173, 189, 206, 210–11
importance of, 34
and self-effacement, 105

in *Zaddiqim*, 5, 95, 100, 131–32, 190, 192–95, 197, 200, 209, 216
fasting
and asceticism, 30, 48, 231n
"of the limbs," 21
and repentance, 35–36, 215n, 258n
"female waters," 71, 137, 272n
Fridel of Brody, 14, 15

gadlut, 71–72, 245n
Gallico, Elisha, 46
Gaon of Vilna. *See* Elijah ben Zalman of Vilna
gavhut, 57–58
Gehinnon, 155
gematria, 134, 262n
Gershon of Kutov, 14
Gershon of Lutzk, 37, 174–75
Gevurah, 154, 268–69n, 271n
Gikatilla, Joseph, 265n
Ginat Egoz, 146
Green, Arthur, 8
Gries, Zev, 92, 221n

HaBaD, 239n, 250n, 272n
and *hitbonenut*, 256n
and Schneuer Zalman, 28–29
School of Hasidism, 1, 4–5, 52, 217n
hafizah, 48
hakarah, 114, 116, 118, 141, 262n
hakhna'ah, 163–64
halakhah, 32, 64
Halperin, David, of Ostrog, 15
Hannover, Nathan, 147
hashiqah, 48
hashmal, 69
Hasidism, Between Ecstasy and Magic, 8
Hasidism Reappraised, 8
hayot, 85
heleq eloha mi-ma' al, 54
Heller, Noah Abraham, 31–32
Heller, Yom Tov Lipman Ha-Levi, 2, 31

Heschel, Abraham Joshua, of Apt, 1, 29–
        30, 232n, 235n
Hesed, 21, 76, 154, 178, 263n
    divine grace, 174
    divine mercy, 158–59, 210, 271n
Hesed le-Avraham, 81, 132
hieros gamos, 151, 257n, 269n
hishtalshelut, 150
hishtavut, 49, 56–57
hitbodedut, 47, 49, 61–62, 237n, 242n
hitbonenut 256n
hit' orerut, 48, 54, 155, 183
hitpashtut ha-gashmiyut. See under
        corporeality
hitqarevut, 164
hitqashrut, 119, 132–43, 151, 184, 195
Hiyyut, 51, 60–61, 64, 173–74, 194–96
Hokhmah, 247n, 263n
    and *Ayin*, 77–78, 84, 169–70
    and *Da'at*, 114–16
    and *Zaddiqim*, 175, 279n
Horodenker, Nahman, 2, 14–16, 213,
        222n
Horowitz, Isaac, of Hamburg, 24, 25
Horowitz, Isaiah
    and *devequt*, 46, 48, 268n
    and prayer, 137
    and Safedian Kabbalah, 81, 83, 86–
        87, 213, 250n, 270n
Horowitz, Pinhas ha-Levy, of Frankfurt,
        26, 29
Horowitz, Shmelka, 29
humility, 17, 210, 241n, 252n
    and awe, 47, 169
    and *Ayin*, 57–58, 88, 90
    and prayer, 128, 164
    and pride, 36, 96–105, 140–42
    and *reshimu*, 138
    and self-annihilation, 168, 172
    and self-effacement, 6, 22, 47, 96–105
    and *Zaddiqim*, 196, 199, 200–202,
        213–14
Hyle, 169–71, 273n

Idel, Moshe, 1, 92
    and *devequt*, 44, 234n
    and Safedian Kabbalah, 46, 238n, 263n
imago mundi. See Ez Hayyim
imitatio dei, 43
Isaac of Acre, 49, 56, 238–39n
Isaac of Drohobitch, 24, 25, 27
Israel, Rabbi, 14
Israel ben Eliezer
    and *Ayin*, 171
    and *devequt*, 56, 210–11, 238n, 255n
    disciples of, 9–14, 16–17, 23–24,
        27–32, 37–38, 163, 185–86, 188,
        190, 198–200, 207, 213, 227n,
        231n, 279–80n, 281–82n
    and divine immanence, 60
    learning *li-shemah*, 63–65, 67, 123–
        24, 140–44, 147, 243n, 258n,
        265n, 281n
    and origins of Hasidism, 1–2, 4, 6,
        219n, 244n
    and prayer, 69–71, 74–77, 246n
        avodah be-gashmiyut, 178–80
    elevation of wayward thoughts, 22,
        127, 182, 192, 283n
Israel of Kozhenitz, 221n
Issachar Ber of Zlotchov, 24, 26, 37, 135
Isaac of Radvil, 27, 28, 31

Jacob Joseph of Lublin, 30
Jacob Joseph of Polnoy
    and *devequt*, 44, 52–53, 57
    learning *li-shemah*, 64–65, 243n
    influence on early Hasidism, 2–3, 5–6
    and Menahem Mendel of Premishlan,
        14–19, 213
    and Meshullam Feibush Heller, 34–
        35, 37, 278n
    and prayer, 263n
    and Yehiel Mikhel of Zlotchov, 29–30
    and *Zaddiqim*, 78–79, 185–86, 231n,
        246n, 278n
    See also Toledot Ya'aqov Yosef

Joel, 3, 39
Joseph of Pistyn 24
Joseph of Yampol, 17, 30, 31
Joseph of Zemigrad, 31
Judah the Hasid, 32

Kahn, Abraham Isaac, 42
Kalisker, Abraham, 210, 278n, 283n
Karo, Joseph, 46
kavvanah, 7, 41, 70–75, 84–85, 87,
        224n, 233n, 245n, 248n, 259–60n
    and detachment from corporeality,
        18, 115
    and *devequt*, 127–33, 176–77, 260n,
        269n
    and *mizvot*, 258n
    and prayer, 25, 68, 146–47, 189, 262n
    and *ruhaniyut*, 62, 137
Keter, 47
Kloyz. See under Brody
Kohelet, 192
Korah, 201
Kosov-Vizhnitz Hasidic Dynasty, 38

Landau, Ezekiel, 24, 25, 26, 227–28n,
        281n
Landau, Joseph, 39–40
Landau, Zvi Aryeh, of Alik, 31
lema' lah me-ha-tev' a-, 52
Levi Isaac of Berdichev, 11, 12, 221n, 278n
Levushey Serad, 33
Liqutim Yeqarim
    and *avodah be-gashmiyut*, 178
    and awe, 167
    publication history, 4, 35, 38–42, 92–
        93, 231n
Luria, Isaac
    and *berur*, 60, 138, 178, 214, 241n
    cosmology of, 81–93, 266n, 271n
        and *shevirah*, 241n, 249n
        and *zimzum*, 155, 158, 248n, 266n,
            269–70n
    and *Da'at*, 117–18

and *devequt*, 63, 66–75, 114–15
and *hieros gamos*, 267n
influence on Early Hasidism, 7–8, 51,
        244–47n
and *kavvanah*, 25, 127–32, 145–47,
        176–77, 196, 233n, 275n
and Meshullam Feibush Heller, 263n
and Moses Cordovero, 247n
and prayer, 244n, 259–60n
and *reshimu*, 163
schools of interpretation, 248n
and Torah study, 242n
and wayward thoughts, 22, 283n
and *yihudim*, 241n
and *Zaddiqim*, 188–90, 227n
Luria, Solomon, of Lublin, 31
Lurianic Kabbalah. *See* Luria, Isaac
Luzzatto, Moses Hayyim, 171, 240n,
        249n, 254n

Maggid of Mezeritch. *See* Dov Ber of
    Mezeritch
Maggid of Slutzk. *See* Rabbi Israel
Maggid of Zlotchov. *See* Yehiel, Mikhel,
    R., of
MaHaRSHaL. *See* Luria, Solomon, of
    Lublin
Mahler, Raphael, 217n
Maimon, Solomon, 3
Maimonides. *See* Moses ben Maimon
Malkhut, 110, 247n
    and awe, 166–68, 273n
    and *Binah*, 65
    and *Shekhinah*, 91, 244n, 273n
    and *Yesod*, 257n, 279n
    and *Zaddiqim*, 185
Maor ve-Shemesh, 30
marah adumah, 167
Mayim Rabbim, 24, 92–93
Mayyin Nuqbin, 167
Meir ben Samson, 31
Mei' rat Eynayim, 49
Meisels, Uziel, 23, 26

Menahem Mendel of Kosov, 38
Menahem Mendel of Lubavitch, 29
Menahem Mendel of Premishlan
    and *Ayin*, 171
    biographical, 2, 9–23, 37, 41, 199–201,
        221–22n, 224n
    and Brody *Kloyz*, 200–1
    and corporeality, 115, 124
    and *Da'at*, 117, 119
    and elevation of wayward thoughts,
        208, 213, 225n, 277n
    and Meshullam Feibush Heller, 208–
        9, 213, 216, 280n, 283n
    and Torah study, 139, 144
    and Yehiel Mikhel of Zlotchov, 23, 30,
        34
    and *Zaddiqim*, 197
    See also Darkhey Yesharim
Menahem Mendel of Vitebsk, 4, 12,
    220n, 228n
Menahem Mendel of Vizhnitz, 221–22n
Menahem Nahum of Chernobyl, 11,
    228n
Menuhah, 172–73
*R. Meshulam Feibush Heller and his
    Place in Early Hasidism*, 8
metinut, 98
Mevasser Zedeq, 26, 37
mohin, 72
Mordecai of Kremenitz, 31
Mordecai of Neshkiz, 28, 30
Moses of Bialetserkov, 25
Moses ben Maimon, 43, 45, 49–50, 53,
    111, 117
Moses ben Nahman, 49–50
Moses of Pistyn, 23
Moses of Zevil, 31
Moshe de Leon, 268n
Moshe Hayyim Ephraim of Sudilkov, 23
mutatis mutandis, 53, 89, 136

Naftali of Ropshitz, 30
Nahman of Bratslav, 14, 38, 218n, 232n

Nahmanides. *See* Moses ben Nahman
Nathan of Gaza, 74
nefesh, 48, 160, 184–85, 268n
neshamah, 48, 73, 160, 184–85, 268n
Nezirut Shimson, 33, 41
Nigal, Gedalyah, 234n
nistar, 23, 211
    and creation, 148–51, 173, 266n, 274n
    and *devequt*, 117, 129, 135, 214
    and Torah study, 139, 142, 145, 174–
        76, 204
    and *Zaddiqim*, 192, 195, 274n, 275n
Noda bi-Yehudah, 24
Nuqba, 269n

ofanim, 61, 85
Orah le-Hayyim, 26, 110
Or ha-Emet, 13
Orhot Zaddiqim, 197

Pardes, 117
Pardes Rimmonim, 45, 137, 248n, 263n,
    270n
parzuf, 72, 82, 263n, 269n, 280n
Pechter, Mordecai, 46, 234n, 237n
peniyah
    and *devequt*, 59, 67
    and *gavhut*, 57
    and *pilpul*, 64
    and separation from God, 53, 62–63
    and Torah study, 143, 165
perishut, 204
Piekarz, Mendel, 8, 218n, 234n, 236n,
    275n
pilpul, 64–65
Pinhas of Koretz, 3, 15, 29, 38, 232n
pride
    barrier to divine aid, 95–105, 107,
        123, 161, 252n
    and Torah study, 138, 140–41
    and *Zaddiqim*, 191, 195–96, 199–201,
        204
    See also devequt, barriers to

qal ve-homer, 179–80, 192
qatnut, 71–72, 198, 256n
qelipah
    and *berur,* 114, 138, 178, 214
    and evil, 102–3, 152, 212
    and *hashmal,* 69
    and *mizvah,* 62

Ra'aya Meheymna, 109, 113
Rabbenu Tam, 191
Raphael of Bershad, 23
Rapoport-Albert, Ada, 8, 223n, 278n
Rappoport, Hayyim, 32
Rashi. *See* Yitzhaqi, Shlomo
Rava, 145
Reishit Hokhmah
    and awe, 168
    and *devequt,* 46–49, 57, 83, 136, 192
    and prayer, 25
    and Safedian Kabbalah, 81, 155
    and Torah study, 145
    and *unio mystica,* 53
    and *Zaddiqim,* 196–97
repentance
    and *devequt,* 164, 177
    and divine aid, 157–60
    and judgment, 168n, 271–72n
    and Shabbat, 172–74
reshimu, 118, 179–80
    and prayer, 138, 163, 263n
    and *zimzum,* 82, 263n
ruah, 48, 160, 184, 268n
Rubenstein, Abraham, 16
ruhaniyut
    and corporeality, 111, 133
    and creation, 148, 150
    and *devequt,* 60, 83
    and prayer, 134–37, 139–40, 242n,
        248n, 263n
    and *unio mystica,* 62–63
RYVaSH. See Israel ben Eliezer

Sabbateanism, 205, 240n, 246n, 275–
        76n, 281n
Sack, Bracha, 238n
Safedian Kabbalah
    and *devequt,* 43–51, 55, 59, 63, 66,
        132, 146–47
    influence on early Hasidism, 7, 20,
        199, 257n, 263n
    and wayward thoughts, 213
    See also Abulafia, Abraham; Azulai,
        Avraham; Luria, Isaac;
        Cordovero, Moses
salvation. *See* divine aid
Samson of Kolymyja, 40
Samson of Ostropol, 230n
Samson of Uziran, 33, 41
Samuel of Zalishtik, 35
Samuel Shmelke of Nikolsburg, 11–12,
        278n
Sanzer, Hayyim, 281n
Schatz-Uffenheimer, Rivka, 1, 92, 217n
    and *devequt,* 65, 234n, 255n
    and Dov Ber of Mezeritch, 219n,
        221n, 282n
    and Meshullam Feibush Heller, 218n,
        231n
Schneuer Zalman of Liadi, 3, 4, 12, 28,
        29, 216. *See also* HaBaD; *Tanya*
Scholem, Gershom, 1, 6, 43, 46, 49,
        217n, 237–38n, 251n
    and *devequt,* 43, 46, 234–35n
Seer of Lublin. *See* Jacob Joseph of
        Lublin
Sefer Ez Hayyim, 69
Sefer Haredim, 46, 57, 59
Sefer Hesed le-Avraham, 46
Sefer Sha'arey Orah, 146
Sefer Vikuah, 14
Sefer ha-Yashar, 191, 197
Sefer Yezirah, 120, 136, 195
sefirot, 240n, 246–47n, 262n–263n,
        265n
    and *berur,* 178–79
    and *devequt,* 47–48, 72, 76, 151

sefirot (continued)
  and the sacred calendar, 268n, 271n,
       266n
  and Safedian Kabbalah, 45, 82–84
  and *unio mystica*, 91, 109
  See also Binah; Keter; Malkhut;
       Tif'eret; Yesod
serafim, 85
Sha'ar ha-Shamayim, 137
Sha'arey Qedushah, 45–49
Sha'arey Zion, 147
shame, 165–68
Shefa, 51, 68, 69, 171
Shekhinah, 51, 30, 247n, 251n, 256n
  and *devequt*, 44, 54–55, 57, 244n,
       273n
  and divine immanence, 51
  and prayer, 68–69, 71, 77–79
  and Shabbat, 151
  and Torah study, 66, 140, 147
  and *unio mystica*, 48, 53, 91
  and *Zaddiqim*, 77–79
Shem ha-Gedolim he-Hadash, 92
Sheney Luhot ha-Berit, 20, 81, 86, 213,
       237n, 247n, 277n
  and *devequt*, 46, 48, 57, 59, 63, 83,
       268n
  and *Zaddiqim*, 197
shevirah, 58, 82–87, 241n, 249n
Shimon ben Yohai, 67, 100
Shivhey ha-BeSHT
  and Menahem Mendel of Premishlan,
       13–14, 17–20, 213
  and Yehiel Mikhel of Zlotchov, 24,
       27–31
Shmelke of Nikolsburg. *See* Samuel
       Shmelke of Nikolsburg
shofar, 78, 159–160
Shor, Abraham Hayyim, 33. *See also*
       Zon Qodashim
Shulhan Arukh, 110, 144
Sidduro shel Shabbat, 32
sitra ahara, 159–60

Solomon of Lutzk, 28
Swierze, Rabbi of. *See* Moses of Pistyn

Tanya, 5, 216, 260n, 284n
Tefillah le-Moshe, 155
temimut, 134
Terumah, 151
Tevele, David, 26, 227n
Tif' eret, 49, 91, 183, 279n
Tiferet Uziel, 26
Tiqquney Zohar, 151
Tiqqun Hazot, 19
Tiqqunim, 146
Tirer, Hayyim, of Tchernowitz, 31–32,
       34, 227n, 278n
Tishby, Isaiah, 1, 217n, 234n, 277n
Tohu, 169
Toledot Ya'aqov Yosef, 2, 4, 15, 26, 178,
       218n, 276n
Tosefot Yom Tov, 31
Tractate Bezah, 152
Tzanzer, Hayyim, 25

unio-mystica, 211, 237n, 239n, 250n,
       253n
  and *Ayin*, 58, 90–93
  and detachment from corporeality,
       109–10, 112–13, 123–24, 172,
       204
  and *devequt*, 5–6, 45–48, 53–54, 78,
       237n
  and Shabbat, 150
  and Torah study, 63

Vilner, Solomon, 17, 37, 223n
Vital, Hayyim, 45, 48, 249n

Walden, Aaron, 92
Weiss, Joseph, 1, 92, 217n, 276n
  and *devequt*, 245n, 253n, 255n

Ya'aqov Yosef of Polonoy. *See* Jacob
       Joseph of Polonoy

Yehiel Mikhel of Zlotzhov
  biographical, 2, 4, 8–9, 11–13, 15, 17–
    18, 20, 23–34, 37, 41–42, 62, 221n,
    225–28n, 232–34n, 280n, 284n
  and creation, 87
  and *unio mystica*, 90–93
  and *devequt*, 178
  and *hitqashrut*, 132–33
  and Meshullam Feibush Heller, 203–
    9, 212–13, 216, 230n, 253n,
    272n, 282–83n
  and Torah study, 145, 281n
  and *Zaddiqim*, 186, 189–90, 197–99,
    201, 218n, 261n, 280n
Yerushalmi, Israel Moses, 31
Yesod, 257n, 263n, 279n
yezer ha-ra, 101
yezirah, 71, 77
yihud, 24, 237n, 241n
  and detachment from corporeality, 77
  and *devequt*, 47, 59–60, 82, 137
  and *kavvanot*, 70
yir'ah, 155, 166–70, 175, 262n, 269n,
    273n
  and *berur*, 180
  and *devequt*, 117, 128, 137, 139, 142,
    177, 204, 211, 254n
  and *Zaddiqim*, 131–34, 192–93, 200
Yisrael Ba'al Shem. *See* Israel ben
    Eliezer
yissurin, 55
Yitzhak Isaac ha-Kohen of Koretz, 31
Yitzhaqi, Shlomo, 23, 113
Yosher Divrey Emet, 32–33, 36–38,
    189–91, 203–9
  and prayer, 19, 214
  publication history, 38–42, 230–31n,
    233n
  and Safedian Kabbalah, 22, 81
  and *unio mystica*, 92
  and *Zaddiqim*, 201, 214, 216
Yospe, 24

Zaddiq, 220n, 279–80n
  and *berur*, 172
  characteristics of, 34, 42, 93, 170,
    185–86, 203–4, 207–16, 231n,
    250n, 266n
    detachment from corporeality, 107,
      112, 151–53
    humility, 17, 99–101, 104
  and *devequt*, 77–79, 122, 237n
    and *Da'at*, 117, 119–21
  and divine aid, 95–101, 104, 126,
    181–82
  and Dov Ber of Mezeritch, 163
  and Elimelekh of Lizhensk, 11–12,
    231n, 284n
  faith in, 95, 99–101, 131–32, 134–35,
    209, 216, 261–62n
  importance of, 187–202
  and prayer, 126, 131–32, 247n
  and Torah study, 174–75, 185
  and Yehiel Mikhel of Zlotchov, 2, 9,
    19, 178, 186, 212–13, 231n,
    261n, 284n
Zava'at ha-RYVaSH, 4
zedaqah, 20
Ze'ev Wolf (Velvele) of Charny Ostrog,
    38, 232n
Zekhariah Menahem Mendel of
    Yaroslav, 12, 40, 190
Zerizuta de-Avraham, 32
Zev Wolf of Zbarazh, 31, 33
zimzum, 82, 86, 173, 248–49n, 263n,
    266–67n, 269n
  and divine judgment, 155–56, 158,
    271n
ziyyur, 116
Zon Qodashim, 33, 230n
Zusya of Anipol, 12
Zvi Hirsh of Nadberna, 29, 31, 37
Zvi the Hasid of Zlotchov, 13, 15, 17, 26,
    37